The Koran For Dummies®

D1283427

The Five Purposes of the Koran

The Koran has five essential purposes:

✔ **The Guidance:** The Koran serves as a guide to belief in the Oneness of God, and leads to an ethical life defined as Submission or Surrender to the Will of God (Islam). This complete way of life offers guidance through both personal and communal laws.

✔ **The Criterion:** The Koran distinguishes between moral and immoral, ethical and unethical, good and evil. The Book helps Muslims make ethical choices in their daily lives.

✔ **The Reminder:** The Koran confirms and reminds the world of the teachings of past Prophets. The stories of the Prophets form an essential part of the Koran's narrative.

✔ **Spiritual healing:** The Book helps Muslims turn away from their lower passions, towards the higher aspirations of worshiping and obeying God.

The Koran presents a personal relationship with the Divine, a God-consciousness that elevates the soul and frees the mind from moral diseases, such as materialism, jealousy, and anger.

✔ **Social change:** The Scripture serves as a roadmap for social change built on social justice, economic equity, racial harmony, human rights, and dignity. The Koran calls the Muslim community to actively enjoin that which is right, good, and just, and to struggle against that which is wrong, evil, and unjust.

Three Basic Features of the Koran

Keep these features of the Koran in mind when reading the Scripture:

✔ **The oral tradition:** The Koran's oral tradition gives the Book its aura. The recited word of the Koran is much more powerful than its printed form, especially if the text has been translated from Arabic into another language.

✔ **The non-linear approach:** The Koran doesn't follow a systematic historical or thematic approach. Rather, stories from the past, laws, and moral teachings drive the Book's narrative.

✔ **The non-historical story:** The Koran doesn't include specifics of history, including times, places, and lineage. The moral of the story, which transcends time and space, trumps the details of history.

For Dummies: Bestselling Book Series for Beginners

Quoting the Koran on Major Themes

These Koranic passages give you a glimpse of some major themes presented in the Book:

✔ **God:** "Say, He is God, the One. God, the Eternal, Absolute. He gives not birth, nor is He born. And there is none like unto Him (*Surah* 112)."

✔ **Prophets:** "Say, we believe in God, and in what has been revealed to us and what was revealed to Abraham, Ishmael, Isaac, Jacob, and the Tribes, and in the Books given to Moses, Jesus, and the Prophets from their Sustainer. We make no distinction between one and another (3:84)."

✔ **Beliefs and actions:** "It is not righteousness that you turn your faces towards East or West. But it is righteousness to believe in God and the Day of Judgment, and the Angels, and the Book, and the Messengers. To spend of your sustenance out of love for Him, for your kin, for orphans, for the needy, for the wayfarer, for those who ask, and for the freeing of slaves. To be steadfast in prayer, and give purifying alms. To fulfill the contracts which you have made. And to be firm and patient, in suffering and adversity, and through all periods of panic. Such are the people of truth, the God-conscious (2:177)."

✔ **Mankind and life:** "By the time, verily, man is in loss, except those who have faith and do righteous deeds, and join together in the mutual enjoining of truth, and of patience and perseverance (*Surah* 103)."

✔ **The Day of Accountability:** "When the earth is shaken to her convulsion, and the earth throws up her burdens, and man cries 'What is the matter with her?' On that day will she declare her tidings, for your Sustainer will have given her inspiration. On that day will men proceed in groups to be shown deeds that they have done. Then anyone who has one atom's weight of good shall see it. And anyone who has done an atom's weight of evil shall see it (*Surah* 99)."

✔ **Human relations:** "O mankind! We created you from a single [pair] of a male and a female, and made you into nations and tribes, so that you may know each other. Verily, the most honored of you in the sight of God is [the one who] is most conscious of God. And God has full knowledge and is fully aware (49:13)."

✔ **Gender relations:** "The believers, men and women, are friends of one another. They enjoin what is just, and forbid what is evil. They observe regular prayers, pay purifying alms, and obey God and His Messenger. On them God will pour His Mercy, for God is Exalted in power, and is Wise (9:71)."

Copyright © 2004 Wiley Publishing, Inc.
All rights reserved.

Item 5581-2.

For more information about Wiley Publishing, call 1-800-762-2974.

The Koran
FOR
DUMMIES®

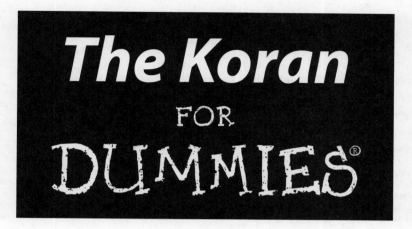

The Koran
FOR
DUMMIES®

by Sohaib Sultan

WILEY

Wiley Publishing, Inc.

The Koran For Dummies®

Published by
Wiley Publishing, Inc.
111 River St.
Hoboken, NJ 07030-5774
www.wiley.com

Copyright © 2004 by Wiley Publishing, Inc., Indianapolis, Indiana

Published by Wiley Publishing, Inc., Indianapolis, Indiana

Published simultaneously in Canada

For general information on our other products and services or to obtain technical support, please contact our Customer Care Department within the U.S. at 800-762-2974, outside the U.S. at 317-572-3993, or fax 317-572-4002.

Wiley also publishes its books in a variety of electronic formats. Some content that appears in print may not be available in electronic books.

Library of Congress Control Number: 2004103140

ISBN: 0-7645-5581-2

Manufactured in the United States of America

10 9 8 7 6 5 4 3 2 1

1B/RZ/QV/QU/IN

WILEY

About the Author

Sohaib Nazeer Sultan has studied traditional Islam for several years while living in the Middle East and the United States. He has studied, both formally and informally, with esteemed scholars of Islamic theology and Islamic law.

During his undergraduate studies at Indiana University, Sohaib played a leadership role in the diverse religious community of Bloomington, Indiana, serving as Public Relations Chair, Vice President, President, and Student Advisor for the Muslim Students Union. Sohaib also organized and participated in numerous interfaith dialogues throughout the state of Indiana, including a forum called Healing Our Community in the wake of the tragic events of 9/11. Upon graduating, Sohaib was honored by Indiana University for his cultural diversity efforts and was asked to offer a Muslim prayer at the pre-graduation ceremony of the 2002 graduating class.

Currently, Sohaib lives in Chicago, Illinois, where he works on independent projects as a freelance journalist. He is often invited by churches and synagogues to speak about the Islamic faith and its role in the world today. Most recently, he served as an Islamic affairs analyst for the British Broadcasting Corporation (BBC) Radio in a series of dialogues on Muslim-Christian relations in the United States. Sohaib plans to begin his masters in Islamic Studies in the Fall of 2004.

The author invites and encourages constructive dialogue with his readers. You can contact him through e-mail at koranfordummies@yahoo.com.

Dedication

I dedicate this book to my family — my mother, Amra Sultan; my father, Talat Sultan; my sister, Sohaira Sultan; and my brother-in-law, Zubair Saeed. I will be forever grateful for their unceasing support, encouragement, and love.

Author's Acknowledgments

I want to thank my Acquisition Editor, Kathleen M. Cox, who initially contacted me about writing this book. Her encouragement and help in the first phase of the book convinced me that Wiley Publishing is the best publishing company to work for. Kathy did a marvelous job of introducing me to the unique, reader-friendly style of the *For Dummies* series. Thanks to my wonderful Project Editor, Mary Goodwin, this project has been completed on time. I am truly indebted to Mary for her excellent review of the chapters, brilliant new ideas, and patience throughout the project.

I greatly appreciate the work and dedication of the technical reviewer, Dr. Dany Doueiri, a scholar of Arabic and Islamic Studies at University of Southern California San Bernardino. Without his scholarly review of this book, this project could never have been such a success. I deeply respect his sincere advice in every chapter of this book.

I owe a great deal to all of my friends who helped me with this book and enlightened me with their conversations and ideas about Islam and the Muslim world. I would like to especially thank my former roommate and good friend, Jermey Burcham, who suggested my name for this project, and diligently reviewed several chapters in this book. Also, I thank my relatives from all around the world who sent their encouragement and good wishes as I completed this project.

Finally, I send my deepest respects to all the scholars that I have ever learned from. Attending their classes changed my life. Their vast knowledge of the Islamic sciences and ability to teach the Islamic tradition is a reflection of their illuminated hearts, beautiful character, and deep intellects.

Publisher's Acknowledgments

We're proud of this book; please send us your comments through our Dummies online registration form located at www.dummies.com/register/.

Some of the people who helped bring this book to market include the following:

Acquisitions, Editorial, and Media Development

Project Editor: Mary Goodwin

Acquisitions Editor: Kathleen Cox

Technical Editor: Dr. Dany Doueiri

Senior Permissions Editor: Carmen Krikorian

Editorial Manager: Michelle Hacker

Editorial Assistant: Elizabeth Rea

Cover Photos: © Robert Berger/ImageState/ PictureQuest

Cartoons: Rich Tennant, www.the5thwave.com

Illustrator: Lisa S. Reed

Composition

Project Coordinator: Adrienne Martinez

Layout and Graphics: Andrea Dahl, Kelly Emkow, Denny Hager, Michael Kruzil, Shelley Norris, Lynsey Osborn, Heather Ryan, Brent Savage, Rashell Smith

Proofreaders: Laura Albert, Carl Pierce, TECHBOOKS Production Services

Indexer: TECHBOOKS Production Services

Publishing and Editorial for Consumer Dummies

> **Diane Graves Steele,** Vice President and Publisher, Consumer Dummies
>
> **Joyce Pepple,** Acquisitions Director, Consumer Dummies
>
> **Kristin A. Cocks,** Product Development Director, Consumer Dummies
>
> **Michael Spring,** Vice President and Publisher, Travel
>
> **Brice Gosnell,** Associate Publisher, Travel
>
> **Kelly Regan,** Editorial Director, Travel

Publishing for Technology Dummies

> **Andy Cummings,** Vice President and Publisher, Dummies Technology/General User

Composition Services

> **Gerry Fahey,** Vice President of Production Services
>
> **Debbie Stailey,** Director of Composition Services

Contents at a Glance

Introduction 1

Part 1: Revealing the Word of God: The Book 7
Chapter 1: Getting to Know the Koran 9
Chapter 2: From Revelation to Written Book 21
Chapter 3: Mapping Out the Structure of the Book 37
Chapter 4: Discovering the Language of the Koran 53
Chapter 5: Relating the Koran to Abrahamic Revelations 65

Part II: Searching for the Soul of the Koran 79
Chapter 6: Interpreting the Koran 81
Chapter 7: Understanding Interpretations of the Koran Today 93

Part III: Seeing the Koranic Worldview 107
Chapter 8: Meeting God, Prophets, and Mankind 109
Chapter 9: Divining Nature, the Universe, and the Unseen 133
Chapter 10: Taking the Koranic View of Other Faith Traditions 147

Part IV: Living the Koran 157
Chapter 11: Following in the Footsteps of Muhammad 159
Chapter 12: Putting Meaning into Ritual 169
Chapter 13: Understanding the Koranic View of Self 191
Chapter 14: Achieving Koranic Ethics and Morality 203
Chapter 15: Raising a Family the Koranic Way 215

Part V: Relating the Koran to the World 231
Chapter 16: Connecting the Koran to Society 233
Chapter 17: Purifying Society through Islamic Law 255
Chapter 18: Struggling for God: Jihad 273
Chapter 19: Discussing Women in the Koran 283
Chapter 20: The Koran and Modernity 295

Part VI: The Part of Tens **309**
Chapter 21: Ten Misconceptions about the Koran 311
Chapter 22: Ten Ways to Dig Deeper into the Koran 321

Appendix A: Glossary of Koranic Terms....................**331**

Appendix B: Finding Prophets in the Koran...............**339**

Index **341**

Table of Contents

Introduction 1

   About This Book 1

   Conventions Used in This Book 2

   Foolish Assumptions 3

   How This Book Is Organized 4

      Part I: Revealing the Word of God: The Book 4

      Part II: Searching for the Soul of the Koran 4

      Part III: Seeing the Koranic Worldview 4

      Part IV: Living the Koran 5

      Part V: Relating the Koran to the World 5

      Part VI: The Part of Tens 5

   Icons Used in This Book 5

   Where to Go from Here 6

Part 1: Revealing the Word of God: The Book 7

   Chapter 1: Getting to Know the Koran 9

   Receiving Revelation Straight from the Source 9

   Guiding the Way: Prophet Muhammad 10

   Discovering the Basic Messages of the Koran 11

      The unity of God 11

      Worship and service to God 11

      Prophets to teach and guide 11

      Completion of past revelations 12

      Guidance to a spiritual path 12

      Movement for social change 12

      Accountability of deeds 13

   Naming the Revelation 13

      The Guidance 13

      The Criterion 14

      The Proof 14

      The Reminder 15

      The Healing 16

   Hearing the Words: The Audience of the Koran 16

   Knowing the Essentials about Islam and Muslims 17

      The Six Pillars of Belief 17

      The Five Pillars of Islam 18

      Muslims: The followers of Islam 19

Chapter 2: From Revelation to Written Book .21

Revealing the Koran to Muhammad 21
    The beginning of revelation 22
    The stages of revelation 24
    The Meccan and Medinan periods 24
    Transmitting revelation to the community 26
Collecting the Koran as a Book 27
    Conforming the Koran's dialects 28
    The Koran in modern-day print 29
Memorizing Miracles: Preserving the Koran throughout History 31
Experiencing the Koran as Divine Art 32
    Recitation 32
    Calligraphy 35

Chapter 3: Mapping Out the Structure of the Book 37

Discerning the Structure of the Koran 37
    Ayat 37
    Surahs 38
    Juz' 39
Discovering Surah Names and Themes 40
Finding Your Way Through the Moral Narrative 46
    Through divine signs 47
    Through laws 47
    Through stories of the past 48
Simplifying the Moral Narrative of Shorter Surahs 52

Chapter 4: Discovering the Language of the Koran 53

Arabic: Plain, Clear, and Eloquent 53
    Digging down to the roots 54
    Reading translations of the Koran 56
Literary Style in the Sacred Scripture 57
    Key literary elements of the Koran 58
    Clear and figurative passages 60
Hearing the Voice of the Koran 62

Chapter 5: Relating the Koran to Abrahamic Revelations 65

Previous Revelations: Between Sacred and Corrupted 65
Linking the Three Faiths: Common Experiences in the Scriptures 66
    Uniting faiths with belief in One God 67
    Bridging the gap between divine laws 67
    Sharing the legacy of prophetic stories .69

Contrasting the Koran with Judeo-Christian Scriptures 70
    Finding a worldview of history in the Scriptures 70
    Reforming laws 72
    Reforming religious rituals 72
    Extending God's covenant to all peoples 73
    Giving a new angle on prophetic stories 73
    Checking the prophetic pulse of Muhammad in the
      Biblical Scripture 75
    Differing on Mary and the message of Jesus 76

Part II: Searching for the Soul of the Koran 79

Chapter 6: Interpreting the Koran 81
Coming to Know the Guidance 81
    Having room for interpretation 82
    Knowing the key terms of Koranic interpretation 82
    Finding the Tasfir that fits 84
Drawing Out Interpretations 85
    Looking at clear and ambiguous passages 85
    Interpreting outer meanings 86
    Interpreting inner meanings 88
    Examining general and specific passages 88
    Keeping circumstances behind revelation in mind 90
    Abrogating passages 90

Chapter 7: Understanding Interpretations of the Koran Today 93
Getting to Know Famous Commentators of the Koran 93
    Among the companions 94
    In successive generations 95
    Classic works of Koranic interpretation 96
Influential Movements of the Twentieth Century 98
    Mawdudi: Framework for a movement 99
    Qutub: The controversial revolutionary 101
    Muhammad Rida: The influential reformer 103
    Muhammad al-Ghazali: Thematic Tafsir 103
Another School of Thought: The Shi'ites 104
    Ali 104
    Two famous Shi'ite Koranic interpreters 105

Part III: Seeing the Koranic Worldview 107

Chapter 8: Meeting God, Prophets, and Mankind 109
Conceptualizing God 109
   "A" is for "Allah" 109
   Exploring the concept of God 110
   Experiencing God through divine attributes 113
   Knowing God 117
Prophets of God: Preaching a Divine Message 119
   Prophets and messengers 119
   Abraham: Beloved Friend of God and Father of Faith 120
   Moses: The Liberator 122
   Jesus: The Spirit of God 125
The Status and Nature of Man 128
   Human nature through Adam 129
   The purpose of human life 131

Chapter 9: Divining Nature, the Universe, and the Unseen 133
The Divine Ways of Nature 133
   Patterns of creation 134
   God's creations in the skies 134
   Earthly creations 136
Inheriting the Earth: The Role of Mankind in Nature 139
The Unseen World: Angels versus Satan 140
   The angels: Pure creations of God 141
   Satan: An avowed enemy 142
Accounting for the Soul 143
   The Day of Judgment 143
   The eternal bliss of heaven 144
   Hell: Torment of the fire 145
   God's Mercy, God's Wrath: Reconciling the two 145

Chapter 10: Taking the Koranic View of Other Faith Traditions 147
Islam: One Religion under God 147
   A brotherhood of Muslims 148
   Limits to an inclusive theology 149
Honoring Freedom of Choice and Respecting Diversity 151
   Protecting freedom of choice 152
   Embracing diversity as the Will of God 152
Examining Some Controversial Passages on Interfaith Relations 153
   Fighting against "unbelievers" 154
   Forbidding "friendship" with People of the Book 156

Part IV: Living the Koran *157*

Chapter 11: Following in the Footsteps of Muhammad 159

The Scripture Speaks about Muhammad 159
    Servant of God and mortal man 160
    Muhammad's divine mission 160
    Muhammad as the best example for humanity 161
    Muhammad's mercy for humanity 161
    Muhammad as a seal of the prophets 162
Doing as God and His Messenger Do 163
Looking at Some Key Prophetic Sayings 165
    Muhammad speaks about God 165
    Muhammad speaks about virtue 166

Chapter 12: Putting Meaning into Ritual 169

Declaring Faith: More than Just Words 170
Conversing with the Divine: Prayer 170
    Understanding the purpose of prayer 171
    Approaching prayer: Purity of mind and body 172
    Let the prayer begin! 175
Raising the Soul Over the Ego: Fasting 180
    Remembering and thanking God 180
    Enjoying the communal aspects of fasting 182
Purifying Wealth, Uplifting the Needy: Almsgiving 183
    Opening your wallet and improving the world 183
    Receiving alms 184
Journeying to the House of God: Pilgrimage 186
    Following the path of Abraham 186
    Journeying through the pilgrimage 186

Chapter 13: Understanding the Koranic View of Self 191

Connecting the Three Dots of Self Awareness 191
    The wild horse and the rider 192
    The three states of self 193
The Seven Gates to the Heart 194
    The ears and tongue 194
    The eyes 195
    The hands and legs 196
    The stomach 197
    The sexual organs 197
Blessed Is the Baby's Soul, a Soul without Sin 198

The Soul's Journey: From Pre-Birth to the Hereafter 199
  Pre-worldly existence 199
  Earthly life 199
  The grave 200
  The Day of Judgment 200
  The final abode 201
The Muslim Self: A State of Being 201
The Kafir: A Faithless Self 202

Chapter 14: Achieving Koranic Ethics and Morality **203**
Discovering Ethical Principles in the Koran 203
  Preserving religion 203
  Preserving life 204
  Preserving lineage 205
  Preserving property 206
  Preserving honor 206
Leading the Life of Good Virtue and Character 207
  Discouraged behaviors 207
  Encouraged behaviors 210
Purifying the Heart 212
  Remembering the Divine: Dhikr 212
  Following God's laws 213
  Keeping company with pious people 214
  Controlling passion and struggling for good 214

Chapter 15: Raising a Family the Koranic Way **215**
Healthy Family Equals Healthy Society 215
Looking for a Spouse: Let the Search Begin 216
  Looking beyond the surface 216
  Making sure the marriage is legal 217
  Giving equal time: Polygamy for men 218
Celebrating Marriage as the Basis of Family 219
  Practically speaking: Basic functions within a marriage ..220
  Intimacy: Both spiritual and physical 222
  Preserving modesty through Scriptural teaching 223
Bringing Up Children 224
  Treating parents well: The best act of piety 225
  Raising children with wisdom 226
  Parental responsibilities to their children 227
A Matter of Inheritance: Who Gets What 228
Tackling Divorce in the Koran 229

Part V: Relating the Koran to the World *231*

Chapter 16: Connecting the Koran to Society 233
Divining a Community of the Middle Path 233
    Having a balanced approach to the Divine 234
    Balancing the worldly and the spiritual in society 234
    Managing justice and mercy in society 235
    Avoiding extremes in religious practice and manners ...236
Witnessing the Truth 237
Enjoining Good and Forbidding Evil 238
Uniting a Community with the Rope of God 240
    Equality of mankind before God 240
    The brotherhood of man 241
Leadership and Citizenship in the Koran 243
    Forming a political identity 244
    Governing by the Book 245
    Living up to citizenship 246
    Receiving the rights of citizenship 247
    Non-Muslims living in Muslim lands 249
Jihad: Struggling in the Path of God 252
    Struggling against evil 252
    Jihad as armed struggle 253

Chapter 17: Purifying Society through Islamic Law 255
Defining Shariah 256
Extracting and Interpreting Sacred Law 257
Searching for Rulings and Principals 258
    In the Koran 258
    In the prophetic tradition 261
    In the consensus of the scholars 263
    In juristic analogy 264
Exploring the Contents of the Sacred Law 264
Understanding the Islamic Penal Code 265
    Punishing murder 266
    Punishing the spreading of violence 267
    Punishing theft 268
    Preventing unlawful sexual relations 269
Looking at the Four Schools of Law 270
    The Hanafi School of Law 270
    The Maliki School of Law 271
    The Shafi'i School of Law 271
    The Hanbali School 272

Chapter 18: Struggling for God: Jihad **273**

Finding the Spirit of Jihad 274
　Defending life and religion 274
　Defending human rights and freedom of worship 275
　Dispelling the myths behind passage 9:5 276
Connecting Qital with Islamic Law 279
Understanding Martyrdom 279
Looking at Jihad in Today's World 280

Chapter 19: Discussing Women in the Koran **283**

Finding Equality in the Scripture 284
　Eve: A model for gender equality 284
　The Virgin Mary: A divinely inspired woman 286
　Other famous and infamous women in the Koran 288
Discerning Women's Rights in Divine Law 290
　Right to inheritance 291
　Right to own property, manage business, and control wealth 291
　Right to work and equal pay 292
　Right to education 292
　Right to social and political participation 293
　Rights of marriage 293
　Right to initiate divorce 293
　Right to bear witness to business transactions 294

Chapter 20: The Koran and Modernity **295**

Differentiating between Modernity and Modern Culture 295
Promoting Social Progress 296
Focusing on Issues of Modernity 297
　Science 298
　The arts 298
　Human rights 299
　Economics and free trade 300
　Morality and secularism 301
Imagining an Islamic Democracy 302
　Debating the rule of law between citizenry and God 303
　Expressing the will of the people through elections 305
　Holding public officials responsible 305
　Liberty and Koranic ideals 306
　Social equality and Islamic law 307

Part VI: The Part of Tens **309**

Chapter 21: Ten Misconceptions about the Koran **311**

Misconception #1: Muhammad Wrote the Koran 311
Misconception #2: The Koran Is Incoherent and Unorganized 312
Misconception #3: The Koran Is Void of Reason 313
Misconception #4: The Koran Espouses Polytheism 314
Misconception #5: The Koran Says That God Belongs to One People 315
Misconception #6: God Is Wrathful and Unloving in the Koran 316
Misconception #7: The Koran Preaches Fatalism 316
Misconception #8: Jihad Means "Holy War" 317
Misconception #9: The Koran Discourages Interfaith Dialogue
   and Cooperation 318
Misconception #10: The Scripture Values Men More Than Women 319

Chapter 22: Ten Ways to Dig Deeper into the Koran **321**

Comparing "Translations" 321
Listening to the Koran 323
Looking at Different Interpretations 324
Reading Books 325
Studying Arabic 326
Studying the Koran 326
Surfing Web Sites 327
Taking Classes 328
Talking to Muslims 328
Visiting Your Local Mosque 329

Appendix A: Glossary of Koranic Terms **331**

Appendix B: Finding Prophets in the Koran **339**

Index **341**

Introduction

· ·

*L*et the exciting journey begin! *The Koran For Dummies* introduces you to the sacred Revelation revered by over 1.4 billion men and women worldwide.

The chapters in this book also guide you through the often complex and controversial perspectives of the Koran that has come under new scrutiny in a post-9/11 world.

I hope that this book answers all your questions about this sacred Book and provides you with a renewed understanding of the Islamic faith and the Muslim tradition.

About This Book

The Koran has been at the heart of Muslim life and culture for over 1,400 years. Interpretations of Islam and its role in the world today gain legitimacy among Muslims only when those ideas and theories can find their roots in the sacred Scripture.

As such, the Koran is probably the most used and misused Book in the world, not only by Muslims, but also by non-Muslim activists and intellectuals. By reading this book, you can gain basic, necessary, information on the teachings of the Koran that continue to shape the debate on the world's future.

Muslims often claim that Islam offers a complete way of life that intertwines inner experiences with outer realities. Through this book, you can come to appreciate the Koran's intimate role in individual and communal Muslim life — a role that gives rise to intense spiritual treasures and core community values. The importance of this subject has taken on new meaning as Islam has emerged as the second largest world religion; many experts consider Islam the fastest-growing religion in the United States and Europe.

The Koran For Dummies provides a basic, practical understanding of the Koran's role in Muslim life and society. This book, as an introduction to the Scripture, doesn't discuss every interpretation found about the Koran in Muslim and non-Muslim circles.

I wrote this book as an American Muslim; my own religious experiences played a part in the writing of this book. However, *The Koran For Dummies* offers an objective, accurate portrayal of traditional Islamic views about the Koran.

Most books that you find on the Koran are either too academic for the average reader or too short for a comprehensive discussion of the Koran's style and content. This is what makes *The Koran For Dummies* unique. This book is organized in a simple, easy-to-read style that tells you what you want to know about the Koran in a straightforward, but complete, way.

As a companion to this book, I recommend *Islam For Dummies,* by Malcolm Clark, published by Wiley. This book does an excellent job of explaining Muslim history, culture, and politics. It also includes a great introduction to the various sects within Islam.

Conventions Used in This Book

As you read this book, you should keep the following points in mind.

Muslims strongly believe that the Koran is the actual living word of God that was revealed through Angel Gabriel to Prophet Muhammad. Muslims use expressions like "the Koran says . . ." and "God says . . ." interchangeably to mean the exact same thing. Throughout this book, I write from the Koran's perspective, keeping in mind that most people who read this book are not Muslim. However, you should remain aware that for Muslims, the Koran represents God's unaltered and eternal word.

I use three different words to refer to the sacred Revelation: Koran, Book, and Scripture. These three words mean exactly the same thing — there is no difference between them whatsoever.

In this book, most Koranic passages that I explain are not direct quotations, but rather paraphrases of the basic overall meaning. Many of the passages that I do quote directly make up only part of the verse that helps explain any given subject, and not the whole verse, which often includes text that strays from the subject at hand.

The Koran is made up of chapters, called *Surahs,* and verses or lines, called *Ayat* (singular, *Ayah*). When I give references to the Koran, I write them like this: *(Surah: Ayah)* or *(Surah*: *Ayah-Ayah)*. For example, if I quote *Surah* 1, *Ayat* 1 through 3, I cite the passage as (1:1–3).

The beautiful and unique Arabic language has amazing depth. Arabic words can be translated in more than one way. In this book, I translate concepts in a way that non-Muslims will find easy to understand. I could write an entire chapter, or even a whole book, to explain the complexity of some Arabic words (such as *Taqwa* — God-consciousness), but, for reasons of space, I use only a few words to reference each Arabic word.

When transliterating Arabic terms into English phonetics, I use transliterations commonly found in the West, so that you can recognize the word. For example, the proper transliteration of "Koran" is "Qu'ran." And, the proper transliteration of "Mecca" is "Makkah." But, for the sake of recognizability, I use the transliterations that may be most familiar to Western readers.

At times, to fully understand the Koran, you have to venture to outward sources. The most important of these sources is Prophet Muhammad, the primary interpreter and teacher of the Book. Throughout this book, I refer to the sayings of Muhammad to expand on basic ideas presented in the Koran. Sometimes I also refer to the words of Muhammad's close companions and famous scholars of the Islamic tradition.

Finally, this book doesn't necessarily tell you about your Muslim neighbor, friend, or co-worker. Nor do these chapters always reflect the condition of the Muslim world today. In fact, most Muslims contend that many in the Muslim world have stopped practicing the authentic teachings of the Koran and instead rely on their own tribal cultures for individual and communal guidance. This book seeks to present the Koranic ideal, which doesn't always translate into practice. However, if you want to understand the role of the Koran in society, and its ability to bring reform to the Muslim world, you must understand the ideals of the Scripture.

Foolish Assumptions

You don't have to be familiar with the Islamic faith or Muslim practice to read and enjoy *The Koran For Dummies*. In each chapter, I tell you the fundamentals that you need to understand what the Koran teaches and how it perceives the seen and unseen world.

If you're already somewhat familiar with the Koran, you'll enjoy an added experience of simplifying and breaking down major concepts and themes in the Koran that you may have questions about. Also, this book will provide you with valuable insight into the Koran's literary structure that will help you to feel more comfortable with the Book's narrative style. Finally, you'll find out about the basics of classical and modern interpretations of the Scripture, which will give you an added perspective into your experience with the Koran.

You have many questions about the Koran. You may have heard many stories and controversies in the media and don't know where the Koran stands on these issues. I answer frequently asked questions and respond from an Islamic perspective to common misconceptions that you may have come across.

I assume that you want an introductory look into the most essential issues related to the Koran. I don't offer you an academic critique that dissects every theory, view, and interpretation about the Koran. Instead, I explain traditional views and interpretations of the Scripture. But please remember, as you dig deeper into your exploration of the Book, that interpretations of its text are as diverse as the Muslim population that comes from every culture possible.

How This Book Is Organized

The Koran For Dummies is not a textbook. You don't have to read it from A to Z or even start from the beginning.

If you want to read about a particular topic regarding the Koran, you can find that subject in the Table of Contents or Index, flip to those pages, and get a quick explanation of the topic.

You don't have to read this book from cover to cover, starting with Chapter 1 and going straight through to the end. However, if you are just starting out in your exploration of the Koran, I advise you to look through the chapters in Part I of this book to get up and running.

Part I: Revealing the Word of God: The Book

This opening part introduces you to the basic themes of the Koran, and the history of its compilation. Here, you also discover the Book's unique style and language. Finally, you get a look into how the Book relates to Judeo-Christian Scriptures.

Part II: Searching for the Soul of the Koran

The Koran has always been open to interpretation and reinterpretation. This part surveys traditional methods of interpreting the Koran, and takes a look at modern movements of thought that seek to define the Will of God through the Koran.

Part III: Seeing the Koranic Worldview

This part of the book explores the Koran's view of the seen and unseen worlds, including the concept of God and angels to the role of man on earth. It also looks at the Scripture's relationships with traditions other than its own.

Part IV: Living the Koran

This part explains the Koran's role as a living Book that guides towards a spiritual life and seeks to create moral-ethical civilizations. It also looks at the teachings of the Book on shaping a good family life.

Part V: Relating the Koran to the World

In this part, you can discover how the Koran plays a dynamic role in shaping modern events and belief systems. This part looks at Koranic teachings on society, law, war and peace, women, and modernity.

Part VI: The Part of Tens

The first chapter in this part addresses ten misconceptions about the Koran, explaining how these wrong ideas about the Book differ from reality. The second chapter gives you ten great ways to continue your exploration of the Koran long after you have read this book.

I end the book with a short glossary of Koranic terms, and a list of references to the prophets throughout the Koran.

Icons Used in This Book

The following icons make your reading of *The Koran For Dummies* even easier:

Points to essential information about the Koran that you may want to remember in the future.

Highlights an example that may help you better understand a particular Koranic concept. Also, leads you to further reading.

Alerts you to important differences of opinion that can be found in the interpretation of the Koran.

Emphasizes sayings of Prophet Muhammad, his companions, or scholars of the Koran to further your insight.

Tells you how Muslims practice their faith in their day-to-day lives.

Points out mistakes that readers of the Koran often make, or common misconceptions that people hold about the Book.

Where to Go from Here

You can begin this book from wherever you like, or simply use it as a reference whenever the need arises. You may also want to start by checking out the following:

- If you're interested in the Koran's most basic message and teachings, then go to Chapter 1. Also check out Appendix A to become familiar with some fundamental Koranic terminology.

- If you want to know how the Koran relates to other faiths, go to Chapters 5 and 10.

- If you're interested in the history of the Koran, its organization, and literary style, then turn to Chapters 2, 3, and 4.

- To read about the Koran's belief system and its worldview, see Chapters 8, 9, and 10.

- To find out how Muslims put the Koran into practice, go to Chapters 11 through 15.

- To discover the Koran's views on contemporary issues and debates, turn to Chapters 16 through 20.

- Finally, if you want to explore the Koran beyond reading this book, see Chapter 22.

Part I
Revealing the Word of God: The Book

The 5th Wave   By Rich Tennant

"I told him we were lost and needed directions. He offered a road map for the former, but suggested the Koran for the latter."

In this part . . .

Although you can begin reading this book from any chapter that interests you, you may want to begin with this part if you are completely new to the Koran.

In this part, I focus on the dynamic style, language, and construction of the Koran. I introduce you to its overall message, and tell you how the Koran came together in book form. I also compare the Book with the Judeo-Christian Scriptures.

Chapter 1

Getting to Know the Koran

In This Chapter

▶ Defining the Koran

▶ Summarizing the Koranic message

▶ Zooming in on the audience for the Koran

▶ Discovering the basics about the Islamic faith and Muslims

As you begin the exciting journey into one of the world's most respected and sacred texts, you need to become familiar with some basics regarding the divine revelation known as the Koran.

In this chapter, I address the meaning of the Koran and explore its divine message to readers and followers alike. I also point out some key information about the Islamic faith and the Muslim community that should help prepare you for a look into the Koranic worldview.

Receiving Revelation Straight from the Source

Muslims view the Koran in its original form and language as the literal and unaltered word of God, preserved for all times to come. When Muslims say, "God says," or "the Koran says," they are in fact using different words to quote one source — namely God Himself.

The Koran provides a direct relationship from its source (God) to its audience (humanity). As such, Muslims have a deep reverence for the Koran. In fact, in traditional understandings of Islam, if you express doubt that the Koran is the word of God, then you have uttered words of disbelief.

Finding meaning in the word "Koran"

Linguistically, the word *Koran* (pronounced *Qur'an*) comes from several roots that shed some light on the significance of the Book to Muslim culture and identity.

Koran comes from the root word *Qara'a,* which means "to read" or "to recite." The word *Koran,* therefore, means "recitation." (Interestingly, the very first word revealed to Prophet Muhammad was *Iqra,* meaning "read" or "recite.") This definition points to the nature of the Koran as an oral tradition that is understood and preserved with the majestic voice of God through the human voice of recitation (see Chapter 2).

Koran also comes from the root word meaning "city," which denotes civilization. The Koran is the foundational book for Islamic civilization, just as the Bible is for Western civilization or the Torah is for the Hebrew people. For Muslims, the Koran forms Islamic identity in individuals and societies alike.

The Koran is also referred to as the Book, which in itself was a revolutionary concept for pre-Islamic Arabs. Up until the Koranic revelation, the Arabs didn't transmit knowledge through writings, but mostly through oral culture. The Koran was literally the first book for the Arabs.

The root word for *book* in Arabic means "to bind." The Koran served, and to this day serves, as the Book that unites hearts all around the Muslim world, irrespective of language or cultural origin. Muslims have different cultural attitudes and lifestyles, but all Muslims can understand one another through a shared Scripture that transmits the same basic ethics and morals. This shared experience facilitated the spread of Islam throughout Asia, Africa, and parts of Europe.

Guiding the Way: Prophet Muhammad

Muhammad is the final prophet and messenger of God, through whom the Koran was revealed and taught to the people of Arabia. As such, he has a very important role in the Koran and Islam.

The Koran describes Prophet Muhammad as a mercy to mankind (21:107) and the best example to be followed in worshipping God (68:4). Muslims seek to emulate Muhammad's nature, character, and actions on a daily basis as the best of God's servants.

The role of Prophet Muhammad is extremely important in Islamic law because his sayings and actions are considered only second to the Koran in the interpretation and development of Islamic law (see Chapter 17). Furthermore, the life example and teachings of the Prophet supplement Koranic teachings by clarifying or expanding on ideas and concepts.

Muhammad preached the message of Islam, which means submission to God alone; he never asked to be worshipped himself. In fact, worshipping Muhammad would immediately place you outside the Islamic faith. Therefore, the term *Muhammadanism,* which some people use to describe the Koranic message, is not only incorrect, but also offensive to Muslims.

In this book I quote sayings and examples of Muhammad, wherever appropriate, to provide further explanation of Koranic concepts. See Chapter 11 for more about Muhammad and his role in Islam.

Discovering the Basic Messages of the Koran

This section gives you a brief glimpse into the different themes covered in the Koran.

The unity of God

The Koranic message centers around the teaching of God's unity as One, known as *Tawhid* in Arabic. This concept says that God is the Creator of all beings, the Sustainer of each living creature, and that He has power over all things (see Chapter 8).

Worship and service to God

The Koran teaches that all creations on earth and in the universe submit to God in worship by following His laws. So, the sun and the moon, the plants and the trees, and the animals bow down in praise of God for sustaining them with His mercy and compassion (24:41) (see Chapter 9).

In this theatre of divine creation, humans play a unique role. God chose humans, over all His creations, as His vicegerents and representatives on earth (see Chapter 8 for more information on the purpose of human life). Human beings, then, must nurture civilization into a God-conscious society by establishing God's laws, known as *Shariah* in Arabic (see Chapter 17).

Prophets to teach and guide

Humans are endowed with reason, superior thought, articulation, and free will that allow them to work for the betterment of humanity. To guide humans in this daunting task, God sent prophets, throughout history and to every community on earth, who taught mankind the ways of spiritual, moral, and ethical excellence (16:36). Muslims show their reverence for these prophets by saying, "Peace be upon him," after mentioning any one of them by name.

From time to time, God also sent down His revealed Books, such as the Psalms and the Torah, to teach humans the difference between right and wrong, and the application of divine laws on earth.

Completion of past revelations

The message of God's Oneness, and the belief system it entails, remained the same with each prophet, but the laws of God changed for each community and time period, ending in the Koranic revelation and prophethood of Muhammad (see Chapter 11). The prophets who preached this message, and their subsequent followers, are all known in the Koranic worldview as Muslims — those who submit willingly to God's will (22:78).

The Koran doesn't preach a new message or even introduce a new religion. Instead, the concept of Islam as submission to the will of God has existed from day one and was taught to Prophet Adam as the first man on earth. The message was introduced in different time periods to each community on earth, specific to the condition of those people and relevance of their time.

According to the Koran, God chose the Koranic revelation as the final message that completes the teachings of all previous revelations, both in theology and law. As the final message, the Koran provides guidance not only for a specific community or time, but for all of humanity.

Guidance to a spiritual path

Submitting to God creates peace and harmony within an individual that then spreads to society. In submission to God, people are free from servitude to other people and to their own lower desires (9:31). Through service to the Divine, people can reach heights of spiritual and moral success. (See Chapter 13 for more information on the Koranic view of the self.)

Followers of this path of enlightenment, described as Light upon Light, constantly seek ways to earn the good pleasure of God that spiritually feeds the soul throughout their lives.

Movement for social change

The Koran places heavy emphasis on using divine revelation as a catalyst for establishing justice in all its forms, and struggling against injustice in all its forms. (See Chapter 16 for more info on relating the Koran to society.) At the center of this teaching is the concept of *Jihad*, which means to struggle in the path of God, both inwardly and outwardly, for good against evil.

The Koran focuses much of its attention on warning against the mistreatment of the poor, orphans, widows, and all those who are oppressed in society (5:8). In fact, almost every story of past prophets focuses on the theme of establishing justice and fighting against evil.

These social teachings make it impossible for Muslims to separate their religious lives from their social responsibilities (6:162–164). The Koran teaches that such a distinction is wrong, and preaches that not only individuals, but also social institutions, should serve God as a means of producing an equitable society.

Accountability of deeds

Carrying out the teachings of the Koran is a trust from God, about which every single individual will be asked on the Day of Judgment and rewarded accordingly (17:13–14). The Koran teaches that God is the most Just, and that those who are punished on that day will only be punished because of what their own hands have sent forth. Those who will be granted paradise will be granted this prize based on their faith in God and righteous deeds. (See Chapter 9 for details on the Day of Judgment.)

Naming the Revelation

To understand what the Koran is and the purpose for its revelation, you need to look at how the Koran identifies itself using various names and qualities in the revelation. The Book uses 50 different names for itself; I describe five of the most-telling and encompassing names in the following sections.

The Guidance

The Koran introduces itself to the reader as a Book of Guidance (2:2) for those who are conscious of their Sustainer. The Koran, therefore, isn't a book of history, science, or even of philosophical arguments — although it has an element of each in it — but is meant, at its very core, to guide human life towards the "straight path" (1:6) of worship and service to God alone.

You can think of the Koran as a kind of user's manual for everyday living. Devout Muslims remember its teachings and guidance in almost every step they take throughout the day. Muslims don't recite the Koran throughout the day for ritualistic purposes, but rather to serve as an internalizing voice of God that directs believers to make ethical and moral choices in every aspect of life, be it in personal worship, family relationships, or social interactions. (See the chapters in Part IV for more information on the Koran as a source of guidance.)

Each verse of the Koran teaches the ways to spiritual and moral success through stories of past prophets and peoples. The Book also warns mankind against the destructive paths that previous generations took.

Establishing the Koran as a Book of Guidance also gives meaning to Koranic laws and prescribed rituals, which guide human actions in ways that benefit both the individual and society. (See Chapter 17 for more about Islamic law.)

The Criterion

The Koran says, "Blessed is He who from on high, step by step, has bestowed upon His servant the standard by which to discern the true from the false (The Criterion), so that to all the world it may be a warning" (25:1).

The Koran, in other words, makes clear distinctions between right and wrong, righteousness and impiety. The Book rejects *moral relativism,* in which cultural attitudes or the trends of time blur the concepts of good and evil. Rather, morality and ethics are based on a divine revelation that judges good and evil on universal, unchanging principles (see Chapter 14). These ethical principals seek to preserve religion, life, intellect, human dignity, wealth, and lineage — rather than maintain the status quo or service to temporal, worldly objectives.

The Proof

The Koran doesn't expect people to blindly follow the Koranic message without using the faculty of thinking and reasoning. In fact, the Koran heavily criticizes those who simply do things because they saw their forefathers doing the same (2:170).

The Koran acts as a kind of proof (4:174) for God's message. In almost every chapter, the Book goes into deep discussions about the wonders of God's creation, asking the reader to reflect on the universe, the plants, animals, and mountains of the earth, and upon the creation of humanity (2:164). All of this is a means of affirming God's true existence, His favors on mankind, and due submission to His divine laws and message alone.

The Koran as proof also has a historical implication regarding people who doubted Muhammad's claims to prophethood. The Jews and Christians asked Muhammad to bring some miracles as proof of the divine inspiration he claimed to receive from God. After all, if Muhammad was a prophet, then he should be able to perform miraculous magic, like Prophet Moses, or instantly cure the sick, like Jesus. The Koran responds to this challenge by exhibiting the highest form of literary Arabic ever to appear in the history of the language.

The majestic words of the Koran changed the face of the Arabic language, outclassing all the famous poetry that was at its height before the Koranic revelation. To this day, the Koran serves as the standard by which all other Arabic is judged. The Book's language proves especially remarkable since it was transmitted through Prophet Muhammad, who was illiterate and was not known for his recital of poetry. (The sayings of Prophet Muhammad, known as *Hadith,* are full of wisdom, but don't come close to the majestic literary standards of the Koran, which comes directly from God.)

In short, the primary miracle and proof that defines Muhammad's prophet-hood is the Koran itself.

The Reminder

The Koran says that the divine revelation is no less than a reminder to all the worlds (6:90). The Book reminds its followers and readers of three things in particular:

- ✔ Of the original, pure teachings and struggles of past prophets who preached submission to God's Will alone (Islam) as a way of life. Also, of the original laws and moral teachings of previous divine scriptures, such as the New Testament and Old Testament.

- ✔ Of the natural, pure state of the human soul that is in tune with the ethical teachings of God. The Book is a reminder of that which the soul already knows and accepts, but may have deviated from after a life without awareness of divine presence.

- ✔ Of God's constant presence from which mankind can hide nothing. Believers should live their lives in full awareness of this reality.

As a reminder to the world, the Koranic message advocated throughout the scripture is universal. The Koran wasn't sent for one nation or time period, but for all peoples until the end of time. (See Chapter 5 for more information on the Koran as a universal message.)

The Koran also sees itself as a reminder because it continues and confirms previous revelations that preach God's Oneness (21:25). The Koran teaches that this message was revealed to the world's communities through various prophets and messengers throughout history, ending with Prophet Muhammad as the last prophet and messenger of God.

Due to the universality of the prophetic message, you can find a lot of similarities between the Koran and the revealed scriptures of Prophets Moses and Jesus (see Chapter 5 for more on the similarities between Koran and Judeo-Christian scripture). However, the Koran was also revealed to clarify theological misunderstandings that developed in previous divine faiths, and to call people towards the reformed laws of God.

The Healing

The Koran describes itself as a healing cure for the hearts of men and women (17:82). This Koranic quality illuminates a spiritual path for the heart's purification through the remembrance of God. The revelation attempts to soften hearts that have become hardened, in order to reclaim and preserve the humanity of people.

The Koran in this role seeks to elevate the spiritual human heart to a level that is in love with the Divine, and therefore submits the soul into a constant state of gratitude to God, known as *Shukr,* during the best and worst of times (2:152). The teachings of healing guide the perception of mind and heart into a state of contentment that allows God's light to enter the soul, so that a person's every word and action are in tune with deep awareness of divine presence.

Hearing the Words: The Audience of the Koran

The Koran's audience is universal, without limitation on gender, culture, or religious beliefs. However, the Koran specifically addresses six general groups of people in various passages and at varying lengths:

- ✔ **Humankind:** These verses usually carry universal teachings, warnings, and glad tidings. Such passages usually begin with "O mankind" or "O Children of Adam." You find most of these addresses in the earlier periods of revelation, known as Meccan Chapters (see Chapter 2).

- ✔ **Believers:** These verses address Muslim behavior and etiquette and often introduce a law. You also find warnings of falling into the wrong path and glad tidings for those who are steadfast and patient in faith. Such passages usually begin with "O you who believe" or end with "this is for those who believe."

- ✔ **People of the Book:** The Koran gives a lot of attention to Jews and Christians as recipients of earlier revelations. When the Koran addresses both religious communities, it uses the term "People of the Book." The Koran uses stories of the respected prophets that all three faiths share to remind People of the Book about the universal message of submission to God alone.

  The Koran sometimes addresses each group separately. For example, after the historic migration of the early Muslim community from the city of Mecca to the city of Medina, Prophet Muhammad interacted with Jewish tribes in discussions and debates about the Koranic revelation. The Koran contains several passages that answer the questions of the

Jews and also highlight some of the tensions that existed between the two communities. (I tell you more about this dialogue between the Koran and the Jews in Chapter 5.)

✔ **The hypocrites:** The Koran finds hypocrisy detestable and uses strong language to condemn it. Usually these verses warn about what awaits hypocrites in the Hereafter and call such people to change their ways from hypocrisy into true belief.

✔ **Rejecters of faith:** The Koran speaks extensively about those who reject the Koranic message with philosophical arguments and warnings of disbelief.

Referring to such people as "unbelievers," or even worse, "infidels," is a serious mistranslation of the Koranic concept of disbelief. The word used in Arabic is *Kafir,* which is a very comprehensive term, but at its core means someone who is ungrateful. From the Koranic standpoint, the greatest ingratitude is to reject the Truth of the Creator (God) after it has been made manifest. However, someone who has never heard the message of the Koran, or only a misrepresentation of its teachings, has never had the opportunity to accept or reject. Therefore, "rejecter of faith" or "denier of God's Signs and Blessings" are more accurate translations of this Koranic term.

✔ **The reader:** When reading the Koran, you can literally find yourself having a conversation with the Scripture as thought-provoking questions come up, one after the other. In one chapter alone the Koran asks 31 times, "Then which of the favors of your Sustainer will you deny?" (55) after recounting the blessings that come from God for mankind.

The Koran also poses questions to capture the full attention of its readers in an intimate way, such as "Has He not found you an orphan and given you shelter? And found you lost on your way, and guided you? And found you in want, and given you sufficiency?" (93:6–8).

Knowing the Essentials about Islam and Muslims

Understanding some fundamentals about Islam helps you more fully investigate the Koran.

The Six Pillars of Belief

Islam has six pillars of belief that altogether are known as *Iman.*

The first pillar of faith is belief in One God, complete monotheism, without any doubt or exception.

Coming to God with an attitude

Both the Pillars of Islam and the Articles of Faith can't be complete unless they are practiced and followed in a most beautiful and perfect way, known as *Ihsan.* Prophet Muhammad defined *Ihsan* as worshipping God as if you see Him, and to know that He truly sees you. This is the essence of God-consciousness, which nurtures a feeling of humility and thankfulness before God. Practicing and believing with this spirit leads to the full fruits of this way of life known as Islam.

The second pillar of faith is belief in angels (Chapter 9), who perform various functions based on God's instructions. Through these angels, God revealed His Books or Revelations to various prophets throughout time. Muslims must believe in God's Revelations and respect without distinction of any prophet who preached the unity of God as One. Belief in these Books and prophets make up the third and forth pillars of faith.

Fifthly, Muslims must believe in accountability of their actions, both good and bad, and subsequent rewards and punishments for those deeds. This concept manifests itself in the belief of the Day of Judgment (Chapter 9), about which there can be no doubt, as the Koran says.

The sixth and last pillar of faith is to believe in the divine Decree of God, by which God's presence is understood as timeless. This belief also teaches God's perfect knowledge, and complete Power and Will over all things.

The Five Pillars of Islam

Muslims often compare Islamic practices to a well-built structure with a solid foundation and four supporting pillars (see Figure 1-1).

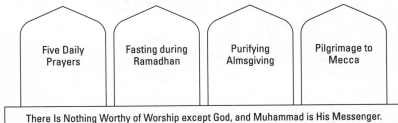

Figure 1-1:
The Five
Pillars of
Islam.

| Five Daily Prayers | Fasting during Ramadhan | Purifying Almsgiving | Pilgrimage to Mecca |

There Is Nothing Worthy of Worship except God, and Muhammad is His Messenger.

The foundation, and first pillar of Islam, is the declaration of faith, known as *Shahadah.* The declaration is that "I bear witness that there is nothing worthy of worship except God, and I bear witness that Muhammad is His servant and messenger." Muslims repeat this declaration several times throughout the day and are expected to speak and act with the *Shahadah's* spirit in mind.

The declaration of faith comes to life through the four supporting pillars. The second pillar is prayer, *Salat* in Arabic, which is offered five times throughout the day between dawn and night. The usual prayer lasts about ten minutes and consists of Koranic recitation, bowing, and prostration before God.

During the month of *Ramadan* — the ninth month of the Islamic calendar and month in which God began revealing the Koran — all able-bodied Muslims who have reached the age of puberty practice Islam's third pillar, fasting, known as *Sawm.* The fast begins at sunrise and ends at sunset each day of the month. The fast consists of avoiding food, water, and sex. Muslims are expected to be on their best behavior during this month.

The fourth pillar of faith is almsgiving, known as *Zakat.* Every financially-able Muslim must give to the poor and needy in society once every year.

The final pillar of faith is pilgrimage, known as *Hajj,* which consists of going on a once-in-a-lifetime journey to visit the city of Mecca and its surrounding areas. Here Muslims visit the *Ka'ba,* the first House of God built by Prophet Abraham and his son, Ishmael. Also, Muslims stand on Mount Arafah where Adam and Eve are believed to have descended to earth from heaven. The pilgrimage has several steps and is very challenging physically and emotionally. Millions of Muslims go each year for this rite that commemorates the life and struggles of Prophet Abraham, his wife Hagar, and son Ishmael, as a way of coming closer to God.

See Chapter 12 for more information on prayer, purifying alms, fasting, and pilgrimage.

Muslims: The followers of Islam

The term *Muslim* refers to anyone who follows Islam as a way of life and declares faith in God alone and in the prophethood of Muhammad. (Linguistically, the word "Muslim" means one who submits in worship to the Will of God alone.)

Since it is impossible (and not the job of humans) to see what is in the hearts of men and women, anyone who declares himself or herself as a follower of Islam is called a Muslim. However, this title of Muslim doesn't guarantee success in this world or in the Hereafter. Only a person's faith in God and righteous actions bring him or her closer to the eternal home of paradise.

Not all Arabs are Muslims, and more importantly, not all Muslims are Arabs. While Arabia is the birthplace of Islam, there are many Jewish and Christian Arabs as well. Moreover, Arabs constitute only about 18 percent of the entire Muslim population of approximately 1.4 billion people. Muslims are the majority population in much of Africa, the Middle East, South Asia, and even some parts of Europe; the highest population of Muslims is in Indonesia. Muslims are a strong and vibrant community in many Western societies, including the United States, which is home to approximately 7 million Muslims.

Please refer to *Islam For Dummies,* by Malcolm Clark, published by Wiley, for more information about Islam and Muslims around the world.

Chapter 2

From Revelation to Written Book

....

In This Chapter
▶ Understanding the story and nature of revelation
▶ Compiling the Book
▶ Preserving the Scripture for over 1,400 years

....

*T*he Koran criticizes previous recipients of divine revelation (such as Jews and Christians) for altering their Scriptures after their prophets passed away (2:75, for example). As such, Prophet Muhammad and his companions were extremely diligent with the proper collection and authentication of the Koran as a Book, so that they would not fall into the same errors as did people of previous faiths. Muslims strongly believe that God fulfilled his promise to protect the Koran from any human corruption.

In this chapter, I talk about the traditional understandings of how Prophet Muhammad received revelation and how the revelation was spread among the people. I also look at the history of the Koran's collection into a Book and its preservation over time.

Revealing the Koran to Muhammad

Like the Torah in the Jewish faith, the Koran claims that it has existed eternally with God in a "preserved tablet" (85:22). Once the time came for revealing the Book to the world through Prophet Muhammad, the Koran descended to the lowest heavens *(Bait al-izza)* in preparation for its revelation. The Koran describes this event, known as *Lailatul' qadr,* in one of the most beautiful *Surahs* of the Book:

> "We have indeed revealed this (Book) in the Night of Power: And what will explain to you what the Night of Power is? The Night of Power is better than a thousand months. Therein comes down the Angles and the Spirit by God's permission on every affair. Peace, until the rise of dawn" (*Surah* 97).

The beginning of revelation

Muhammad, a deeply reflective person since his childhood, spent days in complete seclusion while meditating and worshipping God in the Cave of Hira. According to Muhammad's own account, one day while he was meditating, a spirit spoke to him with the word, "Read!" Muhammad was startled by the voice and replied, "I do not know how to read." Suddenly, the spirit caught a hold of Muhammad, squeezing him until he could bear it no more, and once again urged Muhammad to read. Muhammad was shaken by the experience, and repeated his honest claim, "I do not know how (or what) to read!" Once again the spirit took hold of Muhammad, squeezing him tightly, then finally letting him go. This time, the spirit, known as Angel Gabriel, revealed the first words of the Koran to Muhammad: "Read, in the Name of your Sustainer, who created, created man from a clot. Read! For your Sustainer is the most Bountiful One, who has taught man the use of the pen — taught man what he did not know" (96:1–5).

This experience marks the beginning of a divine revelation, the finality of Islam, and the Prophecy of Muhammad, who continued to receive the Koran in stages through Angel Gabriel over a span of 23 years (610–632 of the Common Era).

After Muhammad experienced revelation for the first time, he returned to his wife, Khadija, seriously unnerved by the experience. His wife comforted him and believed that Muhammad had just received a divine message. Khadija took Muhammad to her cousin, Waraqa ibn Nawfal, a learned Christian monk who converted to Islam, for advice. After hearing Muhammad's experience, Waraqa reassured him by saying:

"Surely, by Him in whose hand is Waraqa's soul, you are a prophet of this people. There has come unto you the greatest Angel (Gabriel) who came unto Moses. Like the Hebrew prophets, you will be called a liar, ill-treated, and they will cast you out and make war upon you."

The Koran reflects this concept of revelation or divine inspiration, known as *Wahy* in Arabic. The Book asserts in several passages that the inspiration Muhammad received came from the same source and experience as those Messengers who came before, such as Prophets Noah, Abraham, Moses, and Jesus.

Muslims believe that the Koran is divinely created in form, content, message, and actual words. Muhammad provided the vehicle for spreading this divine message to the world by imparting revelation; however, he is not, Muslims believe, the author or editor of the Scripture. In fact, the Koran describes Muhammad and his people as unlettered (7:157; 62:2). The Koran also refutes the notion that Muhammad wrote the Koran by saying, "And you were not a reader of any Scripture before it, nor did you write it with your right hand. In that case, indeed, would the talkers of vanities have doubted" (29:48).

Wealth, women, and wine in Pre-Islamic Arabia

Historians use two primary sources to know what life was like in Pre-Islamic Arabia: the Koran and famous poetry of that time. Both of these sources paint a picture of a society that was in love with wealth, women, and wine. The culture reflected an over-indulgence in worldly affairs, social injustice, and economic disparity. The Koran was revealed into these social conditions.

Many early chapters, or *Surahs* in Arabic, in the Book passionately speak out against the period's arrogance and materialism, both of which lead to social injustice, which impacted mostly the poor, destitute, orphans, widows, and women.

Surah 107 illustrates this disdain for arrogance and materialism: "Have you seen one who denies the True way of life *(Din)*? Behold, it is the one who turns away the orphan, and encourages not the feeding of the needy. Woe, then, unto the worshippers who are neglectful (in spirit and mind) of their prayers. Those who want only to be seen and praised but refuse even neighborly needs."

In order to rectify the situation, the Koran instituted a pillar of faith, known as *Zakat,* to bridge the gap between the rich and poor by making almsgiving obligatory. Also, the Koran created laws to end unethical business practices and economic corruption. For example, the Koran made usury unlawful because the practice drew the poor into unending debt.

Pre-Islamic Arabia was a harsh place for women. The citizens grieved over the birth of baby girls, and even buried baby girls alive in order to save face in society. The Koran strongly condemns this immoral behavior in several passages (16:59 and 81:8–9, for example).

Also, like most other societies at the time, women were denied such basic rights as inheritance, owning property, and equal status under the law. The Koran elevated the status of women by providing them with inheritance rights, rights to ownership of property and businesses, and equal status under the law and in religion (see Chapter 19 for more about women in the Koran). Women were often harassed in society and sexually preyed upon. The Koran honored the position of women in society by encouraging modesty in clothing and behavior (24:31–33:59), and commanding men to respect the women.

Similarly, orphans were stigmatized and mistreated in Pre-Islamic society. In response, the Koran encouraged kind treatment of orphans, protection of their wealth until they reached a mature age to take care of themselves, and marriage with them despite the lower social status given to them in Pre-Islamic Arabia (4:1–10).

Wine and other intoxicants were also a major part of Pre-Islamic culture. The prevalence of alcohol created an obstacle towards the spiritual and moral development of man, and distracted members of society from the serious issues of their time. The Koran forbade alcohol in order to develop God-conscious individuals who had the ability to make moral and ethical choices in life.

Obviously, these and other laws seriously challenged the status quo of Pre-Islamic Arabia. They were met with stiff resistance, especially from tribal leaders who benefited the most from the unjust institutions of society. Muslims were persecuted, mocked, and eventually driven from their homes in Mecca, because of their call for a just society built on divine laws.

Please see *Islam For Dummies,* by Malcolm Clark, published by Wiley, for more information on the history of Islam.

The stages of revelation

Muhammad told his companions that divine inspiration came to him in two primary ways through Angel Gabriel:

- Revelation came "like the ringing of a bell" until he grasped all that was revealed.
- Revelation came through Angel Gabriel taking the form of a man who would then impart divine inspiration to Muhammad.

The Islamic tradition says that Angel Gabriel visited Prophet Muhammad every Ramadan (the month of fasting in which the revelation of the Koran began) to review whatever had already been revealed of the Koran with Muhammad. The year Muhammad died, Angel Gabriel came twice during Ramadan to review the Koran, thereby finalizing its content and organization.

The Prophet received revelation in stages, and not all at once, for a number of reasons:

- **To relate revelation to Prophet Muhammad's life and experiences as a Messenger of God.** For example, stories of past prophets and their difficulties in preaching God's messages are constantly told throughout the Koran as a way of strengthening the resolve of Muhammad and his companions.

- **To gradually apply divine laws on a community that was not used to the practice of divine ways.** If the Koran were revealed all at once, it would surely have been difficult for the believers to completely change their lifestyles overnight. For example, the ban on alcohol was revealed in three different stages — first limiting its use all the way to forbidding consumption — because alcohol was a big part of Pre-Islamic Arabian culture; it would have been impossible to impose this religious ban cold turkey.

- **To make memorization of the Koran and its application by the community as easy as possible.** Since the Koran was revealed a few verses at a time, it was easier for believers to commit the Scripture to memory and implement its teachings in society.

The Meccan and Medinan periods

Prophet Muhammad first received revelation while he was in Mecca, which marked the first 13 years of his life as the Prophet. The *Surahs* and passages revealed to him during this time are known as *Meccan Surahs*. The next period of revelation occurred after Muhammad and his companion migrated from persecution to Medina, which lasted ten years. Passages and *Surahs* revealed during the Prophet's time in Medina are known as *Medinan Surahs*.

Seven dialects of the Koran

According to the *Hadith,* Angel Gabriel recited the Koran to the Prophet in seven different ways that reflected the diversity of dialects in Arabia. Muhammad told one of his companions, "This Koran has been revealed to be recited in seven different ways (modes), so recite of it whichever is easier for you."

Today, Muslims conform to reading the Scripture in the same dialect that Prophet Muhammad read it, with very few exceptions. (See the section "Collecting the Koran as a Book," later in this chapter, for more information.)

The Koran is not organized chronologically. Meccan passages and Medinan passages appear intermixed in many *Surahs,* especially the longer ones. (See Chapter 3 to find out which *Surahs* were revealed during the Meccan phase, and which ones during the Medinan phase.)

Meccan phase of revelation

Interestingly, the majority of Meccan *Surahs* appear at the back of the Book, and they are usually pretty short. Eighty-five of the 114 *Surahs* were revealed during the Meccan phase, accounting for 11 out of 30 parts, or *Juz'* (see Chapter 3), of the Book.

During this phase of Muhammad's prophetic life, the Koran focused most of its attention on calling people to Islam. Mankind as a whole was addressed more than the community of believers. As such, the subject matter of the Meccan *Surahs* can be categorized as follows:

- **God's Oneness (Tawhid):** *Surahs* during this period introduced a radical notion about God that was quite alien to the Pagan Arab majority. Much of the Koran's early attention focused on convincing the Pagans that God was in fact One. As such, worship and obedience is due to Him alone without any partners. This was the primary message of the Koran during this phase.

- **Day of Judgment and Afterlife:** The second most important doctrinal teaching during the Meccan phase regarded the preaching of the Day of Judgment and an Afterlife. This was a radical departure from Pagan beliefs that did not recognize an accountability of moral actions after death.

- **Pious conduct:** A major emphasis of the Koran during this phase was the upright conduct and manner of the believers who accepted Islam. These teachings sought to transform personalities from rigid, harsh, and impatient into tranquil, merciful, and patient human beings. The Koran also took issue with unethical practices of economic and social injustice that were manifested by materialism and arrogance. During this phase, the Koran called on the freeing of slaves and proper treatment of orphans, the poor, and women.

Medinan phase of revelation

Even though these *Surahs* were revealed after the Meccan *Surahs,* a majority of them are found at the beginning of the Book. These *Surahs* are usually much longer than the Meccan *Surahs.* Twenty-nine out of 114 *Surahs* were revealed during the Medinan phase, comprising about 19 out of 30 parts of the Koran. While there are fewer Medinan *Surahs,* they constitute a greater part of the Book due to their length.

The Medinan *Surahs* address the community of believers more than all mankind. These *Surahs* focus on the following subjects:

- **Legal code:** Much of the Koranic laws, known as *Shariah,* developed during the Medinan phase of revelation. At the time, communal laws became as important as individual laws in order to create a morally functioning society. A vast majority of the laws that you find in the Koran are a direct reflection of the experiences of the Muslim community in Medina.

- **Relationship between immigrants and hosts:** The Koran talks a great deal about the relationship between the Muslims who migrated from Mecca *(Muhajirun)* and the hosts of Medina *(Ansar).* Their relationship is solidified as one-brotherhood; mutual rights and responsibilities are also discussed in this context.

- **The hypocrites:** The Koran addresses the issue of hypocrites during this phase as well. These people were those who had infiltrated the Muslim community acting as Muslims, but really serving as agents of Islam's enemies, such as the Pagan Arabs of Mecca.

- **People of the Book:** Prophet Muhammad and the Muslim community come into contact and social-political relationships with the Jews and Christians of Medina. Many passages deal with theological debates between Prophet Muhammad and the People of the Book. The relationship between the two groups is also discussed in these *Surahs.*

Transmitting revelation to the community

Prophet Muhammad transmitted the Koran to his community in two primary ways.

The oral tradition

With the aid of Angel Gabriel, Muhammad first memorized the revelation and then taught it to his followers. Arabian society at the time had a very strong oral tradition, whereby memorization of poetry and stories was the primary form of education, especially in the absence of a literate written tradition.

When Muhammad recited and taught the Koran, his companions committed the verses to memory. Prophet Muhammad encouraged memorization of the

Book in several of his sayings *(Hadith)*. Most of Muhammad's companions memorized large parts of the Koran, and some of his companions, including three of his wives, memorized the entire Koran.

The Prophet encouraged those who memorized the Koran to teach it to others. Muhammad sent special delegates to various communities for this purpose once Islam began spreading far and wide.

Memorization is absolutely necessary to carry out the five daily prayers that in part require recitation of passages from the Koran. As such, memorization of the Koran remains an important part of the Muslim experience to this day.

The written tradition

The Koran is unique among religious scriptures of the world in that the entire Book was written down by several scribes during the lifetime of Prophet Muhammad, who directed its organization himself. The *Hadith* say that in Medina, Muhammad had over 29 scribes who wrote down every revelation that the Prophet received. The Prophet himself directed which verse belonged in which *Surah*.

Some Western historians doubt that the Koran was written down during the Prophet's lifetime. But Muslims believe that the *Hadith* (which also serve as historical documents) make clear that the Koran was indeed written during Muhammad's lifetime. The Koran itself also hints at the presence of a written form when it says, "None shall touch it but those who are pure" (56:79).

Collecting the Koran as a Book

Two years after Prophet Muhammad died, the Muslim community under the Caliphate of Abu Bakr was drawn into a few internal and external battles. In one such battle, known as the Battle of Yamama, several companions who had memorized the Koran were killed. Umar, who succeeded Abu Bakr after he passed, feared that as these companions died, preservation of the Koran would weaken, since the written pages existed with individual scribes and not as a collected Book. Umar advised Caliph Abu Bakr that the Koran should be collected in book form in order to preserve the Scripture.

Abu Bakr hesitated at first to take on this enormous project, because he feared venturing into an area that Muhammad did not, nor did he instruct his companions to produce the Koran as a book after his passing. However, Umar slowly convinced Abu Bakr that compiling the collections of the scribes into book form would preserve the Koran from any future corruption or tragedy. Abu Bakr employed Zaid bin Thabit, one of the greatest learned men among the companions who had served as the Prophet's primary scribe, to collect manuscripts of the Koran and prepare them for collection as a Book.

Zaid bin Thabit called for all those with written records of the Koran to bring their collections forward. The submissions had to meet four criteria:

- ✔ The recordings must have been written originally in the presence and with the instruction of Prophet Muhammad.
- ✔ Two witnesses had to testify that the writings were indeed made in the presence of Muhammad.
- ✔ The writings could not include passages of the Koran that were clearly abrogated by the Prophet.
- ✔ All recordings had to be checked against the memory of those who had memorized the entire Koran.

Scribes gathered and copied all the manuscripts that passed the submission requirements. This one Book was then given to Abu Bakr. When Abu Bakr passed away, the Book was given to Umar, as the succeeding Caliph. After Umar's assassination, the Book went to Hafsa, the daughter of Umar and widow of Muhammad.

Conforming the Koran's dialects

As the borders of Islamic civilization grew beyond the Arabian Peninsula, and more and more non-Arabic speakers embraced Islam, new challenges began to emerge. The seven dialects in which the Koran was revealed (see the sidebar "Seven dialects of the Koran" earlier in this chapter) began causing some confusion among the Muslims, as the recitation of certain passages differed from one group to another.

During the Caliphate of Uthman, the third Caliph of Islam, unity was undermined between Muslims who ignorantly claimed superiority of one dialectical recitation over another. One of Uthman's advisors, Hudhayfa bin al-Yaman, sent an urgent message to the Caliph: "Quick! Help the Muslims before they differ about the text of the Koran as the Jews and Christians differed about their Scriptures."

Uthman and his council decided to restore unity among the Muslims by producing a Book that followed only the Quraysh dialect — the same dialect that Prophet Muhammad used. The original transcription of the Koran, made during the time of Caliph Abu Bakr, served as the primary source for this new version. This time, however, the Quraysh dialect was given preference over recordings of any other dialect. A council of companions who were most knowledgeable about the Koran, including Zaid ibn Thabit, oversaw the project and approved its final version. This version, known as "Uthmani," exists up to this day.

Uthman ordered the burning of all other copies of the Koran, so that the Muslim community could unite in its recitation of the Koran under a single dialect. This Koran was copied and sent to the major centers of the Islamic world along with learned men who taught its proper recitation to the people, to great success. Today, Muslims have absolutely no dispute about the wording or recitation of the Koran.

Three copies of the original Uthman Koran remain preserved today. Also, the seven dialects of reciting the Koran are still known, taught, and documented in written and oral form in different regions of the Muslim world. However, the Uthmani recitation serves as the unifying dialect of recitation for all Muslims.

The Koran was compiled, authenticated, and spread throughout the Muslim world within 20 years after the Prophet's death. Today, Muslims employ people who have memorized the Koran to authenticate the correctness of the printed Word before it goes for publication. Unlike other religious traditions, memorization remains the primary method for preserving the Koran.

The Koran in modern-day print

The earliest written copies of the Koran didn't contain any vowel marks (*Tashkil*) or diacritical marks (*I'jam*). People at the time learned the Koran orally, and the written copy only served as a reminder for those who had memorized the Koran. However, the science of vowel marks on the Koranic text developed within the first two centuries after the Prophet's death.

With the invention of the printing press, copies of the Koran appeared at a faster rate and spread to the farthest parts of the world. The Arabic of the printed Koran needed vowel marks and diacritical marks to assist primarily non-Arabs in pronunciation and distinguishing letters.

Reading with the wrong vowels or diacritical marks can lead to serious errors in meaning. For example, in 9:3, if the word for *Apostle* is read wrongly as "*Rasulihi*" instead of correctly as "*Rusuluhu,*" then the meaning changes from "God and His Apostle dissolve all obligations with the Pagans," into "God dissolves obligations with the Pagans and the Apostle."

Also, in earlier versions of the Koran, letters with the same shape could not be distinguished one from the other. For example, the letters *Ba, Ta,* and *Tha* are all shaped as a line. In earlier versions, no dots distinguished these three letters — since the oral culture did not necessitate it. But, today, with a more literary culture, these letters need to be clearly distinguished in the Scripture. As such, modern-day prints mark:

- *Ba* with a dot below the line
- *Ta* with two dots on top of the line
- *Tha* with three dots on top of the line

These marks help guide readers through the Scripture. The only difference between earlier and latter versions of the Koran is these guiding marks or dots for the reader's aid (see Figures 2-1 and 2-2).

Figure 2-1:
Letters of
the earliest
written
Koran.

© Neema Frederic/CORBIS SYGMA

Figure 2-2:
Letters of
the Koran
that exists in
print today.

© Harold Naideau/CORBIS

Handling the Book

Muslims have great reverence for the Book and treat it with respect. The Koran itself only makes only one requirement for touching the Koran: that a worshipper be pure when he or she touches it (56:79). Scholars of the Koran take this to mean that the reader must be in a state of ritual purity (see Chapter 12) when holding the Book.

However, other traditions of showing respect have also taken root in Muslim culture. For example, Muslims place the Koran on the highest shelf in their homes, and they consider it sacrilegious to place the Book under any other books. Similarly, Muslims never place the Koran on the ground. Instead, Muslims elevate the Koran on a well-designed wooden structure (see Figure 2-3) or table when reciting its passages.

Many Muslims carry the Koran around with them so that they can read or refer to it whenever they want or need to. Also, Muslims display verses, such as 2:255, of the Koran on the walls of their homes, inside their cars, and in lockets in an effort to gain God's protection.

Muslim culture calls forth the Koran during both happy and sad occasions. For example, the Book is often raised over a bride and groom as they enter their new home. At funerals, some Muslims place the Koran over the coffin, and a group of people often read the entire Koran on behalf of the deceased after the funeral. This is all done in the spirit of gaining God's blessings, mercy, and forgiveness.

However, scholars point out that the greatest reverence Muslims can show to the Koran is believing in its message and following its teachings with complete submission to God.

Memorizing Miracles: Preserving the Koran throughout History

In the tradition of Prophet Muhammad and his companions, Muslims all over the world continue to memorize passages of the Koran. Many Muslims memorize several parts of the Book, while some memorize the entire Koran. Those who commit the entire Koran to memory are honorably known as *Hafidh* (plural, *Huffadh*) or traditionally as *Qari* (plural, *Quraa*), or preservers of the Koran.

The *Huffadh* have the responsibility to help others memorize the Koran. This teacher-student tradition goes all the way back to Prophet Muhammad, who memorized the Koran with Angel Gabriel as his teacher; the companions then memorized the Book with Muhammad as their teacher. In successive generations, other young Muslims memorized the Koran with those companions as their teachers. This oral tradition continues even today.

After a person memorizes the Koran, with the aide of a teacher, he or she appears before a group of senior *Huffadh* who administer a test. One *Hafidh* randomly selects a passage of the Koran and recites the first line. The student carries on the recitation of that passage either to the end of the *Surah* or until the group of testers indicates that they are satisfied. The *Hafidh* then chooses another passage for recitation.

In many Muslim countries, this test appears every Friday on national television. It's a very powerful testimony to the dedication that Muslims have in preserving their Scripture.

Experiencing the Koran as Divine Art

The language of the Koran is expressed in Islamic culture and civilization through beautiful recitation or chanting, known as *Qira'ah,* and through the beautification of Koranic verses in calligraphy.

Recitation

The science of reciting the Koran is known as *Tajweed* in Arabic. Young students learn this science from professional teachers. Muslims recite the Koran all their lives (see Figure 2-3).

© Dean Conger/CORBIS

Figure 2-3:
A man sits with the Koran as he practices the oral tradition of recitation.

Hearing the Word

Since the Koran has a natural rhyme and rhythm to it, reciting the Scripture with a beautiful voice is not as difficult as you may think. Once, I remember leading the prayer at my local mosque when a group of non-Muslim visitors came to visit the Center. After the prayer was over, one of the guests said, "Wow, learning to recite the Koran must have taken you forever!" In reality, the Muslims there knew that my voice was only mediocre compared to the eloquent recitations you can hear all across the Muslim world. The naturally beautiful voice of the Koran comes out when the Book is recited with a pure heart and mind.

Good reciters of the Koran are as well known in the Muslim world as pop stars are in the West. People talk about the qualities of these reciters at the dinner table, and when they appear on television, people on the streets gather around TV screens as if a major sporting event were taking place.

God taught Muhammad to "recite the Koran in slow, measured, rhythmic tones" (73:4). There are four modes of recitations in the science of *Tajweed:*

✔ *Hadr:* Reciting the Koran at normal talking speed.

✔ *Tartil:* Reading slowly with a sense of deep reflection.

> ✔ *Tajweed Tahqiq:* Reading slowly, but with more care. Usually used for teaching recitation to others.
>
> ✔ *Tajweed:* Reading at a pace between normal and slow. Most prayer leaders *(Imams)* use this mode when leading prayers at the mosque.

If you want to listen to recitation of the Koran, you can find some great audio files on the Internet that offer recitation in Arabic and many other languages. Check out my recommendations for these sites in Chapter 22.

Navigating through recitation notes

If you look at a printed copy of the Book, you notice several diacritical marks (see the section "The Koran in modern-day print" earlier in this chapter). These marks serve almost like musical marks that navigate the recitation of the Koran.

These marks help the reader of the Koran to properly pronounce the assimilation of words into each other in the Scripture, so that the rhythmic flow remains constant and undisturbed from word to word. Diacritical marks also tell the reader where to pause within a long verse, where to raise the voice, and where to lower it. The marks also navigate prolongation of letters that produce a more powerful affect for the listeners.

Diacritical marks were not included in the earlier written Book, but eventually became necessary as the number of non-Arab Muslims grew. These marks helped non-Arab readers recite the Koran properly and serve the same purpose today. Those who have memorized the entire Koran also memorize diacritical marks and how to apply them with every passage of the Scripture. As such, the voice during recitation also alternates with emotions of the Koran that are represented by these marks.

Savoring the majestic oral voice of the Koran

Reciting the words of God, as Muslims believe the Koran to be, internalizes divine speech in the human heart. Prophet Muhammad described the heart of a believer who does not recite and memorize the Koran as a "deserted house."

Hearing the words of the Koran has been known to bring even the burliest of followers to their knees — it's that intense of an experience for many Muslims. Your basic understanding of the Koran can't be complete without listening to the oral recitation of the Koran (see Chapter 22 for recommendations). Even if you don't understand the Arabic words, the recitation can give you a feel for the voice of the Book that evokes such emotions in the Muslim experience.

Calligraphy

Unlike the pre-Islamic period of Arabia, when people drew pictures and made statues of their gods, Muslims are completely prohibited from making any physical representation of God or His prophets. Doing so is considered sacrilegious.

The art of calligraphy was developed as an artistic form to express the beauty of divine words. This beautiful tradition appears throughout the Muslim world, on the walls of mosques — most famously at the *Ka'ba* in Mecca and Dome of Rock in Jerusalem — and on the pages of the Koran. You can also find calligraphy of Koranic verses at the gates of Muslim owned shops, homes, schools, and hospitals.

Calligraphy is known in Arabia as "Music for the eyes." Usually the beauty is expressed by the eloquent display of letters (see Figure 2-4). Other times, letters join together to form an object, such as a mosque or an animal, such as a peacock.

Figure 2-4: Beautiful Islamic calligraphy appears on many mosques.

© Lindsay Hebberd/CORBIS

If you want to find out more about Islamic calligraphy and art, I encourage you to check out the following sites on the Internet:

✔ **Islamic Art Network:** www.islamic-art.org

✔ **Famous photographer of the Muslim world, Peter Sanders:** www.petersanders.co.uk

✔ **Famous Islamic Calligrapher, Muhammad Zakariya:** www.zakariya.net

Chapter 3

Mapping Out the Structure of the Book

In This Chapter

▶ Finding out about the Book's organization

▶ Experiencing the Koran's narrative style

▶ Illustrating the difference between early *Surahs* and later ones

In this chapter, I explore the idea behind the Koran's narrative style and show some examples of early *Surahs* and later *Surahs*. I also look at some interesting facts about the Book's organization. All of this information should help you feel more at home when you pick up a copy of the Koran.

Discerning the Structure of the Koran

Today's written Koran has three major organizational elements: phrases, sentences, or verses, known as *Ayat;* chapters, known as *Surahs;* and parts, known as *Juz'.* I tell you about each of these in the following sections.

Ayat

Ayat are of various lengths; they can be as short as one letter or as long as several dozen words, which make up the verses *(Ayat)*. In the printed edition of the Koran, all verses have a number (1, 2, 3, and so on) to make them easier to locate; you can find several of these verse references throughout this book. Every *Ayah* in the modern printed Book is clearly marked with an imprinted symbol that contains the number of the appropriate verse.

Ayah means "sign" in Arabic, which fits in with the concept that every word, and indeed every sentence, of the Koran is a sign of God. In each *Ayah*, Muslims find wisdom, beauty, and spiritual teachings that represent God's Wisdom and Beauty.

Surah 2, *Al-Baqara,* contains the most *Ayat* — 286. You find the shortest number of *Ayat* in *Surahs* 98, 103, and 110, which all have 3 *Ayat.* In total, the Book contains 6,240 *Ayat.*

Surahs

A *Surah* is a body of words that form one chapter or part distinguishable from the next *Surah.* (In Arabic, *Surah* means "rows" or "fence.") The *Surahs* vary in length between 3 *Ayat* (*Surah* 108) and 286 *Ayat* (*Surah* 2). In total, the Book has 114 *Surahs.*

Each *Surah* begins with the words "In the Name of God, the most Gracious, the most Merciful," except for *Surah* 9. Even when people recite the Koran, they start each *Surah* with this phrase, which reminds them of God's dominant attributes.

All *Surahs* have a number. When you see a reference to a passage in the Koran, the *Surah* number appears first, then the verse, or *Ayah,* number. For example, a reference to the Opening *Surah, Ayah* 3 would read as (1:3).

Each *Surah* also has a name that derives from the central idea or story of the *Surah,* or simply from the first few words of the *Surah.* Sometimes you may find it difficult to see the central topic or story that gives the *Surah* its name. For example, *Surah* 2 is named *Al-Baqara,* or "The Cow." This *Surah* describes how the Children of Israel took the golden calf for worship when Prophet Moses left them for 40 nights; however, this story only makes up a short part of the *Surah's* 286 *Ayat.*

Generally, but not always, *Surahs* are arranged according to their respective lengths:

- ✔ The longest ones — with over 100 *Ayat* — are known as *Al-tiwal.* You find these in *Surahs* 2 through 10.

- ✔ *Surahs* with about 100 *Ayat* are known as *Al-mi'un;* they can be found in *Surahs* 10 through 35.

- ✔ *Surahs* that consist of fewer than 100 *Ayat* are known as *Al-mathani.* These are found in *Surahs* 36 through 49.

- ✔ The last set of *Surahs,* which usually run fewer than 50 *Ayat* long, are known as *Al-mufassal.* These are found in *Surahs* 50 through 114.

Juz'

Juz' literally means "part" or "portion." *Juz'* is an artificial construct that was introduced to make the reading of the Koran easier over a period of one month; especially in Ramadan, congregations recite one *Juz'* each day in order to complete the recitation of the Koran over the period of the month. As such, the Koran is divided into 30 parts, which you can see in Table 3-1.

Table 3-1	**Juz' in the Koran**
Juz' Number	*Surah and Ayah*
Juz' 1	1:1–2:141
Juz' 2	2:142–2:252
Juz' 3	2:253–3:92
Juz' 4	3:93–4:23
Juz' 5	4:24–4:147
Juz' 6	4:148–5:82
Juz' 7	5:83–6:110
Juz' 8	6:111–7:87
Juz' 9	7:88–8:40
Juz' 10	8:41–9:93
Juz' 11	9:94–11:5
Juz' 12	11:6–12:52
Juz' 13	12:53–14:52
Juz' 14	15:1–16:128
Juz' 15	17:1–18:74
Juz' 16	18:75–20:135
Juz' 17	21:1–22:78
Juz' 18	23:1–25:21
Juz' 19	25:22–27:59
Juz' 20	27:60–29:45

Table 3-1 (continued)	
Juz' Number	**Surah and Ayah**
Juz' 21	29:46–33:30
Juz' 22	33:31–36:27
Juz' 23	36:28–39:31
Juz' 24	39:32–41:46
Juz' 25	41:47–45:37
Juz' 26	46:1–51:30
Juz' 27	51:31–57:29
Juz' 28	58:1–66:12
Juz' 29	67:1–77:50
Juz' 30	78:1–114:5

Discovering Surah Names and Themes

The Koran consists of 114 chapters, known as *Surahs* in Arabic, which run as long as 286 verses or as short as 3 verses.

Table 3-2 identifies the names of each *Surah*, in English and Arabic, and describes the overall theme(s) of each *Surah*. This list also identifies whether a *Surah* was revealed in Mecca (MC) or in Medina (MD).

Table 3-2		*Surah* Names and Themes
Surah Number	**Names in Arabic and English**	**Major Theme(s)**
1	Fatihah: The Opening (MD)	Introduction to the overall message of the Koran
2	Al-Baqarah: The Cow (MD)	Nature of man; Israel's story; Abraham's story; *Ka'ba* and Islamic community; struggle in God's path; nature of God
3	Al-Imran: Family of Imran (MD)	Jews and Christians; lessons from battles of Badr and Uhud; internal and external responsibility of Muslims

Surah Number	Names in Arabic and English	Major Theme(s)
4	An-Nisa: The Women (MD)	Treatment of women and orphans; inheritance, marriage, and family; community of Medina and hypocrites; People of the Book
5	Al-Ma'ida: The Table Spread (MD)	Fulfillment of obligations; manners; righteousness; critique of Jews and Christians; justice and brotherhood; life and miracles of Jesus
6	Al-An'am: Cattle (MC)	Nature of God and His signs; Paganism
7	Al-A'raf: The Heights (MC)	Man's religious history; prophets' lives
8	Al-Anfal: Spoils of War (MC)	Defining success; the power of Truth
9	At-Tuaba: Repentance (MD)	Treaties; ethics of war; the power of Truth
10	Yunus: Jonah (MD)	Signs of God; ungratefulness of man
11	Hud: Hud (MC)	Mercy and Patience; Noah, Hud, Lot
12	Yusuf: Joseph (MC)	Story of Joseph; forgiveness
13	Al-Rad: Thunder (MD)	Revelation; righteousness versus evil
14	Ibrahim: Abraham (MC)	Darkness versus Light; Abraham's story
15	Al-Hijr: The Rocky Tract (MC)	Evil of Satan; Abraham; the Koran
16	An-Nahl: The Bee (MC)	All creation glorifies God; the Koran
17	Bani Israel: Children of Israel (MC)	Prophets; service to God; pride; the Koran
18	Al-Kahf: The Cave (MC)	Timeless time; teachings of wisdom
19	Maryam: Mary (MC)	Mary and Jesus; Abraham and family
20	Ta-Ha: Ta-Ha (MC)	Revelation; the life of Moses; the Last Day
21	Al-Anbiyaa: The Prophets (MC)	Day of Judgment; work righteousness
22	Hajj: Pilgrimage (MD)	Pilgrimage; Mercy and Truth of God
23	Al-Muminun: The Believers (MC)	Faith and practice; unity of the prophets

(continued)

Table 3-2 *(continued)*

Surah Number	Names in Arabic and English	Major Theme(s)
24	An-Nur: The Light (MD)	Modesty and privacy laws; God's Light
25	Al-Furqan: The Criterion (MC)	The Koran as Criterion; contrast of Signs
26	Ash-Shu'araa: The Poets (MC)	Prophetic struggles; truth versus falsehood
27	An-Naml: The Ants (MC)	Moses, Solomon, Salih; God's Glory
28	Al-Qassas: The Narration (MC)	Pharaoh versus Moses; Muhammad
29	Al-Ankabut: The Spider (MC)	Trials in preaching; the nature of the Koran
30	Ar-Rum: The Romans (MC)	God's creation; man brings corruption
31	Luqman: Luqman (MC)	Imparting wisdom to children; parents
32	As-Sajda: Adoration (MC)	Symbols before man; Revelation
33	Al-Ahzab: The Confederates (MD)	Men and women; the Prophet's wives
34	Saba: The City of Saba (MC)	Power and justice; faith versus unbelief
35	Fatir: The Originator (MC)	God's creation and praise; good versus evil
36	Ya-Sin: Ya-Sin (MC)	Revelation; nature; the Day of Judgment
37	As-Saffat: Ranks (MC)	Peace and victory; evil; the prophets
38	Sad: Sad (MC)	Spiritual power versus worldly temptation
39	Az-Zumar: The Groups (MC)	Unity in creation; revelation; guidance
40	Gaffir: Forgiving (MC)	Good versus evil
41	Fussilat: Detailed verses (MC)	Mankind in relation to faith and revelation
42	Ash-Shura: Consultation (MC)	Defending revelation; evil versus guidance
43	Az-Zukhruf: Gold Adornments (MC)	Revelation; Abraham; Jesus
44	Ad-Dukhan: Smoke (MC)	Revelation; pride versus a spiritual truth

Surah Number	Names in Arabic and English	Major Theme(s)
45	Al-Jathiya: Bowing the Knee (MC)	Results of mocking faith and unbelief
46	Al-Ahqaf: Winding Sand-tracts (MC)	Purpose of creation
47	Muhammad: Muhammad (MD)	Defending faith against hostility
48	Al-Fath: The Victory (MD)	Elements of ultimate victory; Hudabiya
49	Al-Hujurat: Inner Apartments (MD)	Healthy communal laws for coexistence
50	Qaf: Qaf (MC)	God's Signs; the Day of Judgment
51	Az-Zariyat: Scattering Winds (MC)	Winds; Signs; the Reminder; the hereafter
52	At-Tur: The Mountain (MC)	Good deeds versus evil deeds
53	An-Najm: The Star (MC)	Revelation; the nature of God; disbelief
54	Al-Qamar: The Moon (MC)	The Day of Judgment nears; heedlessness
55	Al-Rahman: Most Merciful (MD)	God's favors on humanity
56	Al-Waqia: The Inevitable Event (MC)	The Day of Judgment and hereafter
57	Al-Hadid: The Iron (MD)	God's Power and Knowledge
58	Al-Mujadila: Pleading Woman (MD)	Rejection of falsehood and mischief
59	Al-Hashr: The Gathering (MD)	Expelling the treacherous Jews of Medina
60	Al-Mumtahana: Examining Woman (MD)	Enemies of faith; Abraham's example; marriages of believers and non-believers
61	As-Saff: Battle Aray (MD)	God's Signs; helping God's cause
62	Al-Jumma: The Assembly (MD)	Purity and wisdom; Friday prayers
63	Al-Munafiqun: The Hypocrites (MD)	The nature of hypocrites

(continued)

Table 3-2 *(continued)*

Surah Number	Names in Arabic and English	Major Theme(s)
64	Tagabun: Mutual Loss & Gain (MD)	The Creator is one; the hereafter
65	At-Talaq: Divorce (MD)	Some laws regarding divorce
66	At-Tahrim: Forbidden (MD)	Harmony in family life
67	Al-Mulk: The Dominion (MC)	Outer shadows versus inner truth
68	Al-Qalam: The Pen (MC)	Good prevails; God's Justice
69	Al-Haqqa: The Sure Reality (MC)	Truth prevails over falsehood
70	Al-Ma'arij: The Ascension (MC)	Patience in time leads to heaven
71	Nuh: Noah (MC)	Struggles of Prophet Noah
72	Al-Jinn: The Jinn (MC)	Nature and story of Jinn
73	Al-Muzammil: Garments Folded (MC)	Prayer and humility in spiritual life
74	Al-Mudathir: One Wrapped Up (MC)	Prayer and patience in spiritual stress
75	Al-Qiyamat: The Resurrection (MC)	The Day of Judgment; inner psychology
76	Al-Insan: Man (MD)	Arguing against the atheist
77	Al-Mursalat: Sent Forth (MC)	The hereafter for rejecters of faith
78	An-Nabaa: The News (MC)	God's loving care and future promise
79	An-Naziat: Tear Out (MC)	Death; the fall of pride
80	Abasa: He Frowned (MC)	Reminding the Prophet; the hereafter
81	At-Takwir: Folding Up (MC)	The Last Day; the Day of Judgment; the Koran
82	Al-Infitar: Cleaving Asunder (MC)	The Last Day; the Day of Judgment
83	Al-Mutafifeen: Dealing Fraud (MC)	Strongly condemns dealing in fraud
84	Al-Inshiqaq: Rendering Asunder (MC)	The Last Day; the Day of Judgment

Surah Number	Names in Arabic and English	Major Theme(s)
85	Al-Buruj: Zodiacal Signs (MC)	God defends his believers
86	At-Tariq: The Night Visitant (MC)	Protection for every soul
87	Al-A'la: The Most High (MC)	Purification of the soul
88	Al-Ghashiyah: Over-whelming Event (MC)	Good versus evil; Signs of God
89	Al-Fajr: The Dawn (MC)	Spiritual truths; inner psychology
90	Al-Balad: The City (MC)	Nature of man; inner psychology
91	Ash-Shams (MC)	Reflection on God's creation; purifying the soul; rejection of arrogance
92	Al-Lail: The Night (MC)	Striving for God's pleasure
93	Ad-Duha: Morning Light (MC)	God's intimate relationship with man
94	Al-Sharh: The Expansion (MC)	With every hardship comes ease
95	At-Tin: The Fig (MC)	Nature of man
96	Iqraa: Recite (MC)	Humble origins of man; preaching
97	Al-Qadr: Night of Power (MC)	The Night of Power (revelation of the Koran)
98	Al-Baiyina: Clear Evidence (MD)	The fate of those who reject faith
99	Al-Zilzal: The Convulsion (MD)	The Day of Judgment
100	Al-Adiyat: Those That Run (MC)	Spiritual power; man's ingratitude
101	Al-Qari'ah: Day of Clamor (MC)	The Day of Judgment
102	At-Takathur: Piling Up (MC)	Man's love for wealth; death
103	Al-Asr: Time through the Ages (MC)	The nature of time; the nature of good
104	Al-Humaza: Scandal-monger (MC)	Condemnation of the scandal-monger and backbiting

(continued)

Table 3-2 *(continued)*

Surah Number	Names in Arabic and English	Major Theme(s)
105	Al-Fil: The Elephant (MC)	Defense of Mecca against the Christian army of Abraha the year Prophet Muhammad was born
106	Quraish: Custodians of Kaba (MC)	An appeal to the Quraish to accept God's Oneness and His Message
107	Al-Ma'un: Neighborly Needs (MC)	True meaning of worship; requiring faith for good deeds; love for those in need
108	Al-Kauthar: Abundance (MC)	Spiritual riches through devotion
109	Al-Kaffirun: Rejecting Faith (MC)	No compromise for the Truth
110	An-Nasr: Help (MC)	All victory comes from God
111	Lahab: Lahab (MC)	Fate of the cruel Lahab who persecuted Muhammad and his followers
112	Al-Ikhlas: Purity of Faith (MC)	Short summation about God in the Koran; Oneness of God
113	Al-Falaq (MC)	Seeking refuge in God
114	An-Nas (MC)	Appeal to trust in God for protection from all evil

Finding Your Way Through the Moral Narrative

Surahs in the Koran are built around a moral narrative. In the longer *Surahs* that dominate much of the Book, the moral narrative is presented in three primary ways:

✔ Signs of the Divine in the universe followed by moral teachings, arguments, and premises

✔ Teachings that set into motion a law or set of laws that seek to put a moral lesson into practice or show ways of preserving the moral teaching

✔ Moral teachings or premises followed by a story or series of stories that provide historical references to past prophets and civilizations to prove a moral argument

In the following sections, I present some examples of how the moral narrative generally works in the Koran.

Through divine signs

Look at the first 13 passages of *Surah* Al-Rahman (55), which is famous for its extraordinary eloquence and beauty. This *Surah* provides a great example of how moral narrative is developed in the Koran through discussion of God's divine signs.

The moral narrative in this *Surah* is introduced with a series of divine signs in the universe, a moral truth about justice that is reflected in God's creation, and finally the moral question that demands an answer. This format then repeats throughout the *Surah,* and many others.

The first seven *Ayat* describe proofs or signs of God in the universe:

> "The Most Merciful! It is He who has taught the Koran. He has created man. He has taught him speech, an intelligent speech. The sun and the moon follow courses computed. And the herbs and the trees both bow in adoration. And the firmament has He raised high, and He has set up the just balance (in the universe)" (55:1–7).

Then, the next two *Ayat* introduce the moral truths of balance and justice:

> "So that you too might never transgress just balance (in life). So establish weight with justice and fall not short in the balance" (55:8–9).

The next three verses return to the signs of God:

> "It is He who has spread out the earth for all living beings. Therein are fruit and date palms, producing enclosed dates. Also corn, with its leaves and stalk for fodder, and sweet-smelling plants" (10–12).

Finally, a question, which is asked 30 times over the course of this *Surah,* presents a moral argument:

> "Then which of the favors of your Sustainer will you deny?" (55:13).

The signs of God's wonder in the world lead to this powerful question, which inspires deep contemplation, reflection, and gratitude in many readers.

Through laws

Some *Surahs* present moral laws and truths one after the other. These laws and truths often relate to a moral teaching presented in the *Surah's* first few

Ayat, which establishes such lessons as human rights and kinship ties. The *Surah* goes on in this pattern, but with new moral propositions, then laws, combined with truths.

As an example, *Surah* Al-Nisaa' (4) presents the moral narrative as a moral teaching followed by supporting moral laws.

Ayat 1 begins with a universal moral declaration:

> "O mankind! Be conscious of your Guardian Sustainer, who created you from a single soul, created out of it, his mate, and from them two spread countless men and women. Be conscious of God through whom you demand your mutual rights and of these ties of kinship. For, verily, God is ever watchful over you" (4:1).

This passage, which speaks of mutual rights, goes on to call for a series of laws that implement social rights for the weakest members of society — orphans (4:2–9). Then, out of these laws, a moral truth is presented: "Those who unjustly eat up the property of orphans, eat up a fire into their own bodies. They will soon be enduring a blazing fire" (4:10).

Then, the moral narrative moves into the laws of inheritance, but with an eye on the very first verse of this *Surah* that speaks of kinship ties. These laws seek to establish justice between family members so that wealth is spread among the deceased's lineage (4:11–12). Again, the narrative uses this opportunity to expound another moral law that describes the fate of those who obey God and His Messenger as opposed to those who willfully disobey the teachings (4:13–14).

From there, the Koran expands on the preservation of lineage by introducing laws that punish sexual lewdness, which threaten the moral foundations of family life (4:15–18). Then, the same theme of mutual rights and honoring of family is once again taught by instructing men to treat their wives with kindness and justice (4:19–21). The sanctity of family life is further explored by a list of prohibitions on who a Muslim male or female cannot marry (4:22–25).

Again, the Koranic narrative turns from moral laws to moral truths that say God only wishes to guide humanity to a good life, but those who follow their lower passions wish only to turn away from that guidance. Also, God wishes to make laws easy for humankind seeing that "man was created weak" (4:26–28).

Through stories of the past

In this narrative form, the Koran often begins with a moral or set of moral teachings that are then explained through stories of prophets or other wise characters, and concluded by a moral truth or set of moral truths.

For example, *Surah* Hud (11) in the Koran presents a moral narrative through the experiences of prophets that strengthen the moral premise of the *Surah*.

The opening passages of the *Surah* present its moral argument:

> "(The Koran teaches) that you should worship none but God. (Say:) Verily I am sent unto you from Him to warn and to bring glad tidings. Seek you the forgiveness of your Sustainer and turn to him in repentance that He may grant you enjoyment, good for a term appointed, and bestow His abounding Mercy on all who abound in merit. But if you turn away, then I fear for you the chastisement of a Great Day. To God is your return, and He has power over all things" (11:2–4).

Then the *Ayat* go on to say that God knows all things, whether they are open or hidden, since He who created the earth will give judgment in the future (11:5–8). From this, the *Surah* begins to talk about the nature of man, where he tends to fall into despair when joy is followed by sadness. And, man tends to fall into arrogance when a period of sadness or suffering is followed by divine favors of joy. But, those who escape this hypocritical nature are those "who show patience and perseverance, and work righteousness" who are then forgiven for their sins and granted happiness (9:11).

After this, the *Surah* warns its believers not to leave the teachings of the Book even when the rejecters of faith belittle them for their beliefs and practices. The *Surah* goes on to defend the sanctity of the Koran, and how it conveys only the Truth. Believers should not worry or get distracted from their objective of worshiping God, despite the efforts of those who lie about God and "hinder men from the path of God" (11:12–23).

The *Surah* then presents a similitude as its first step in explaining with clarity the moral lessons of the past 23 *Ayat*. "These two kinds may be compared to the blind and deaf, and those who can see and hear well. Are they equal when compared? Will you not then take heed?" (11:24).

The *Surah* builds to this point: That God alone should be worshiped, and to achieve a happy state of bliss, you must practice patience, perseverance, good deeds, and humility. But, those who are impatient, arrogant, reject faith, and work to prevent man from walking God's path will be punished in the hereafter.

Now, with this moral premise in mind, the Koran then ventures into a series of stories about past prophets who struggled to preach God's word, but each time were met with opposition to the Truth.

The experience of Prophet Noah

First up is Prophet Noah, who declares his prophetic mission to warn his people, and to serve God alone. The rejecters of faith mock Noah as a liar. Noah tells his people that he has indeed come in Truth, does not ask for any material gain, and only seeks to save them from this state of unbelief (11:25–35). Then,

Noah is told to construct an ark that will save him from the great flood. Most people reject his warnings, including his own son. And, when God's word comes true, Noah's people perish, except those who accepted the prophetic teachings of Noah (11:36–48).

The moral of Noah's experience ties back directly to the moral argument or premise in opening passages of this *Surah*. "Such are some of the stories of the unseen. . . . So persevere patiently, for the end is for those who are deeply conscious of God" (11:49).

Prophet Hud and his people

Hud was a prophet sent to the People of 'Ad as their own brother. He also says to his people, just as Prophet Noah before him, that he seeks no material reward for urging his people to turn in repentance to God and to turn away from sin. But, the People of 'Ad reject his message and prefer to continue in their idol worship while claiming that Hud had been seized by evil (11:50–54).

Prophet Hud responds by saying that he calls only to the worship of One God and puts his trust in the Divine, because only God knows all things. He then warns his people of God's punishment if they persist in sin. Finally, God decrees that the People of 'Ad be destroyed, except Prophet Hud and those who followed him (11:55–60).

Prophet Salih and the people of Thamud

Prophet Salih, like Noah and Hud before him, was sent to his people with the same message to worship God alone and to turn to him in repentance. Again the People of Thamud, like the past peoples, accuse Salih of lying and ask for a clear proof. God sends this proof with the miraculous birth of a unique and beautiful she-camel (the Koran is vague on the exact nature of this miracle, but some stories say that the she-camel suddenly appeared from the earth). Salih tells his people to let the camel wander freely without harming her in the least. But, since they are bent on rejecting faith, they kill the camel and reject the clear proof sent by God (11:61–64).

Salih warns them that a day will soon come where they will be destroyed for their persistent rejection of faith. The People of Thamud were eventually destroyed with a mighty blast (11:65–68).

The patience of Abraham and story of Lot

Tying the moral narrative back to patience, this *Surah* tells of the time when Abraham and his wife receive the good news of a son after patiently trusting in God for years (11:69–73).

Abraham pleads with the angels who bring him good news, to help Prophet Lot's people, who prefer men instead of the pure women in the town. The angels tell Prophet Lot that his people will not turn away from indecency, and therefore they will be destroyed. He is told to leave with his family, but his wife does not heed his call, and is also destroyed along with the town's people (11:74–83).

Prophet Shu'aib and the people of Madyan

Prophet Shu'aib was sent to the People of Madyan as one of their own, and he, like all past prophets, urged his people to worship God alone and to practice economic justice — which was a particularly unethical practice of his people. Like past peoples, the People of Madyan mock Shu'aib's call to prayer and away from over indulgence in materialism (11:84–88).

Prophet Shu'aib warns his people not to reject his message just because of their hate for his dissent against the status quo of social and economic injustice that benefited the powerful and wealthy. And, he warns them of receiving a fate that is similar to the peoples of Noah, Hud, Salih, and Lot. He asks them to turn in forgiveness to God. Shu'aib is then mocked by this materialistic society as a man with no wealth and with lowly social status (11:89–93).

Finally, after persistent rejection of faith and extreme love of materialism, the People of Madyan are destroyed, except for Shu'aib and those who followed him (11:94–95).

Prophet Moses confronts the tyrant Pharaoh

This *Surah* only briefly mentions the case of Prophet Moses and his struggle against the tyrannical forces of Pharaoh. Moses came with clear signs, but Pharaoh and his Chiefs followed the wrong path, and for this they were destroyed like the non-believers before them. On the Day of Judgment, Pharaoh will lead his followers into the hellfire (11:96–99).

Conclusion of the moral narrative

After briefly mentioning the stories and struggles of the heroic and pious prophets, the Koran returns to the premise of the moral narrative. All these stories find one thing in common: Truth is always at odds with falsehood. The people of Truth are rejected, mocked, and oppressed by rejecters of faith. But, in the end, Truth and patience win out over the delusion of falsehood.

The Koran explains its historical analysis of these prophets and civilizations by saying, "It was not we who wronged them. They wronged their own souls. The deities other than God whom they invoked did not profit them when there issued the decree of your Sustainer. Nor did they add anything but perdition" (11:101). The *Surah* goes on to say that this historical account is a sign for those who are conscious of God, and that all unjust communities must eventually meet their downfall because of their persistent arrogance. But, those who do good will be rewarded in this world and in the hereafter (11:102–109).

Finally, the *Surah* advises the believers to take a path that will protect them from arrogance and disbelief: Stand in faith with those of faith, incline not towards those who practice evil, establish regular prayers, and remain steadfast in patience (11:115).

Simplifying the Moral Narrative of Shorter Surahs

Shorter *Surahs,* usually less than 50 *Ayat,* cover most of the latter sections of the Koran. Their moral narrative is much simpler than the longer *Surahs* because they focus on a central moral theme that is presented as a teaching, usually without long references to past prophets and divine laws.

Most of these *Surahs* focus on belief in the Oneness of God, the Day of Accountability, paradise and hellfire, good spiritual qualities, and condemned moral evils.

Since these *Surahs* present the premise of the Koranic message, you may want to begin from the back of the Book and familiarize yourself with these basic teachings before reading the longer *Surahs* found earlier in the Book. Any *Surah* from *Juz'* 30 of the Koran (see the section "Juz'," earlier in this chapter) provides a good starting point.

Here's an example of just one *Surah* to give you a basic idea:

> "Woe to every scandalmonger and backbiter who piles up wealth and lays it by thinking that his wealth would make him last forever. By no means! He will surely be thrown into that which breaks to pieces. And what will explain to you that which breaks to pieces? It is the fire of God kindled, which does mount to the hearts. It shall be made into a vault over them, in columns outstretched" (*Surah* 104).

This short *Surah* makes the moral narrative pretty simple: The moral evils of spreading scandals, backbiting, and materialism are condemned as acts that lead to the hellfire. You can find this same sort of simple narrative in most of these shorter *Surahs*.

Chapter 4

Discovering the Language of the Koran

In This Chapter

▶ Unearthing the roots of Arabic

▶ Unlocking key literary devices

▶ Hearing the voice of God

*T*he Koran's unique literary style makes it a Scripture that is admired and revered, yet sometimes difficult to grasp, especially for predominantly non-Arab readers.

In this chapter, I give you an analysis of the Arabic language and what it means for your understanding of the Koranic message. Then, I examine the Koran's narrative on history, sacred law, and pious expressions of faith.

Arabic: Plain, Clear, and Eloquent

The Arabic language has a unique depth, breadth, and power that expand outer meanings into inner meanings. Any commentator or interpreter of the Koran must have a mastery of the Arabic language that enables him or her to tap into the Koran's inner and outer meaning.

The Koran itself shows great reverence for the Arabic language, which it calls "plain and clear" (26:193–195). According to Muslims, God chose Arabic as the language of final revelation because it reached beyond communicating in the language of its original audience (41:44; 42:7).

Arabic remains a living language that millions of people around the world use every day. Unlike Aramaic, Latin, old Greek, and other languages, the Arabic of the Koran is still preserved, taught, and learned today. In addition, other classical languages, such as Urdu, Persian, Berber, Turkish, and even Spanish, find their basis in Arabic. The influence of Arabic across the globe is perhaps the greatest of any language that exists.

Building on the roots

The triliteral roots that form the basis of the Arabic language make it an easy language for children and non-Arabs to learn. Students can add letters at the beginning, in the middle, and at the end of the roots to create well-structured meanings.

For example, the letters "Mu" in Arabic at the beginning of a word express the notion of acceptance. So, when you replace the "I" of "Islam" with "Mu" it becomes "Muslim," which means one who has accepted Islam, or has submitted to the Will of God. Similarly, the word for belief in Arabic is *Amin.* By putting "Mu" in place of "A" you get *"Mumin,"* which means one who has accepted belief, or a believer.

The Arabic language at first seems quite alien and difficult for any non-Arab, especially those who don't share Arabic script. However, structurally, linguists agree that Arabic is one of the easiest languages to learn, because of its simple and logical pattern in forming words through their triliteral roots.

The following sections look at different aspects of the Arabic language that may aid in your understanding of the Koran's message.

Digging down to the roots

Arabic words are built on triliteral (sometimes four-literal) roots from which a constellation of meanings emerge. Each word relates to a root of usually three letters that serve as the philosophical basis of that word. These roots provide depth in meaning, and also a vast ocean of words that can describe every thought, human feeling, or new phenomenon in an ever-evolving world.

Translating the Koran from its original Arabic into another language proves difficult, because Arabic terminology usually expresses more than one idea or one corresponding word. Each Arabic word carries a philosophical thought that is expressed through its roots.

For example, the Koran contains many words for sin, but all of them express a central idea that means to rebel or corrupt. The Koran's philosophy on sin also relates to the idea of rebelling or corrupting the original nature of humanity that is in harmony with God's Will. Interestingly, the word for repentance in Arabic is *Tawba,* which literally means "to return." The Koran's philosophy on repentance is expressed as a return to the original pure self in which God created all men and women.

The following list gives you three illustrations of important words in the Koran that can only truly be understood by an examination of their triliteral roots:

✔ **Islam:** The world uses this word to name a religion followed by over a billion people. However, most non-Muslims, and even many Muslims, don't know what it really means in Arabic. "Islam" is often translated as "submission" or "surrender," which is fairly accurate in its intensive (active) form.

When you look at its triliteral roots, "Islam" comes from the letters "SLM," which in turn produce a vast array of words related to the philosophical concept of Islam. For example, the roots "SLM" form the basis of the word "Salaam," which is usually translated as "peace," but expresses much more than an absence of conflict. "Salaam" also suggests the idea of goodness, prosperity, completeness, wholeness, and health. The word "Salim" also derives from the root SLM; Salim expresses purity and absence of fault, corruption, and immorality.

The philosophical roots of the word "Islam" mean much more than submission or surrender. In its wholeness, the word Islam means an inner and outer peace and wholeness through submission or surrender to the Will of God.

✔ **Taqwa:** This extremely important word appears throughout the Book to describe the relationship between God and man. It is often simply translated as "God-fearing" or "God-consciousness."

The word "*Taqwa*" comes from the triliteral roots "WQA." This root brings forth words with meanings such as "to protect," "to save," "to guard against evil," "to be secure," and "to take as a shield." The word "*Taqwa*" expresses a spirit of God-consciousness that shields, wards off, and saves the soul from inner and outer evil. People who strive toward this spiritual quality increase the strength of this shield that protects them from evil in all its forms.

✔ **Jihad:** This word has wrongly become synonymous with "Holy War." However, if you examine the word "*Jihad*" with its root words "JHD," you arrive at an entirely different literal and philosophical meaning. The roots of "JHD" express meanings such as "to toil," "to exert effort towards," and "to struggle," among others. As such, "*Jihad*" can be expressed philosophically in the Koran as a struggle or striving for faith and purity against disbelief and evil.

Interestingly, the word that describes progressive thinking in the Islamic tradition also comes from the same roots. This word philosophically means to take up a scholarly struggle in knowing the Will of God on any given issue.

The philosophical understanding of the word "*Jihad*" is vast, and is certainly not limited to the arena of war.

Preserving the Koran's Arabic

Most languages evolve over time. Reading a classical work of Shakespeare, for example, is a different experience than reading any modern day novel in English. To a lesser extent, the same holds true for Arabs who read the classical Arabic of the Koran and the modern day Arabic.

However, because of the triliteral roots that form Arabic, even Koranic words that may eventually die out with modern Arabic will remain preserved in basic meaning and spirit, if not in actual definition. For example, imagine hypothetically that the word *Kitab,* meaning Book, is eventually replaced with another word in modern Arabic. Students of the Arabic language could look at the triliteral roots of *Kitab,* which are *KTB.* From this root emerges a plurality of meanings that express the idea of a book, such as "to write," "to bind together," amd "to collect." Even if you have no notion of what *Kitab* means, by looking at the triliteral roots and other words formed from those roots, you can trace the original basic meaning of *Kitab* in the Koran.

The meanings of the Arabic words in the Koran are also historically preserved through scholastic interpretation *(Tafsir)* of the Scripture, authentic sayings of Prophet Muhammad *(Hadith),* and classical dictionaries of the Koranic language that are recorded in over 30 published volumes.

The Arabic language is self-preserving because a word can never be lost completely even if it is no longer used in modern Arabic. This is an essential characteristic of Arabic, because the Koran strongly argues that the Koran is unchangeable and protected from corruption by God. So, the language itself acts as an essential vehicle through which God's promise to preserve the Koran in its original form as revealed to Prophet Muhammad can be fulfilled.

Reading translations of the Koran

Even if you don't plan to read the Koran in the original Arabic, you need to remain aware of the triliteral nature of the language, and especially its implications when it comes to "translations" of the Book.

Because each word in Arabic derives from a root, there is no such thing as one absolute translation for any word.

Any good translation of the Book acknowledges that the Koran's Arabic can never be fully translated, but only interpreted into another language. In the end, all "translations" are really interpretations.

The best "translations" of the Koran use *several* words to translate a single Arabic terminology in the Scripture. The author must eventually decide, based on his or her philosophical bias, on a word or set of words that express the vast Arabic terminology of the Koran.

Most translations, especially those done by Muslims, place something like "The Message of the Koran," "Towards Understanding the Koran," or

"Translation of the Meanings of the Koran" on the cover to avoid the idea that the book provides a literal translation of the Koran's Arabic.

Early translations of the Koran done by Christian missionaries did a poor job of translating the Book into English. Most of them introduced alien and sometimes derogatory words into the Scripture, such as "infidel" for the word *Kufr,* which denotes rejection of faith, that are unfortunately still in circulation. Some translations in English today are extremely inaccurate and even damaging to the Koran's message.

I recommend three translations which I think do as good of a job as can be done:

- *Message of the Koran,* by Muhammad Asad (published by Maktaba Jawahar ul uloom Publishers and Distributors)

- *The Holy Koran,* by Yusuf Ali (published by King Fahd Holy Qur'an Printing Complex)

- *The Meaning of the Holy Koran,* by Marmaduke Pickthall (published by UBS Publishers & Distributors Ltd.)

Comparing and contrasting all three translations as you read through the Book may help you see different ways in which Koranic concepts are translated and explained. Also, doing so may give you greater insight into the discourse of scholars who have interpreted the Koran with the useful footnotes present in each translation.

I recommend that you do the following to help you acquire a sound grasp of the Scripture's basic content, literary structure, and language:

- Read through this book to give you an introduction to the Book.

- Study the Koran with a group of friends to help you look at the Scripture from different perspectives and to provide an avenue for further discussion about ideas presented in the Book.

- Keep a reading journal of the Koran to help express your feelings and questions about the Koran, which may prove to be very useful in your future study or research on the Book. Go back to your journal often to see if any of your previous questions have been answered as you become more familiar with the Koran.

Literary Style in the Sacred Scripture

Rhythmic tone and style adorn much of the Koran's beauty. However, the Koran itself takes great pains to dismiss the idea that its text is poetry (69:40–43).

If the Koran was merely poetry, then critics of the Book would call it a work of art, rather than a true Book of Guidance. Regarding the Koran as poetry creates the danger that it becomes a source of wise quotations and beautiful rhyme, rather than a source of moral truths and divine laws that guide human life. So, Muslims don't regulate the Koran to the works of poetry that are usually quoted more than lived by individuals and society alike.

Also, poetry is most often characterized as a literary method of conveying experiences, ideas, or emotions of the poet through powerful, rhythmic language. But, the Koran is not the experience or emotion of a single person. Rather, it is a divine Scripture that provides concrete laws and teachings that are to be applied and not just talked about.

Rather than poetry, a better description of the Koran's literary style is rhythmic prose, known as *Saja'* in Arabic. The Koran lacks the specific meter and consistent rhythmic pattern that you can find in traditional Western poetry. However, the Book does manage to produce an irregular rhythmic style that brings to life even the most complicated laws.

In fact, the Koran's rhythmic prose is so eloquent that reciting one word incorrectly disturbs even an untrained ear. When such a mistake occurs, you hear a pause in the Book's eloquence as if oxygen has been sucked out of a living vessel. In other words, it is like a wrong note being struck in the middle of eloquent music. Take the example of a short *Surah,* 112, in Arabic:

> *Qul huwa llahu ahad:* Say, "He is One God."
>
> *Allahus samad:* God the Eternal, Absolute.
>
> *Lam yalid wa lam yulad:* He begetteth not nor is He begotten.
>
> *Wa lam yakun lahu kufwan ahad:* And there is none like unto Him.
>
> *If someone were to wrongly recite Wahid in the first verse instead of Ahad, you would hear a loss of rhythm. Even though the two words mean the same thing, only Ahad fits into the rhythmic prose of the Surah.*

The Book doesn't allow the human ear to accept words that are out of sync. This attribute of the language makes the Koran a self-preserving Book; listeners of the recited Koran can immediately catch the deliberate or accidental replacement of the original words.

Key literary elements of the Koran

You find three primary literary elements throughout the Koran: similes, known in Arabic as *Mathal;* sayings, known as *Qawl;* and oaths, known as *Qasm.* In the following sections, I give you a brief description and examples of all three elements.

Similes

A *simile* compares one thing with another of a different kind to illustrate a point. The Koran uses similes to simplify spiritual truths, or to drive home important theological and legal teachings. Similes are so prevalent because the Koran seeks to make its meanings clear to the reader in order to convince him or her of the Truth.

Passages with this intent usually begin with something like, "The parable of . . ." or these passages end with something like, "Thus, does God set forth parables."

Almost every *Surah* of the Book makes use of simile. *Surah* 10:24 contains a typical example:

> "The parable of the life of this world is as the rain that We send down from the skies. By its absorbing arises the produce of the earth, which provides food for men and animals, until when the earth is clad with artful adornment and is decked out (in beauty). The people to whom it belongs think they have all powers of disposal over it. There reaches it Our command by night or by day, and We make it like a harvest clean-mown, as if it has not flourished only the day before. Thus do We explain the signs in detail for those who reflect."

Sayings

Sayings are a literary device that responds to theological questions or arguments.

The Koran uses this literary device to respond to opponents or critics of the Koran's message, or those who would debate with Prophet Muhammad and his companions. Sayings primarily appear in response to the questions and arguments of the Arab polytheists and People of the Book. However, at times saying surface to address the Muslim community. Passages that use Sayings always begin with "Say. . . ."

You find examples of sayings throughout the Koran. For example, in *Surah* 10, you find an interesting passage that uses this literary element to respond to the beliefs of Pagans:

> "Say: 'Of your partners can any originate creation and they repeat it?' Say: 'It is God who originates creation and repeats it: Then how are you deluded away (from the Truth)?' Say: 'Of your partners is there any that can give guidance towards Truth?' Say: 'It is God who gives guidance towards the Truth. Is then He who gives guidance to Truth more worthy to be followed, or he who finds not guidance unless he is guided?' What then is the matter with your judgement?" (10:34–35).

Oaths

Oaths are a literary device that presents a formal declaration or a pledge made by God in the Koran.

The Koran uses oaths as a way of exemplifying how serious or how powerful a specific teaching is. The Scripture also uses this literary device to show the greatness of God's creation and wonders in the universe. These types of passages usually open with "Indeed, I swear . . ." or "By your Lord. . . ."

Examples of oaths are much harder to find in the Book than similes or sayings. The later *Surahs* contain more oaths than the beginning or middle ones. Here is an example of God's oath:

> "Furthermore, I swear by the setting of the stars, and that is a mighty oath if you but knew — that this is indeed a Koran (recitation) most honorable, in a Book well-guarded, which none shall touch but those who are pure: A Revelation from the Sustainer of the Worlds" (56:75–80).

The Scripture has God swearing or taking an oath by the following creations of His wonders: God Himself (16:56); the Koran (36:2; 44:2; 50:1); the winds (51:1); the sky (51:7; 52:5); the mountain (52:1); the *Ka'ba* or House of God in Mecca (52:4); the ocean (52:6); the stars (53:1); the pen (68:1); the night (74:33); the dawn (74:34); the angels who draw out the souls (79:1–2); the Day of Judgment (85:2); the earth (86:12); the city of Mecca (90:1); the soul (91:7); the creation of male and female (92:3); and the fig and olive (95:1).

Clear and figurative passages

The Koran itself identifies two types of verses in the Scripture: absolutely clear verses, known as *Muhkamat,* and unclear verses open to more than one interpretation, known as *Mutashabihat.*

The *muhkamat* verses form the foundation or essence of the Book, and should be strictly followed. On the other hand, only God knows the true meaning of *mutashabihat* verses, and therefore they should not be used as a basis for discord. In fact, the Koran says that only those who have corrupt hearts seek final answers and follow the *mutashabihat* verses over the *muhkamat* (3:7). The following two sections discuss these two types of verses in more detail.

Muhkamat: Clear verses

These verses are entirely clear within themselves. In other words, their meaning is one-dimensional and there is no need for further explanation or clarification. Most laws in the Koran fall under the category of *muhkamat.*

For example, in the laws about impermissible food, the Koran says: "He has only forbidden you dead meat, and blood, and the flesh of swine, and that on which any other name has been invoked besides that of God. But if one is forced by necessity, without willful disobedience, nor transgressing due limits, then he is without guilt. For God is oft-Forgiving, most Merciful" (2:173). This verse offers absolute clarity about what food is forbidden and the law of necessity.

Another obvious, clear teaching concerns "God is One" (112:1, for example). There is no if or but about it. God is one without any partners.

Mutashabihat: Figurative verses

Some verses need further explanation, with the possibility of more than one interpretation. Muslims believe that only God knows the full and true meanings of such verses. These verses concern some aspects of theology, spiritual truths, and stories of prophetic miracles.

For example, the following verse about God's nature has caused a lot of intellectual discourse about its meaning:

> "God is the Light of the heavens and the earth. The parable of His Light is as if there were a niche and within it a lamp. The lamp is enclosed in glass. The glass is as if it were a brilliant star, lit from a blessed tree — an olive, neither of the East nor of the West, whose oil is well-nigh luminous, though fire scarce touched it. Light upon Light! God does guide whom He will to His Light. God does set forth parables for men. And God knows all things" (24:35).

This verse, and many like it, contains spiritual truths and wisdom, while obviously creating multiple interpretations. For example, some mystical interpretations say that the niche mentioned describes divine reality in the heart of a pious believer. Others have argued that the niche is God's gift to humanity in Prophet Muhammad's life that brings divine Light to life. And, many other similar interpretations have been offered. In fact, the famous jurist and theologian, Al-Ghazali, wrote an entire book on this *Ayah* alone, called "The Niche of Lights," which was translated by David Buchman.

The disjointed letters in the Book

Among the verses categorized by scholars of the Koran as *mutashabihat* are those that begin with the so-called disjointed or mysterious letters, known as *Al Muqatta'at*. These letters are found at the beginning of 28 *Surahs*. For example, in the second *Surah*, the opening letters are ALM, pronounced in elongation as *Alif-Lam-Mim*. Similarly, all the *Surahs*, 40–46, begin with HM, pronounced in *elongation* (extending each letter in high tone) as *Ha-Mim*.

Bearing in mind that Muslims believe only God truly knows what these abbreviated letters mean, four sound theories exist about the meaning behind these letters:

✔ **Abbreviation for sentences:** Some scholars of the Koran believe that these letters are abbreviations for entire sentences. For example, they argue that *Alif-Lam-Mim* is an abbreviation for *Ana Allah A'lamu,* which means "I am God, the All-Knowing."

✔ **A symbol:** Other scholars argue that these are in fact symbols of God or of Prophet Muhammad. For example, many Muslims believe that the letters *Ya-Sin* at the beginning of *Surah* 36 are a name by which God calls Muhammad. As such, children in Muslim households are often named *Ya-Sin* or *Ta-Ha* — names thought to refer to Muhammad.

✔ **Calling attention:** Some scholars believe that these letters could be a means of calling attention to Prophet Muhammad as he received revelation, and then to his people as revelation was then subsequently recited. This is a sound interpretation, because these letters create an awesome echo when read aloud in elongation. These letters may very well be a means of attracting attention to the announcement of new revelation.

✔ **Orientalist thought:** Students of the Islamic tradition from the West believe that these letters represent the names or signatures of the scribes who wrote the Koran under Muhammad's supervision. Other Orientalists believe that the letters signal the beginning of a new *Surah* that was especially important in the oral tradition or in the original written copies of the Koran that were not divided by *Surah* names. However, this is a weak theory, because if it were true, then all *Surahs* would begin with these abbreviated letters.

Hearing the Voice of the Koran

Unique among religious Scriptures, the Koran's entire narrative is told from the perspective of God — not, as many would expect, from the perspective of Prophet Muhammad.

✔ **God addresses Muhammad:** Whenever the Prophet is specifically addressed, he is addressed in second person. For example, the Koran says, "O Prophet! Truly We have sent you as a witness, a bearer of glad tidings, and a Warner, and as one who invites to God by His permission, and as a lamp spreading light" (33:45–46).

✔ **God speaks of Himself in first person form:** Sometimes He uses the royal "We" and sometimes just "I." For example, the Koran says, "When My servants ask you concerning Me, I am indeed close (to them). I respond to the prayer of every supplicant when he calls on Me. Let them also, with a will, listen to My call, and believe in Me. So that they may walk in the right way" (2:186).

✔ **God speaks of Himself in third person form:** There are also times when God refers to himself in third person form. For example, the Koran says, "It is God who has subjected the sea to you, that ships may sail through it by His command, that you may seek of His bounty, and that you may be grateful" (45:12).

The Koran establishes a concrete relationship between God and the reader by sometimes replacing the abstract, third-person "He" with God's Attributes. For example, the Koran introduces God by Names such as "The Merciful" or "The Compassionate" in order to establish a stronger relationship to the Divine. You can find numerous examples of these divine Attributes throughout Koranic passages.

✔ **God recounts historical conversations:** God narrates conversations that took place in history, usually between the prophets and their people. For example, take part of the conversation between Prophet Moses and Pharaoh:

"Pharaoh said: 'And what is the Sustainer and Cherisher of the Worlds?' (Moses) said: 'The Sustainer and Cherisher of the heavens and the earth, and all between — If you had but sure belief.' (Pharaoh) said to those around him: 'Do you not listen?' (Moses) said: 'Your Sustainer and the Sustainer of your fathers from the beginning.' (Pharaoh) said: 'Truly your messenger who has been sent to you is a veritable madman.' (Moses) said: 'Sustainer of the East and the West, and all between. If you only had sense.'" (26:23–28).

Remembering morals, not dates

The Koran is a living Book that finds the details of history irrelevant. The Koran emphasizes the moral of the story — not the who, where, and when of it. The Koran doesn't list dates, rarely uses proper names, and hardly ever describes the historical setting of the story.

For example, *Surah* 36:13–32 tells the story of a man who came to a city to preach God's message. The people of the city reject and mock the man when he tries to convince them of the Truth. God then rewards the man for his efforts, while the city's people are destroyed for their rejection of God's message. This story never names the man, the city, or the time period.

The story focuses on accepting the message; the non-historical narrative form supports the idea that spiritual truths transcend time, place, and even personalities. In fact, the Koran speaks of these stories as if they occurred during modern times, by beginning some stories with "Remember when. . . ."

At times you find a story, theological doctrine, or ethical teaching repeated more than once in different parts of the Book. For example, the attributes of God appear in almost every *Surah*. The Koran discusses various topics throughout the Scripture, and doesn't limit any particular topic to a single *Surah* or passage.

Chapter 5

Relating the Koran to Abrahamic Revelations

In This Chapter

▶ Knowing the Koran's view of other revealed Books

▶ Looking at similarities and differences between the Torah, Bible, and Koran

*I*nterestingly, the three Abrahamic faiths — Judaism, Christianity, and Islam — share much in common, including a lineage of noble prophets sent by God. At the root of commonality lies a deep connection to the legacy of Prophet Abraham and a belief in One God. However, the Testament's narrative and the Koran's narrative differ on some key issues.

In this chapter, I look at how the Koran views previous divine revelations. Then, I examine the theological and practical similarities and differences between the Scriptures of Judaism, Christianity, and Islam.

Previous Revelations: Between Sacred and Corrupted

The Koran has an unambiguous view of previous revelations. From the beginning, the Book makes it clear that Muslims must believe not only in the Koran, but also in Books that were revealed to past prophets (2:4). In fact, the Koran speaks of itself as a confirmation of the Torah and Gospel (3:3).

The Koran holds the Torah in great esteem by saying, "It was We (God) who revealed the Torah. Therein was guidance and illumination. By its standard have been judged the Jews, by the prophets who bowed to God's Will, by the Rabbis and scholars of law: For to them was entrusted the protection of God's Book, and they were witnesses to that" (5:44).

However, the Koranic view also maintains that the Jews did not properly guard their Book from human changes and corruption. The Koran argues that the Children of Israel introduced new laws into the Torah that were not revealed to Prophet Moses, simply to reflect their whims and desires (3:93–94). As such, when the Koran refers to the Torah, it speaks of the original revelation that came down to Prophet Moses, and not the Old Testament or the Pentateuch.

In the Koran, Prophet Jesus reaffirms the message of the Torah, while reforming some of its laws by making permissible what in the past was impermissible (3:50). Prophet Jesus comes with a revelation referred to in the Koran as the *Injil,* which can be best translated as Gospel. This Gospel is revered as "guidance and illumination," "confirmation of the Torah," and "admonition to those who are God-conscious" (5:46).

However, the Koran believes that the original Bible as revealed to Jesus has been lost. As such, the four accounts of Jesus' life that appear today in Mark, Matthew, Luke, and John are not considered to be a fully accurate recollection of the *Injil* that the Koran so fondly speaks of.

The passage that may best reflect the Koran's view of what Jews and Christians did to their revealed Books appears in 3:78: "There is among them (Jews and Christians) a section who distort the Book with their tongues so that you would think it is part of the Book, but it is no part of the Book. And they say, 'That is from God.' But it is not from God. It is they who tell a lie against God, and they know it" (3:78).

The Koran views the Bible and Torah in the following way: Moses received divine revelation in the form of the Torah. Jesus received divine revelation in the form of the Gospel. Both of these Books were corrupted by human changes, and are therefore no longer reliable as the words of God. Each Book does contain within it the original Truth, but not all of it. The Koran sets the record straight by including the portions of Torah and Gospel that are valid and still relevant, while correcting mistakes and excluding that which is no longer relevant.

Linking the Three Faiths: Common Experiences in the Scriptures

The Koran finds common ground with Christians and Jews (known as *'Ahl Al-Kitab,* or People of the Book) in three broad ways:

- ✔ Theological belief in the Oneness of God
- ✔ Common divine laws
- ✔ A shared narrative of prophetic stories

Uniting faiths with belief in One God

The Koran addresses the Jews and Christians by saying, "O People of the Book! Come to common terms as between us and you: That we worship none but God; that we associate no partners with Him; that we erect not from among ourselves, Lords and patrons other than God . . ." (3:64).

The Koran finds commonality with Jews and Christians in the belief of strict monotheism, by which no prophet or saint is to be worshipped or venerated as divine alongside God.

Muhammad is also told by the Koran to remind People of the Book that God alone is "our Sustainer and your Sustainer" (2:139). As such, there is no need for dispute between the Muslims and their fellow monotheists, says the Scripture.

The Koran also attempts to fulfill its role as "The Reminder" (see Chapter 1) by reminding Jews and Christians of their holy covenant with God, which among other things establishes belief and worship in God alone. The Koran confirms and praises the first Biblical covenant that says, "You shall have no other gods before me. You shall not make for yourself an idol in the form of anything in the heaven above or on earth beneath or in the waters below. You shall not bow down to them or worship them . . ." (Exodus 20:4–5). This same understanding surfaces many times in the Koran (4:48, for example).

The Koran also shares the Biblical understanding of God as Creator of the universe (7:54), and reflects the same comprehension of God's sovereignty (6:59) as the Bible's insistence that everything is run by divine Will (Matthew 10:29–31).

With this spirit of unity in theological belief, the Koran encourages healthy dialogue (29:46) and coexistence in the form of marriage and the sharing of meat (5:5).

Bridging the gap between divine laws

Western commentators on religion and civilization often make it sound as if Islamic and Judeo-Christian laws are polar opposites. This is simply untrue. The Koran includes many of the same laws that you find in the Torah and Bible. In fact, the Koran is viewed in the Islamic tradition as a confirmation and reformation of previous divine laws.

The Ten Commandments

The Ten Commandments shared by Jews and Christians are almost identical to the laws found in the Koran, but the Koran doesn't list them as systematically as you find them in the Old Testament (Exodus 20:2–17):

- The first commandment in the Old Testament forbids taking any gods beside God. The Koran also strictly forbids associating partners with God, known as *Shirk*. It is considered the only unforgivable sin for one who dies without repenting (4:48).

- The second commandment forbids making images of God. The Koran too warns against idolatry and making images of God (6:103; 14:35).

- The third commandment forbids using God's name in vain. The Koran also prohibits Muslims from using God's name in casual swearing (2:224).

- The fourth commandment says that the Sabbath must be kept holy. This is the only commandment that the Koran does not include, because it believes that the Sabbath was prescribed only for the Children of Israel (16:124).

- The fifth commandment says to honor your parents. The Koran says that honoring your parents means not even expressing a word of frustration with them, such as an "uff," or its English equivalent of "ugh" (17:23).

- The sixth commandment prohibits unjust killing or murder. The Koran also prohibits murder and compares the unjust killing of one life to be equivalent to the murder of all of humanity (5:32; 17:33).

- The seventh commandment prohibits adultery, which is also equally prohibited by the Koran (17:32).

- The eighth commandment prohibits stealing. The Koran condemns the act of stealing as one of the worst crimes and punishes it severely (5:38–39).

- The ninth commandment prohibits lying and giving false testimony. The Koran also strongly condemns lying and false testimony (2:283; 24:7). And, the Koran commands Muslims to speak the truth even if it is against their own selves or their own family (4:135).

- The tenth commandment forbids coveting. The Koran also forbids the evil practice of coveting the possessions of others (20:131).

Other laws

Everyday laws prescribed in Islamic law often resemble similar laws in the Torah. For example, the laws of purity after sexual intimacy between a husband and wife are almost exactly the same in Islamic law and the Torah as taught in Leviticus (16–18).

The penal codes of the Koran and Torah also have overlap. For example, Islam is often criticized for including the death penalty for adultery as part of its penal code (see Chapter 17). However, the Torah establishes the same punishment for sexual immorality, such as adultery and incest (Leviticus, 20:10–16). Also, the Koran follows basically the same law in the cases of murder and killing — acts that prescribe the death penalty in both Scriptures (Koran, 2:178–179; Genesis, 9:6).

Same laws, different reasoning

Sometimes, the same laws appear in both Scriptures, but the wisdom or reasoning behind the laws may be different. Take for example the law requiring women to cover their hair. People often condemn Islam for requiring women to wear the headscarf, or *Hijab* in Arabic. However, if you read Corinthians, 11:3–10, it says that when a woman prays, she must either cover her hair or shave it. Also, traditional Rabbinical law states that modesty and nobility required covering the hair. Even modern paintings of traditional Jewish and Christian women, including the Virgin Mary, reflect this modest dress.

The required head-covering in Islam and Judaism share the same spirit — the desire to sanctify a woman's modesty and nobility. However, the Biblical passage on head-covering reasons it in the woman's position as "the glory of man."

Laws in the three faiths may overlap, but the wisdom and reasoning behind them can differ. This may explain why the West wrongly views the *Hijab* as a symbol of oppression, and even as a controversial legal issue in modern secular Europe.

Sharing the legacy of prophetic stories

According to the Book, Abraham's path is defined as "Islam," meaning "submission or surrender to the Will of God," which in spirit describes the universal religion of all prophets.

The Book teaches Muslims, "Say you: 'We believe in God, and the revelation given to us, and to Abraham, Ishmael, Jacob, and the Tribes, and that given to Moses and Jesus, and that given to (all) prophets from their Sustainer. We make no difference between one and another of them. And we submit to God'" (2:136).

The Koran views Prophet Abraham as an "ideal model" (60:4) for all three faiths, because of his determined struggle to obey and serve God alone. Abraham's total and complete submission before God makes his path or way (*Millat*) the model for the righteous servants of God (2:130–131). The Koran insists that Abraham's sons, who continued the prophetic mission, followed this same path, and that from them came other prophets who also continued in the path of Abraham (2:132–133).

Of the 26 prophets mentioned in the Koran, only five are non-Biblical characters. You can find the names of all other Koranic prophets in the Bible, although their stories are often presented from a different angle. Of course, the collection of stories about the prophets in the Koran also includes Jesus, unlike the Torah that was revealed before the time of Jesus.

Prophet Moses in particular receives much attention in the Koran (he is mentioned 44 times), because his prophecy draws important parallels to the prophetic experience of Prophet Muhammad:

- ✔ Both prophets suffered oppression at the hands of tyrant governments, and both migrated in order to practice their faith freely.
- ✔ Both prophets received revealed Books that not only deal with personal spiritual ethics, but also communal laws that establish order and justice in society.
- ✔ Both prophets found themselves in the role of statesman that required defense of the homeland, war, and other political roles.

Many similarities between Moses and Muhammad exist, and the Koran constantly draws on that connection both explicitly and implicitly.

The greatness of prophets throughout history is a shared experience that can firmly establish a shared wisdom among all three faiths. More interfaith dialogues among the Abrahamic faiths can cultivate these shared stories and the wisdom they offer. In my personal experience, such discussion has proven a much more productive and worthwhile endeavor than simply exchanging respective doctrines.

Contrasting the Koran with Judeo-Christian Scriptures

While the three Abrahamic faiths enjoy much in common, some key differences in the Scriptures exist, which I tell you about in the following sections.

Finding a worldview of history in the Scriptures

While the Koran and Judeo-Christian Scripture share much of the same content regarding stories of the prophets, they differ on how they present historical narrative.

The Torah, which possesses most of the stories about prophets, begins quite literally with the "beginning" and proceeds from there into a chronological sequence of the first man and his children. Then come the rise of the prophetic mission and guidance on earth, along with the lives of these intriguing prophets. In essence, the Torah brings forth an inspired message of theology, morality, ethics, and divine laws in a historical format up until the time of Prophet Moses. The Gospel more or less follows the same historical narrative.

The Koran, however, offers a subtle and yet intriguing shift in narrative perspective. The Book literally begins with a powerful prayer that introduces the nature of God and man's relationship with the Divine. "In the Name of God, most Gracious, most Merciful. Praise be to God, the Sustainer of all the worlds. Most Gracious, Most Merciful. Master of the Day of Judgement. You do we worship and Your aid we seek. Show us the straight way. The way of those upon whom You have bestowed Your Blessings, not of those who have been condemned, nor those who go astray" (1:1–7).

Then, beginning with *Surah* 2, the Koran delves into a deep discussion of the nature of belief, rejection of faith, and hypocrisy. The Koran goes on to urge its readers to believe in One True God, while issuing a challenge to those who disbelieve in the Koran. Finally, 30 *Ayat* (see Chapter 3) later, the Koran introduces the story of creation in Adam, the philosophical question about the nature of man expressed through the angels, and an introduction to the mischief-spreading character known as Satan. However, only ten verses later, the Koran switches its historical narrative from the creation of Adam to reminding the Children of Israel of their covenant and the life of their prophet, Moses.

The Koranic narrative style differs vastly from the Biblical in that the Koran's approach is non-chronological. The Koran's primary concern is with humanity's faith and obedience to God. This moral theme develops throughout the Book through a series of teachings, reminders, and philosophical arguments. History is not the structural narrative, but rather simply an important tool in drawing out lessons of past prophets and civilizations. In other words, the Koran doesn't focus on the intricacies of history, but on the moral and ethical spirit of historical experiences.

While the Biblical narrative relates the location, lineage, and offspring of most characters, the Koran doesn't emphasize such "facts." One passage in the Koran even shows distaste for historical intricacies when relating the story of the People of the Cave *(Ashab Al-Kahf)*. There was a dispute among the People of the Book about the number of men in the cave, and the Koran simply says, "Enter not, therefore, into controversies concerning them, except on a matter that is clear . . ." (18:22). In other words, the Koran says to keep your eye on the ball and don't fall into unnecessary arguments about historical facts that distract you from the moral narrative.

In general, the historical perspective (if not the narrative) of the Koran more closely resembles traditional Judaism than traditional Christianity. The Koran, like the Torah, presents history as a continuing saga of human disharmony, which divine intervention rectifies through tranquility and wrath. Neither tradition believes in the original sin of man that can only be cleansed by accepting Jesus as the savior. That belief fits the Christian historical worldview that man was created in sin, and that Jesus sacrificed his life for the sins of humanity — an alien concept for both Jews and Muslims.

Reforming laws

Many divine laws overlap in the Jewish and Muslim Scriptures. Most Christians today believe that Jesus abolished most of the sacred laws found in the Torah. Muslims do not agree with this analysis. Instead, they believe that Jesus was sent to remind and fulfill the laws for the Children of Israel (5:46) — the same concept that is taught in Matthew 5:17–20. However, the Koran says that it reforms laws of past revelations "with something better or similar" (2:106).

The laws of purity, which are quite sophisticated and complex in orthodox Judaism, offer an example of how the Koran simplifies laws. If you look at books of Jewish law, you find chapters dedicated to the laws of bodily purification. However, in the books of Islamic law, you find only a few pages worth of material on this subject. The Book simplifies the Jewish series of laws on ritual impurity into a simple method that says when you are ritually impure, you wash your body and your clothes, and immediately you become ritually pure without any waiting.

Similarly, on the issues of women's monthly courses, the Torah suggests that women separate from the household for seven days before regaining their purity (Leviticus, 15:19–33). Islamic law simplifies this process so that women can coexist with society and carry out their normal daily work, except for the obligatory five daily prayers and sexual intercourse with their husbands.

Sometimes Islamic law completely removes certain practices that were made obligatory on the Children of Israel. For example, the Koran completely eliminates the Sabbath, or day of rest. On Fridays, Muslims attend large congregational prayers that involve a religious sermon. As such, most Muslim countries make Friday a public holiday. However, Islamic law doesn't attach further laws or restrictions to Friday, other than attending the congregational prayer. Other than that, Muslims continue on with their daily lives on Friday.

Reforming religious rituals

The Koran firmly believes that prayer, purifying alms, and fasting are a part of all divine religions. However, the practice of each institution has been reformed with the teachings of Islam.

For example, the practice of fasting has been reformed from a 24-hour fast into a fast that lasts from dawn to sunset. Similarly, the prayers in Islam have been institutionalized to five times a day, instead of the three daily prayers that you find in orthodox Judaism.

Extending God's covenant to all peoples

The covenant of God through Islam extends beyond the Children of Israel to cover a truly multinational, universal family in which genetics or inheritance play no role whatsoever. The Koran refers to the body of believers worldwide as an *Ummah* or Muslim community, which holds no ethnic boundaries.

The Islamic tradition believes that all previous faiths came to specific places and peoples. Jesus' saying in the Bible, "I am not sent but to the lost sheep of Israel," also reflects this. But, the religion taught by Prophet Muhammad is universal, since Muslims regard him as the last Messenger of God. As such, Muhammad said: "Every prophet before me was sent only to his people, but I was sent to all mankind." The Koran reiterates this point by stating, "We have not sent you but as a mercy to all mankind" (21:07).

In other words, the Koran doesn't believe in a "chosen people" that are exclusively responsible for carrying out God's mission, as is commonly believed in Judaism about the Jews. The Koran believes that God's message and laws are universally beneficial. The covenant extends to every person who declares faith in Islam and becomes a part of the *Ummah*.

Giving a new angle on prophetic stories

The shared stories of the prophets bring forth a common experience of faith and ethics through great historical figures. However, the Koranic and Biblical narratives of the prophets differ in some important ways.

Some Jews and Christians, along with some academics, feel that the Koran has taken existing stories of the Old and New Testament and changed them to fit its own worldview. Firstly, the Koran makes no apologies or does not try to hide the fact that many stories are similar if not the same, because the Koran is not a new revelation, but rather a continuation and finality of previous revelations.

Also, the Koran does not claim to be from a new source, but rather from the same source as previous divine revelations — namely God. At the same time, the Book is convinced that some stories of prophets found in the Bible and Torah must have been corrupted, because God sent prophets with the highest of spiritual and moral qualities to lead their respective communities onto the right path. As such, these prophets must have been the noblest men to ever walk the earth in order to be considered heroes and role models in the religious experience of human beings.

Presenting the prophets as sinless

The Koran believes that every prophet sent by God with a divine mission carries the quality of *Masum,* which means innocence or protection from God against major sins. As such, the Koran always mentions prophets with an aura of nobility and pious character that serves as a beautiful role model for all of humanity. There's never even a hint that prophets commit any sort of vice. On the other hand, the Biblical account includes several instances of prophets committing immoral acts, which are not always repented for.

Take for example the narrative of Prophet Joseph, which the Koran calls the most beautiful story. The Koranic account of the story and the Biblical account are nearly identical, and surely the moral of the story is the same. But one part of the story illustrates how the two traditions view prophets differently.

When Joseph is tempted by his master's wife, the Bible leaves it unclear whether Joseph fell into temptation or not. In contrast, the Koran makes a serious effort to absolve Prophet Joseph of any immoral conduct by adding the following key details to the narrative: The master's wife tries to seduce Prophet Joseph by locking the doors and trapping him in her room. Joseph responds by saying, "God forbid. . . . Truly no good comes to those who do wrong" (12:23). Then, the Koran says that Joseph would have desired the woman as well, "but that he saw the evidence of his Sustainer. Thus (We ordered) that We might turn away from him evil and indecent deeds. For he was one of Our chosen servants" (12:24). Then, when Joseph tries to escape the woman's temptation, she grabs him from behind, ripping the back of his shirt. The master then suddenly opens the door to find his wife and Joseph in a conflict situation. The wife immediately accuses Joseph of trying to seduce her (12:25). Joseph fights back, saying that the wife tried to seduce him, and that the evidence was in the torn shirt. If Joseph's shirt were torn from the front, the evidence would indicate that she was trying to escape him. But, since the shirt was torn from behind, it was clear that Joseph tried to get away from her. The master accepts the evidence and condemns his wife for her actions (12:26–29).

With this added narrative, the Koran goes out of its way to defend the honor and chastity of Prophet Joseph. Clearly, the Koran wants to defend the innocence and role model capacity of the noble prophets.

Sometimes, rather than adding details to the narrative, the Koran rejects stories that appear in the Biblical narrative to preserve the honor of a prophet. For example, in the Bible, Prophet David is accused of watching Queen Sheba showering and then committing adultery with her. The Koran finds that completely unimaginable in its understanding of Prophecy. As such, the Koran relates the story of David's heroism in defeating Goliath and praises his sense of judgment, but completely rejects any reference to his alleged adulterous affair with Sheba. In fact, David is among the greatest prophets, because he is also a recipient of a divine Book, called the Psalms, or *Zabur* in Arabic.

Shaping Prophet Abraham's life in the Islamic tradition

Some interesting details are added to Prophet Abraham's life in the Koran that connect his life and works with the Islamic faith. For example, the Koran tells a story of Abraham as a wise youth who tries to convince his father and community to turn away from idol worship (21:51–70). They reject Abraham and even persecute him for preaching God's Oneness. This story does not exist in either the New or Old Testament. The Koran presents this story as a direct parallel to the experience of Prophet Muhammad, who also rejects idol worship and is chased out of the city because of his preaching.

Also, significantly, the Koran intimately attaches Prophet Abraham to the city of Mecca, where he builds the Ka'ba with his son Ishmael. Here Abraham also makes a passionate supplication, calling on God to deliver a noble prophet and civilization of believers to the city of Mecca (2:125–129). This helps establish Abrahamic roots in the lineage of Prophet Muhammad, through Prophet Ishmael, and founds Islam's legitimacy among the monotheistic faiths. Although this exact story is not told in the Torah's narrative on Abraham's life, it does reflect Abraham's prayer to raise a great nation from the seed of Ishmael, and God's resulting promise to bless the earth with Abraham's family (Genesis 12:1–3 and 17:4).

Checking the prophetic pulse of Muhammad in the Biblical Scripture

The major point of contention between Jews and Christians is over the authenticity of Jesus as the Messiah. Jews strongly believed that no prophet would come after Moses, and no divine Book would come after the Torah. The Koran, in contrast, finds itself defending Jesus' authenticity as a prophet to the Jews, and Muhammad's authenticity as a prophet to both Jews and Christians.

The Koran confidently argues that the prophecy of Muhammad was foretold in the original Scriptures of the Torah and Gospel. The Book quotes Prophet Jesus as saying to the Children of Israel, "I am the Messenger of God sent to you, confirming the Torah before me, and giving glad tidings of a Messenger to come after me, whose name shall be Ahmad" (short for Muhammad) (61:6). This passage has led commentators of the Koran to dig for evidence of Prophet Muhammad's coming in the sacred Scriptures of the Old and New Testament. Some interesting theories have emerged from this research.

Researchers of the Torah argue that Deuteronomy 18:18 foretells the Prophecy of Muhammad when it says, "I will raise them up a prophet from among their brethren, like unto you, and will put my words in his mouth; and he shall speak unto them all that I shall command him." Christians argue that this passage speaks of the coming of Jesus. However, some scholars on the Testaments argue that Prophet Moses and Prophet Muhammad are more alike in their nature and prophetic mission than Moses and Jesus. Also, these scholars say that the rise of a prophet from "their brethren" indicates Muhammad's lineage with brother Ishmael rather than Moses' and Jesus' lineage through Isaac.

Other scholars of the Testaments point to the original Greek term in the Gospel, *Periclytos,* which is now translated as "comforter" in English. However, scholars have pointed out that this word in fact has almost the same meaning as the Arabic for Ahmad or Muhammad, meaning "the Praised One" and does mean "comforter." As such, the Greek word means "the Much Praised" — which is also the meaning of "Muhammad."

Also, these commentators point out that the "comforter" mentioned in the Bible, whom Christians take to be the Holy Spirit, is spoken of in future tense, and not in present tense. As such, it can't refer to the Holy Spirit that was supposedly present with Jesus. Commentators of the Testaments and the Koran, then, argue that in fact the "comforter" refers to the coming of Prophet Muhammad (John, 14:16; 15:26; 16:7).

Differing on Mary and the message of Jesus

The Koran holds Mary and her son Jesus in great esteem. However, these two characters both unify and divide Christians and Muslims.

Contrasting Mary in the Islamic and Christian traditions

The Koran has such high regard for Mary that God describes her as chosen "above the women of all nations" (3:42). *Surah* 19 is even named after her. Interestingly, the Koran talks more about Mary than the Bible does, and presents some new details concerning her virgin birth of Jesus, which are not told in the Bible.

These passages say that "the pains of childbirth drove" Mary under a palm-tree, where she cried out for her own death because of the pain and from the dishonorable accusation of adultery. Here, a voice responds to her saying, "Grieve not! For your Sustainer has provided a stream beneath you. And shake towards yourself the trunk of the palm-tree. It will let fall fresh ripe dates upon you. So eat and drink and cool your eyes." Mary is also instructed to remain silent before returning with baby Jesus to her people (19:22–26).

However, the Koran states that Mary's childbirth experience was a miraculous sign from God, nothing more and nothing less. Muslims don't attribute any divinity to Mary whatsoever.

Koranic and Biblical views on Jesus

Jesus miraculously speaks from the cradle as a Babe in defense of his mother's chastity, and also as a Messenger of God. In his address to the Children of Israel, the Koranic Jesus defines himself in three ways, two of which oppose traditional Christian views.

Firstly, Jesus says in an eloquent passage, "I am indeed a servant of God. He has given me Revelation and made me a prophet" (19:30). So, here the Koranic Jesus claims that he is not God, but instead in submission to God. He also confirms his status as a prophet and receiver of a divine Book.

Then, the Koran goes on to say that God, in his Majesty, doesn't "beget a son." Rather, he simply creates by saying, "Be," and it is. So, the Koranic Jesus is also not the son of God.

The Islamic doctrine views Jesus as a prophet and Messenger of God who came with many miracles to prove his message to the Children of Israel. Also, Jesus is considered as the Messiah, though not the savior of humanity (3:45). But, Jesus in the Koran is not God or the son of God or in any way divine.

Finally, the crucifixion presents a major doctrinal difference between Christianity and the Koran. Christianity believes that Jesus was crucified on the cross for the sins of humanity. However, the Koran says that God saved Jesus from crucifixion by raising him up to the heavens; God only made it seem as if he had been crucified. Because the Koran doesn't adhere to the belief of original sin, there is no reason for Jesus to die on the cross for the sins of humanity, according to the Islamic tradition.

The Islamic tradition also believes, like the Christians, that Jesus will return towards the end of time to fight the antichrist. However, Muslims believe that in returning, Jesus will proclaim his true nature as a Messenger of God, confirm the teachings of Prophet Muhammad, and die as a human being on earth. This belief of Jesus' return is vaguely referred to in the Koran (43:61), and confirmed in the *Hadith* (sayings of Prophet Muhammad).

Part II
Searching for the Soul of the Koran

The 5th Wave   By Rich Tennant

"I'm listening to a golden oldie. Recitations of the Koran."

In this part . . .

As soon as the Muslim community was deprived of Prophetic guidance after the passing of Prophet Muhammad, the tradition of interpreting the Book, known as *Tafsir,* developed. Interpretation of the Koran lies at the heart of all beliefs and actions for a devout Muslim.

In this part, I tell you about traditional methods of interpretation and famous classical commentators of the Book. I also look at how commentators emerging from the post-colonial experience have interpreted the Koran.

Chapter 6

Interpreting the Koran

- -

In This Chapter

▶ Introducing the science of Koranic interpretation
▶ Understanding traditional methodologies used in interpreting the Scripture

- -

Throughout Islamic history, Muslims have consulted the Scripture to reaffirm traditional teachings and to find new meanings that address the challenges that emerge with each new generation.

Some aspects of the Koran are crystal clear and firm in meaning *(al-muhkamat)*. However, room for differences of opinion exists on some matters, which is considered a blessing for the Muslim community, and not, in most cases, a hindrance to progress.

In this chapter, I talk about the important science of interpreting the Koran. Then, I examine the classical techniques scholars use in understanding the Scripture.

Coming to Know the Guidance

The Koran teaches its followers an active lifestyle that requires a struggle to come closer to God. Every single *Ayah* in the Book offers wisdom of spiritual truth, pious belief, and moral law. These *Ayat* shape the individual life and collective body of Muslims *(Ummah)*.

Proper interpretation of the Scripture proves essential to developing the correct belief system and moral character of Muslims.

Having room for interpretation

The majority of Muslims view the Koran as the undisputed word of God. As such, all authentic teachings must find their proof at the very least in the spirit of the Koran, if not in its exact wordings. The Koran provides the standard, or criterion, by which all other ideas are judged. If an idea, religious ruling, or any aspect of modernity conflicts with the spirit of the Book, then it doesn't have the moral authority to work as a model for success.

Muslims have historically acknowledged, as well as encouraged, differences of opinion in most non-fundamental religious matters. Muslims appreciate that the Koran possesses enough depth and breadth to be viewed from various angles.

However, these differences of opinion must be solidly based in the teachings of the Book. You can't just offer a new perspective or idea about the Koran (and thus Islam) that finds no legitimate moral basis in the Scripture, or clearly contradicts fundamental teachings of the Scripture.

Muslim and non-Muslim intellectuals who try to promote certain ideas, such as democracy, tolerance, and so on, must make Koranic teachings a focal part of their argument. Similarly, any ideas that intellectuals want to discourage, such as unjust violence, must be proven to be antithetical to the wording or spirit of the Book.

No religious body regulates Koranic interpretation, and, therefore, people can offer their own interpretations. However, they may have a difficult time gaining legitimacy without the necessary qualifications. And, the Muslim community usually shuns interpretations that offer unorthodox or clearly faulty explanations.

The Koran is a Book of guidance. Interpreting the Koran helps believers come to know that guidance.

Knowing the key terms of Koranic interpretation

In order to discover the science of Koranic interpretation, you need to know the following words and their meanings:

- ✔ *Tafsir* **(plural, *Tafaseer*):** Means "explanation" or "interpretation." Refers to the science of Koranic interpretation.

- ✔ *Ta'wil:* Differs from *Tafsir* in that it interprets the deeper meanings of the *Ayat* through sophisticated application of Arabic linguistics and other methods.

- *Mufasir* **(plural,** *Mufasirun*)**:** One who does *Tafsir;* an interpreter of the Koran. Muslims all over the world have a great affinity for the famous *Mufasir* and honor their important contributions.

   Traditionally, only those scholars who spent almost all their lives studying the Koranic sciences would venture into writing volumes of *Tafsir;* those interpretations find legitimacy among most Muslims.

   Beyond scholarship, the character of a *Mufasir* is important. He or she should have a pure and sound heart free from arrogance, self-desire, and innovation. People usually study the biographies of famous classical interpreters along with their *Tafsir.*

- *Sunnah:* Practice or way of Prophet Muhammad. Considered the second most important source of *Tafsir* after the Koran itself. (*Sunnah* should not be confused with *Sunni,* which is the largest group of Muslims in the world.)

- *Sahaba:* Refers to the first generation of companions who lived and breathed with Prophet Muhammad. Their *Tafaseer* are held in high esteem, and even considered authoritative by some. Considered the third source of *Tafsir* after the *Sunnah.*

- *Tabi'un:* The generation that succeeded the companions of the Prophet. The reports and opinions from the scholars of this generation form an important part of *Tafsir* literature.

- *Tafsir bi'l-ra'y:* A *Tafsir* that relies on reason and intellectual struggle (*Ijtihad*) to come to know the meaning of the Koran. Of course, this *Tasfir* doesn't involve mere guesswork or random opinion, but reason based on sound sources.

- *Tafsir mahmud:* Refers to the *Tafsir* of reason that comes from well-established roots in the Koran itself, in the *Sunnah,* or in Islamic law.

- *Tafsir madhmum:* *Tafsir* of reason which is condemned or disliked because it occurs without the proper consultation of authentic sources.

- *Tafsir bil-'Ishara:* Refers to *Tafsir* based on the "indication" or "signs" of the *Ayat* in the Koran; the inner reading of the Scripture. This form of *Tafsir* occurs most commonly among Islamic mystics who contend that some people have hearts and minds so pure that they can see the inner dimensions of the Koran coupled with the outer dimensions.

Some scholars consider this contentious form of *Tafsir* forbidden. Also, this form of *Tafsir* adds meaning and depth to the discourse on the Koran, but it can't be used to interpret Islamic law, since it usually lacks solid evidence. This *Tafsir* must not contradict the plain or clear meaning of the *Ayah* it applies to; it must have one of the words used in that specific *Ayah* as its root.

✔ *Isra'ilyat:* Traditions and stories found in Jewish (and some Christian) sources that build on the stories of the Koran. The first generation of Muslims rarely used *Isra'ilyat,* but it gained some popularity later on.

The Koran states that both the Jews and Christians added stories to their tradition that have no sound basis — and are even sometimes outright fables. As a result, this *Tafsir,* especially today, is not held favorably. Many scholars see it as an effort by *Mufasirun* to reconstruct the missing history of the prophets in the Koran.

Generally, scholars have taken three approaches to the *Isra'ilyat* traditions:

- Some are absolutely true, because they confirm the Koran.

- Some are absolutely false, because they clearly contradict the Koran.

- Some are neither absolutely true nor absolutely false; while the Koran doesn't confirm them, they don't contradict the Koran, either.

Finding the Tasfir that fits

Many Muslim countries have television and radio programs that teach various interpretations, and many Muslims choose to study it themselves. However, no authoritative body of religious scholars sanctifies or forces a certain interpretation.

Various cultures find specific interpretations most fitting for their community's time and place in the world. For example, Muslims who live in Saudi Arabia often rely heavily on *Tafsir mahmud,* because Muslims there are very conservative about following only those sources that are firmly established as authentic. Muslims who live in West Africa, on the other hand, are usually attracted to *Tafaseer* that draw out inner meanings and spirit of passages in the Koran.

Unfortunately, the amazing tradition of scholarship and education on Islam has drastically fallen off in the past century or so. As a result, many Muslims today simply follow the interpretations prevalent in their communities without taking the time or effort to study the *Tafaseer* themselves.

Language presents a major barrier for some because most classical *Tafaseer* are in Arabic and have not, for the most part, been translated (at least properly) into other languages. Many communities are influenced primarily by the *Tafaseer* that exist in their own respective languages.

Drawing Out Interpretations

I could fill an entire book describing each tool used in *Tafsir,* because of the science's sophistication and complexity. Here, I just want to touch on the basics of some commonly-used methods in interpreting the Scripture.

The Koran, when read in full, clarifies many of its own theological and moral teachings.

Looking at clear and ambiguous passages

The Koran says regarding its own *Ayat* that some passages are clear and unambiguous *(muhkamat),* while others are ambiguous or metaphorical in nature *(mutashabihat)* (3:7).

The clear *Ayat* form the foundation of the Book. They include passages about fundamental beliefs (such as God is One), pious rituals (such as prayer and almsgiving), and explicit laws (such as the prohibition of stealing).

The ambiguous *Ayat* describe aspects of faith whose nature can't be truly known (such as the angel blowing the trumpet on the Day of Judgment). Muslims accept these passages on faith, and hold a number of interpretations about them.

The Koran explains itself

The Koran's depth allows each *Surah* to explain, expand, and redefine its own *Ayat.* As such, an interpreter of the Koran must have a thorough knowledge and understanding of the Scripture in order to explain a single passage.

For example, passage 2:37 relates the story of creation; it only says that after Adam sinned, he received "words of inspiration" by which he (and Eve) earned the Mercy of God. Then, five *Surahs* later, passage 7:23 clarifies these words of inspiration: "Our Sustainer! We have wronged our own souls. If You forgive us not, and bestow not upon us Your Mercy, we shall certainly be lost."

If an interpreter doesn't have complete knowledge of the Book, then he or she can make a serious mistake by prematurely drawing some important conclusions on a certain subject. Only when a *Mufasir* can fully read and understand the Koran can he or she interpret the Koran's message on any given topic.

Although the Koran encourages interpretation, Muslims shouldn't over indulge in theories about the ambiguous *Ayat,* because only God knows what they truly mean. Doing so can cause Muslims to fall into schisms about the ambiguous *Ayat,* while ignoring adherence to clear beliefs and laws (3:7).

The interpretation of these two types of passages falls into the following two categories:

✔ **Tafsir al-dhahir,** or interpretation of clear, outer *(dhahir)* meanings

✔ **Tafsir al-baatin,** or interpretation of hidden, inner *(baatin)* meanings

Tafsir on *dhahir Ayat* comes in two types. The first one is known as *Tafsir bil mathur* or *Rewiyah,* which are commentaries based on the explanation of Prophet Muhammad, his companions, and their respective students. The second one is known as *Tafsir ra'i* or *Dirayah,* which are commentaries based on reflection on the Arabic language, different reading styles, jurisprudence, history or cause of revelation, and deep knowledge of interpretive methods.

Dhahir Ayat are first examined in their clear, outer meanings. Then, their metaphorical meanings are based on sound knowledge of Arabic or proof in the tradition handed down from Prophet Muhammad and his companions.

Tafsir baatin are much more controversial in nature since they deal with *Ayat* that are by their very nature metaphorical and philosophical. Admirers of this *Tafsir* find the tradition an eye-opening experience offering vast meanings that a single *Ayah* can provide. However, this tradition of *Tafsir* also has many critics. The critics feel that these interpretations are rather stagnant in that they don't contribute to the Book's purpose of serving as a guide for human life.

Interpreters who have legal inclinations, or who are most interested in the Book as guidance for living life, focus much of their attention on *dhahir Ayat.* Those who are interested in the spiritual and inner meaning of the Koran focus much of their attention on the *baatin Ayat.*

Many *Mufasirun* attempt to explain both the outer and inner meaning of a passage. Most interpreters focus more heavily on the outer meaning than inner meaning. Those who focus more on inner meaning are usually mystics or are influenced by mystical thought.

Interpreting outer meanings

Tafsir of *dhahir Ayat* involves looking at verses from a legal standpoint. The *Mufasir* (interpreter) takes each *Ayah* line by line and extracts laws from the *Ayah.*

The *Tafsir* of a legal-minded *Mufasir* might work something like this:

1. **Examine the passage in question.**

   The interpreter starts with the original text from the Koran.

   For example, passage 2:239 reads: "If you fear (during travelling), pray on foot, or riding. But, when you are in security, celebrate God's praises in the manner He has taught you, which you knew not before."

   Here, the *Mufasir* looks for clear legal injunctions and also legal Koranic principles that he or she can use to extract future laws that are not dealt with in the Scripture.

2. **Draw a general explanation of the text.**

   The interpreter examines the specific conditions relating to the revelation of an *Ayah,* so that he or she can understand and explain the proper use of these legal injunctions.

   For example, passage 2:239 deals with praying while travelling in circumstances that don't permit the normal prayer ritual (see Chapter 12). This passage was revealed at the time of the Battle of Badr, in which Muslims faced grave danger.

3. **Extract the legal principles from the passage.**

   The *Mufasir* seeks to use his or her vast knowledge of the Koran to arrive at an interoperation that produces a law that Muslims can use in their everyday lives.

   For example, the interpreter may extract the following legal principles from 2:239:

   - **First rule:** While travelling in fear, you may turn away from facing the *Ka'ba.*

   - **Second rule:** While travelling in fear, you can pray while in motion — whether on foot or riding.

   - **Third rule:** This law is limited only to fear, and can't be used to justify praying in this manner when travelling in security. Safe travel requires that you pray as you normally would by stopping in a safe location.

4. **Extract actual law.**

   In the case of passage 2:239, the laws may read something like this:

   - **First extraction of law:** God wants safety and security for His servants, and not danger. As such, when a Muslim faces a dangerous situation, he or she should follow the path which provides security.

   - **Second extraction of law:** In the modern age, this law allows Muslims to pray in a car or airplane, if such a need arises.

5. **Confirm the extracted law.**

> The interpreter must provide evidence of how other passages in the Koran expand or limit the law. The *Mufasir* has to look at other *Ayat* in the Koran that pertain to the subject and see if those *Ayat* in any way limit or expand the concept of the legal injunction.

Interpreting inner meanings

Interpreters looking for inner meanings intricately examine each word in a passage using the triliteral roots of the Arabic language. (See Chapter 4 for more information on Arabic and its triliteral roots.) Through this analysis, the passage expands to reflect its inner meanings coupled with its outer meanings.

These commentators also attempt to explain metaphors of the Koran in much greater detail; those who focus on clear explanations (see the preceding section) feel more comfortable leaving metaphors to literal readings — though they too sometimes venture into the interpretations of metaphorical *Ayat*.

The science of interpreting inner meanings often leads to different viewpoints on the same passage. The *Tafsir* of 2:255, which extols God's attributes, provides a good example of this phenomenon. One part of this *Ayah* says, "His Throne encompasses the heavens and the earth."

Interpreters of this *Ayah* have widely debated what "His Throne," or *Kursi* in Arabic, means. Some interpreters reflect on various reports among the Prophet's companions that discuss how long and large God's Throne may be — they focus on the *dhahir,* or apparent meaning. Various interpreters explain the *baatin,* or hidden meaning, as a reflection of God's Knowledge, God's Greatness, and God's Sovereignty. The word *Kursi,* these commentators say, is a literary technique used by God to express His nature with terms that the human mind can grasp. A mystical reading of *Kursi* attempts to look at inner meanings related to the soul and heart. For example, mystics refer to an unauthentic *Hadith* of Prophet Muhammad, when explaining *Kursi,* that says, "The heart of the man of faith is the Throne of God."

Examining general and specific passages

Passages of the Koran can be divided into two further types: those with a general application for wide audience (*'Aam*) and those with a specific application for a limited audience (*Khaas*).

General *Ayat* usually address humanity as a whole ("O mankind . . .") and the Muslim community as a whole ("O you who believe . . ."). For example, the Koran says, "Every soul shall taste (or experience) death" (3:185). Another example is when the Koran says, "O you who believe! Fasting is prescribed on you as it was prescribed on those who came before you, so that you may learn God-consciousness" (2:183).

However, general *Ayat* can have limitations that exclude certain people from the law. For example, continuing with the theme of fasting, the Koran says, "So every one of you who is present during that month (Ramadan) should spend it in fasting. But, if anyone is ill or on a journey, the prescribed period (should be made up) by later days . . ." (2:185). The general ruling of fasting has limitations for those who are ill or travelling.

Also, some general *Ayat* provide for an alternative if the first law cannot be met for some reason. For example, in the verse on ritual purity, the Koran says that you should wash yourself with water. However, in the same passage it then says, "And if you find no water, then take yourselves clean sand or earth and rub therewith your faces and hands" (5:6). This *Ayah* provides an alternative to the general rule.

Ayat that are *khaas,* or limited, usually address a small group of people or the Prophet Muhammad (33:50, for instance), or are limited in applicability to a specific event during the revelation of the Koran. For example, the Koran vaguely addresses an event during the lifetime of Prophet Muhammad where his wife, Aisha, was falsely accused of adultery. "Why did not the believers, men and women, when they heard of the affair think well of their people and say, 'This charge is an obvious lie?' Why did they not bring four witnesses to prove it?" (24:12–13).

This *Ayah* addresses a specific event that took place. However, this does not mean that its wisdom is limited to history. Rather, from this Muslims are taught that when they hear a rumor, they should give the benefit of doubt to the person who has been accused of something. Also, from this scholars of Islamic law derive the principal of "Innocent until proven guilty" — similar to the law in the United States.

Mufasirun spend a lot of time examining which passages are considered *'aam* and which are considered *khaas,* sometimes with differences of opinion. Based on their conclusions, they determine which legal injunctions, commandments, and moral and spiritual teachings apply for all of humanity, all Muslims, or a specific group and time.

Keeping circumstances behind revelation in mind

The Koran is universal and eternal in its meaning and guidance, according to the Islamic tradition. However, interpreters of the Koran must also study the circumstances, reasons, or causes behind the revelation of passages *(Asbab al-Nuzul)* in order to yield accurate interpretations.

Generally, most *Ayat* were revealed in one of three circumstances:

- ✔ In reaction to a specific case or general circumstance
- ✔ In reaction to a question people asked Prophet Muhammad
- ✔ In reaction to events unknown (a general teaching)

To give you an example, the Koran says that "To God belongs the East and West. Wherever you turn your face is the presence of God . . ." (2:115). You could look at this *Ayah* and think that it's okay to pray in whatever direction you want! However, the historical context related by the Prophet's companions shows that this *Ayah* was revealed when a group of Muslims got stuck in a dark area and couldn't figure out the direction of the *Ka'ba*. So, they just made an estimate and prayed in that direction.

The historical context of this *Ayah* explains that if a Muslim has no way of knowing the direction of the *Ka'ba*, he or she can pray according to their best estimate.

Sometimes doubt exists about the historic conditions under which *Ayat* were revealed. Therefore, Muslims don't consider this method of interpretation as reliable as other methods, unless they are related in fully authentic *Hadith*. Also, sometimes more than one tradition exists about the circumstance or reason behind the revelation of an *Ayah*.

Abrogating passages

The Koran provides a code of law that leads to a good, pious life. Since God revealed the Koran in stages over a period of 23 years (see Chapter 2), the moral laws that stem from the Koran also developed over time. As a result, passages of the Koran regarding specific laws sometimes also developed in two or more stages. The Koran itself recognizes this phenomenon when it says, "None of Our revelations do We abrogate or cause to be forgotten, but We substitute something better or similar" (2:106).

Abrogation means replacing certain legal injunctions or commandments with another legal injunction or commandment regarding the same issue. An *Ayah* that was revealed in the latter stages of revelation usually replaces an *Ayah* revealed in the earlier stages of revelation.

Varying opinions exist as to which *Ayat* have been abrogated and which have not, making abrogation a complex science. At times, the Koran offers two competing worldviews or attitudes that reflect two different contexts. This situation doesn't automatically lead to abrogation of one of the passages. Both teachings should be applied with the wisdom of Scriptural and historical contexts.

Examining two passages in *Surah* 73 illustrates the concept of abrogation. *Ayat* 1–4 of this *Surah* say, "O you enwrapped in your robes. Stay up the night, except a little, half of it, or a little less or a little more, and recite the Koran in slow, measured rhythmic tones." Read in isolation, Muslims could interpret this passage to mean that they should spend most of the night in prayer. But, *Ayah* 20 says: "Your Sustainer knows that you remain up nearly two-thirds of the night, or half of it, or a third, and a party of those with you likewise, and God determines the night and the day. He knows that you will never count it up, so He has turned towards you in mercy. So recite what may be convenient (for you) of the Koran; He knows that some of you will be sick and others journeying about in the land, seeking the bounty of God, and others engaged in armed struggle in the cause of God. So recite what is convenient of it, and establish regular prayer, and pay the purifying alms. . . ."

Clearly, the latter *Ayah* abrogates the former *Ayat* on this subject. Through this science of abrogation, Muslims know that it is not obligatory for them to pray most of the night, as may be understood if the first four *Ayat* were read in isolation.

The rules of abrogation

Without abrogation, interpreters can't derive moral laws. Scholars use three criteria to judge which passages have abrogated other passages:

- ✔ **An authentic report from the Prophet Muhammad or the companions:** This reliable tradition clearly indicates that Prophet Muhammad taught his companions about certain abrogation in the Scripture.

- ✔ **The consensus of the scholars (*Ijma*):** Occurs when scholars of a certain time period are in complete agreement about the abrogation of an *Ayah* or some *Ayat*.

- ✔ **The historical order of passages:** The later law or commandment abrogates the one revealed earlier in the process of revelation.

For example, the first law that appears in the Koran regarding inheritance says that before dying, a Muslim should leave his or her will in charge of someone, and the will should be "according to reasonable usage" for parents and kin (2:180). However, later, as the moral law developed, the law of inheritance was divided equitably between family members (4:11–12). The law in *Surah* 4 cancels out the law in *Surah* 2.

Specification, not abrogation

Some laws don't abrogate earlier laws, but rather expand on or limit earlier laws.

For example, 2:183 makes fasting obligatory on Muslims. However, 2:184 says that those who face physical hardship have the alternative of "freeing a slave or feeding one that is indigent." Instead of abrogating 2:183, 2:184 specifies the law for people who can't fast without undue hardship, such as the old and sick.

Chapter 7

Understanding Interpretations
of the Koran Today

In This Chapter

▶ Examining classical interpretations of the Koran

▶ Understanding post-colonialist understandings of the Scripture

▶ Looking at the Shi'ite tradition in relation to Koranic interpretation

Today, the Muslim world has reached a critical period in its history. An intellectual, spiritual, and sometimes emotional search is underway to define the religious, social, and political landscape of a civilization that was once considered the guiding light of humanity.

In this chapter, I trace the history of Koranic interpretation by looking at some of the earliest companions who studied and taught the Koran. Then, I look at some famous personalities associated with the science of Koranic interpretation, and briefly discuss their respective approaches to the Book. Finally, I examine the influential work of two intellectuals — Sayyid Qutub and Sayyid Mawdudi — and their impact on post-colonial Muslim thought.

Getting to Know Famous Commentators of the Koran

The day Prophet Muhammad died, the Muslim community faced a state of chaos; for the first time, Muslims had questions that couldn't be answered directly by God through the Prophet.

During this critical time, Abu Bakr (a close companion of Prophet Muhammad and first *Caliph* after the Prophet's death) stood in front of the Muslims and emotionally recited a passage of the Koran that suddenly came to life: "Muhammad is no more than a messenger. Many were the messengers that passed away before Him. If he died or was slain, will you then turn back on your heels?" (3:144). Then, Abu Bakr said, relating the meaning of this passage to his people, "If you worshiped Muhammad, then know that Muhammad has died. But, if you worship God, know that God is living and He lives forever."

With these beautiful words, Abu Bakr began the science of *Tafsir,* a science that continues to this day.

In the following sections, I introduce some of the great interpreters of the Koran in history and their contributions to the science of *Tafsir.*

Tafsir from the first generation and successive generations was largely, if not strictly, based on *Tafsir bil-riwaya,* or *Tafsir* transmitted through a chain of narration to Prophet Muhammad and the teachings of his companions. This makes these *Tafaseer* the most authentic in the eyes of the majority of Muslims.

Among the companions

In order to understand the Scripture, Muslims referred to many of the famous companions of Prophet Muhammad, such as Abu Bakr, Umar, Uthman, and Ali. The closest companions basically lived and breathed with the Prophet, and were therefore most intimately aware of the Koran's meaning.

The companion Ibn Abbas spent much of his childhood under the teaching of Prophet Muhammad. Muhammad praised Ibn Abbas's wisdom, and the other companions deeply respected him, even though he was considerably younger than most of them.

Other young companions who grew up in Prophet Muhammad's presence were Al-Abadillah, Ibn Zubair, Abdullah ibn Umar, and Abdullah ibn Al-As. These companions were among the greatest teachers of the Koran; references to their traditions are highly revered.

The Prophet's wives also made outstanding contributions to *Tafsir* because they experienced his everyday life and most of his private actions and concerns. These women, known as the Mothers of the Believers, related many of Muhammad's practices.

Interestingly, while the companions experienced the revelation through the Prophet at the same time, their *Tafsir* often differed. For example:

✔ **Ibn Abbas:** Known to be very accommodating and flexible in his opinions on sacred law. He is recognized today for his progressive understanding of the Koran, especially on matters dealing with the rights of women.

✔ **Abdullah ibn Umar:** His personality was more conservative and strict. Umar complained once to Ibn Abbas that his opinions (or *Fatwas*) were too flexible and lenient. Umar was known for his strict interpretation of the Koran and sacred law.

Despite their differences, the companions had great respect for each other and always acted in mutual consultation. They lived the tradition that says, "Difference of opinion among the *Ummah* is a blessing from God." But, these differences of opinions do not exist on fundamental teachings, but rather on minor issues.

In successive generations

The generation that followed Muhammad's companions *(Sahabah)* is known as *Tabi'un.* These interpreters came mainly from three locations:

✔ **Mecca:** The group from Mecca was considered most knowledgeable and trusted, because they were students of Ibn Abbas (see the preceding section). From among them, Mujahid was considered the wisest interpreter. People visited from all across Islamic civilization to learn from him. His was also the first written book of *Tafsir* collected.

✔ **Medina:** The students from Medina also learned from some of the greatest companions. Ubay bin Ka'b's students — Zaid bin Aslam and Ka'b Al-Quradi — count among the great interpreters from this school.

✔ **Iraq:** The group of interpreters from Iraq benefited greatly from the companion Ibn Mas'ud, who moved to Iraq. Basra and Kufa were the two great cities of knowledge. The most famous students from this school were Al-Hasan al-Basri and Ibrahim al-Nakhai'.

Collecting the companion's *Tafsir*

Early *Tafsir* was primarily transmitted as an oral tradition, meaning that very few writings of *Tafsir* exist from the companions of Muhammad. However, their students transmitted knowledge to their children and kept their interpretations alive through the generations. As such, collections of interpretations from these early companions exist today. Unfortunately (and sadly), almost none of these interpretations have been translated into English.

Classic works of Koranic interpretation

The following classic works of *Tafsir* have been collected into books. Unfortunately, almost none have been translated into English to this date, so I can't refer you to their books for the most part.

Muslim scholars refer to these works heavily, even today.

Tafsir of al-Tabari

The work of Ibn Jarir al-Tabari (died 922) is the best, most comprehensive, and most detailed work in the history of *Tafsir*. All other *Tafaseer* rely heavily on al-Tabari's work, since he is the first to complete the *Tafsir* in book form.

Al-Tabari's work transmits knowledge of the past and offers original critical insights on the tradition. He is also known for his mastery of Arabic grammar, which he uses quite effectively in interpreting the Scripture.

Jarir al-Tabari's book includes the controversial *Israliyat,* stories and traditions found in Judaism, but not necessarily confirmed in authentic Islamic sources.

Collection of history in the book of Al-Wahidi

Abu al-Hasan 'Ali ibn Ahmad al-Wahidi (died 1076) wrote a *Tafsir* that became an extremely useful resource for future commentators.

Al-Wahidi did a brilliant job of collecting the history or primary reasoning (*Asbab an-Nuzul*) behind passages in the Koran, which helps explain the primary reason and wisdom of its meaning. His *Tafsir* is most famous for its monumental work in this area. He is also known for his excellent knowledge of Arabic grammar.

Ibn Kathir: Interpreter of the conservative school

Ismail "Imad al-Din Abu al-Fida" ibn Kathir (died 1373) backed Ibn Taymiyah, a famous scholar in the conservative school of thought. Ibn Kathir's *Tafsir* offers an excellent collection of historical analysis on the Koran, and his mastery of Islamic law makes his insights especially interesting.

Many people consider Ibn Kathir's work the second best *Tafsir* after al-Tabari's book. Ibn Kathir proves more strict in his use of traditions, sticking to those that are considered authentic.

Ibn Kathir rejects any foreign sources in his interpretation, such as the *Israliyat.* Also, his style is unique in that he gives utmost attention to explaining the Koran through the Koran, and he refers his readers constantly to other passages in the Scripture. His is one of the few works that is currently translated into a 24-volume English translation: *Tafsir Ibn Kathir,* published by Darussalam Publications.

Al-Qurtubi: The pious jurist

Muhammad ibn Ahmad Abu 'Abdullah al-Qurtubi (died 1273) is known for his vast knowledge and expertise in Islamic law. Much of his *Tafsir* looks at the Koran with a legal eye, but his work is extremely eloquent in his use of wise sayings and insight into Arabic grammar. His work counts among the best organized *Tafsir* existing.

Al-Zamakhshari: Interpretation of reason

Abu al-Qasim Jar Allah Mahmud ibn Umar al-Zamakhshari (died 1114) was known in his time as one of the most brilliant thinkers in the Muslim world. His knowledge of Arabic grammar was probably the best in *Tafsir* history. His *Tafsir* relies on reason in the Koran. Critics of his work discount his strong emphasis on metaphoric interpretation in the Koran.

In theology, al-Zamakhshari was a staunch believer that God's features in the Koran could not be taken literally, and should rather be understood as symbols of his attributes. Most orthodox thought does not seriously disagree with this notion, but also does not dare to venture into the power of symbolism in the Scripture.

Muhammad Asad was greatly influenced by this *Tafsir*. His translation and commentary of the Koran also borrows heavily from al-Zamakhshari.

Al-Razi: Renewal of religion

In every century, God sends a scholar who renews the faith. Many consider Fakhr al-Din al-Razi (died 1209) to be the reviver of the seventh century, according to the Islamic calendar.

Fakhr al-Din al-Razi is known as the most brilliant scholar to have ever existed. Before he was an interpreter, he was a great philosopher. As such, Al-Razi focuses much attention on Islamic philosophy in the Koran, something earlier commentaries rarely expounded on.

Like many philosophers, al-Razi fell into endlessly debating points about various verses, which makes his *Tafsir* difficult to follow. His critics say that his *Tafsir* is more a book of theology and philosophy than an explanation of the Koran.

Al-Suyuti: Seeker of knowledge

Jalal al-Din al-Suyuti (died 1505) traveled to almost every great center of learning in Islamic civilization to gain knowledge about the Islamic tradition. He was a jurist of the highest order, a brilliant historian, and a pious mystic *(Sufi)*.

Some consider him in such high esteem as to argue that he was a reviver of religion for the tenth century (Islamic calendar). However, his mystical interpretations make him as controversial as he is loved.

Al-Nisaburi: The mystical interpreter

Nizam al-Din al-Nisaburi (died 1327) is a popular author of *Tafsir* among *Sufis* (mystics) even today. His collection of *Tafsir* reflects the thoughts of al-Zamakhshari and al-Razi, but he does an excellent job of explaining the Koran through the lens of popular mysticism.

Some feel that he relies too heavily on unauthentic sayings of wisdom rather than authenticated sources.

Ibn Arabi: The famous mystic

Perhaps the greatest work of *Tafsir* from a *Sufi* is the comprehensive work of Muhyi al-Din ibn Arabi (died 1240). His unique *Tafsir* views the explanation of the Koran as less of a science and more of a spiritual experience.

In defense of his work (from traditionalists), Ibn Arabi argues that interpreting the Koran based on mere opinion or guesswork is forbidden *(haraam)*. But, discovering the inner or hidden *(baatin)* meaning of the Koran does not harm Muslim thought, even if it does not benefit it.

Influential Movements of the Twentieth Century

With the collapse of the Ottoman Empire in 1923, Islamic civilization began to deteriorate. For years, Muslims suffered continuous defeats, leading to the colonization of most of the Muslim world by European powers, such as England and France. Almost a century before colonialism finally ended in about 1945, social, political, and religious movements started to fight colonial rule — thus opening a new phase in the ever-evolving history of Koranic interpretation.

From this chaos emerged the real need for an Islamic identity. In an effort to return Islam to its former glory, revivalists began appearing all over the Muslim world, declaring a vision for political and social change through Islam. These revivalists believed that Islamic civilization fell because Muslims had abandoned the true, authentic teachings of Islam. The *Tafsir* from this era reflects this social and political reality.

Revivalists draw parallel after parallel with the condition of Muslims today and the condition of Muslims at the time of Prophet Muhammad. Also, interestingly, these movements remain open in their interpretations of Koranic law in order to support their claims to Islam's universality. For example, women, such as Zain ibn Ghazali — an Egyptian scholar of the Koran and Islamic law — have played an active role in many of these movements. Also, there is a broad vision for non-Muslims in their vision of an Islamic state, taking the constitution of Medina as the ideal document laying out the way to a healthy religious community.

In the following sections, I look at the Koranic interpretation of Sayyid Abul Ala' Al-Mawdudi, who founded the Islamic movement in Pakistan known as *Jamaat Islami* (Group of Islam). I also talk about Sayyid Qutub, an influential member of the Egypt-based *Ikhwan al-Muslimeen* (Muslim Brotherhood). Both of these interpreters have a major influence in the American Muslim community today.

The core argument of these two influential personalities, in their *Tafsir,* is that the world has fallen into the same darkness of *Jahiliyya* (ignorance) that marked the period before the coming of Islam in Arabia. Both men, and the movements they inspired, see parallels in the moral corruption of pre-Islamic Arabia and the modern world (including the Muslim world, not only the West). As such, both view Islam as the force that will bring light into a world turned dark.

Mawdudi: Framework for a movement

Sayyid Mawdudi's great explanation of the Koran, known as *Tafhim al-Qur'an,* or *Towards Understanding the Qur'an,* is most influential on the Indian Subcontinent, but is also well received in other places.

Mawdudi's *Tafsir* resembles no other because he focuses on the dynamic themes of the Koran, rather than undertaking an *Ayah*-by-*Ayah* detailed analysis into various traditions.

Mawdudi talks about man's relationship to God, and his role as God's representative on earth. He articulates, better than anyone else in *Tafsir,* the history of the universal message and appeal of the Koran for humanity. Mawdudi constructs the life stories of the prophets in the Koran as a growing movement to establish God's way of life *(Deen)* on earth. Every prophet, Mawdudi argues, was sent to struggle for good against evil, Truth against falsehood, and faith against rejection of faith (the essence of *Jihad*).

This influential thinker also gave special emphasis to the role of man on earth as representative or vicegerent of God on earth. Mawdudi, like very few before him, argued that this role of man was the key to human moral and social progress.

Here's an example of how Mawdudi taught the idea of man's relationship with God. It also highlights his ability to relate to the simple man:

"Take, for example, the case of an estate which someone has been appointed to administer on your behalf. You will see that four conditions are met. First, the real ownership of the estate remains vested in you and not in the administrator. Second, he administers your property only in accordance with your instructions. Third he exercises his authority within the limits prescribed by you. And, fourth, in the administration of the trust, he executes your will and not his own. These four conditions are so inherent in the concept of "representation" that if any representative fails to observe them he will rightly be blamed for breaking the covenant which was implied in the concept of "representation." This is exactly what Islam means when it affirms that man is the vicegerent of God on earth. Hence, these four concepts are also involved in the concept of *Khilafat* (God's vicegerent on earth)."

In his reading of the Koran as a guide to an Islamic movement, Mawdudi ignores, if not rejects, the idea of abrogation (see Chapter 6) as it was traditionally understood. Mawdudi *did* accept the notion that the Koran was revealed in steps, and that laws therefore developed over time. However, he sees these changes as a process of *gradualism,* by which the pure and greatest Islamic state was formed — the state of Medina under Prophet Muhammad.

Mawdudi didn't accept tradition on face value. For example, regarding the Koran's discussion on the change of prayer direction from Jerusalem to Mecca, most classical commentators explained this move as Islam's return to Mecca in the tradition of Prophet Abraham. Mawdudi agreed with this explanation, but expanded this theory further. He argued that the change in the direction of praying was God's sign that He had shifted the responsibility of implementing His Will on earth from the Children of Israel to the Muslim community.

Mawdudi argued that all those who declare belief in the Oneness of God and the Prophecy of Muhammad had the responsibility to struggle in a *movement* for the sake of good against evil. This concept of movement in particular represents a shift from classical interpretations that did not carry this idea of a dynamic movement with them.

The strength of Mawdudi's work rests on his unique ability to communicate the message of the Koran to the intellectual as well as the layman. Through the use of simple metaphors and reason, Mawdudi effectively articulated the relationship between God and man, and man's subsequent role on earth. His *Tafsir* focuses on Islam as a complete way of life, and his work attempts to explain Islam's teachings on social interaction, economic principles, and political theory.

Mawdudi's interpretation of the Koran is being translated into English, with several volumes already complete. Look for *Towards Understanding the Qur'an,* by Sayyid Abdul A'la Mawdudi, translated by Zafar Ishaq Ansari; published by The Islamic Foundation.

Qutub: The controversial revolutionary

Sayyid Qutub's works on the Koran count among the most controversial writings that exist in the modern Muslim experience. Since the tragic events of September 11, academics have, unfortunately, come to the conclusion that his work forms the basis for some terrorist movements, such as Al-Qaeda.

However, a non-ethnocentric view of his work shows that Qutub was a much more complex man than many give him credit for. While he supported social change, by lawful force if necessary, he also believed in the strict ethical code of *Jihad* (see Chapter 18). It would be incorrect to classify him as a terrorist or supporter of terrorism.

Qutub was born to a poor family in Egypt, but he rose quickly among the intellectuals of his time because of his thoughts on the modern world. Interestingly, Qutub was not praised, early on, for his revolutionary ideas about the Koran and Islam, but because of his attachment to Western ideology, which he said should be implemented in Egypt. Qutub was pro-Western during the early part of his activist life.

Qutub decided to study abroad in the United States. There he confronted, as a dark-skinned man, the racism of Jim Crowe laws. Suddenly, Qutub's image of the West and its ideals was shattered. Qutub returned to Egypt after only about two years and surprised everyone with his change of heart. Qutub was deeply affected by his experience in the West, and returned to his homeland advocating an Islamic revolution.

More than any *Tafsir,* Qutub's work undoubtedly reflects his own life into reading the Scripture. His writings, including his large volume on interpretation of the Koran, center around a few key points, many of them passionately reflecting the time period in which he lived.

Qutub took the concept of *Jahiliyya,* which traditionally means ignorance about God's ways, and transformed it into what he saw as the problem with the entire world. *Jahiliyya,* for Qutub, meant the rule of man over man. He introduced this concept as antithetical to Islam, which he argued offered mankind freedom from every authority, except God. Qutub sincerely came to believe that as long as man ruled over man, racism, inequality, and injustice would reign supreme. Qutub argued that moral and spiritual chaos could only disappear when humanity freed itself from earthly authority and turned to God.

Qutub felt that mankind had no right to legislate moral laws on society, because once humans submitted to man-made moral laws, they could no longer be free to submit to the sole authority of moral laws — God. This also meant that any government that advocated laws other than God's were in essence committing *Shirk*, or the act of associating partners with God, which is the only unforgivable sin in Islam.

He argued that two institutions could free mankind from the rule of man:

- ✔ *Jihad:* Qutub argued that the movement must present Koranic teachings to the world through words and actions. So long as the movement could freely preach its message and practice its faith, then this struggle of words and deeds would continue.

  However, a second stage of *Jihad* would come into play, Qutub argued, if the movement lost its freedom to preach its message or its freedom of worship. Then, Qutub said, armed struggle would be permissible against the forces of oppression, and the struggle would have to continue until mankind was free from the institutions of oppression.

  Qutub also made clear that Muslims must honor the Koran's divine commandment, "Let there be no compulsion in religion," without compromise. In fact, Qutub writes in his *Tafsir* of 2:192 that ". . . forced religious conversion is the worst violation of a most inviolable human right. It is, therefore, a much more heinous offence than murder, regardless of the form that coercion takes or how it is exerted."

  In his *Tafsir,* Qutub also lays down ethics of warfare in response to 2:191, which introduces the concept of armed struggle. In these ethics, Qutub does not stray from the high ethical standards of armed struggle in the classical Islamic tradition. On this point, Qutub vastly differs from modern-day terrorist groups like Al-Qaeda.

- ✔ **Gradual law:** Qutub wrote that Muslims must honor the Koranic concept of *gradual law,* meaning that he opposed the sudden implementation of Islamic law on people without their understanding of God's religion. Qutub argued that only once the people were ready to submit to God's Will, could Islamic law be implemented.

  He saw the gradual application of laws over a 23-year period as the ideal standard that the Islamic movement should follow. His beliefs on this matter stand in stark contrast to radical groups that want to impose sudden and strict Islamic laws on Muslims and non-Muslims alike.

Some people say that radical terrorist groups have used Qutub's arguments for an Islamic state for their own agenda. However, to argue that Qutub and the terrorists share the same ideology and objectives is false.

Qutub was a man of his time. Whether you agree with his views or not, his writings express the Muslim world's passionate desire to live in freedom, especially from its own tyrant regimes.

If you're interested in reading Qutub's interpretation of the Koran, it has been translated into English. Look for *In the Shade of the Qur'an*, by Sayyid Qutub, translated by M.A. Salahi and A.A. Shamis; published by The Islamic Foundation.

Muhammad Rida: The influential reformer

Muhammad Rashid Rida came from Egypt and was a student of the Koranic scholar Muhammad Abduh. Rida wrote an interpretation of the Koran known as *Tafsir al-manar,* which proved to be as influential as it is controversial. Rida only interprets 12 parts *(Juz')* of the Koran, but his work offers some important insights into how Muslims continue to grapple with questions of modernity.

Many praise Rida for his vision in critically interpreting the Koran in the context of modernity. However, his critics feel that Rida went overboard in trying to reconcile Koranic ideals with modernity. For example, Rida famously argues that the Koran in fact outlaws polygamy, because it is impossible for any man to live up to the Koran's teaching of treating wives equally. He is highly quoted among many modernist-thinking Muslims, but since he presents some unorthodox views, many Muslims are cautious of his *Tafsir.*

Muhammad al-Ghazali: Thematic Tafsir

Shaykh Muhammad al-Ghazali, an Egyptian *Mufasir,* is one of the most highly respected scholars today. His work on *Tafsir* is known as much for its content as it is for its new style — a thematic commentary of the Scripture. It's the first of its kind, one that mixes classical interpretations with post-colonial thought and his own deep reflections. Al-Ghazali's brilliant work effectively links all the passages of the Koran's moral narrative together to show how the Koran is indeed a cohesive and comprehensive Scripture.

Fortunately, this *Tafsir* does exist in English, and it serves as an excellent, easy read if you're interested in finding out more about Koranic interpretation. Look for *A Thematic Commentary on the Qur'an,* by Shaykh Muhammad al-Ghazali, published by the International Institute of Islamic Thought.

Another School of Thought: The Shi'ites

Shi'ites comprise about 15 percent of the entire Muslim population. Shi'ite means "follower of," and implies, "Followers of Ali," referring to Prophet Muhammad's first cousin and close confidant, the fourth Caliph of Islam.

The split between the *Sunni* majority of Islam and the Shi'ites began with the passing of Prophet Muhammad. Immediately, the question arose as to who would succeed Muhammad as leader of the *Ummah*. The Shi'ites strongly believed that the successor should come from within the house of Muhammad *(ahl' al-bayt)*. The obvious candidate, then, was Ali.

Ali

Sunni Muslims highly revere Ali as the last of the rightly-guided *Caliphs,* and love him as the "Gate of Knowledge." However, the Shi'ites, with their belief that leadership must stay within the family of Prophet Muhammad through his daughter Fatimah and cousin Ali, disregard the first three *Caliphs* (Abu Bakr, Umar, and Uthman) as illegitimate. Instead, they believed that Ali was the *Imam* and spiritual head during this whole time period.

Sunnis contend that Ali was supportive of the three *Caliphs* and had no aspirations to the responsibility of office. In Shi'ite Islam, Ali is considered the perfect Muslim and is often called the Commander of the Faithful. Also, Shi'ite commentators believed that when the Koran spoke about a spiritual being or the height of righteousness, it was in fact reflecting on Ali. For example, 2:177, one of the most comprehensive *Ayat* on righteousness, is said by Shi'ite commentators to describe all the qualities that Ali possessed.

The *Sunni* tradition relies heavily on reports coming from Abu Bakr, Umar, and Uthman. However, the Shi'ites are hostile to these companions, and their *Tafsir* books are dominated by sayings of Ali. Along with the collection of sayings of Muhammad, the sayings of Ali form an important part of Shi'ite tradition.

While *Imam* in the *Sunni* tradition implies prayer leader, community role model, teacher, legal and spiritual adviser, and judge, *Imam* in the Shi'ite tradition means head of the entire community of Muslims. *Imams* are not only pious figures, but are also known to have communication with the angels and deep knowledge of the Scripture by which they come to know both the inner *(baatin)* meaning as well as the outer *(dhahir)* meaning of the Book. As such, Shi'ite *Tafsir* refers much more often to inner meanings than does classical *Sunni Tafsir*.

After Ali was martyred, his sons (and grandsons of Prophet Muhammad) became known among the Shi'ites as the next *Imams*. Soon thereafter, both sons were also martyred in what amounts to a very sad period in the Islamic tradition for both Shi'ites and *Sunni*.

Sunnis too hold the Prophet's grandson in high esteem. Shi'ites blamed themselves for the death of Imam Hussein as they failed to protect him. To this day, Shi'ites grieve over this event by showing physical expressions of grief such as hitting their chests, known as *Matam*, or mourning processions. However, most Shi'ites do not participate in this ritual.

Shi'ites believe that, including Ali and his two sons, there are 12 *Imams* who will come to the world with special guidance of inner and outer meanings of the Koran. However, it is believed that the twelfth *Imam* is alive, but in hiding (occultation) and has communication with the prophets in heaven. He is anticipated to arrive near the end of time to restore justice to the world. All *Imams* are considered, like prophets, to be innocent or free of major sin *(Masum)*.

As such, the Shi'ite *Tafsir* of the Koran is inundated with references to the eleven *Imams* — their sayings, actions, and experiences. The *Imams* are all connected in a line right through Ali to Prophet Muhammad, and therefore are considered to have special knowledge that can only come as a direct successor of the previous *Imam*. It is also believed that the Koran first pertains to the *Imams* and then by extension to the rest of the Muslim community.

This is where the Shi'ite and *Sunni* schools differ widely, since the *Sunni* school has no concept of a class of religious men that are in any way, shape, or form in divine communication.

Two famous Shi'ite Koranic interpreters

The Shi'ite tradition has produced a number of Koranic interpretations, which actually don't differ vastly from the majority *Sunni* tradition — except for a few key differences mentioned in the previous section.

Here I briefly mention two Shi'ite *Tafsir* that are deeply respected among Shi'ites — one classical and one modern.

Tafsir of al-Tabarsi: Classical Shi'ite tradition

Abu Ali al-Fadl ibn Hasan al-Tabarsi (died 1153) is one of the greatest *Mufasir* in the classical Shi'ite tradition. Tabarsi was well-known as a brilliant jurist, theologian, and expert of the Arabic language.

As is the case with Shi'ite thought, Tabarsi focuses much of his *Tafsir* on Mu'tazali theology, which is known for its ultra-rational, deeply philosophical explanations of the Koran and Islamic tradition. Tabarsi does an incredible job with analysis of Arabic words and their relationship to the Koranic worldview.

Tafsir al-Tabataba'i: Modern Shi'ite interpreter

Sayyid Muhammad Husayn al-Tabataba'i (died 1981) produced probably the most influential *Tafsir* for young Shi'ite intellectuals and reformers. The *Mufasir* combines classical interpretations, social realities, and philosophical reflections on modern society — which makes it very attractive for young men and women trying to find their way in life.

You can read Tabataba'i's interpretation for yourself in English, because his entire *Tafsir* is conveniently published on the Web at www.almizan.org/. This site provides an excellent resource, although not all volumes of his work are available at this stage.

Part III
Seeing the Koranic Worldview

The 5th Wave   By Rich Tennant

©RICHTENNANT

"These drives to the mosque always remind me of what unites Muslims: submitting completely to Allah, praying five times per day, and that arriving early will assure you the best parking space."

In this part . . .

Have you ever wondered what Muslims believe and how they view the world? Well, with over a billion Muslims worldwide who belong to such diverse cultures as Africa and North America, I can't generalize an answer to that question. But, the Koran, as the Book of guidance for all Muslims, provides unique insight into the generally shared world-view of devout followers.

In this part, I explain Koranic teachings on God, prophets, and the purpose of life on earth. I examine how the Koran views other faith traditions and the spiritual, unseen realm of the universe.

Chapter 8

Meeting God, Prophets, and Mankind

In This Chapter

▶ Exploring God according to the Koranic worldview

▶ Understanding the nature and roles of prophets and messengers

▶ Zooming in on the purpose of human life

The entire Koranic narrative revolves around God, prophets, and mankind. You must understand the nature and purpose of these Koranic players to grasp the Book's message for humanity.

In this chapter, I explain the concept of the Divine, and the role of prophets and humans as vehicles for understanding God's Will and applying His divine ways to earthly life. I also show how these Koranic characters are deeply interconnected in fulfilling the Koran's mission of guiding societies towards God-conscious living.

Conceptualizing God

In this section, I discuss the linguistic implications of the term "God" in Arabic, and then explore two important passages from the Koran that give special insight into the nature of the Divine.

"A" is for "Allah"

Every language has a word to describe the Divine. In English it is "God," in Persian it is "*Khudah,*" and in Hebrew it is "*Eloh,*" to name just a few. The Arabic word for God is *Allah.* (Arab Christians and Arab Jews also call God by *Allah.*)

The word *Allah* holds a special place in the study of the Koran. *Allah* is a beautiful and unique word in many ways:

- You can't pluralize *Allah* as more than one, as you can make the English word "God" into "gods." There is only one *Allah.*

- The Koran often refers to God by naming one of His attributes, such as Knowledge, Power, or Mercy. *Allah* unites all the attributes of divinity used for God in the Koran. When the Koran says *Allah,* it calls the Divine by all the Beautiful Names that are attributed to Him.

- *Allah* as a proper name has no gender associated with it. Also, you can't "genderize" the word Allah, as you can turn "God" into "goddess" in English. This underscores the point of God's uniqueness; He is not like His creation. The Koran uses the second-person "He" only because there is no "it" in the Arabic language.

Exploring the concept of God

The Koran is full of passages that speak of God's attributes and nature. However, Muslim theologians look especially to the two following passages for understanding the concept of God.

Purity of Faith

Surah 112, called "Purity of Faith," is only four verses long, but Prophet Muhammad described it as one-third of the entire Book, because of the meaning it carries:

> "Say: 'He is One God: God the Eternal, the Uncaused Cause of all being. He Begets not, and neither is He begotten; and there is nothing that could be compared with him'" (112:1–4).

This short *Surah* summarizes God's nature found throughout the Koran. The *Surah* contains four essential elements. The first two affirm qualities of God, while the latter two reject certain theories about God found in other religious traditions:

- The word *Tawhid,* which means unity of God as One, or simply One God, perfectly describes God's nature. The concept of God advocated in the Koran doesn't belong to any one race or religion. Rather, the Divine is a universal Deity that sustains every living creature in the high heavens and on earth, and is the Lord of the East and the West, as the Koran puts it.

   The scripture also says that this revelation is from the same source as the inspiration given to all past prophets, including Abraham, Moses, and Jesus. As such, there is only one Creator, and only one Master. Therefore, all gratitude, worship, and obedience are due to Him alone.

The first verse of the Purity of Faith completely rejects polytheism in all its forms and functions.

✔ God is eternal and therefore lives outside the realm of time. The Divine exists outside the science of cause and effect, because every caused (living) thing goes back to Him as its original source of life. In this reasoning, God is completely independent and self-sufficient, while all creation is dependent on Him for their continued existence and sustenance.

God's eternal nature also gives eternal meaning to His Knowledge, Power, Compassion, and all other divine attributes. Therefore, from a Koranic standpoint, God's ethical teachings must also be universal and eternal.

✔ This passage rejects the Christian doctrine of God having a begotten son. The Koran argues that God is above and beyond the need for having a son. God doesn't have parents, nor does he produce children.

The Koran also rejects the notion found in the common saying that "we are all God's children." The Koran argues that humans are the servants of God, united as the children of Adam.

✔ The Koran makes it clear that God is completely unlike His creation in bodily form. The last verse of this passage warns against thinking of God in anthropomorphic terms, such as having hands and eyes. Muslims have no visual concept of God, and any drawings or paintings of the Divine are considered highly blasphemous.

Umar ibn Al-Khattab, the second Caliph of Islam and one of the closest companions to Prophet Muhammad, said it best when he said, "Your inability to perceive God is your perception of God."

The Verse of the Throne

Surah 2 of the Scripture, called the "Verse of the Throne," also contains some key concepts regarding the nature of God. Some elements of this verse resemble those found in the Purity of Faith (see the preceding section), so I don't repeat them here.

The Verse of the Throne reads as one of the most eloquent and beautifully rhyming verses in the Book:

> "God! There is no deity except Him, the Ever-Living, the Self-Subsistent Fount of all being. Neither slumber overtakes Him, nor sleep. Who is there that could intercede with Him, unless it be by His permission? He knows all that lies open before men and all that is hidden from them, whereas they cannot attain to anything of His knowledge except that which He wills (them to attain). His Throne overspreads the heavens and the earth, and He feels no fatigue in guarding and preserving them. And, He is the Most High, The Supreme (in glory)" (2:255).

The vast meaning found in the Verse of the Throne could fill an entire book. The following points focus on a couple of the passage's key concepts:

- ✔ The Koran rejects the concept of God's share in human limitations, such as getting tired or feeling pain. Instead, God has unique power and strength that He uses to sustain and govern the universe.

  The Koranic understanding of God denies the Biblical notion that God created the world in six days and took rest on the seventh day. The Koran argues that God needs no rest, as He feels no fatigue in carrying out divine functions. If God slept or took rest, then the entire universe would cease to exist, since everything runs on His Sustenance.

- ✔ This passage argues that everything in the heavens and on earth belongs to God, because He is the Creator of all things. Therefore, everything runs according to His divine will. The sun rises each morning and sets each evening, not based on its own strength or will, but based on God's Power and Will.

  When it comes to human beings, despite an intriguing element of free choice and independence, the Koran argues that God can take away a person's strength, knowledge, and life at any time. Therefore, all uniquely human qualities are also a part of God's Will, and He is Owner over them.

  This concept of God's ownership has strong implications for Muslims, because it says that God is the owner of life and any blessings that He chooses to give. Attitudes such as, "It's my money and I'll spend it however I choose," are incompatible with this concept. Instead, a devout Muslim says, "This money comes from God, and I will spend it in ways that are pleasing to Him alone." This spirit constantly encourages devout Muslims to look beyond their own egos for ways to help other human beings and draw nearer to God.

  The Koran rejects the concept that everything is He (God); the Koranic truth is expressed as everything is His (God's).

- ✔ In the middle of this passage you find the concept of an *intercessor,* or intermediary, between God and His servants (such as a priest).

  From the Koranic concept of God, humans don't need intercession for salvation to occur, because God's Mercy, Compassion, and Forgiveness are above anyone's intercession. God can forgive when He wants and whom He wants, without the need for an intercessor.

  However, this verse does point out that God can accept the intercession of those whom He chooses on the Day of Judgment. Scholars of the Koran have a difference of opinion as to exactly who can intercede. Some commentators believe only Prophet Muhammad could hold this role. Others say that true martyrs in the path of God could also act as intercessors; others believe that all extremely pious worshippers of God will have the ability to intercede with God's permission on the Day of Judgment. Similarly, there is a difference of opinion on the degree of intercession that each holds, with scholars agreeing that prophets have a higher degree of intercession than do pious people.

✔ With God lies all the treasures of knowledge both in the seen and unseen worlds. As such, divine knowledge is perfect and eternal. As the Koran puts it, "Not a leaf falls but He knows it" (6:59). This is a very powerful reminder for Muslims to be in a state of constant awareness of divine knowledge in all that they say and do.

✔ This verse speaks of God's Throne, which has caused some debate among commentators of the Koran as to whether this verse should be taken literally or metaphorically. In any case, the scholars agree that the Throne represents God's Power, Will, Authority, and — probably most importantly — His Sovereignty over creation.

God's Sovereignty and His Knowledge have a direct and important connection. The theory goes that if God is all Knowing, then He must know what is best for human development and progress. Divine laws are based on benefit for humanity, and can't by their very nature intend harm for the human race.

This understanding of God's nature as Sovereign becomes extremely important in understanding the concept of an Islamic state. The entire governance of an Islamic state revolves around the concept of God as the giver of law upon which societies are formed. An Islamic state must be governed by divine laws and principles. As such, an "Islamic secular state," as there is a "Jewish secular state" in Israel, would be a contradiction of terms.

Experiencing God through divine attributes

In a famous *Hadith*, Prophet Muhammad said, "God has ninety-nine names . . . and whoever enumerates them will enter paradise."

Seeking divine advice

Muslims find faith in divine knowledge to guide them towards the right path in all decisions made throughout life. The following supplication, taught by Prophet Muhammad, illustrates the trust Muslims place in God's knowledge:

"O *Allah!* I seek your counsel by Your Knowledge and by Your Power. I seek strength and I ask You from Your immense favor, for verily You are able and I am not, and You know while I do not, and You are Knower of the unseen. O *Allah!* If you know this affair to be good for me, in relation to my religion, life, and end, then decree and facilitate it for me, and bless me with it. And, if you know this affair to be ill for me towards my religion, my life, and end, then distance it from me and remove me from it. And, decree for me what is good wherever it be and make me content with such.'"

The Koran refers to these names as "the most beautiful names" (see Table 8-1). With each name, the Koran unlocks secret doors that provide readers of the Scripture with a taste of God's divine attributes and nature, through which humanity comes to know God from the Koranic worldview.

Table 8-1	Ninety-nine Names of God in the Islamic Tradition
Arabic Name	**English Meaning**
Allah	The proper name for God in Arabic
Al-Rahman	The Compassionate
Al-Rahim	The Merciful
Al-Malik	The King or Sovereign
Al-Quddus	The Holy
Al-Salaam	The Source of Peace
Al-Mumin	The Giver of Faith
Al-Muhaymin	The Protector
Al-'Aziz	The Strong
Al-Jabbar	The Almighty
Al-Mutakabbir	The Majestic
Al-Khaliq	The Creator
Al-Bari'	The Maker
Al-Musawwir	The Fashioner
Al-Ghaffar	The Forgiving
Al-Qahhar	The Dominant
Al-Wahhab	The One who Bestows
Al-Razaq	The Provider
Al-Fattah	The Opener or The Reliever
Al-'Alim	The All-Knowing
Al-Qabid	The Restrainer or The Withholder
Al-Basit	The Expander
Al-Khafid	The Humbler

Arabic Name	*English Meaning*
Al-Rafi'	The Exalter
Al-Mu'izz	The Empower
Al-Mudhill	The One who Humiliates
Al-Sami'	The All-Hearing
Al-Basir	The All-Seeing
Al-Hakam	The Judge
Al-'Adl	The Just
Al-Latif	The Kind
Al-Khabir	The All-Aware
Al-Halim	The Forbearing
Al-'Azim	The Mighty
Al-Ghaffur	The Forgiving
Al-Shakur	The Grateful
Al-'Aliyy	The High or The Sublime
Al-Kabir	The Great
Al-Hafiz	The Preserver
Al-Mughit	The Sustainer
Al-Hasib	The One who Judges
Al-Jalil	The Revered
Al-Karim	The Generous
Al-Raqib	The Watchful
Al-Mujib	The Responsive
Al-Wasi'	The All-Embracing
Al-Hakim	The Wise
Al-Waddud	The Loving
Al-Majid	The Most Glorious
Al-Ba'ith	The One who Resurrects

(continued)

Table 8-1 *(continued)*

Arabic Name	English Meaning
Al-Shahid	The Witness
Al-Haqq	The Truth
Al-Wakil	The Most Trustworthy
Al-Qawwiy	The Most Strong
Al-Matin	The Firm or The Authoritative
Al-Waliyy	The Protector
Al-Hamid	The Praiseworthy
Al-Muhsi	The One who Reckons
Al-Mubdi'	The Originator
Al-Mu'id	The Restorer of Life
Al-Muhy	The Giver of Life
Al-Mumit	The Giver of Death
Al-Hayy	The Ever-Living
Al-Qayyum	The Self-Existing
Al-Wajid	The Self Sufficient
Al-Majid	The Glorified
Al-Wahid	The One
Al-Samad	The Eternal
Al-Qadir	The Omnipotent
Al-Muqtadir	The Powerful
Al-Muqaddim	The Expediter
Al-Mu'ahkhir	The One who Delays
Al-Awwal	The First
Al-'Akhir	The Last
Al-Zahir	The Manifest
Al-Batin	The Hidden

Arabic Name	English Meaning
Al-Wali	The Protector or The Friend
Al-Muta'ali	The Most Exalted
Al-Barr	The Source of All-Goodness
Al-Tawwab	The Acceptor of Repentance
Al-Muntaqim	The Avenger
Al-'Affuw	The Pardoner
Al-Rauf	The Clement
Malik ul-Mulk	Owner of the Kingdom
Dhul Jalal wal Ikram	Possessor of Majesty and Honor
Al-Muqsit	The Equitable
Al-Jame	The Gatherer
Al-Ghaniyy	The All-Sufficient
Al-Mughni	The One who Enriches
Al-Mani'	The One who Prevents Harm
Al-Darr	The One who Afflicts
Al-Nafi'	The One who Benefits
Al-Nur	The Light
Al-Hadi	The Guide
Al-Badi'	The Originator
Al-Baqi'	The Everlasting
Al-Warrith	The Ultimate Inheritor
Al-Rashid	The Guide to the Right Path
Al-Sabur	The Patient

Knowing God

Scholars of the Christian tradition often challenge Islamic thinkers with the following question: If God is Other, then how do humans relate to the Divine?

To study this question, you need to know two central philosophical ideas that are presented about God in academic literature:

✔ **Transcendence:** The otherness of God. Those qualities that are outside the realm of human experience. Certain qualities of God in the Islamic tradition fit under this category.

✔ **Imminence:** The avenue whereby God is known and His presence felt in the human experience on earth.

Muslims feel God's imminence through divine attributes that have their signature throughout the wonders of creation. The Koran speaks of God as the Most Merciful, the Most Compassionate, the Most Forgiving, the Most Just, and so on.

With each of these attributes, you can relate to the Divine in knowing that every act of mercy, beauty, forgiveness, love, and wisdom represent manifestations of the Divine. The Koran says that humans come to know God and feel His divine presence by reflecting on His signs and wonders all around.

In as much as God constantly manifests His presence through creation each day, imminence of God in the life of a personal worshipper must require struggle and active participation.

The Koran says that at the time of birth, God blows some of His spirit into each and every soul, meaning that God created His spirit in every person (4:171). Every human being has a share — albeit very little in comparison with God — of qualities that define the Divine. By harvesting these qualities in your soul and in your outward practices, you continue to come closer to God in the relationship leading to mutual love.

For example, God is The Generous, and with every act of generosity by a person, he or she comes closer to The Generous. God is The Forgiving, and every time that a person forgives another person, he or she comes closer to The Forgiving.

The effort that a person must take in achieving nearness to God is probably best articulated through a *Hadith Qudsi,* in which Prophet Muhammad quotes God as saying: "I am as My servant thinks I am . . . And if he draws near to Me a hand's span, I draw near to him an arm's length. And if he draws near to Me an arm's length, I draw near to him a fathom's length. And if he comes to Me walking, I go to him running."

Not all attributes of the Divine are imminent. Humans have no share in those qualities that are transcendent in nature, such as The Creator, The Powerful, The Unique, The Eternal, and so on.

From the Koranic worldview, nearness to God requires gratitude to the Divine in every aspect of life. Distance from the Divine is a result of ingratitude towards the blessings and favors of God.

Prophets of God: Preaching a Divine Message

Through the stories of prophets and messengers of God, readers of the Scripture find ways to reach the Divine, understand the Will of God through sacred law, and discover the ways of spiritual, moral, and ethical success.

As you read the stories of the prophets, you may notice that they mention very few historical dates and place names. The prophetic stories center around moral teachings, and as such, places and timelines are usually of no significance in the Koranic narrative.

After telling you a little about what it takes to be a prophet or messenger of God, I focus on the stories of Abraham, Moses, and Jesus.

Prophets and messengers

A *prophet* receives divine inspiration about the theological and ethical teachings of God, and then relates that inspiration to his people. A *messenger* is very similar to a prophet, but also has an added quality of receiving a divine Book, such as the Psalms of David or the Torah.

All messengers are also prophets, but not all prophets are messengers.

Two universal characteristics describe all prophets according to the Islamic tradition:

✔ **All prophets preached the same message.** Each prophet brought the same divine message to the world: "There is nothing worthy of worship except God."

With this worldview in mind, each prophetic community called on the establishment of a just social system based on divine teachings and principles. Each prophet taught his people Islam (submission to One God), and their subsequent followers are called Muslims (those who submit to One God) in the Koran.

> ✔ **All prophets were innocent of major sin.** Islamic tradition gives the status of *maasum,* or "innocent of any major sin (such as adultery and murder)," to every prophet.
>
> The prophets had flaws, but whatever mistakes they committed were very minor in nature, and were immediately made known to them by divine inspiration. (Sins such as those committed by Prophet David or Prophet Lot in the Bible are completely unacceptable in the Koranic worldview.)

The Koran recognizes the existence of prophets outside of the Koranic narrative. The Koran says that "Of some Messengers We have already told you the story, and of others We have not" (4:164). Several thousand prophets (124,000 according to some weak *Hadith*), who taught the worship of God alone as a way of life, were sent to each community on earth. In fact, some Islamic scholars argue that pure teachings from other religions, such as the teachings of Buddha, are part of the universal Islamic legacy.

Abraham: Beloved Friend of God and Father of Faith

Abraham (pronounced *Ibraheem* in Arabic), plays an essential role in the Koranic narrative in three ways:

- ✔ Abraham ties Prophet Muhammad to the family of prophets through a supplication (plea to God).
- ✔ Abraham and his son Ishmael built the first House of God (known as the *Ka'ba*). Some scholars say that the two prophets reconstructed the *Ka'ba,* which was originally built by Prophet Adam.
- ✔ Abraham universalizes the concept of a Muslim. He serves as the prime example of the status Muslims strive to reach, namely becoming a friend of God.

Building a house, praying for a prophet

The story of Abraham begins with verse 124 of *Surah* 2, which places the prophet in Mecca (by all historical accounts) with his son Ishmael. Father and son build a House for the service of One God, a temple which Muslims call the *Ka'ba,* known to be the first place of worship and meditation built for God alone.

As Abraham and Ishmael raise the foundations of the temple, Abraham makes a passionate plea to God in a supplication that Muslims still recite almost every day. In this supplication, Abraham asks God to sustain the land with fruits and provide security to its people. After begging God to raise up a community of believers that submit to no one but God, Abraham then says:

"O our Sustainer! Raise up from the midst of our offspring an apostle from among themselves, who shall convey unto them Your messages, and impart unto them revelation as well as wisdom, and cause them to grow in purity: for verily, You alone are Almighty, truly Wise" (2:129).

This supplication becomes very important theologically for Muslims, because they see the birth and prophethood of Muhammad as an answer to Abraham's supplication. This supplication ties the Islamic community to the Abrahamic tradition and legacy.

Following the path of Abraham

Immediately after his supplication (see the preceding section), Abraham answers God's call for submission by saying, "I have surrendered myself unto You, the Sustainer of all the worlds" (2:131).

Abraham's surrender makes him quite literally the father of faith as he tells his children (who are future prophets) to follow "the purest faith," and to not die without having submitted to God alone. Muslims define the teachings of the Koran as the path or creed of Abraham.

Passing the test and becoming God's friend

God chooses Abraham to become His prophet. God gives Abraham a series of difficult tasks to test his faith and to teach Abraham the spiritual truth that says, "Never shall you attain to true piety unless you give (freely) out of that which you love" (3:92).

Abraham's first test is to leave his child, Ishmael, and wife, Hagar, in the middle of a deserted land with no provisions, seeking only the trust of God. This test was especially difficult because Abraham had waited many years until his old age to have children, and finally when God grants him this blessing, Abraham must leave Ishmael in the valley of Becca (more commonly known as Mecca).

Claiming Abraham

In passage 3:65–68, the Koran answers the criticisms of Jews and Christians who held that Abraham was exclusively part of their traditions. The Koran points out that Abraham could not have been a Christian or a Jew, because the Torah and Bible, as the basis of the two faiths, were revealed long after Abraham. Instead, the Koran insists that Abraham was a Muslim because he surrendered himself to the teachings of God alone.

The Koran ends this passage by trying to reclaim Abraham as a universal figure that belongs to anyone who follows his pure path of submission to God alone. The Koran, while laying claim to Abraham's place in the Islamic tradition, also attempts to universalize Abraham as a spiritual and moral model for all of humanity.

The next test proves even more difficult. God reveals to Abraham in a dream that he should sacrifice Ishmael. Abraham passes this difficult test by his willingness to sacrifice his beloved son.

According to the Koranic and Biblical stories, God shouts out to Abraham before the sacrifice, telling him that he has already passed God's test in his willingness to let go of even that which he most loved for the sake of God. While Jews and Christians believe that Prophet Isaac asked to be sacrificed, the spirit and moral of the story is a shared tradition in all three Abrahamic faiths.

Because of his willingness to follow God's commands, the Koran describes Abraham as "most tender hearted, forbearing" (9:114), by which he reaches the exalted status of God's friend (4:125).

Abraham's example serves as a strong spiritual teaching in the lives of Muslims, who are told that they must be willing to strive and sacrifice their egos and other spiritual obstacles to reach a beautiful relationship of friendship with God.

Moses: The Liberator

Prophet Moses (Musa in Arabic) is the most often-mentioned of all the prophets in the Koran. His life parallels the life and prophetic experience of Muhammad in many ways.

Both prophets offer spiritual teachings and model ethical lives, and both have the responsibility of state leadership. As such, both prophets are given social laws from God through divine revelation that impact beyond individual lives, and move into the social realm of community ethics.

The Koran also reveres Moses because he received divine revelation in the form of the Torah, and because he is the only prophet God spoke to directly.

I describe Moses as "The Liberator" because the Koranic narrative of his life revolves around two major events:

✔ Moses liberates his people from Pharaoh's oppression and cruelty.

✔ Moses frees his people from worship of gods other than God.

You can find a good summary of Moses' life in *Surah* 28 of the Koran.

Preparing for prophethood

Moses, from the days of his youth, yearns to learn the ways of wisdom and true knowledge. He hears of a man, known as Al-Khidr, who has deep knowledge and understanding of the Divine.

Moses finds his way to Al-Khidr and requests to join him on a journey, so that he can learn the ways of wisdom. The sage agrees to take Moses on the condition that Moses ask no questions about Al-Khidr's actions.

On the journey, Al-Khidr makes a hole in the boat of some poor and needy people. Alarmed, Moses complains that anyone who takes the boat after them will drown. The sage reminds Moses of their agreement, and Moses apologizes.

After some time, Al-Khidr meets and kills a boy. Once again, Moses protests by decrying the killing of an innocent human being. Al-Khidr begins to lose patience, but Moses convinces the sage to be patient with him.

Finally, Al-Khidr and Moses approach a town in which the people treat them poorly and refuse them food. Nonetheless, Al-Khidr takes it upon himself to rebuild a wall that is about to tumble. Moses finds this odd and asks Al-Khidr why he doesn't take any payment in return so that they can feed themselves. Al-Khidr ends their journey, but first provides Moses with an explanation of his actions.

The sage explains that he destroyed the boat to protect people from an oppressive king on the other side of the sea. As for the boy he killed, Al-Khidr had received inspiration that the boy treated his righteous parents in the most wicked manner, and Al-Khidr wanted to save his parents from their oppressive son.

Finally, the sage explains that he rebuilt the wall because underneath it lied treasures for two orphan boys in the town; had the wall fallen, the town's people would surely have stolen from the orphans' property (18:60–82).

Scholars differ on what teachings to draw from this Koranic narrative. Generally, commentators of the Koran say that this story teaches Moses (and all humanity) that an inner or hidden reality lies inside everything that happens in the world, and that the naked or outer eye can only understand the outer meanings of worldly experiences. What may appear on the surface may not be the ultimate reality.

For others, in particular Muslim mystics, known as *Sufis*, this story teaches that to achieve the spiritual path of knowledge and wisdom, believers must obey a trusted teacher with patience in the knowledge that the teacher has certain knowledge which they have yet to acquire.

Becoming a prophet

The prophethood of Moses in the Koran begins with Moses receiving revelation from God as he stands in the valley of *Tuwa,* or the Hallowed Valley. Here, Moses learns of his prophecy and receives three teachings:

- To believe in no deity except God alone
- To establish prayers as a means of remembering the Divine
- To believe in the Last Hour when every soul will be rewarded according to its deeds

Moses then discovers the powers of his staff, which is inspired by God to perform miracles (28:32–36). The staff plays an important role during Moses' visit to Pharaoh.

Meeting Pharaoh

God tells Moses to go on a mission to preach the divine teachings to Pharaoh, who is described as a tyrant, an arrogant king who spread corruption on the earth.

Moses speaks kindly to Pharaoh, first calling him to accept faith. When Pharaoh arrogantly rejects this message, Moses informs the tyrant that as an apostle of God, he has been sent to liberate the children of Israel, and that he carries with him signs of God. Upon Pharaoh's request for proof, Moses throws down his staff, which becomes a serpent. Moses then draws forth his hand from his chest to show a shinning white light.

Despite the clear signs, the king says that all of this is mere magic. Moses then challenges Pharaoh to match these miracles with the best of magicians that can be found in the city. In this competition, Moses clearly wins when his divinely inspired staff outclasses all the other magicians. The city's sorcerers become convinced of the truth and proclaim their belief in God alone.

Infuriated by the conversion of the magicians without his permission, Pharaoh begins persecuting all the followers of Moses. This persecution leads to God's wrath and the utter destruction of Pharaoh's kingdom. On the other hand, the Children of Israel are saved by the parting of the seas with Moses' staff; they also receive the trust of living according to divine laws in the land of Israel.

Leading the Children of Israel

Much of the Koranic narrative on Moses as the leader of the Children of Israel centers around Moses' struggle to deal with elements within his own community that constantly called people back to the ways of idol worshipping.

Drawing inspiration from Abraham and Moses

Both Prophets Abraham and Moses had experiences with conversations with arrogant kings.

Abraham received the divine gift of reason, and Moses was blessed with magic. Abraham reasoned with the king by arguing that if he was more powerful than God, the king would be able to give life and death. The arrogant king responded by saying that he can give life by conception and death by killing. Then, Abraham argued, "But it is God that causes the sun to rise from the East. Can you then cause it to rise in the West?" As such, the king was then defeated by the use of Abraham's reason (2:258).

In both cases, the kings persisted in arrogance even after they were shown clear proofs of God, and such are the ways of arrogance according to Koranic teachings.

In the Koranic worldview, these stories serve as a model for the struggle between good and evil. Muslims find great inspiration in these stories for the struggles of their own socio-political condition.

The Children of Israel are reminded in the Book to remember the time when they were saved from their enemy, the Pharaoh, and given the covenant on Mount Sinai, which was as follows:

> "You shall worship none but God, and you shall do good unto your parents and kinsfolk, and the orphans and the poor; and you shall speak unto all people in a kindly way; and you shall be constant in prayer; and you shall spend in charity . . . We accepted your solemn pledge that you would not shed one another's blood, and would not drive one another from your homelands" (2:83–84).

The Koran tells of the rebellion against this covenant once God had placed His blessings over the Children of Israel. Interestingly, the Koran makes the same covenant with the Muslim community in various passages, and warns against taking the path of transgression against any of these laws, by relating the story of the Children of Israel.

The Koran uses the example of this rebellion to warn against the nature of human beings, who the Koran says call on God in times of hardship, and then forget the source of their blessings once they have been given ease.

Jesus: The Spirit of God

Prophet Jesus is revered as one of the greatest prophets in the Koranic tradition — he is honored by God as the "Spirit of God."

The Koran doesn't deal with the life and prophecy of Jesus in much detail, but places emphasis on his birth through the Virgin Mary. Most of the Koranic discourse on Jesus is about absolving him from the status of "son of God," which the Koran completely rejects.

Jesus is also recognized in the Koran as being a recipient of a divine Book, called the *Injil,* which is not the same thing as today's New Testament (see Chapter 5).

Jesus is born to Virgin Mary

The Koran holds Mary as the mother of Jesus in very high esteem by stating that she was made pure and "raised above all the women of the world" (3:42).

The Koran depicts Mary as an extremely pious worshipper who God blesses with constant sustenance through the angels. One day, Angel Gabriel appears with a "glad tiding, through a word from Him, (of a son) who shall become known as the Christ Jesus, son of Mary, of great honor in this world and in the life to come, and (shall be) of those who are drawn near unto God" (3:42).

Obviously, this news shocks Mary, because no man had every touched her, according to the Koranic narrative. The angel responds to this shock by reminding Mary that God can simply will a thing to be.

Christians see this miraculous birth as a sure sign of Jesus' divinity. The Koran argues otherwise, by saying that the birth of Jesus is like that of Adam: God said "Be" and it is. In other words, the Koran argues that if Jesus is divine based on only having a mother, then what about Adam who had neither a mother nor a father? That's even more miraculous according to Koranic reasoning.

Also, scholars of the Koran suggest that with the miraculous birth of Jesus, God completes his signs in creation. Adam was created without a mother or father; Eve was created from a man (father), but without a woman (mother). And, finally Jesus was created with a mother (Mary), but no father.

Miracles and the message of Jesus

Jesus receives the ability to perform several miracles in the Koran:

- Jesus speaks as a newborn baby from his cradle, proclaiming his prophethood and human nature as the servant of God (not son of God), calls people to the worship of God alone, and clears his mother from the false accusation of adultery. From the cradle, Jesus also teaches his people to establish regular prayer and purifying almsgiving (19:27–37).

- Jesus takes clay and breathes life into it.

- Jesus cures the blind.
- Jesus cures the leper.
- Jesus brings life back to the dead.

From the Koran perspective, these miracles are meant as signs of God to convince the Children of Israel as to the prophecy of Jesus. Furthermore, with each miracle, the Koran says "by God's permission." The Koran makes clear that none of these miracles could have occurred without God's permission, and therefore Jesus acted only in complete obedience to the Will of God.

The Koran articulates Prophet Jesus' message and mission in three ways:

- Jesus is taught the Torah and given revelation of the Gospel (see Chapter 5).
- Jesus comes as an apostle to the Children of Israel with a reminder of the pure teachings of God, and a reformed law. Jesus defines this law as a confirmation of the laws that still hold true from the Torah, but with ease of some legal restrictions that were no longer relevant.
- As with all prophets from the Koranic perspective, Jesus says, "God is my Sustainer as well as your Sustainer; so worship Him alone: This is a straight way" (3:51).

The Koran says that Jesus finds few followers to his path during his lifetime, and soon his people turn against him and seek to kill him on the cross.

Jesus teaches God's Unity

The Koran rejects the notion of trinity (Christian theological concept of Father, Son, and Holy Spirit forming one Union in One God), arguing that Jesus preached obedience and worship to God alone (5:72–73). The Koran says that "Christ, the son of Mary, was no more than a Messenger; many were the Messengers that passed away before him" (5:75). The *Ayah* goes on to say that a clear sign of Jesus and his mother's human nature is found in the fact that both had to eat food to live, just like other mortal creations of God, and unlike God, who is Self Sustaining.

The Koran finds the notion of God having a son as blasphemous, and the argument against this

concept evokes some of the most powerful language in the Koran, such as this passage: "As it is, some assert, 'The Most Merciful has taken unto Himself a son!' Indeed, you have brought forth something monstrous, whereat the heavens might well-nigh be rent into fragments, and the earth be split asunder, and the mountains fall down in ruins!" (19:89–90).

Interestingly, the Koran records a dialogue that will take place in the future between Jesus and God on the Day of Judgment where Jesus denies asking to be worshipped or claiming partnership with God (5:116).

Jesus and the cross

In the Koranic narrative, God tells Jesus before the crucifixion that his people would turn against him and seek to kill him. God also tells Jesus that the plot against him would ultimately fail, as God planned to bring Jesus up to the heavens without facing any humiliation. The Koran says that although he seemingly was put on the cross, Jesus was actually saved by God from the plotters of evil.

Koranic commentators debate two points the Koran makes in 4:157–158: Firstly, the passage "it (the crucifixion) only seemed to them;" and secondly, "God raised him unto Himself."

The majority of classical commentators believe that the story of crucifixion is true, but God placed someone on the cross (Judah, according to many versions), who looked like Jesus. Therefore, it seemed as if Jesus was killed, but in reality, it was not him on the cross.

As for the second part of the issue, classical commentators believe that Jesus was literally raised to the heavens in bodily form, and is awaiting return to earth in the "second coming of Christ."

Some modern commentators, beginning with Sheikh Muhammad Abduh, point out that the Koran says that the crucifixion only made it *appear* as if Jesus was killed. These commentators argue that the entire story of crucifixion was made up, and with tales that passed through generations, this story became real in the lives of people and is reflected as such in the New Testament.

As for the second issue, these modern commentators feel that Jesus died a natural death, and the raising up that the Koran speaks of is in fact the exalted status of Jesus in the sight of God. However, both of these interpretations are minority opinions, even among modernist-thinking Muslims, because it contradicts authentic *Hadith* that say Jesus did not die and will return towards the end of time to confirm God's Oneness.

In any case, the theological implications for Muslims are obvious: If Jesus did not die on the cross, then the Christian doctrine of "dying for the sins of man" becomes impossible to accept from the Koranic point of view. Instead, salvation comes through belief in God alone and righteous deeds, the message preached by Jesus himself, according to the Koran.

The Status and Nature of Man

The entire purpose of the Koran would be void if the Book did not address the status, nature, and purpose of human life. The Koran itself says that this revelation is for the guidance of humanity.

In this section I discuss the status of man through the prism of Adam's experience as the first man created by God. I also look into the purpose of human life from the Koranic understanding.

Human nature through Adam

You need to examine the Scripture's version of creation to understand the nature and role of mankind from the Koranic standpoint. In the Koranic narrative, three events in particular define man's nature.

Adam's ability to name things

The angels were quite skeptical about God's decision to create humans, who unlike angels, have the ability to disobey God. However, God sees another side to the human race — the power of intellect and articulation.

Adam is brought before the angelic audience and asked to name things, which he successfully does (2:30–33). In naming things, he shows humanity's unique status among God's creation in the ability to use reason and to acquire knowledge, which have been an important element of all successful civilizations.

For this reason, the Koran calls man by the best description: "Indeed, We have honored the children of Adam (humanity) (17:70)."

Satan lures Adam into sin

God gives Adam and his wife, Eve, a beautiful garden where they experience their original nature as spiritually pure and innocent in the delights of God-consciousness.

However, God tells Adam not to approach a forbidden tree, known as "the tree of life eternal." Satan (see Chapter 9) whispers into Adam's heart, tempting him to discover "eternal life in which his kingdom will never decay" (20:120). Adam and Eve succumb to Satan's temptations and eat from the forbidden tree.

This passage provides some very interesting insights into the human soul. Before Adam sins, he is in spiritual bliss and completely devoted in nature to the Divine. This, from the Koranic view, is the original nature of human beings when they are born, and they too, as with Adam, can become corrupted by following in the footsteps of Satan (see Chapter 9).

The Koran teaches that the essential, dominant nature of humans is pure and good. However, the deception of Satan can change all that, and can lead man to turn against his very nature.

The question of Eve

The Koran doesn't share the Biblical view that Eve played a major part in tempting Adam to eat from the forbidden tree. Instead, the Book depicts the two as partners who fell into temptation together and asked God's forgiveness together. Adam and Eve came to earth in progressive roles as complementing one another.

As such, the Koran attaches no stigma to the woman's menstrual cycle or the pain she feels in pregnancy, both of which are sources of punishment for the woman in the Biblical narrative. See Chapter 19 for a more in-depth conversation about the theological implications of this story for women.

This passage also speaks to the human nature of denying mortality. The tree that Satan tempts Adam to has a deceptive quality of eternality. Human nature is obsessed with this feeling of immortality, which leads people to sin, without believing that they will soon die and have to account for their sins.

When man reaches this state, the Koran takes him out of the honored status, and places upon man the description of "lowest of the low" (95:6), for corrupting the original fair nature that God created.

Adam falls out of bliss

As soon as Adam and Eve eat from the tree, they become ashamed of their nakedness. (This nakedness is both physical and spiritual according to the Koranic terminology "the garment of God-consciousness" (7:26–27). Thereafter, Adam and Eve recognize their great sin, and ask for repentance. God forgives them and promises guidance in the new role that has been given to humanity as inheritors of the earth.

The Koran completely rejects the concept of original sin. Instead, the Koranic narrative says that Adam was forgiven, and sent to earth not as a punishment, but as part of God's plan to open up a new stage of human development with all the awareness of the moral implications of free will. In this sense, the Koran views man's role not as regressive, but as progressive.

The Koran says that for spiritual and moral development, people must learn that there are consequences to their actions, and without experiencing those consequences, growth can't occur. This may be why, at least from my experience, some of the most spiritual people are those who have experienced the darkest ways of life, and are now committed to pursuing the path of the divine light called for in the Koran.

The purpose of human life

The Koran describes two concepts related to the purpose of human life: vicegerent and worship.

Vicegerent

The Koran says that humans have been given the responsibility to represent or act as the deputy of the Divine on earth, in both words and deeds. This responsibility asks human beings to develop the imminent divine qualities of God, and to spread those qualities of mercy, compassion, and justice to society at large.

The role of vicegerent calls on human beings to become active participants in the enjoining of good and forbidding of evil, which the Koran describes as an obligatory social role.

Part of enjoining good and forbidding evil is the struggle towards implementing divine laws on earth, whereby societies live under a system of justice and righteousness.

Worship

The Koran says, "I have only created *Jinn* and men that they may serve me."

Many outside observers of the Islamic tradition have trouble with this verse because it conjures a flawed image of Muslims constantly praying to God, with no other purpose in life.

Passages such as 2:177 of the Book make it clear that worship is more than routine ritualistic practices. Rather, worship is a constant state of thankfulness to God, and showing this gratitude by seeking to spend every minute of life in the service of that which is good.

For this reason, when someone asks me how Muslims worship, I usually answer by describing a series of righteous actions, such as smiling at another person or sharing food. Rituals provide a means of achieving a state of constant desire to participate in good works.

The purpose of life from the Koranic worldview is to draw near to God by becoming godlike in His imminent attributes, so that life becomes a vehicle for spreading divine qualities on earth, both at the individual and societal levels. By doing this, you perfect your worship of God, and therefore fulfill the purpose of life.

Chapter 9

Divining Nature, the Universe, and the Unseen

In This Chapter

▶ Connecting the Divine to nature

▶ Defining the unseen in the Koran

▶ Getting the Koranic perspective on heaven and hell

The Koran urges reflection on nature and the universe to fulfill the desire of the human heart to see God, either out of love for the Divine or doubt about His existence. Belief in the Divine requires belief in good versus evil in the form of a battle between angelic and satanic forces. The Scripture then teaches that the path you choose between these two forces determines your fate in the next life, which is defined by a contrast between bliss and torment.

In this chapter I explore how the Koran views the universe in relation to the Divine and in relation to the purpose of life outlined for human beings. I also look at how the unseen world plays an important role in the human experience. Finally, this chapter explores the Koranic narrative on the Day of Judgment and the Hereafter, both of which motivate the soul towards accountability.

The Divine Ways of Nature

"Are you not aware that before God prostrate themselves all that are in the heavens and all that are on earth — the sun, and the moon, and the stars, and the mountains, and the trees, and the animals? . . ." (22:18). This important passage provides a good basis for the study of nature in the Koran. I focus on several aspects of this verse in the following sections.

The Scripture warns that in the reflection of nature, humans must not become so awed by what they see and discover that they take to worshiping those things. The Koran argues that God created nature, and therefore praise and worship should be due to Him alone. This warning applies especially to astrology and the worship of science, which is very common today (41:37).

While I focus some attention on scientific revelations in the Scripture, you must understand that the Koran is not a book of science. Some students of the Koran become so intrigued with scientific discoveries that they forget to focus on the moral message of the Book. Furthermore, sometimes scientific-minded students of the Scripture tend to over imagine that which really isn't there and begin to fit scientific theories into the verses.

Patterns of creation

The Koran asks its readers to reflect on two universal patterns of creation:

- ✔ The Koran describes God's design of the universe as "created in proportion and due measure (54:49)." If you look at any creature, you see that its bodily pattern is completely consistent with its ability to survive and function. Perhaps this concept is best reflected in the creation of the human body, which functions as a complementary unit for the survival and success of the entire human being.

- ✔ The entire universe consists of opposite pairs that create a just balance between extremes in creation (51:49). These pairs take the form of dominant and recessive traits, as found in the human genetic pattern, or in the domination of the sun over the moon, and even in societal relationships such as parent to child. The Koran points out that both members of these pairs prove absolutely necessary for the continued survival of the earth and proper function of its inhabitants.

God's creations in the skies

In this section I focus on the Koranic perspective of how the universe was created, including the complementing sun and moon and the navigation of the stars.

Creation of the universe

There is a great deal of debate and discussion within the scientific community about the creation of the universe. One of those theories, the one most accepted by scientists today, is the Big Bang Theory. This theory states that the universe was all one mass, and a violent, massive explosion caused the gradual expansion of this mass into galaxies, solar systems, stars, and planets.

Scientific-minded commentators of the Koran feel that the Book teaches the Big Bang Theory when it says, "Are then, they who are bent on denying the truth not aware that the heavens and the earth were once one single entity, which We then parted asunder? . . ." (21:30). The Koran also describes the universe as "steadily expanding" (51:47).

The last part of verse 21:30 points to another scientific aspect of the universe's creation: "We made out of water every living thing" (21:30). Today, the role of water in creation is considered a universal scientific truth. The microscope has made it possible to observe that water contributes 50 to 90 percent of a living organism's weight.

The stars and planets

The majestic nature of stars in the Koranic worldview is highlighted by God saying, "Furthermore I swear by the setting of the stars, and that is indeed a mighty appeal if you but knew" (56:75–76). Interestingly, the stars provide a secondary source of light after the sun, and humans use the stars as guides to travel the earth.

So, as you can see, the stars have played a major role in the development of human progress, especially in areas of navigation and geography. This is why the stars in particular have been mentioned as being among the signs of God.

The Koran talks about planets as swimming in their own orbits (36:40), which accurately describes how scientists today believe planets move in space.

The sun and moon

The Book almost always mentions the sun and the moon together as complementary signs of God. The Scripture gives honor to the sun and moon as one of God's most majestic signs (91:1–2).

The Koran shows an innate knowledge of astronomy in pointing out that the sun and moon alternate by day and night in a "rounded course" (21:33), which alludes to the fact that both the sun and moon rotate around the earth, a "scientific" discovery that was made well after the Koran's revelation.

Here on earth, the sun and moon fulfill important function for mankind. The sun and moon help people keep track of time and the number of months in a year (10:5). As such, the Islamic calendar, like the Jewish calendar, runs on a lunar system.

Also, traditional Muslim cultures still measure the time of prayer by the position of the sun:

- First prayer is offered at daybreak.
- Second prayer is offered at noon.
- Third prayer is offered when the length of the shadow doubles.
- Fourth prayer is offered at sunset.
- Fifth prayer is offered about one and a half hours after sunset.

The sun and moon act as everyday guides from the Divine among Muslims today.

Earthly creations

The Koran speaks of divine ways in the seas, sky, mountains, plants, and animal life, and especially in the creation of human beings. I talk about each of these in this section.

The deep seas

The Koran encourages man to study the ocean and all the blessings that are carried in it as means of becoming thankful to God:

> "The two great bodies of water are not alike — the one sweet, thirst allaying, pleasant to drink, and the other salty and bitter: and yet, from either of them do you eat fresh meat, and you take gems which you may wear; and on either you can see ships plough through the waves, so that you might go forth in quest for some of His bounty, and thus have cause to be grateful" (35:12).

This verse and other passages (25:53; 55:19–20) speak of a dividing barrier between seas. Modern oceanographers have echoed this observation through the scientific discovery that each sea has its own density, temperature, and salinity, which do in fact "divide the seas."

The Koran also shows knowledge about the depths of the sea, which it describes as "overwhelmed with waves, one over the other, and above it is a cloud of darkness upon darkness, one above the other" (24:40). With the invention of the first nuclear submarine, the wonders of deep-sea waves were discovered. This discovery disproved the theory that water lying underneath the sea's surface is calm and tranquil. Rather, the study showed that the sea consists of waves upon waves, now known as deep-sea currents, as described in 24:40.

The waves also fulfill the divine function of allowing humans to travel by sea. This blessing alone, as the Koran points out, is responsible for major developments in human civilization by helping humans reach out beyond their shores and providing the freedom to trade with other nations.

The divine sky: Cloud formations and thunder

The Koran asks its readers to reflect on the cloud formations through which rain comes to revive the land and end drought. The Koran describes cloud formations as the slow coming together of clouds that join together to make heaps of layers that then causes rain to come to the earth (24:43).

In another verse, the Koran describes the phenomenon of winds that plays a major role in raising and spreading the clouds over land to ensure that rain and shade spreads out over the land (30:48).

The Scripture speaks of lightening as a sign of God that instills both fear and hope. And, the Book uses rain as a powerful sign of God's ability to bring life to that which is dead as a parable for the resurrection of all living things on the Day of Judgment (30:24).

The fixed mountains

The Koran describes the divine structure of the mountain as firmly rooted in the earth, "standing firm" so that the mountain does not shake with the rest of the earth (31:10). Today, geologists have also come to the conclusion that mountains are rooted in the earth with hard sediments, like the roots of trees, which play an essential role in securing the earth.

The Koran uses the mountain to describe the awesome nature of the Koran and the Day of Judgment; the Koran says that the mountains crumble by the weight of responsibility that comes with divine Revelation and the day of questioning (59:21; 73:14).

The Plant Kingdom

Just as mountains (see the previous section) are held up as a sign of divine power and strength, plant life is a manifestation of God's beauty, according to the Koran. The Scripture describes plant life as bowing in adoration of the Most Merciful (55:6).

Interestingly, the Koran reflects on plant life as a sign of beautiful diversity that is part of God's plan and will for his creation.

The Scripture also shows a deep understanding for the way plant life is formed and reproduced. Firstly, the Koran points to the fact that plants are created with a gender, which allows for the reproduction of plant life (31:10). Secondly, the Koran describes the phenomenon of pollination through wind that causes such diversity in plants (15:22).

The mighty olive

Muslim culture enjoys the olive as a fruit of divine blessings. The Prophet Muhammad taught his companions, "Anoint yourselves with olive oil because it comes from a blessed tree."

Intellectual communities in the Muslim world have also drawn great inspiration from the analogy that the olive tree presents in the Koran. One of the oldest, best and most famous Islamic universities, located in Tunisia, is known as *Zaytuna* (olive tree in Arabic). Following this tradition, Muslims have built the Zaytuna Institute in Hayward, California, under the leadership of Sheikh Hamza Yusuf. (You can find out more about the Zaytuna Institute at www.zaytuna.org.)

The Koran gives special attention to the olive tree (24:35; 95:1) as a manifestation of the Divine. The olive is one of the unique fruits that can be found in abundance in both the east and west, such is the universal Light of God according to the Koran. Also, the olive is a majestic tree in that its roots run so deep into the earth that even in times of drought when other trees die off, the olive tree stays standing. Furthermore, these roots allow for olives to continue growing for hundreds of years, even after the tree looks to have no life in it. All these characteristics of the olive tree are analogies for the Divine.

The Animal Kingdom

The Koran asks its readers to reflect on the way God has organized animals into communities and taught them the ways of worship and survival: "There is not an animal (that) lives on earth, nor a creature that flies on its wings, but (forms) communities like you" (6:38).

The Book also points to the miracle of how animals have the ability to survive on their own. For example, the cow produces pure milk to feed its children and also humans. The Koran also talks about bees in this context:

> "And your Lord inspired the bee, saying: Take your cells in hills, on trees, and in habitations. Then eat of all fruits, and follow the way of your Lord made easy (for you)" (16:68–69).

This intriguing passage shows that animals, too, receive inspiration and messages from the Divine, and they submit to His Will in return. Also, this passage continues to say that bees produce "a drink (honey) of varying colors wherein is a healing for men." Muslim cultural dishes often include honey, and Islamic medicine uses honey effectively as a cure for some ailments.

Humans

The Koran often asks human beings to think about their own origins before claiming independence from the Creator (76:1–2). The Koran, in its self-described role as a reminder to humanity, reminds its readers that every single person was created from a single sperm drop that was then divinely fashioned into stages in the womb (22:5).

Many, including non-Muslims, in the scientific community strongly believe that the origins and stages of embryonic development described in the Koran are extremely accurate. Passage 22:5 most thoroughly analyzes the process of human development:

> "O mankind! If you have a doubt about (the truth) of Resurrection, (consider) that We created you out of dust, then out of a drop of sperm, then out of a germ cell, then out of a morsel of flesh, partly formed and partly unformed, in order that We may manifest (your origin) clear unto you. And We cause whom We will to rest in the wombs for an appointed term, then do We bring you out as infants so that you may reach maturity. And some of you are called to die, and some are sent back to the feeblest old age so that they know nothing after having known much. . . ."

Inheriting the Earth: The Role of Mankind in Nature

God created and organized the entire universe, and, in turn, each living creature turns to Him in submission. Humans play a special role in this divine creation and organization — humans inherit the earth as deputies or vicegerents of God on earth (27:62).

From the Koranic perspective, everything in creation serves man's need for survival and development towards that which is good. For example, with the turning of night into day, the human need for both sleep and rest are fulfilled. In the creation of animals, some provide food for the human body, and others carry people to great distances in search of noble goals, such as knowledge and trade (16:5–8).

The Koran warns humans not to regard their special role in the universe as a right, but rather as a responsibility. God placed upon the shoulder of human beings the responsibility to work for righteousness and build civilizations; He also provided the means to properly carry out these functions.

Showing kindness to animals

Prophet Muhammad once saw a donkey that was bleeding from the nostrils and side of its face. Upon witnessing that, Muhammad said, "Curse is upon the person who has done it." He then ordered his companions to never beat any living creature on its face.

In another teaching, Muhammad's companions reported that a camel came running to the Prophet and sat down by his side with tears overflowing. The Prophet searched for the camel's owner, and upon finding him, asked why the camel was crying. The owner replied that the camel had grown old after many years of service, and now the man wanted to slaughter it and distribute the camel's meat. Muhammad said, "Don't slaughter it. Give it to me with price

or no price." The man then offered the grieving camel to the Prophet as a gift.

Hunting for the sake of sport is strictly prohibited under Islamic law because Muhammad said, "Whoever kills (even) a sparrow for no reason, it will complain to God on the Day of Judgment: O God! This man killed me uselessly and not for the sake of meat."

In cases when humans must kill an animal for food, the Prophet ordered that it should be done with the sharpest knife possible, and without the presence of other animals, so that the least amount of pain could come to the animal. So, while Muslims are permitted to eat lawful meat in order to provide strength for life, the sacrifice of animals must take place in the quickest and least painful way.

Humans are the caretakers of the earth and its inhabitants. Abuse of the dominant position that God has given to human beings in strength, intelligence, and free will violates that role of caretaker. When humans rebel against this duty by mistreating the earth, the Koran says that creation literally turns against humanity to give a taste of the evil and pain that it sometimes causes (30:41).

These extremely powerful teachings call Muslims towards the kind treatment of animals and proper care for the environment. Sadly, some in the Muslim world ignore these great ethical teachings.

The Unseen World: Angels versus Satan

In the role of earth's caretaker (see the previous section), the human heart faces a major test of will and faith: choosing worship of God or rebellion against God's laws and order. This battle for the spiritual human heart takes place between two Koranic characters: angels and Satan. The following sections look at the nature and purpose of these two forces.

The angels: Pure creations of God

Muslims believe in angels, which, according to Islamic tradition, have wings and are made out of light, and can also appear in the form of human beings. Angels perform the following function, according to the Koran:

- Angels appear by God's command to inspire and guide devout men and women, foremost among these being the prophets and messengers (for example when the angel visits Mary — 19:17).

- Angels appear to execute just punishment against evil and transgression (15:7–8; 16:2; 25:21–22).

- Angels warn humans against worship of anything else other than God (16:2).

- Angels, as representatives of the most noble and pure of God's creation, pray to God for the forgiveness of all beings on earth (42:5).

- Angels act as agencies of physical and spiritual protection for whomsoever God chooses (82:10–12). From the Koranic point of view, people survive the worst of accidents or mishaps not by a miracle, but by divine decree carried out by angels. Furthermore, God sends angels to help those who fight for good and against evil.

- Angels sit on the right and left of each person to record every single action and word uttered, whether good and bad. This book of deeds will be presented on the Day of Judgment in front of God (50:17–18).

- Angels will blow the trumpet that calls for the Day of Judgment (20:102), take each soul out at the time of death (6:61), and guard the doors of heaven and hell (39:71–75).

The Koranic narrative on angels begins with a surprise reaction that these pure beings have to God's announcement that He was going to create Adam. The Koran quotes the angels as asking, "Will you place therein (on earth) one who will make mischief therein and shed blood, while we do celebrate Your praises and glorify Your holy name?" (2:30). God then assigns angels as protectors over human beings to show them that there indeed is another side to the coin, where humans are capable of much good and virtue, not only evil and destruction.

The pure power of angels calls for purity in the human soul and seeks to protect humans from the satanic forces that beckon towards transgressing God.

Satan: An avowed enemy

Unlike the Bible, the Koran does not describe Satan, called *Iblis* in Arabic, as a fallen angel. Instead, the Book believes that Satan comes from a community known as *Jinns*, or invisible spirits created from fire that can travel far distances in short times. *Jinns* can also take human form, just as angels can.

Not all *Jinns* are devilish in their ways. Some *Jinns* practice good works and are considered to be Muslims.

These Satanic forces have the following major purposes according to the Scripture:

- ✔ Satan causes animosity and hatred between people by encouraging them to indulge in actions that tempt the soul to submit to lower passions, such as intoxicants and gambling (5:91). Satan seeks to take men out of the remembrance of God and into a state of delusion in which the soul can't recognize the difference between good and evil, reality and falsehood.

- ✔ Satan is described as the "deceiver" in the Koran (4:120). Satan can indeed make sin look extremely alluring to the eyes, ears, intellect, and hearts of humans (8:48). As such, many people who recognize that they are on a path that leads them towards an unhealthy life find it very difficult to leave that path because of its temporal, deceptive pleasure.

- ✔ Satan whispers to the human heart to turn away from God towards a spiritually downward state. The Koran accuses Satan of changing the fair nature of men into a state that opposes the very nature that God instills in humans at the time of birth. The last chapter of the Koran contains a prayer, that among other things, seeks protection from Satan's whispers (114:4).

The Koran sees Satan as an important character in the human experience; without this "avowed enemy" (2:168), humans could never be tested in sincerity of faith. It is one thing to say you believe, but do your actions back up your testimony? That's the question presented to the human soul, and without an evil path, that test would be void. Also, without evil, the human experience of good would not be complete. Much of our affection for good comes because it is the opposite of evil.

The Scripture provides an interesting dialogue between Satan and his followers on the Day of Judgment, when Satan disassociates himself with the actions of all those who followed in his footsteps. Satan will say that he had no power over humans other than to call them to the misleading path, and it is their fault for responding to that call (14:22).

The Koran spells out the choice between the Angelic and the Satanic messages when it says, "Satan threatens you with poverty and bids you to be miserly. God promises you His forgiveness and bounties. And God cares for all and He knows all things" (2:268).

Accounting for the Soul

All societal functions entail responsibilities, accountability, and finally reward or punishment in one form or the other. For example, school students have a responsibility to learn and grow intellectually, and exams test the students' commitment to their studies. In the end, good students earn scholarships, admission to top universities, and other rewards. Poor students often find these rewards unattainable.

Try applying this analogy to the human spiritual experience. If humans have the responsibility to play a progressive role on earth as servants of God and builders of righteous societies, then a day must come when their commitment to that responsibility is either rewarded or punished. Similarly, if God has given human beings the faculty of reason and a pure soul that recognizes God's Oneness, then it is only reasonable that men and women will be tested for their beliefs on the Day of Judgment.

The Day of Judgment

The Koran discusses the Day of Judgment throughout the Scripture, but the last part of the Koran deals more heavily with this event than other parts do.

The Koran uses the strongest literary devices to draw a picture of the Last Day, when the earth will be folded up and creation will cease to exist. English translations of the Koran come close to reproducing the powerful language and awesome feeling that is inspired in the original Arabic text. Here's an example:

> "When the sun is folded up, when the stars lose their light, and when the mountains are made to vanish; and when the she camels big with young, about to give birth, are left untended, and when all beasts are gathered together; and when seas boil over, and when the souls are sorted out, and when the girl-child that was buried alive is made to ask for what crime she had been slain, and when the scrolls (of men's deeds) are unfolded; and when the heavens is unveiled, and when the blazing fire is kindled to fierce heat, and when paradise is brought near: then shall each soul know what it has put forward" (81:1–14).

The Koran says that a trumpet blown by one of the angels will cause life to cease and the entire earth to literally crumble up, and humanity will run in fear — so much so that the pregnant woman will drop her unborn child. Then a second trumpet will sound and all life that has ever existed will reemerge from the earth like scattered moths in a state of confusion and disarray. Thereafter, souls will be separated into three categories:

✔ Those foremost in faith

✔ Companions of the right hand (righteous souls)

✔ Companions of the left hand (evil souls)

On the Day, God's Justice will rule, and no excuses or bribes will be of any use. A weight balance will be filled with a soul's good and bad deeds. If the good deeds outweigh the bad deeds, then that soul experiences paradise. If the bad deeds outweigh the good deeds, then the soul experiences the fire, unless it be by the Mercy of God. Sincere faith in God alone is equally, if not more, important in the judgment that each soul receives on the Day of Judgment. In fact, Prophet Muhammad said that every action is judged by its intention. So, faith, sincerity of intention, and good actions all go hand-in-hand.

The Koran and *Hadith* contain many descriptions of the Day of Judgment, if you want to read more about it. For example, see the following:

✔ *Ayat* 20:102–127

✔ *Ayat* 23:101–104

✔ *Ayat* 39:71–75

✔ *Surah* 82

✔ *Surah* 84

The eternal bliss of heaven

Perhaps the best description of heaven in the Koran is, "that which is beyond human perception" (19:61). However, the Koran does put into words a picture of heavenly bliss; the Koran's images of paradise are as beautiful as they are sensational. For example:

> "The description of the garden which the righteous are promised: In it are rivers of water which time does not corrupt; rivers of milk wherein the taste never alters; rivers of wine delightful to those who drink it; and rivers of honey of all impurity cleansed, and the enjoyment of all the fruits and of forgiveness from their Sustainer . . ." (47:15).

The Koran presents a dialogue between the angels and inhabitants of paradise as they enter the gates of heaven. The angels will say, "Peace be upon you! Well have you done: enter, then, this paradise, herein to abide . . . " The righteous souls reply to the angels in peace and thank God for His promise that has now come true (39:73–75).

Hell: Torment of the fire

The Koran places equal emphasis, both in content and in literary language, on describing the hellfire for the souls that reject faith out of arrogance, deny the hereafter, and sin against themselves. Here's one example of how the Koran describes the hellfire:

> "Suffering in hell awaits all who are bent on rejecting their Sustainer: and how vile a journey's end! When they are cast into that (hell), they will hear its breath drawing in as it boils up, near bursting with fury; and every time a group (of sinners) is flung into it, its keepers will ask them, "Has no warner ever come to warn you?" They will reply: "Yes, a warner did indeed come unto us, but we denied him and said, 'Never has God sent down anything, you are but lost in a state of delusion!'" And they will add: "Had we listened to those warnings, or used our own reason, we would not be among those who are destined for the blazing flame!" (67:7–10).

Some scholars of the Koran believe that the hellfire will not be eternal for all souls. These scholars believe that there may come a time after which souls that had much evil in them, but also some good, will be sent to paradise after being purified for their sins in the hellfire. I think verse 11:107 certainly supports this theory.

God's Mercy, God's Wrath: Reconciling the two

Islamic thinkers often get this question: If God is the Most Merciful, then why does the Koran place such a heavy emphasis on God's wrath towards people who reject Him?

Before you can understand the answers to that question, you need to look at the Koranic perspective on the notions of Mercy and Wrath.

Mercy

The Koran introduces God to the reader of Scripture as the Most Merciful, the Most Compassionate; each *Surah* of the Koran begins with this declaration.

The Koran's version of God's accountability is overwhelmingly merciful. Both the Koran in 6:160 and various *Hadith* make it clear that if a person does something good, then he or she receives rewards tenfold or more for that righteous deed. But, if a person does something evil, then only the sin of that evil is accounted for.

Furthermore, the Koran says that even for the worst of sins, such as associating partners with God, murder, and adultery, God is still willing to forgive those who return to Him in humility and commit themselves to working righteous deeds (25:68–70). Along the same lines, the *Hadith* say that even if a person has a mountain full of sins, God would forgive, if he or she returns to God asking for His Mercy.

From the Koranic perspective, God's greatest sign of Mercy is in the sustenance that He provides equally for both those who worship Him and those who reject Him. However, persistent ingratitude leads to God's wrath.

Wrath

The Koran says that God's wrath is for those who are persistent in sin, those who practice oppression and rebel against the cause of justice. Those who transgress all bounds in violating the laws of God also receive the wrath.

The Koran sees wrath as something that is literally earned by the hands of those who sin. As such, the Koran refers to sinners as "those who oppress their own souls."

However, the Koran says that because of God's Justice, He does not bring wrath on a person, or on a people, until they are given the message and given time to return to God.

The Islamic tradition does not recognize wrath as one of God's attributes. Rather, Muslims see wrath as an important component of God's justice in His attribute as The Just.

Tying the knot

The marriage between mercy and wrath comes in the Koranic understanding that the universe is made of opposites. For the first to hold true, the second must also be true. Mercy towards creation is incomplete if justice in the form of wrath is not held for those who are victims of evil.

Chapter 10

Taking the Koranic View of Other Faith Traditions

In This Chapter

▶ Understanding the place of religious tolerance in Koranic teachings

▶ Discovering Scriptural teachings on freedom of choice

▶ Discussing interfaith relations in the Book

▶ Looking at some controversial verses in the Koran regarding other faiths

A recent poll conducted by the Pew Research Foundation found that 44 percent of Americans believed Islam to be an intolerant religion. Certainly, recent events around the world have caused this belief to grow. However, as you discover in this chapter, Islam is a universal faith that embraces the divine teachings of all previous prophets and faith traditions. Jews and Christians are especially addressed as People of the Book *(Ahl' al-Kitab),* and Moses and Jesus are highly revered in the Scripture as prophets of the Islamic tradition.

In this chapter, I look at how Islam acts as an umbrella for all other faiths in history. I also reflect on Koranic teachings that talk about how Muslims should treat people of other faiths, and discuss some controversial verses in the Koran that people often misunderstand and misconstrue.

Islam: One Religion under God

Islam, unlike any other faith, is named not after a prophet or a group of people, but rather after a universal concept that means "Submission to the Will of God." This name recognizes faith in One God as a historical movement in the human experience, one that takes many forms while containing the same essential Truth.

A brotherhood of Muslims

All prophets of God and their followers constitute a historical brotherhood of faith as Muslims (those who submit to God's Will). Accordingly, Prophet Abraham, as the father of all prophets, and all those who follow him are called Muslims in the Koran (3:67–68).

These prophets, the Scripture teaches, were sent to all nations at various periods throughout history, speaking in the same language as the people, and carrying the same message of submission to the Will of God (14:4; 16:36; 35:24).

One of the fundamental requirements of faith, then, is to believe in all prophets that are mentioned in the Koran, without exception (2:285). In fact, if someone declares that he or she does not believe in any of the prophets, they cease to be Muslim. The Koran also says that only *some* of the prophets are mentioned in the Book (4:164), which leaves open the possibility of all faiths finding their roots in divinely-authentic teachings. The *Hadith* say that God sent about 124,000 prophets, beginning with Adam and ending with Muhammad.

The Koran deconstructs the universal essentials of spiritual success and salvation into three broad Truths:

- ✔ Belief in One God (including the prophets of God who teach divine laws and ways)
- ✔ Belief in the Last Day (the accountability of beliefs and deeds)
- ✔ The practice of good works

The Scripture quite emphatically states that "Those who believe (the Muslims) and those who follow the Jewish faith (followers of Prophet Moses), and the Christians (helpers of Jesus) and the Sabians, any who believe in God and the Last Day, and work righteousness, shall have their reward with their Sustainer: On them shall be no fear, nor shall they grieve" (2:62, 5:69).

The Koran calls Jews *Yahud,* which means "repenting" or "the ones who repented" by following Prophet Moses and living by the guidance of the Torah. Christians are known as *An-Naasara,* which derives from the word meaning "helpers." They are known as such because they are helpers of Jesus in God's cause. *Sabians* refers to those in Pre-Islamic Arabia who worshipped One God and rejected idolatry. The Koran doesn't refer to religious groups as such, but rather to the true followers of divine guidance.

The Koran even urges those who have received previous divine revelations to adhere to the teachings and laws of their faith, and to not stray away from the guidance of their divinely-revealed Books (5:44–50; 5:68).

The Koran preaches an inclusive theology, rather than an exclusive theology. Religions throughout history that have taught worship and obedience to God alone emanate from the same prophetic tradition and can be summarized as Islam. Their followers can be categorized as Muslims.

Limits to an inclusive theology

The Koran doesn't espouse all religious beliefs. Rather, it strongly opposes certain theological beliefs, which I talk about in the following sections.

The Koran says that while these beliefs and practices theologically contradict the Islamic way of life, it is not the responsibility of the Muslims to judge others. Rather, the Book says that God alone has the responsibility and right to judge "Muslims, Jews, Sabians, Magians (fire worshippers), and Polytheists" on the Day of Judgment, since only God is aware of all things (22:17). God's condemnation and punishment of certain souls should not be misunderstood as a call for Muslims to take these souls to account in this world. Muslims themselves are to be judged by God, and are in no position to judge others.

Associating partners with God

The Koran adamantly opposes any belief about God that denies His absolute unity as One Deity. The act of associating partners with God in worship and obedience is considered the greatest act of disbelief and the only unpardonable sin. Polytheism, which was the dominant faith and practice in pre-Islamic Arabia, is strongly rejected and condemned in the Book (48:6, for example).

Polytheism is considered a corruption of the original true faith instilled into every human soul to worship and obey God alone (30:30). The Scripture describes someone who associates partners with God as a soul snatched up by birds or thrown far away by a strong wind (22:31). Those who die believing in polytheism are destined to the Hell fire, the Koran states in many passages.

The Koran defines associating partners with God as much more than outward worship of idols or the worship of the natural order, such as the sun or moon. Polytheism also includes worship and obedience of the lower self or ego that calls to the obedience of illicit sexual temptations, greed, anger, and arrogance.

Of course, everyone, at times, falls short in his or her obedience to God. However, the Koran reproaches a life dominated by obedience to the ego.

Jesus as the Son of God and the Trinity

The status of Jesus may create more debate between Muslims and Christians than any other issue.

Most Christians today regard Jesus as God or the son of God. However, the Koran clearly states that Jesus was a noble prophet sent by God to the Children of Israel. The following passage best reflects the Koran's belief about Jesus and the Trinity:

> "The Christ Jesus, son of Mary, was but a Messenger of God — His promise that He had conveyed unto Mary — and a soul created by Him. So believe in God and His Messengers. Say not 'Three (as in Trinity)': Desist for your own good. God is One God: Exalted is He above having a son. To Him belong all things in the heavens and on earth. And enough is God as a trustee of affairs. Never did Christ feel too proud to be a servant of God" (4:171–72).

The Koran quotes Jesus as miraculously preaching from his cradle to the Children of Israel, saying that he was a servant of God who had received revelation as a prophet and came to enjoin prayer and purifying alms (19:20–33). In another passage, the Koran quotes Jesus as absolving himself and his mother (Mary) on the Day of Judgment from being associated as a partner with God (5:116). Instead, the Scripture says that Jesus taught his followers to "worship God, my Sustainer and your Sustainer" (5:117).

The theological belief of *trinity,* which places Jesus as the son of God, is completely unacceptable according to the Koranic perspective. The Book teaches that Jesus was a servant and prophet of God, and that some of his followers falsely attributed worship to him after God took him up.

The Koran recognizes the fact that many of Jesus' followers among the early Christians never took or accepted Jesus as divine, but simply as a messenger of God (3:49–53).

Limiting God's attributes and Sovereignty

The Koran argues that God's attributes — knowledge, power, mercy, and generosity — are limitless, even if He chooses to wait in applying them to His creation (2:255, for example).

The Jews who argued with Prophet Muhammad are especially criticized for making fun of the poor status of the Muslims, saying that God's generous hands are tied from helping the community of believers (3:181; 5:64).

Rejecting the Truth

To be ignorant or truly misinformed about the teachings of the Koran is one matter. But, to understand the Truth of the Koran and to know it to be the word of God, and to still continue rejecting it, is a grave sin.

People sometimes translate the word *Kafir* as "unbeliever" or "infidel," both inaccurate translations of the Koranic concept. Rather, those condemned as *Kafir* are people who knowingly reject, conceal, and oppose Islam even though they know it to be true.

This rejection often takes place because of sectarian pride, unwillingness to give up an esteemed position in the community, or blindly following the ways of forefathers without thought or reflection on what the Koran says.

Passages that condemn People of the Book relate to those who know that the Koran is true, but continue to oppose the message and Prophet Muhammad and his followers. The Koran even states that the religious leaders from among the People of the Book know the truth of the Koran as "they know their own sons," but conceal the truth knowingly (2:145–146). The prophetic tradition *(Hadith)* has many examples of Jews and Christians privately acknowledging the truth of Muhammad's message, but concealing that knowledge from their people.

Rejecting the truth also includes rejecting God's presence and existence altogether. The Koran points to the signs of God in the heavens and on earth as a proof of his existence, and argues that it is unacceptable to deny the presence of God in life. Those who do await painful punishment in the hereafter (22:18–22, for example).

The Koran obligates those who know the truth of Islam to accept it, even if doing so means sacrificing personal prestige and status in society (3:85). However, private acknowledgement and practice of Islam is permissible if a person's life is at risk by publicly declaring faith *(Shadah)*.

Honoring Freedom of Choice and Respecting Diversity

Like the Torah, the Koran declares a single life, regardless of religion or culture, as sacred as all of humanity. The unjust taking of a soul is like killing all of humanity, and saving a single soul is like saving all of humanity (5:32).

Each soul is sacred. The Book says that God breathes His own spirit into every soul (every soul contains awareness of God) (32:9), and instills in it the natural way of life *(Fitrah)* that is to worship (through belief and good actions) God alone (30:30). As such, the human soul itself is a bearer of divine faith.

Protecting freedom of choice

The defining characteristic of all human beings is honor, which Islamic law specifically protects (17:70). This protection includes the intellectual capacity to make moral and ethical choices, which by its very nature requires the freedom of choice to believe or not to believe in God and His laws. Restricting this freedom violates this ennobling quality in the human soul.

The Koran declares: "Let there be no compulsion in religion: Truth stands out clearly from falsehood" (2:256). The Book warns against forcing others to accept Islam, because doing so diminishes their intellectual capacity to distinguish between Truth and falsehood.

The Scripture constantly argues that to accept guidance benefits your soul, and to reject guidance hurts your soul. Therefore, no one is responsible for another person's acceptance or rejection of the message (10:108; 27:92; 39:41; 34:50).

However, the believer can righteously call people towards faith — not through force, but through wisdom, beauty, and kindness (16:125). If people accept the call, then it is for their own good (10:108). If people reject the call, then the Book simply instructs Muslims to leave them to their choice (*Surah* 109, for example).

Embracing diversity as the Will of God

The Koran embraces the diversity of the world's peoples as a sign of God's Will and beautiful design on earth. The Book says that despite the diversity present in the human race, all people came originally from a single soul *(Nafsin Wahidah)*, and, as such, have mutual rights and responsibilities towards each other (4:1).

Far from being a cause for hatred and jealousy, diversity is the result of a divine design that forms nations and tribes in order for humanity to come to know and learn from one another (49:13). In another passage, the Koran says that "Among (God's) Signs is the creation of the . . . variations in your languages and colors: Verily in that are signs for those who posses knowledge" (30:22).

The Koran teaches that religious diversity should not be a reason for conflict, rather an opportunity for working together in good actions: "To each among you have We prescribed a law and way of life. If God had so willed, He would have made you a single community, but (His plan is) to test you in what He has given you. Vie, then, with one another in doing good works" (5:48). In this spirit of cooperation, the Scripture encourages sharing food and permits

Muslim men to marry chaste women from among the People of the Book — calling both of these social constructs among "things good and pure made lawful to you" (5:5).

The Scripture encourages interfaith dialogue and a search for common ground, especially among People of the Book. The Koran calls on Jews and Christians to "come to common terms as between us and you." It goes on to say that the common ground is in worship and obedience to God alone without associating any partners whatsoever with Him (3:64). The Koran also says that Muslims should debate with People of the Book in the kindest manner and should say to them: "We believe in the Revelation that has come down to us and in that which came down to you. Our God and your God is One. And it is to Him that we submit ourselves" (29:46).

The Koran clearly states that Muslims should treat people of other faiths with utmost kindness and justice, so long as they don't persecute or assist in persecuting the Muslim community (60:7–9). The term used for this relationship, *Al-Birr,* is the same term that describes a child's relationship with his or her parents, which constitutes the highest acts of kindness and love in human relations.

Examining Some Controversial Passages on Interfaith Relations

Just as with the Torah and Bible, you can quote passages from the Koran out of context, making it appear that the Book takes an intolerant or even hostile view of other faiths.

Since September 11, 2001, strong critics of Islam in particular have made it their job to quote these passages in order to "prove" that Islam is a violent and intolerant religion. Interestingly, critics of the Islamic tradition and extremist elements within the Islamic tradition loathe each other, but they often share the same method of interpretation — one which uses (or rather misuses) verses in order to prove and back an agenda of hate. Those who try to set the record straight are often called "apologists."

The Koran doesn't deal with issues thematically, but rather in the context of teachings about beliefs and morality. As such, if you quote one verse on a certain topic to the exclusion of all other verses on the same topic, you can't see the full picture.

For example, take the issue of consuming alcohol. The Koran outlines the prohibition of intoxicants in successive stages in various parts of the Book. If you read the verse that only prohibits prayer under the influence of alcohol, but don't read the verse that clearly prohibits alcohol altogether, you would incorrectly assume that the Koran does not prohibit intoxicants outside of the state of prayer.

When looking at passages about interfaith relations, keep this idea of proper context in mind.

In the following sections, I take a look at some of the most commonly misunderstood and misquoted passages about interfaith relations. Of course, space doesn't allow me to go over all the controversial verses, but the following examples illustrate how you should read and understand some important verses in the Scripture.

Fighting against "unbelievers"

Critics of the Koran often misquote verse 9:5, *part* of which reads, ". . . fight and kill the 'infidels' wherever you find them, capture them, and lie in wait for them in every place. . . ."

The term "infidel," is not part of Koranic terminology. The word used in Arabic is *Mushrikun,* meaning "those who associate partners with God," or "polytheists." This verse does not apply to all "unbelievers."

To truly understand the Koranic perspective on this issue, you have to look at the context of this quote. Verse 9:5 begins by saying, "And so, when the sacred months are over," and ends by saying, ". . . but if they repent, and establish regular prayers, and pay the purifying alms, let them go free: For God is oft-forgiving, Most Merciful."

Researching specific Koranic topics

If you want to know the complete teaching of the Koran on a certain topic, I recommend that you make use of the index provided in many translations of the Koran. There you can look up any given topic and see where that subject surfaces throughout the Book. Then, you can gather those verses together to see the complete Koranic teaching on your subject of research.

Also, various search engines on the Internet can provide you with a list of all the verses on any given topic. I recommend using the search engine created by the University of Virginia, which you can find at http://etext.lib.virginia.edu/koran.html. This search engine does an excellent job of providing you with options to help refine your search.

The beginning clause of the verse ("And so") indicates that something precedes this command to fight unbelievers. In fact, reading the first four verses preceding 9:5 shows that this verse is part of a broader issue:

- 9:1 announces a breaking of the treaty between the Muslim community and the Pagan Arabs.

- 9:2 gives a four-month waiting period for the beginning of any hostilities.

- 9:3 further clarifies the intent of breaking the treaty.

- 9:4 says that treaties are not to be broken with those Pagan Arabs who have not broken their part of the agreement, and have not aided any of the enemies against the Muslim community.

The annulment of the treaty and the subsequent call to war responds to the Pagan Arabs breaking the peace treaty by attacking the Muslims and aiding those who want to destroy the Muslim community.

Furthermore, the verse after 9:5 even says that Muslims must grant protection to the Pagans who seek the asylum of the Muslims and end hostilities (9:6). Verse 9:7 further clarifies that ". . . so long as they remain true to you, stand you true to them, for God loves those who are deeply conscious of Him."

Verses 9:8–10 argue that God and His Prophet had to break the treaty because whenever the Pagan Arabs had an advantage over the Muslims, they would try to overcome them and not respect the agreed upon peace treaty. Verse 9:11 once again reminds the Muslims that if the Pagans "repent, establish prayer, and pay purifying alms" all hostilities must end, and they should be embraced as brothers in faith.

From this example, you can see that reading a particular verse in isolation of its surrounding verses gives you a false picture of what the Koran teaches its followers.

Similarly, people sometimes take verses such as 2:191 and 4:76 out to context to claim that Islam preaches violence. But, if you read both those verses in the context of their surrounding verses, you find that they actually teach a very humane concept of warfare — one based on self-defense, freedom of religion, and fighting oppression and tyranny.

See Chapter 18 for a more detailed discussion on *Jihad* and war in Islam, including an explanation of the debate over verse 9:29 requiring payment of tax for non-Muslims living in Muslim lands.

Forbidding "friendship" with People of the Book

Passage 5:51–52 forbids Muslims from taking Jews and Christians as "friends" because the two look only to protect one another rather than the Muslims. The verse goes on to say that Muslims who ally with them have a (spiritual) disease in their hearts whereby they can't trust in God.

"Friend" is an incorrect translation of the Arabic word *Awliya',* which is closer in meaning to "allies" or "protectors."

Critics of the Islamic tradition have held this verse up as proof of Islam's inherent hostility towards Jews and Christians. Extremists within the Islamic tradition also use this verse to argue that Muslims should not associate or befriend non-Muslims. They point to such events in history as the Crusades, colonialism, and the current Arab-Israeli conflict as proof of Jews and Christians opposing the Muslims.

However, in passages that follow this verse, the Koran explains that forbidding alliance with People of the Book does not apply to all Jews and Christians. Rather, it refers, first, to those who make fun of Islam and Muslim practices (5:57–58). And, secondly, it applies to those non-Muslims who commit aggression against the Muslim community, oppose the practice of faith, and drive Muslims out of their homes (60:9).

If the People of the Book, or any other non-Muslims, do not persecute Muslims, then the Koran permits alliance and friendship and enjoins mutual kindness and justice between communities (60:7–8).

As such, passage 5:51–52 once again must be understood within the context of the Koranic revelation and worldview as a whole, and not in a vacuum or in isolation of the overall message of the Book.

If you want to read more on the subject of Muslim and non-Muslim relations, I highly recommend reading *Islam and Other Faiths,* by Ismail Raji al-Faruqi (published by The Islamic Foundation and The International Institute of Islamic Thought). The author gives a brilliant account of teachings in the Koran, prophetic tradition, and Islamic history on how Islam relates theologically and practically with other world faiths.

Part IV
Living the Koran

The 5th Wave   By Rich Tennant

This is our Koran. Its text is most authoritative, powerful, and inviolable.

Yeah. I wish my long distance calling plan was like that.

In this part . . .

The Koran contains several passages that give the keys to spiritual success in this world and in the hereafter: Belief in One God and good works. Muslims compliment their beliefs with a sincere commitment to practice the teachings of the Book.

This part takes a look at the spiritual, ethical, and moral dimensions of Islamic practices and laws taught in the Koran. I examine how the Koran provides an active guide to a moral way, healthy spiritual life, and family relations.

Chapter 11

Following in the Footsteps of Muhammad

In This Chapter

▶ Teachings about Muhammad in the Koran

▶ Understanding Muhammad's position in the Islamic faith

▶ Discovering some key sayings of Muhammad about God, life, and the Hereafter

Muslims revere Muhammad as God's final Messenger, through whom the Koran was revealed and taught. As such, you must understand how Muhammad relates to the Koran in order to fully comprehend the Islamic tradition.

This chapter doesn't present a summary biography of Muhammad, but rather a look into how the Koran describes his role and character as the final prophet of God. (Pick up a copy of *Islam For Dummies,* by Malcolm Clark, for a detailed description of the life of the Prophet.)

In this chapter, I take a look at some verses that describe Muhammad's character and role in the world. I also briefly examine some of Muhammad's sayings that Muslims revere and practice to this day.

The Scripture Speaks about Muhammad

In the following sections, I point out verses in the Koran that express deep admiration and love for Prophet Muhammad, and how those teachings shape Muslim beliefs and practices.

Servant of God and mortal man

Perhaps the most fundamental teaching about Prophet Muhammad in the Koran is that he is His servant. Muhammad's exalted status in the sight of God and in the eyes of Muslims doesn't in any way give him partnership in divine attributes. Rather, the Koran says that Muhammad is a Messenger of God (3:144; 33:40; 48:29), no more and no less.

Worshiping Muhammad is an act of great disbelief that immediately places a person outside the Islamic faith.

Muhammad himself warned his companions, and Muslims of later generations, not to exalt him to the status of divine after his death. Muhammad said, "Do not exceed bounds in praising me as do the Christians in praising Jesus, son of Mary. I am only a servant of God, then call me servant of God and His Messenger."

Muslims believe that Muhammad never acted or spoke on matters of religion from his own will or wisdom, but only in accordance with divine teachings that he received by inspiration as God's Messenger and servant (10:15–16).

Muhammad's words, known as *Hadith,* and his actions, known as *Sunnah,* form an essential part of everyday Muslim practice. They comprise a second source, after the Koran, from which Muslims know divine Will. Muslims practice his words and actions in the form of Islamic law, known as *Shariah* (see Chapter 17).

Muhammad's divine mission

Passage 3:164 describes the various aspects of Muhammad's mission as Messenger of God:

- **To impart revelation:** Muhammad is the vehicle through which God sent down His verses in the form of the Koran. As such, the Prophet developed a relationship with God, which is then felt by Muslims when emulating his path.

- **To purify souls:** Muhammad's second mission is to purify the souls of men and women through divine guidance, so that they can walk on the straight path of living according to divine ethics and morality.

- **To teach the Book:** God sent Muhammad not only to impart divine revelation, but also to teach and explain the verses of the Koran.

  As such, Muhammad's explanation of the Koran's verses serve as the first and most accurate exegesis (Scriptural interpretation) of the Book, known as *Tafsir.*

According to the Scripture, Muhammad taught by conveying both glad tidings of hope in God's Mercy for those who have faith and do good, and by warning of God's punishment for those who reject faith and practice evil deeds.

✔ **To teach the wisdom:** Commentators of the Koran believe that "the wisdom," *Al-Hikma,* means the *Sunnah,* or practice of Prophet Muhammad himself. The life of Muhammad is an embodiment of wisdom, and by living life in his shadow, Muslims attain this divine path of wisdom in their lives.

Muhammad as the best example for humanity

The Koran says, "Verily, in the Messenger of God you have the best example for everyone who looks forward (with hope) to God and the Last Day, and remembers God constantly" (33:21). The Koran also describes Muhammad as having the highest standard of character and morals (68:4).

Devout Muslims express their love for Prophet Muhammad by trying to follow his life example in almost every step they take throughout the day. When they sit down to eat, they try to eat in the same manner as Muhammad; when they talk, they try to talk with the same humility that Muhammad exhibited towards his companions; and when they walk, they seek to walk with the same gentleness as their Prophet.

Muslims do all this, according to the Scripture, because Muhammad's teachings can lead believers "out of the depths of darkness" with faith and righteous deeds (65:11). Muslims view following Muhammad's life example as the best and fastest path towards achieving closeness to God and receiving His divine Blessings.

Muhammad's mercy for humanity

The Book says about Muhammad, "We sent you (O Muhammad) not, but as a mercy for all the worlds" (21:107). This verse has two important teachings about Muhammad from the Koranic perspective:

✔ Mercy defines Muhammad's character, personality, and path.

✔ Muhammad's mercy and message extend to the entire world and to all of creation, including animal and plant life (see Chapter 9), not just to one nation or group of people.

The merciful nature of Muhammad

Muhammad received the honorable title of "Mercy to all the worlds" after his experience in the city of Taif, where the town's people rejected his call to worship One God and physically abused the Prophet.

After a month of abuse, Muhammad prepared to leave the city to return to Mecca. According to Islamic tradition, Angel Gabriel appeared and said that if Muhammad wanted, God would destroy the entire city of Taif and its inhabitants because of the way they treated him.

Instead, Muhammad asked God to forgive the people of Taif. He also asked Angel Gabriel not to destroy the town because Muhammad hoped that, in the future, righteous generations would arise out of the city of Taif.

The Scripture points out that had Muhammad not been gentle hearted, the message of Islam would have never spread as it did (3:159). Muhammad's mercy is seen as a divine gift that was placed in his heart for the purpose of expressing divine will to all of creation.

Universality of Muhammad's teachings

From the Koranic perspective, all prophets were sent for a specific group of people, time, and place, but Muhammad, as God's final prophet, was sent to all of humanity throughout time.

All prophets, beginning with Adam, built up to the moment when the world would be ready for one divine message that would relate and apply to all people throughout the world. Muslims see Muhammad's teachings as the culmination of all prophetic revelations, and as a final guide for all of humanity.

About Muhammad's universal message the Koran also says, "We have not sent you, but as a (Messenger) to all mankind, giving them glad tidings, and warning them, but most men know not" (34:28).

Muhammad as a seal of the prophets

The Koran says regarding the finality of prophets with the coming of Muhammad: "Muhammad is not the father of any one of your men, but is God's Messenger and the Seal of all prophets" (33:40).

Muhammad described his own Prophecy as like a beautiful house that is nicely built, but missing a cornerstone. People pass by this house with great admiration, but see the missing brick and wonder how complete the house would look if that brick were in its place. Muhammad then says, "I am that brick and I am the last of prophets."

Muslims don't consider Muhammad to be a prophet with a new message for humanity. Rather, the Koran repeats again and again that the Book is the final culmination of all prophetic teachings that preach the Oneness of God and establishment of just societies.

As such, Muhammad said that all prophets come from one Father, but different mothers. Scholars of Islam believe that Muhammad meant that all prophets shared one sacred theology, defined by God's absolute Oneness without associating any partners; but, the law (*Shariah*) that each prophet brought from God was different in specifics.

Often, people have difficulty understanding why God would suddenly stop sending prophets and divine revelations to humanity, which clearly needs such guidance in a chaotic world.

From an Islamic standpoint, the purpose of sending prophets was never to fix the world's problems, which man created in the first place. Rather, prophets were sent throughout history to impart divine Revelation, Wisdom, and Will to all of humanity, step-by-step and region-by-region.

When the world was ready to receive a universalized message and law, God sent Prophet Muhammad with the Koran, which serves as guidance until the end of time.

People must carry out the prophetic responsibility of enacting divine guidance in the world. No prophet can simply swoop down and fix what humans have destroyed through the ages.

Doing as God and His Messenger Do

For devout Muslims, it is simply not enough to sing Muhammad's praises and remember him every so often in religious gatherings.

Rather, Muhammad's life example is meant, according to Koranic teachings, to build exalted characters and societies that live divine guidance in all aspects of life. As such, Islamic scholars argue that the greatest way to praise Muhammad is to follow in his footsteps on the path of living life according to divine Will.

The Koran says that obedience to Prophet Muhammad is in fact obedience to God (4:80), because Muhammad taught the ways of divine will and wisdom based on divine inspiration. As such, the Scripture reminds Muslims that "It is not fitting for a believer, man or woman, when a matter has been decided by God and His Messenger, to have any option about their decision: If anyone disobeys God and His Messenger, he is indeed on a clearly wrong path (33:36)."

Devout Muslims, therefore, strongly believe that Islam is a complete way of life that requires obedience to God and His Messenger (Muhammad) in communal laws as well as individual ethics.

Most devout Muslims can't accept the notion that religious laws (see Chapter 17) must be replaced with secular laws in order to live in the modern world. Rather, as representatives or vicegerents of God on earth, Muslims feel a responsibility to live on earth in accordance with divine laws.

As Creator and Sustainer of the world, God alone is law giver, and Muslims (as those who submit to divine Will) must in turn practice and implement those divine laws.

However, this doesn't mean that all secular laws contradict divine religious laws. The overall objective of public benefit is the concern of both systems in an ideal sense. As such, Muslims who live in any given state should follow those laws and traditions that are consistent with the spirit of divine teachings, and peacefully struggle against those laws that contradict the spirit of divine teachings.

When Muslims enter secular lands, they sign an agreement to live according to the laws of the land. Breaking this agreement would constitute a violation of religious teachings that do not permit falsifying oaths and breaking contracts.

For example, although God strongly prohibits alcohol, Muslims can't go around burning down liquor stores when they live in secular lands that allow the sale and consumption of alcohol. Nor can Muslims apply Islamic law to those Muslims in the community who drink alcohol. Both these actions would violate the laws of the land, which Muslims agree to abide by when they become citizens or residents of any given nation.

If Muslims have a real problem following secular laws, they should migrate (make *Hijra)* to Muslim lands where they can freely follow their religion. However, as most Muslims will tell you today, that is nearly impossible because there is not a single government left today that truly practices Islamic law.

Muslims often find more freedom to practice their religion in many secular societies, such as the United States, than they do in some countries that have predominantly Muslim populations.

However, this doesn't mean that Muslims should stand idly by and watch as society transgresses against divine laws. Muslims as citizens on earth are required to enjoin what is good and forbid what is evil, whether it be by hand, or by tongue, or at the very least by heart, according to Prophet Muhammad.

"When in Rome, do as the Romans do," doesn't complement Islamic teachings. Regardless of whether a Muslim lives in Rome or Saudi Arabia, he or she is required to live according to the divine teachings and laws imparted by the Koran and Prophet Muhammad.

Looking at Some Key Prophetic Sayings

In the Islamic tradition, the Koran and *Hadith* (sayings of Muhammad) are both considered to be from divine inspiration. The two complement each other, and as such the sayings of Muhammad form an important part of understanding the Koran.

You simply can't interpret or understand the Koran without knowing some of the basic sayings and teachings of Muhammad that complement the Koran.

In this section, I examine some of Muhammad's teachings regarding theological beliefs and virtuous practices.

Muhammad speaks about God

The following list presents a selection of some of the Prophet's words about God:

✔ **God's Oneness (*Tawhid*):** "The right of God upon His servants is that they worship and serve Him alone, and make none a god beside Him. And the right of servants upon God is that He does not punish those who do not make anything a god beside Him."

✔ **God's Mercy:** "God, the Exalted and Glorious, stretches out His Hand during the night so that the people may repent for the faults committed in the day; and He stretches out His Hand during the day so that people may repent for the faults committed in the night until the sun would rise in the west."

✔ **God's Reckoning:** "A servant of God will remain standing on the Day of Judgment till he is questioned about his life on earth and how he spent it, and about his knowledge and how he utilized it, and his wealth and how he acquired it and in what way did he spend it, and about his body and how he wore it out."

✔ **God's punishment:** "There will be some to whose ankles the fire will reach, some to whose knees the fire will reach, some to whose waist the fire will reach, and some to whose collarbone the fire will reach."

✔ **Relationship with God:** "If someone wants to know what position he enjoys in the eyes of God, he has only to look at what place he gives to God (in his life and heart)."

"One who remembers God and one who does not are like the living and the dead."

✔ **Seeking God's Love:** A man came to the Prophet (Muhammad) and asked: "O Messenger of God, tell me of some deeds that I may do, so that God will love me as people will love me." Muhammad said, "Do not covet this world, and God will love you; do not covet what people possess, and people will love you."

Muhammad speaks about virtue

The following list presents a selection of Prophet Muhammad's words about virtue:

✔ **The heart as source of all good:** "Listen carefully, there is a lump of flesh in the body. If it is set right and made good, the entire body becomes good and healthy. But, if it becomes corrupt, the entire body becomes corrupt: Remember well: It is the heart."

✔ **Obedience to God:** "God has laid down certain duties, so do not neglect them. He has set certain boundaries, so do not cross them; He has prohibited certain things, so do not violate them. About the rest of things He has kept silent — out of compassion for you, not because He has forgotten — so leave them alone and refrain from questioning about them."

✔ **Sincerity:** "God looks not at your figures, nor at your outward appearance, but He looks at your hearts and deeds."

✔ **Condemnation of outward religiosity:** "Many a one fast, but gain nothing from their fasting except hunger and thirst; and many a one pray all night, but gain nothing from their night prayers except sleeplessness."

✔ **The nature of sin:** "When a believer sins, a black spot appears on his heart. But if he repents and seeks God's forgiveness, his heart becomes cleansed and polished. However, if he continues to commit more sins, the spot continues to spread and ultimately covers all of his heart."

✔ **Patience:** "The strong man is not one who is good at wrestling, but the strong man is one who controls himself in a fit of anger."

✔ **Showing mercy to others:** "Only those who are merciful will be shown mercy by the most Merciful."

✔ **Kindness:** "Do not belittle even the smallest act of kindness, even if it were not more than meeting your brother with a smiling and cheerful face."

✔ **Generosity:** "If one gives charity, it does not diminish his wealth; if one forgives others, God bestows more honor on him; and if one humbles himself for God's sake, He exalts him higher."

✔ **Truthfulness:** "He who is not trustworthy has no faith. He who does not keep his word has no religion."

✔ **Human relations:** "Whoever relieves a believer from a distress, God will relieve him for one of his distresses on the Day of Resurrection. Whoever alleviates the hardship of a person in difficulty, God will alleviate his hardship in this world and the next. Whoever covers a Muslim, God will cover him up in this world and the next. And remember, God will help a servant so long as the servant helps his brother."

Chapter 12

Putting Meaning into Ritual

· ·

In This Chapter

▶ Praying in gratitude to God

▶ Fasting as a path to purity

▶ Almsgiving for the sake of others

▶ Making the trip to Mecca

· ·

*P*racticing rituals without an understanding of their spiritual and ethical teachings can foster a false sense of religiosity within an individual and society. Religious practices, and not morality or ethics, come to define the people's tradition. Some parts of the Muslim world struggle with this very problem, by emphasizing the outer forms of worship, such as the five daily prayers, while failing to address poverty and other social injustices with the same fervor.

The Koran argues that piety and righteousness are not found in simply turning your face towards the east or the west (for prayers) (2:177). The Scripture condemns those who pray without true faith and sincerity (13:14). In another passage, the Koran warns people against giving charity, followed by reminders of their generosity or causing pain to those who have benefited from the charity (2:262–265). Yet another chapter of the Book condemns worshipers who pray without the presence of heart and soul, only to be seen by others, and who in turn neglect basic neighborly needs (107:1–7).

The Koran warns against this spirit of religiosity, and instead calls upon its followers to draw meaning and action out of rituals taught by the Scripture.

In this chapter I explore the five pillars of Islam in their outer and inner meanings. I also examine the personal and communal aspects of each obligatory ritual.

Declaring Faith: More than Just Words

The first pillar of Islam is known as the *Shahadah,* which requires all Muslims to say, "I bare witness that there is nothing worthy of worship, except God, and I bare witness that Muhammad is the messenger of God."

The first part of the *Shahadah* affirms God's Oneness, or Unity. The second part affirms that the lives of the prophets, in particular that of Prophet Muhammad, provide examples of how to live according to the Will of God.

The spiritual, ethical, and moral life of a Muslim centers around these concepts. More than just a simple declaration, this pillar represents a serious commitment that seeks to transform life and society from the "depths of darkness . . . into light" (2:257) by following the divine way, known as the "straight path" (1:6).

In the *Shahadah,* Muslims enter into submission to God's Will wholeheartedly (2:208), which means obeying God and His Messenger (24:51–52). The declaration of faith sums up a way of life, known as Islam (surrendering or submitting to God's Will).

The path of God seeks to elevate society through freedom, justice, and equality (9:11–16), while elevating the soul through faith and patience so that individuals can join together in "deeds of kindness and compassion" (90:17).

The remaining pillars of Islam bring the *Shahadah* to life by prescribing a path that aims to fulfill the objectives of this first pillar.

Conversing with the Divine: Prayer

Prayer, known as *Salat* in Arabic, is the first act commanded by God in the Koran (2:3) and the second pillar of Islam.

The word "prayer" evokes different meanings for different people. For some, prayer means a simple supplication, and to others it means going to a place of worship and listening to a sermon. In Islam, prayer denotes an obligatory, organized ritual consisting of various steps and number of cycles (called *Rakat*) that Muslims offer five times a day at set times between morning and night hours (17:78).

The passage 29:45 sums up the purpose of prayer by saying, "And be constant in prayer: for, behold, prayer restrains from shameful and evil deeds; And remembrance of God is indeed the greatest (good). And God knows all that you do."

The *Sunnah* gives the exact details of how you should offer the *Salat,* but the Koran commands Muslims to "bow down, prostrate yourselves and adore your Sustainer," as well as "standing" before God in prayer (25:64). The Koran says that these three steps in prayer constitute a universal act of worship that was taught to past prophets (22:26, for example). In bowing and prostration, you can find the worship of the entire universe in adoration of its Creator (22:18; 55:6).

Understanding the purpose of prayer

Prayer fulfills four primary functions:

- **Showing gratitude to God:** Prayer allows Muslims to show appreciation to the Divine for all the favors and blessings bestowed (32:15). By turning their attention to God alone, and leaving momentarily all other worldly concerns, Muslims return to the ultimate purpose of creation, which is to worship God alone, according to the Koranic perspective (see Chapter 8).

  Commentators of the Koran argue that if a person does a favor for you, you immediately express your gratitude by thanking that person and performing some act of favor to show your appreciation. The least human beings can do to show their appreciation for divine sustenance and mercy is to offer these five daily prayers.

- **Building trust in God:** By constantly turning to God throughout the day, a worshiper acknowledges his or her dependence on God for continued sustenance and help. A worshiper then develops a relationship with God built on complete trust in His power and protection, which is manifested through patience and perseverance (2:45).

- **Creating a God-conscious individual and society:** By turning five times a day in worship to God alone even during the busiest hours of the day, you are constantly reminded of the fact that God is "with you wherever you are" (57:4). This daily interaction through prayer creates a close relationship with God that manifests itself in the Koranic saying that God is even closer to man than his jugular vein (50:16).

  This relationship is built on both love for the Divine and fear (and consciousness) of His justice, and should ingrain in the worshiper a sense of responsibility and accountability before God. This inner consciousness then drives a believer to ward off evil even when it becomes easily accessible or tempting (29:45).

  Prophet Muhammad taught his companions that seven types of people will receive God's shade on the Day of Judgment, and one of them will be a young man who is tempted to commit sexual indecency, but refuses only because he or she fears and is conscious of God's punishment.

Prophet Muhammad conveyed the purity that prayer causes in the heart by asking his companions the following question: If there were a stream outside their homes in which they bathed five times a day, would any impurity remain on their body? The companions of course replied, "No dirt would remain." Muhammad then said that offering the five obligatory prayers cleanses a worshiper's soul much like the stream purifies the body.

✔ **Building community:** Each of the five pillars in Islam has an individual and a communal aspect. The Koran commands the establishment of prayer (4:77, for instance), which is taken to mean praying in congregation. The Koran also commands Muslims to "bow down your heads with those who bow down" (2:43).

Praying together in a community setting is certainly ideal. Of course, praying in a mosque is not always possible, especially in non-Muslim countries that have few mosques. In such cases, Muslims try to pray in congregations inside the home with family and neighbors.

Group prayers (known as *Jammat* in Arabic) bring together members of a community five times a day, building a strong sense of neighborhood and companionship. During the prayer, worshipers line up in straight rows, standing ankle-to-ankle and shoulder-to-shoulder, as they perform each act of the prayer (see Figure 12-1). If you observe the congregation from outside, you see that the group synchronizes with great eloquence, as one great body of worshipers, with each completed cycle.

Congregational prayers also teach worshipers that even when you are at the peak of your spiritual communication with the Divine, you must not forget about your brother or sister on the left and right of you (107:4–7). No matter how devoted you become in the prayer, you must take the comfort of your fellow worshipers into consideration by leaving enough space for comfortable ritual motions and other similar considerations. This same kindness and consideration then extends outside of the formal prayer.

Approaching prayer: Purity of mind and body

The Scripture teaches its followers to come into prayer with a pure body and clean state of mind by ordering two purification acts before starting the prayer.

Calling for prayer: Adhan

Almost all religious traditions have a method of calling people to prayer, such as the use of a bell in Christianity. Before each of the five obligatory prayers, the call to prayer, known as the *Adhan*, echoes throughout Muslim cities. The human voice that makes this call (see Figure 12-2) reflects the Koranic worldview of preserving simplicity and the natural way of life.

Figure 12-1:
Muslims praying in congregation.

© Michael S. Yamashita/CORBIS

Figure 12-2:
A man, known as a *Muadhin,* stands at the top of a mosque and gives the call for prayer.

© David Lees/CORBIS

The *Adhan* purifies a Muslim's mind by turning his or her attention to the worship of God in prayer. The *Adhan* reflects the call of God and His Messenger, and the response of Muslims to that call reflects the nature of those "who do right and refrain from wrong" (3:172). It is also a reflection of Abraham's persistent call to the worship of One God (22:26–27).

The words of the *Adhan* sum up the Koranic message and remind believers of the Divine and of the path of Prophet Muhammad. The *Adhan* calls on its listeners to fulfill life's purpose by worshiping God, and ultimately urges Muslims towards a successful life and hereafter:

> *Allahu'Akbar, Allahu'Akbar:* God is the Greatest, God is the Greatest (recited twice).
>
> *Ash-hadu an- Laa'illaha Illal-laah:* I bear witness that there is no deity worthy of worship except God (recited twice).
>
> *Ash-hadu anna Muhammad-an-Rusoulul Laah:* I bear witness that Muhammad is the Messenger of God (recited twice).
>
> *Hayya 'alas-Salaah:* Come to the prayer (recited twice).
>
> *Hayya alal-Falaah:* Come to success (recited twice).
>
> *Allahu'Akbar, Allahu'Akbar:* God is the Greatest, God is the Greatest (recited once).
>
> *La'ilaha Illal-Laah Allah:* There is no deity worthy of worship except God (recited once).

The *Adhan* has enormous impact on its listeners. I remember, when living in the Muslim world, that when the *Adhan* was called, all business dealings came to a halt and idle talk ceased until after the prayer. The *Adhan* establishes the proper mindset of a worshiper, who after hearing the call responds by preparing himself or herself for the prayer.

Purifying the body and soul: Wudu

The Koran prescribes a process of ritual purity that Muslims must perform before entering into the state of prayer (5:6). This ritual purity constitutes *Wudu*, often translated as "ablution."

In 5:6 the Koran says that the purpose of *Wudu* is not hardship, "but to make you clean, and to complete (God's) favor to you, so that you may be grateful." This same concept on the interrelation between physical and spiritual purity is reflected in one of God's earliest commands to Prophet Muhammad (74:4–5).

Wudu cleanses the body of any impurities so that you approach the prayer in the cleanest possible manner. *Wudu* reflects Prophet Muhammad's assertion that "purification is half the faith."

Wudu purifies the soul from all minor sins that may have been committed. As such, Prophet Muhammad said, "When a believer washes his face (during *Wudu),* every sin which he contemplated with his eyes will be washed away from his face along with the last drop of water; when he washes his hands, every sin which is committed by his hands will be erased from his hands with the last drop of water; and when he washes his feet, every sin towards which his feet have walked will be washed away with the last drop of water; with that he emerges cleansed of all his sins."

Wudu literally wakes the soul up from the remembrance of anything other than God, so that the prayer begins with full concentration and no worldly distraction. This is especially true during the morning prayers and night prayers when the body is usually tired or sleepy.

Wudu also becomes a significant mark for Muslims on the Day of Judgment; Prophet Muhammad said that he will recognize his followers because of the light that will emerge from their faces and limbs by the performance of *Wudu.*

The *Wudu* goes like this, as detailed in 5:6 and supporting examples of Prophet Muhammad (see Figure 12-3):

1. **Begin by washing your hands three times, starting with the right hand.**

2. **Rinse your mouth three times.**

3. **Sniff water into your nose three times.**

4. **Wash your face from forehead to below the chin three times.**

5. **Wash your arms three times, beginning with the right arm first.**

6. **Place your wet hands over your head.**

7. **Place your wet hands around your neck and into your ears.**

8. **Wash your feet up to the ankles three times, beginning with the right foot.**

Let the prayer begin!

Each step of the prayer has special meaning and significance. The Scripture outlines the primary steps that constitute the prayer, but all the details are fleshed out in the *Hadith.* In the following sections, I tell you about the outer and inner meaning of each step of the prayer.

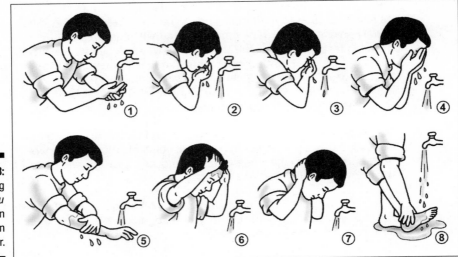

Figure 12-3:
Performing
Wudu
(ablution) in
preparation
for prayer.

Starting the prayer: Takbir

To begin the prayer, a Muslim faces towards the first House of God in Mecca, raises both hands to the ears (see Step 1 of Figure 12-4), and says, "*Allahu' Akbar,*" or "God is the Greatest." This action, called *Takbir,* formally marks the beginning of the prayer.

The *Takbir* signifies two things:

- ✔ **God first:** *Takbir* metaphorically raises God over all other things and affairs. *Takbir* prepares the worshiper to enter divine presence.

- ✔ **The world second:** Raising your hands signifies taking all worldly affairs between your hands and putting them behind you in order to fully concentrate on your worship and communication with God alone.

Standing before God: Qiyam

After *Takbir,* the worshiper stands in divine presence and recites passages from the Koran, known as *Qiyam* (see Step 2 in Figure 12-4). The first passage is the very first chapter of the Koran known as "*Al-Fatihah*" or "The Opener" (1:1–7):

> "In the Name of God, the Most Gracious, the Most Merciful. All Praise is due to God alone, the Sustainer of all the worlds, the Most Merciful, the Most Compassionate, Master of the Day of Judgment. You alone do we worship, and unto You alone do we turn for aid. Guide us the straight way: The way of those upon whom You have bestowed Your blessings, not of those who have been condemned, nor of those who go astray."

Figure 12-4:
The Islamic ritual prayer *(Salat)* offered five times a day.

This chapter is called the "Mother of the Book," because it summarizes the entire Koranic message.

For the second passage read in *Qiyam,* a worshiper may recite any set of verses that he or she has memorized. These can range from as few as three verses to as many as 286 (which make up the entire second chapter of the Koran). Prophet Muhammad encouraged the *Imam,* or congregation prayer leader, to recite short verses that would suit the convenience and comfort of all the worshipers. People usually recite longer passages when they pray alone.

Qiyam allows a Muslim to literally stand before God in the most humble manner (23:2) by looking downwards and reflecting on the divine communication of the Koran. *Qiyam* represents standing before God on the Day of Judgment, when all deeds will be accounted for, according to the Koran (83:6).

Bowing before God: Ruku

After the passages recited in *Qiyam,* the worshiper says, "God is the Greatest" and goes into the bowing position, called *Ruku,* with both hands resting on the knees (see Step 3 in Figure 12-4). In this state a Muslim recites three times, "Glory be to my Sustainer, the Magnificent."

The bowing position represents a universal sign of respect (55:6), and the worshiper uses *Ruku* as a symbol of his or her deep respect for God (3:199).

After rising from the bowing position, the worshiper stands up straight (see Step 4 in Figure 12-4) and says, "God listens to one who praises Him." These words remind the believer that God listens to all his or her prayers, and no prayer is left unheard by God who hears all things (14:39).

Prostrating before God: Sujud

After rising from the bowing position *Ruku,* the worshiper then prostrates, with forehead and nose touching the ground, in a position called *Sujjud* (see Step 5 in Figure 12-4). In this state a Muslim says, "Glory to my Sustainer, the most High," at least three times. The worshiper assumes this position twice within one cycle.

Sujjud represents the ultimate spiritual state of being that all Muslims aspire to: complete submission to God alone without associating any partners. Every single prophet, according to the Islamic tradition, taught this prostration as a universal part of prayer (19:58). There are about 13 places in the Koran that talk about prostrating before God, each one requires Muslims to prostrate themselves upon reading that verse.

Prophet Muhammad said that *Sujjud* was in fact the position in which the worshiper is closest to God, and should therefore supplicate for his or her needs in that state as the best way to achieve nearness to the Divine.

Offering salutations: At-tahiyyat

After the second prostration in the second cycle, the worshiper sits and renews his or her declaration (see Step 6 in Figure 12-4) of faith that "There is no deity worthy of worship except God, and Muhammad is His servant and messenger." In this position Muslims also reconnect with their religious roots by offering prayers of peace and mercy on Prophet Muhammad (33:56) and Prophet Abraham (11:73), and upon all those who follow them.

The *At-tahiyyat* position, the final step in the worshiper's prayer, symbolizes his or her renewed faith in God. The position evokes a commitment to live life according to divine teachings, following the same path of all the prophets and righteous servants of God. This declaration reminds the worshiper before ending the prayer that worship to God is not only for the prayer itself, but must be manifest in actions and words outside of the state of prayer.

Greetings of peace: Salam

After a worshiper completes the *At-tahiyyat,* he or she remains in the sitting position and turns the face towards the right saying, "Peace be upon you and the Mercy of God" (see Step 7 in Figure 12-4). The worshiper then turns his or her face towards the left and repeats those same words. This act of greeting, called *Salam,* completes the prayer.

The *Salam* offers greetings to the recording angels that are positioned on each side of every person (50:17–18). (See Chapter 9.) In congregation prayers, the *Salam* also serves as a greeting to the fellow worshipers who sit on the right and left of you. The Koran says about greeting, that when it is offered you should meet it with an even more courteous or at least equal greeting (4:86) — meaning that kindness should be met with even greater or at least equal kindness.

Blessings on top of blessings

Additional or supplementary prayers outside of the five obligatory prayers are highly encouraged in the Koran, especially those that are offered in the last third of the night (32:16), known as *Tahajud.* The supplementary prayers are well established as the practice of Prophet Muhammad.

✔ **Sunnah Salat:** Prophet Muhammad performed *Sunnah Salat* before and/or after every obligatory prayer in order to come closer to God and gain even more blessings and benefits from this spiritual act. Muhammad highlighted the importance of *Sunnah Salat* by saying that on the Day of Judgment, anyone who is deficient in the obligatory prayers will be rewarded and saved by their supplementary prayers.

The steps for *Sunnah Salat* are exactly the same as for regular prayer, but the number of cycles varies from prayer to prayer.

Worshippers often say these prayers during the last one-third of the night, when God descends to the lowest heavens to hear the supplications of those who call on Him.

✔ **Dua':** These supplications (a humble request made to God) can be offered at any time of the day without going through the ritual steps of the formal prayer. This is a sincere call on God for any need, help, or want that may arise. In the Koran, God promises to respond to every supplicant's prayer (2:186).

Devout Muslims offer these supplications constantly throughout the day before committing to any task — whether it be as small as eating or as important as making a speech — in order to gain God's blessings and support. Established *Dua'* can be found throughout the Scripture, often in the eloquent supplications of Prophet Abraham that are recorded in the Book (26:77–87, for example).

In its inner meaning, the act of turning the face to the left and right offers peace and God's Mercy to all of humanity, whether they are in the East or in the West. *Salam* symbolizes commitment to spread peace and mercy throughout the world, which Muslims are ready to foster after devoting themselves to reflection and communication with the Divine.

Each ritual act of the prayer serves as a reminder of God's attributes and His favors and bounties on every soul. Prayer is also a process through which believers renew and confirm their commitment to serve God alone and follow in the footsteps of the prophets.

Raising the Soul Over the Ego: Fasting

Fasting during the sacred month of Ramadan (2:183) constitutes Islam's third pillar of faith. Fasting requires Muslims to abstain from food, water, and sex from dawn to dusk each day during the sacred month. Muslims are expected to be on their best behavior and adhere to the strongest spiritual and moral practices.

Remembering and thanking God

Ramadan is the month in which the Koranic revelation began to come down to Prophet Muhammad as a "guidance unto man and a self-evident proof of that guidance, and as the standard by which to discern the true from the false" (2:185). Therefore, fasting is a celebration of divine guidance, and it has two primary objectives according to the Scripture:

- ✓ **Fasting makes you conscious of God (2:183):** The Koran says that fasting in one form or the other is a universal teaching of all faiths and was ordered by God for every prophetic community. Fasting, then, is a unique teaching in the human experience that raises the level of God-consciousness through an internal bodily experience.

  By depriving the body of food, water, and sex from dawn to sunset only for the sake of God, the soul becomes deeply aware of divine presence with every feeling of hunger and thirst. The fasting individual is tempted to grab that doughnut in the morning or drink from the water fountain, but restrains himself or herself from desire with the remembrance of God.

  This is important training for the soul from the Koranic perspective, because it teaches human beings that if the soul can deprive itself of the basic necessities of life for a number of hours, for the pleasure of God, then surely the soul can control itself from the passions of lower desire that cause humans to go astray from the divine path (see Chapter 13 for more about the Koranic view of self).

Fasting means more than just abstaining from food, water, and sex. When fasting, Muslims are expected to grow in patience, endurance, and humility — all in the knowledge that God watches over them. As such, Prophet Muhammad said, "Fasting is a shield (against wrong actions). When anyone of you is observing fast on a day, he should neither indulge in obscene language, nor should he raise his voice. And if anyone speaks ill of him or tries to fight with him, he should say: 'I am fasting.'"

Scholars of Islam say that if someone loses his or her patience and fights without justice, or uses obscene language, or tells a lie, then that person's fast becomes void or decreases in reward.

Fasting trains the soul to refrain from doing anything that displeases God and that the Koran prohibits.

✔ **Fasting makes you thankful of God (2:185):** Without doubt, abstaining from food, water, and sex proves a very difficult test for most people. Fasting makes apparent the hardship and suffering that others go through every day of the year because of poverty and drought. As such, the soul feels a great sense of gratitude to God for sustaining him or her each day with the blessings of food and water — things that people often take for granted, but without which human survival becomes impossible.

Thankfulness to the Divine is not shown by constantly chanting His name or spending the entire day praying at a mosque. Rather, gratitude must be shown by sharing your food and sustenance with those around you who have nothing or little to eat once the sun goes down. Muslims are technically allowed to eat as much as they want once the sun goes down, but are highly encouraged to in fact lower their food intake during this month so that they can live physically and spiritually healthier lives.

Fasting, then, becomes a way for even the wealthiest person to share for a moment the experience of those who are less fortunate. As such, fasting should create a feeling of sympathy for the poor, and a sense of responsibility to feed the impoverished, clothe the naked, and provide shelter for the homeless.

The Koran prescribes fasting in celebration of the month in which the Koran was revealed. Koranic commentators have said that the character that a soul develops out of fasting is the very ideal that the Koran asks men and women to aspire towards. Furthermore, the Koran was revealed for the very purpose of reminding and guiding humans towards the God-conscious path, and fasting causes people to make such a remembrance.

The entire month of fasting trains the human soul in self control so that the pure heart that advocates patience and righteousness rises above the ego or lower desires that call the soul towards anger, violence, revenge, and other self-destructive acts.

Enjoying the communal aspects of fasting

The month of Ramadan is a very festive time in the Muslim world, with Muslims feeling a special sense of blessings from God. Islamic teachings say that during this month, the rewards for righteous deeds increase tenfold, the doors of hellfire close, Satan is chained up, and the gates of heaven open wide. Ramadan creates a sense of urgency to do good works, to share food, and to spend long nights in the mosque worshiping God. In addition, families and friends often decide to get together for breaking the fast in the evening, which fosters a nice feeling of brotherhood and sisterhood.

During the month of Ramadan, known as "the month of the Koran," special night prayers, known as *Tarawih,* are offered in mosques throughout the world. Each night the congregation recites about 1/30 of the Koran, so that by the end of the month, the entire Book has been recited and listened to. (See Chapter 3 for a list of which *Surahs* make up these 30 parts, known as *Juz'.*) These long prayers and time at the mosque bring the community closer, providing one reason why Muslims are usually quite sad to see Ramadan end.

Ramadan renews the faith and soul of individuals and communities. Ramadan revives the commitment to follow the ethical and moral teachings of the Koran.

Fasting beyond Ramadan

Many Muslims fast outside of Ramadan as a way to continue the spirit of self-control and development of high spiritual values that comes during this month, a practice that is praised as the quality of the righteous men and women (33:35).

Prophet Muhammad recommended that those of his companions who did not have the means to marry could instead fast in order to control their sexual passions. (Fasting can also help with other passions in the human experience that need to be controlled by the soul.)

Muhammad forbade fasting continuously without any break as that would be going to extremes that could eventually cause the fasting soul to feel overburdened. The maximum fasting outside of Ramadan that is allowed was practiced by Prophet David (Dawud in Arabic) who fasted every other day. Prophet Muhammad fasted every Monday and Thursday, which is why many devout Muslims follow this practice throughout the year.

Purifying Wealth, Uplifting the Needy: Almsgiving

The word for almsgiving in Arabic is *Zakat,* which is the fourth pillar of Islam. The root word of *zakat* means "to purify;" *Zakat* purifies the wealth of Muslims, transforming it into a resource that can aide those who need help (9:103). By helping those in need, Muslims cleanse their money of greed, and also wash from their souls those lower desires that call towards miserliness and selfishness.

Interestingly, the Koran usually mentions *Salat* and *Zakat* together (2:277, for example). This is consistent with the Koranic teaching that individual religion or spirituality is of no use and can't be complete without the righteous works that seek to build God-conscious societies. Individual worship and social work go hand-in-hand, and they serve as supporting pillars for each other. As such, the Koranic formula for worldly success and salvation in the hereafter is found in belief of One God (manifest in the obligatory prayers) and righteous deeds (manifest in almsgiving).

Opening your wallet and improving the world

Those who can afford to feed their families for an entire year are obligated to give a minimum of 2.5 percent of their individual net worth in alms. All members of a family who earn more money than needed to cover basic needs are obligated to pay the minimum. Those who can't afford to sustain their families for an entire year are exempt from giving the purifying alms. The details on *Zakat* amount are not found in the Koran, but in the prophetic tradition. The 2.5 percent may seem like a small amount, but alms are intended to show that if all those who have been blessed with financial resources put their money together, they can in fact considerably help reduce starvation and poverty in the world.

Muslims give their purifying alms at any time during the year. First, almsgivers seek out members within their extended family who may be in need of this money (16:90). Then, barring family members, they look for someone in the community (see the section "Receiving alms," later in this section, for more information); if they still can't find a needy person, they send the money somewhere in the world where it may be needed.

If almsgivers seek to help and empower those closest to them, then one community at a time, the condition of people all around the world will be uplifted.

Zakat, social equity, and the law

Zakat is the primary way in which Islam establishes economic justice and equality for those who are in need, such as orphans and widows. Without alms, Islam couldn't attain the monetary justice and social welfare that the Scripture so passionately advocates.

These alms are so important in Islam that an Islamic government, which legitimately governs with consent of the people and follows Islamic law, has been given the authority to fight those Muslims who refuse to pay this obligatory alms. Since the *Zakat* is usually paid in private, it is not possible to know who has paid and who has not, so rarely are people penalized for not paying the purifying alms. The Koran advises those who don't pay the *Zakat* to follow the "straight path" and warns that in the sight of God, those who refuse to pay *Zakat* are like those who associate partners with Him (41:6–7).

Receiving alms

The Koran categorizes eight different social groups who can receive purifying alms (9:60). I list them as they appear in this Koranic passage:

- ✔ *Fuqara* (the poor): Scholars of the Koran define this group as those who have a limited amount of income and struggle to meet their basic needs, such as food, clothes, and shelter.

- ✔ *Masakin* (the destitute and needy): Those who have no income whatsoever and are therefore in desperate need of financial aid. Some scholars say that this group includes those who are unemployed.

- ✔ *Amilina 'alayha* (the administers of the alms): The salaries of government alms collectors or nonprofit organizations that collect the alms can be paid with alms.

- ✔ *Mu'allafati Qulubuhum* (those who need to be reconciled): Alms for those who support Islam, but who aren't Muslims, in order to tie their hearts to the community and sanctify a solid relationship.

  Another group eligible under this type of alms are those who have recently converted to Islam, especially those converts who sacrifice a lot to become Muslim. For example, even in the United States, you find those who convert to Islam and are subsequently cast aside by their families and friends with at times devastating consequences. Purifying alms can be spent to help such converts.

- ✔ *Fi'r Riqab* (those who need to be freed from slavery or bondage): Slavery was a very serious problem, especially during the time of the Koran's revelation. As such, this category allowed for purifying alms to be spent in freeing slaves, and was a progressive means to ending slavery altogether. Since slavery no longer exists (at least in most of the world), scholars have argued that this category can be extended for those who are imprisoned unjustly, such as political prisoners, or those who have been wrongly captured during a war.

✔ *Al-gharimin* **(those overburdened by debt):** Those whose debts can't be repaid with their own money. However, scholars have warned against giving alms to those who are in debt as a result of extravagant spending on material goods; doing so can inadvertently encourage a pattern of overspending.

✔ *Fi-sabili 'llah* **(those in the way of God):** Generally for people who struggle on behalf of the Muslim community for the preservation and promotion of Islam (such as freedom fighters) and for righteous works (such as a soup kitchen). For example, people who fight for the security of Muslim lands can receive purifying alms. Also, those who run programs and schools where good Islamic values are taught and preached are eligible for the funds collected through alms. Basically, anyone who works for the sake of Islam in a legitimate cause and in a lawful manner can receive alms.

✔ *Ibnu 'Sabil* **(travelers in need):** This category addresses travelers who lose their money or mode of transportation, and are therefore in need of help. For example, if someone goes on vacation or on a business trip and their money gets stolen, then they can receive the purifying alms so that they can safely make a journey back home.

Giving more and more

Muslims are highly encouraged to give more than the obligatory alms throughout the year by helping individuals and by supporting righteous institutions that provide a good service to the community. This type of charity, called *Sadaqa* in Arabic, can be paid anywhere, at any time, and to anyone.

The Koran says that those who spend in charity will be blessed many folds (2:276). The Book also says that hidden charity is better than having people know about it, and the act of charity removes evil from the soul of a person (2:271). But, the Scripture also teaches that "Kind words and covering of faults are better than charity followed by hurt..." (2:263) or reminding beneficiaries of your generosity (2:264).

Prophet Muhammad said that once a man removed a branch from the street so that no injury would come to any pedestrians who walked on that path, and for this God forgave all his previous sins. Similarly, a prostitute once saw a thirsty dog and dipped her shoe in a well to quench the dog's thirst, and for that act of charity all her sins were forgiven by God. Muhammad also taught his companions that even a cheerful smile towards a fellow human being is an act of charity that merits God's reward.

Journeying to the House of God: Pilgrimage

Pilgrimage (called *Hajj* in Arabic) to Mecca, in Saudi Arabia, constitutes the fifth and final pillar of Islam, which is recognized by the Koran as being "in the service of God" (2:196). It is obligatory only on those who can afford to make the travel physically and financially (3:97).

Following the path of Abraham

This sacred pilgrimage originates in the life mission and struggle of Prophet Abraham and his family. *Hajj* celebrates this Prophet, known as the "father of faith" (22:78) and the friend of God (4:125) in the Koran. The Scripture often refers to its own message as the "Path of Abraham, the true in faith" (6:161).

The Islamic tradition believes that Abraham came to the valley of Becca (more commonly known as Mecca) with his son Ishmael (Ismail in Arabic) and wife Hagar.

At Becca, Abraham and Ishmael rebuilt the *Ka'ba* (first House of God, originally built by Prophet Adam) and sanctified it for the worship of God alone (3:96–97). After rebuilding the House, Abraham called on God to raise a group of people in the land who would serve and worship One God without associating any partners (2:128–129). Muslims believe that the two million-plus pilgrims who make the *Hajj* each year fulfill Abraham's supplication and call. This reality is reflected in a passage that assures Prophet Abraham of success in his call: "And proclaim the Pilgrimage among men. They will come to you on foot and (mounted) on every camel, lean through deep and distant mountain highways" (22:27).

Some generations down the line, the descendants of Ishmael began worshiping idols and turned away from the practice of belief in One God. In turn, they also made the House of God a place of idol worship. Muhammad, then, through his Prophecy, is ordered to reclaim the House of God for the worship of Him alone, and to destroy any idols. Prophet Muhammad is successful in his mission, and the original rites of Abraham are restored in the practice of *Hajj*.

Journeying through the pilgrimage

The pilgrimage lasts for four days and is a major physical, emotional, and spiritual undertaking that tests the pilgrim to the limit. Because of the physical struggle and crowding caused by so many people making the *Hajj* at the same time, tragic stampedes and other disasters sometimes occur. For this reason, before Muslims go on the Pilgrimage, they must draw up their wills and reconcile their relationship with anyone who they may have abandoned as a result of some fight or argument.

However, for Muslims, death during Pilgrimage means that they die with the same status as a martyr in the way of God, and such a soul goes back to his Creator completely purified of any sins.

Pilgrimage purifies the soul. Muhammad said, "Whoever performs pilgrimage and does not have sexual relations, nor commits sin, nor disputes unjustly, then he (or she) returns from the pilgrimage as pure and free from sins as on the day on which his (or her) mother gave birth to him (or her)."

The Pilgrimage consists of five basic acts, all of which have an enormous impact on the soul of the pilgrims. In the following sections, I describe each act that a pilgrim must go through for his or her pilgrimage to be complete.

Dressing in humility and equality: Ihram

Before the pilgrimage begins, the pilgrim must take a bath and put on two separate pieces of long white towels (for men) or simple clothes that modestly cover the body (for women). This act of dressing constitutes the *Ihram* and officially places the pilgrim in a state of pilgrimage.

Once this dress has been put on, the pilgrim lives a very pure lifestyle in which he or she must guard every single word and action to be only for the pleasure of God. Fighting, arguing, slandering, lying, and backbiting are strictly prohibited (2:197). Kindness and mercy must become the character and way of the pilgrim, who can't even kill a single ant on purpose, or comb the hair or cut the nails, for that act alone kills living organisms. Pilgrimage means living the purest and simplest lifestyle that is manifest in worship to God, and mercy towards all creation.

Ihram strips away all material indications of a person's wealth or economic class, and thereby the richest person and the poorest person walk side by side as they struggle for the same goal of achieving nearness to the Divine. Peoples of all colors, races, and national origin come with the same purpose and intention, and therefore are united by the same spiritual message and call of Prophet Abraham.

Answering the call: Talbiya

After putting on the *Ihram,* the pilgrims walk towards the House of God (see the following section) chanting aloud in a unified passionate voice, speaking the same spiritual language: "Here I am before You, O God, at Your service. Before You I am, there is no partner unto You, at Your service here I am. All praise and blessings are Yours, and power. There is no partner unto You."

This chant, known as the *Talbiya,* becomes the defining voice of the pilgrimage as it reminds the pilgrims of their status as servants of God (2:196), and therefore as His representatives on earth (see Chapter 8 for more information on the purpose of human life according to the Koran).

Walking around the House of God: Tawaf

When pilgrims enter the sacred Mosque (see "Following the path of Abraham," earlier in this chapter), they walk around the House of God (22:29) seven times, chanting various prayers as well as the *Talbiya,* while raising their hands towards the House in a sign of affection.

Walking around the *Ka'ba,* which is called *Tawaf,* signifies that God and His divine teachings are at the center of life for the individual pilgrim and for the collective body of Muslims who participate in the rite. Furthermore, it symbolizes the pilgrims' submission to God's natural order by following the same motion that the earth follows (rotation) by the command of divine will. Finally, it also symbolizes the way in which angels praise the Throne of God.

Tawaf takes place immediately before pilgrimage, and upon returning from the *Hajj* rites to the House of God for a non-obligatory round of farewell to the place that changes the lives of pilgrims.

Hurrying between two hills: Sa'ee

Next the pilgrim walks at a fast pace seven times between the hills of *Safa* and *Marwah,* two symbols set up by God (2:158). This part of the journey is known as *Sa'ee.* The distance between the two hills is about a 15 minute walk for an average healthy person.

The significance of these two mountains comes from the story of Hagar (Hajar in Arabic) who was left by Prophet Abraham, according to God's command, in the deserted valley of Mecca, trusting in God's sustenance for his wife and child (14:37).

Soon Hagar found herself alone with the baby and quickly running out of water. She began to run between the mountains of *Safa* and *Marwah* looking for help and for God's sustenance. The desperate mother never gave up hope in God and continued to struggle by running between the two mountains a total of seven times. As Hagar became tired and more desperate, she suddenly heard the voice of Angel Gabriel, who hit the earth with his heel causing a fountain of water to gush out from beneath the earth's surface. The water created an abundance of sustenance for Hagar and her child, Ishmael. According to Islamic tradition, this fountain continues to flow in the blessed *Zamzam* water that can be found in Mecca today. Muslims believe that this water has healing powers and consider it a blessing to drink from the *Zamzam.*

Hagar's struggle shows Muslims that with struggle, sacrifice, and unrelenting trust in the Divine, success comes, even though it may take some time. Pilgrims walk between the two mountains to commemorate the struggle of a righteous mother who never gave up hope in God's Mercy and Blessings.

Camping out at Mina: Wuquf

After completing the *Sa'ee,* the pilgrim dons the *Ihram* once again and makes the official intent for Pilgrimage, called *Wuquf.* The pilgrim then walks from the House of God to a place called *Mina,* which is a desert area about six kilometers away from the *Ka'ba.* Pilgrims there stay in white tents to experience a simple life while turning to God in prayer and supplication.

Asking for forgiveness: Arafah

Pilgrims spend a day at Arafah, which is considered the climax of the Pilgrimage (2:198–199). Arafah means "the meeting place," because this is where Adam and Eve met after descending on earth and where all of humanity will be brought together on the Day of Judgment. All the pilgrims turn their attention to asking for God's forgiveness as they stand in an empty area where you can't see anything for miles upon miles (except other pilgrims).

For Muslims, this represents what the Day of Judgment will look like, when all of humanity will gather before God, stripped of any pride in class or race. At Arafat, even the strongest men seem to break down into tears with remembrance of their sins, begging for God's forgiveness.

Stoning the devil: Jamarat

Upon returning from Arafat, pilgrims go back to *Mina* where they visit a place called *Jamarat.* Here, the pilgrims gather seven stones and cast them at pillars that represent Satan.

This ritual reenacts what Prophet Abraham did when he was tested by God to sacrifice his beloved son, and Satan constantly came to tempt him away from following the path of God. Each time, Prophet Abraham picked up a stone and threw it at Satan to ward of the evil temptation. As such, the pilgrim throws stones at the pillars vowing to eliminate the influence of Satan in his or her life.

Making the sacrifice: Udhiya

After the symbolic stoning of Satan, pilgrims sacrifice an animal (usually a sheep), whose meat will be distributed throughout the world to the poor (22:28; 22:36). Pilgrims don't have to do the sacrifice, called *Udhiya,* themselves; they can pay a butcher to do it for them.

The Koran says about the animal sacrifice that "It is not their meat nor their blood that reaches God. It is your piety that reaches him . . ." (22:37). This sacrifice for the sake of God ends the Pilgrimage with a sense of duty and responsibility to help the poor and needy.

At this time, most male pilgrims also shave their heads (2:196) to symbolize a return to a pure, baby-like state devoid of any sin or fault. Shaving also represents a new beginning in life, one dedicated to the worship of God in ritual and in righteous works. Female pilgrims cut only a piece of their hair in the same symbolic act.

The Koran offers a beautiful perspective into the transformation that takes place in the nature of a pilgrim after completing the pilgrimage: "So when you have accomplished your rites, celebrate the praises of God, as you used to celebrate the praises of your fathers (lineage) — yet, with far more heart and soul . . ." (201).

The passage goes on to say that there are those who only pray for the good of this world, but those who are true in faith pray to God for both the good of this life and the hereafter (2:201–202). A true pilgrim turns in humble worship to the Sustainer, fully aware of his or her responsibilities in life and promise of the Hereafter.

Chapter 13

Understanding the Koranic View of Self

In This Chapter

▶ Identifying the three elements of self-knowledge

▶ Distinguishing three types of self

▶ Journeying to five stages of the soul

▶ Exploring the meaning of Muslim and *Kafir*

For an outside observer of Muslim practices, Islam can seem rather ritualistic. However, the rituals taught by the Koran only serve as a means to achieving something much greater: A state of soul that lives in submission to God, and with whom God is pleased.

In this chapter, I explain how the Koran views the concept of spirituality, and the role the heart and soul play in developing a devout worshiper and obedient self that is dedicated to a deep spiritual relationship with God.

Connecting the Three Dots of Self Awareness

The Koran identifies three essential parts to the self:

✔ **Nafs:** The selfish or egotistical self of desire and passion

✔ **Ruh:** The spiritual self of human conscience

✔ **Qalb:** The spiritual heart

Everything in moderation

Three people inquired about Prophet Muhammad's worship. They considered their worship insignificant to his and said, "Where are we in comparison with the Prophet, while God has forgiven his past sins and future sins."

One of them said, "As for me, I shall offer prayer all night long." Another said, "I shall observe fasting continuously and shall not break it." The third said, "I shall abstain from women and shall never marry."

Prophet Muhammad came to them and said, "Are you the persons who said such and such things? By God, I fear God more than you do, and I am most obedient and dutiful among you to Him, but still I observe fast and break it, I offer prayer and sleep at night and marry. So, whoever turns away from my practice is not of me."

The wild horse and the rider

You can't consider these three interconnected elements separately from one another. A famous analogy among classical commentators of the Koran describes the *Nafs* as a wild horse and the *Ruh* as a rider of that horse.

The *Ruh* tames the wild beast into a peaceful, disciplined horse that can carry the rider far distances. The *Qalb* is the driving force inside the rider that determines his or her ability or inability to tame the wild beast.

If the *Qalb* contains excellent spiritual qualities, such as patience and gentleness, it empowers the rider *(Ruh)* to take control of the wild horse *(Nafs)* and direct it towards good. However, if the *Qalb* is spiritually weak, with qualities such as anger and harshness, then the rider *(Ruh)* will lose control of the wild beast *(Nafs)*, leaving it to wander into paths of great danger.

The aim is not to kill the *Nafs,* as in some other spiritual traditions, but rather to use it in moderation and in ways which the Koran permits according to God's laws (91:7–10). For this reason, even sexual intimacy between a married couple is a blessed act of worship that merits God's reward, according to Prophet Muhammad. In the interest of balance, Islamic law prohibits extreme acts, such as celibacy or continuous fasting.

Nevertheless, the Koran warns that if human passions are left unchecked by the human conscience, they will lead to a harmful downward road: "O men! Indeed your transgressions are bound to rebound against your own selves" (10:23).

According to the Koranic perspective, the *Qalb* (heart) is the organ of perception in mankind. If the heart is spiritually strong, it has the ability to empower the human conscience over the affairs of the passionate self. A heart in spiritual darkness weakens the spiritual self and allows the *Nafs* to rule over body and mind, a state referred to when the Koran asks, "Have you seen him who takes his lower passions for his god?" (25:43).

Constant remembrance and awareness of God provides the path to the heart's purity and light (13:28). The Koran teaches that this pure heart wards off the illusions of Satan and gives people the ability to distinguish between good and evil. However, the heart that is open to persistent sin and rejection of faith leads to a distortion of reality that inhibits recognizing right from wrong.

A saying of Prophet Muhammad emphasizes the essential role of the heart for spiritual purity: "Verily, in the body there is a piece of flesh, which if healthy, the whole body is healthy; and if it is corrupt, the whole body is corrupt. Verily, this piece of flesh is the heart."

The three states of self

The Koran identifies three types of self that develop in humans through their actions on earth:

- *Nafs al-Ammarah Bis-sou:* A soul that inclines towards evil and heads towards a spiritually and morally downward state.

- *Nafs al-Lawwamah:* A soul that struggles against the lower self, recognizing evil and wanting to submit to God alone. This is the most sensitive state because of the constant struggle.

- *Nafs al-Mutma'innah:* Best of all souls, which reaches a state of peace and satisfaction with constant remembrance of God.

These states are not fixed in earthly life. You can move from one state of self to the other during your lifetime.

The Koran always leaves open the door for change through God's mercy by saying, "(If) he repents, believes, and works righteous deeds. For God will change the evil of such persons into good, and God is Oft-Forgiving, Most Merciful" (25:70). But, after death, the state of self is fixed, and souls will be raised up on the Day of Judgment in the same state in which their earthly lives ended.

The Seven Gates to the Heart

A common analogy for the heart *(Qalb)*, found in traditional Islamic texts, is that of a city which in its essence is pure and peaceful. Seven gates protect this city from corruption and evil, and welcomingly receive messengers of light and guidance. Satan constantly tries new ways of getting through these gates so that he can attack the city.

The heart is like the city. If not properly guarded, the heart becomes vulnerable to impurity. However, if the defense of the heart remains steadfast against laziness and negligence, then the heart will remain pure and tranquility will reign.

According to classical interpretation of the Koran, the seven gates that the Koran seeks to protect through theology and law are:

- "Ears with which you hear"
- "Eyes with which you see"
- "Tongue with which you speak"
- "Hands with which you act"
- "Legs with which you walk"
- "Stomach with which you take your fill"
- "Sexual organs with which you take pleasure"

The Koran constantly reminds its reader that all seven spiritual gates that protect the heart are gifts from God; they are to be kept as a trust by using them in ways that show gratitude to the Creator (16:78).

I explain these seven gates more fully in the sections that follow.

The ears and tongue

Whenever the Koran calls its readers to self-responsibility and accountability, it begins by mentioning the faculties of hearing. Commentators of the Koran point out that what you allow into your ears is most difficult to protect because of the circular nature of hearing that enables you to listen from all directions, unlike the eye that has linear vision.

The spiritual gates of ears and tongue are interconnected. Everything to be avoided in hearing is also to be avoided in speech. And, everything to be avoided in speech must also be avoided in hearing.

The Koran strongly warns against three types of speech and hearing:

- **Idle talk (23:3):** Idle talk also includes lying, which the Koran strongly condemns: "Shall I inform you on whom it is the evil ones descend? They descend on every lying, wicked person" (26:222).

- **Defaming or insulting another human being:** The Koran prohibits making fun of others: "O you who believe! Let not some men among you laugh at others: it may be that the (latter) are better than the (former). Nor let some women laugh at others: It may be that the (latter) are better than the (former). And neither shall you defame one another, nor insult one another by (offensive) nicknames" (49:11).

- **Backbiting and slandering:** The Koran condemns backbiting and slandering (see the sidebar "Is it backbiting or slandering?" later in this chapter): "Woe unto every slanderer and backbiter" (104:1). However, Islamic law makes some exceptions for informing others about the bad character of people, such as warning or advising people against a fraudulent business dealer, or the immoral character of someone that wants to get married.

Upon hearing these restrictions, some people think that Muslims must live very dull lives without any enjoyment or laughing. Not true! The life of Prophet Muhammad has many examples where he joked with people and laughed at the jokes of his companions.

However, the tongue should be guarded against hurting other people or telling lies for the sake of entertainment. This is why traditionally in the Muslim world you can find many funny stories, but usually they are about a comical character who does silly things. Making offensive fun of a specific person or group is unacceptable.

A golden rule taught by Prophet Muhammad, regarding the tongue, is in his saying: "He who believes in God and the Last Day must either speak that which is good or remain silent."

If Muslims encounter a situation in which their tongues and ears are tempted into sin, they are encouraged to leave that gathering in order to maintain purity of mind and soul (28:55).

The eyes

The Koran reminds mankind to be in a constant state of awareness about God's all-Knowing attribute, by which not even a leaf falls without his knowledge (6:59). The Koran warns that "God knows the faithlessness of the eyes, and all that the hearts conceal" (40:19).

Is it backbiting or slandering?

Prophet Muhammad once asked his companions, "Do you know what is backbiting?" The companions said, "God and His Messenger know better."

Muhammad then said, "Backbiting is talking about your brother in a manner which he dislikes." The companions countered by asking the Prophet, "What if my brother is as I say?" Muhammad replied, "If he is actually as you say, then that is backbiting; but if that (what you say) is not in him, that is slandering."

The spiritual gate of the eyes is strongly connected with chastity and modesty, as the Koran commands its followers: "Tell the believing men to lower their eyes and to be mindful of their chastity: this will make for greater purity for them . . . and tell the believing women to lower their eyes and to be mindful of their chastity . . ."(24:30–31). (This verse also discusses the dress code for women, which I talk about in Chapter 15.)

Several commentators of the Koran have argued that lowering the eyes is as much an emotional lowering as it is a physical one. This command protects the heart from images that can take you away from the remembrance and worship of God, and even lead you to act on the passions of the lower self. This is why Prophet Muhammad said, "The fornication of the eye is the (lustful) look."

Certainly this safeguard has become especially difficult to preserve with the invention of the television and other avenues of advertisement, which constantly spew out sexual messages and innuendoes. As such, the harmful effects of television are widely discussed in the Muslim community; many leading clerics around the world discourage Muslims from watching television. Sometimes, outside observers see this as a lack of ability to "modernize," but Muslims feel that they can embrace modernity and progress without losing the spiritual tradition of Islam.

The hands and legs

The Koran teaches its readers to protect the hands from acts of destruction and to use the hands for giving charity and working for good causes (2:195, for example).

The Koran also reminds the reader of God's sacred trust over the hands, which must not be used in acts that displease God. The Scripture warns that those people who do use their hands for evil will face an unhappy fate in the Hereafter. Those who incline towards evil deeds shouldn't blame their dejected fate in the Hereafter on God; God never acts unjustly and only punishes those who have wronged themselves (8:51).

The spiritual gates of the hands and legs are interconnected. For every evil action committed by the hands, the legs take the hands to that place of evil. The Koran says, "That Day (of Judgment) shall We set a seal on their mouths, but their hands will speak to Us, and their feet will bear witness, to all that they did" (36:65).

For example, if you go somewhere to fight with another person without a just cause, then not only will your hands bare witness to your actions on The Day of Judgment, but also your legs, because your legs carried you to the fight. Similarly, if you go to a soup kitchen in order to help people and come closer to God, not only will your hands bare witness to your good actions on the Day of Judgment, but also the legs that brought you to the place of charity.

The stomach

The Koran calls on man to show an act of thankfulness before eating by recognizing that all sustenance comes from God alone (16:114). Muslims always begin their meals by saying, "In the name of God, the Most Merciful, the Most Compassionate."

The Koran strongly discourages overeating and wasting food (20:81). Commentators of the Koran point out that overeating leads to laziness, which is one of the worst spiritual qualities according to the Koranic perspective.

The Koran prohibits its followers from eating certain meats in order to protect the spiritual gate of the stomach. The Koran says, "Forbidden to you is dead meat, and blood, and the flesh of swine, and that over which any name other than God's has been invoked, and the animal that has been strangled, or beaten to death, or killed by fall, or gored to death, or savaged by a beast of prey, except that which you may have slaughtered while it was still alive; and (forbidden to you is) all that has been slaughtered on idolatrous altars . . ." (5:3).

These Koranic laws make things a little challenging for Muslims living in non-Muslim countries. In such situations, the local Muslim populations usually open meat slaughterhouses in order to provide lawful meat for the community. Most Muslims also accept eating kosher meat because of the similarities in Muslim and Jewish law in preparing the meat.

The sexual organs

One of the worst sins a person can commit, according to Koranic law, is fornication or adultery. The Koran teaches, "(Successful are those) who guard their private parts, except with those joined to them in marriage . . . but those whose desires exceed those limits are truly transgressors" (23:5–7).

Achieving nearness to God

The goal of protecting your heart from Satan and directing your body towards good actions is best understood with a saying from God to Prophet Muhammad, known as Hadith Qudsi, in which God says, "And the most beloved thing with which My servant comes nearer to Me is what I have enjoined upon him; and My slave keeps on coming closer to Me through performing extra righteous deeds till I love him. When I love him I become the hearing with which he hears, his seeing with which he sees, his hand with which he acts, and his legs with which he walks; and if he asks (something) of Me, I give him, and if he asks My Protection, I protect him."

The Koran accords severe punishment to both fornicators and adulterers, not only because of the social consequences of such actions, but also because of the violation of God's institution of marriage in which He places divine mercy and love between the hearts of a man and a woman.

Because of the intense pleasure that comes from sexual experience, the Koran warns that if left unchecked, it can lead a person away from the worship of God and towards the worship of his or her own lower self *(Nafs)*. For this reason the Koran praises those who actively guard the spiritual gate of sexual organs, and counts them among those who will receive the gardens of paradise in the Hereafter (79:40–41).

Blessed Is the Baby's Soul, a Soul without Sin

The Koran rejects the Christian concept of *original sin*, which is, according to Christian theology, the state of sin that marks all humans as a result of Adam's first act of disobedience.

In the story of creation, as told by the Koran, Adam sins by eating from the forbidden tree and has to live with the consequences of his actions by falling out of Paradise. God ultimately forgives and honors him, firstly as His representative on earth, and secondly as the first prophet in a series of prophets that bring constant guidance to humanity. (See Chapter 8 for more about Adam and the creation of mankind.)

The Koran emphatically repeats that "No soul shall bear the burden of another" (6:164). According to the Koran, people don't carry Adam's sins, but only their own good and evil deeds.

For this reason, the purest state a human can achieve is that of a newborn baby, who is sinless and whose heart lives in a complete state of submission to God. Muhammad said that every child is born in a state of natural inclination to worship God alone.

From the Koranic perspective, every soul, regardless of religion or culture, has certain universal ethics that stem from the purity of the original spiritual heart *(Qalb)*. But, when people forget God and sin against their own selves, their souls lose touch with these moral principles.

This original spiritual heart constantly calls man back to the straight path. This inclination is called *Fitrah* in Arabic, and one of the names of the Koranic message is Deen Al-Fitrah, loosely translated as the "Way of Natural Inclination."

The Soul's Journey: From Pre-Birth to the Hereafter

The Koran describes five stages for the life of the soul, which begin before birth and continue until after death. I tell you about each of these stages in the following sections.

Pre-worldly existence

According to the Koran a conversation takes place between every human soul and God before earthly creation: "And whenever your Lord brings forth their offspring from the loins of the children of Adam, He calls upon them to bear witness about themselves: 'Am I not your Lord?' — to which they answer, 'Yes, indeed, we bear witness'" (7:172).

Scholars of Koranic interpretation debate whether the covenant mentioned in 7:172 is pre-existential or at the time of birth. The majority opinion is that this is a pre-existential experience of the soul, because the seed of Adam refers to all of humanity, born or unborn, without any limit of time. Furthermore, the Arabic of the text is in the passive voice of "he brought forth," and "he asked them," which also indicates a pre-existential event.

Earthly life

Babies are born with the original pledge to God in their subconscious. Parents must nurture that spirituality into remembrance. Interestingly, the Koran also calls itself a "reminder" of that which the soul already has knowledge of at the subconscious level.

On earth, the soul faces tribulations that test its commitment to worshipping God by acting as His representative: "And most surely shall We try you by means of danger, and hunger, and the loss of worldly goods, of lives and of (earned) fruits. But give glad tidings unto those who are patient in adversity" (2:155).

The worldly life experience ends with death, of which the Koran promises "every soul shall taste" (3:185). Prophet Muhammad advised his followers to "be in the world as if you were a stranger or wayfarer." The Prophet used to also say, "Remember (frequently) the destroyer of pleasure — death."

The grave

"We came into this world crying, and all of those around us were happy. We should leave this world happy, with those around us crying." This famous Muslim saying summarizes the transition from earthly life to the grave for a righteous soul.

The Koran describes the grave as a place of initial questioning where the soul faces the illusory nature of worldly goods and the reality of God's promise to hold each soul accountable for his or her deeds.

Prophetic sayings of Muhammad make it clear that the grave is also a place of peace and satisfaction for righteous souls and a place of punishment for the evil souls. Also, in the grave there is a period of purification through punishment for souls who had much good in them, but committed evil deeds as well, so that on the Day of Judgment those souls will be forgiven and granted paradise.

The Day of Judgment

The Koran describes the transitory stage from grave to Judgment Day in the following passage: "And verily the Hour will come: there can be no doubt about it, or about (the fact) God will raise up all who are in the graves" (22:7). On this day, souls "will come forth — their eyes humbled, from their graves, like locusts scattered abroad" (54:7).

The Day of Judgment is an awesome event when all souls will be brought from the grave to account for their time on earth. In Arabic, the term literally means "the day the debts fall due." The debt of God's blessings and favors is submission to Him, and the Day of Judgment is when the soul will have to account for "every good it did, and every evil it did" (99:7–8).

For a complete discussion on the Koranic view of the Day of Judgment, refer to Chapter 9.

Don't get lost in the marketplace

The story of the soul's five stages has traditionally been taught to young Muslim children with a tale about a boy who is given some money by a king and asked to purchase some goods from the marketplace (Pre-Worldly Existence). When the young boy reaches the marketplace he becomes fascinated with all the fun toys and begins wasting the money on enjoyment, while forgetting his original purpose of serving the king (Earthly Life).

In the midst of his enjoyment, the marketplace begins to close down. All of a sudden, the boy remembers why he was sent in the first place and frantically runs around trying to purchase the goods, but it's too late (The Grave). The boy returns to the king ashamed at his actions, and when the king asks him what he did with the money, he has no option but to tell the truth (Day of Judgment). The king is disappointed with the boy and sends him to be punished, never asking the boy to serve him again (The Hereafter).

The final abode

After the day of questioning, the soul reaches its final home, either the delights of paradise or the torments of hellfire. The Koran attributes paradise to that soul which was near to God on earth: "And those foremost (in faith and actions) will be foremost (in the Hereafter)" (56:10). Similarly, those for whom the Koran attributes hellfire for are the souls that overindulged in their worldly passions: "For, behold, in times gone by they were indulged in sinful luxury, and persisted in sinning" (56:45–46).

The Muslim Self: A State of Being

Today, people use the term Muslim in social and political contexts to describe a large group of people who share the Islamic faith. However, according to the Koran, the word "Muslim" refers to a state of being.

The Arabic meaning of Muslim is very comprehensive. It can best be described as someone who recognizes God as the Truth and is in a constant struggle to perfect his submission to Him. As the Koran says, "Who can be better in religion than one who submits his whole self to God, does good, and follows the way of Abraham the true in Faith? . . ." (4:125).

Since "Muslim" is a state of being, people are wrong to believe that it only applies to the followers of Muhammad. The Koran makes it clear that all the prophets, messengers, and those who followed them were Muslim because they were in submission to God's Will. A passage from the Koran about the life of the Prophet Jesus makes this concept clearer:

"When Jesus found Unbelief on their part he said: "Who will be my helpers to (the work of) God." Said the disciples: "We are God's helpers: We believe in God, and do bear witness that we are Muslims" (3:52).

The Kafir: A Faithless Self

Just as with the term "Muslim," the term "Kafir" has also been widely used in social and political contexts with a broad brush to mean anyone who is not a Muslim. Nothing can be further from the truth. The Koran uses the term *Kafir* to describe a soul that rejects faith — in other words, a soul which understands the Koranic message, knows it to be true, yet continues to reject it in one form or the other.

The story of Satan, who is the chief of *Kafirs,* gives more insight into the exact nature and personality of a rejecting soul. The sin that Satan committed, according to the Koran, was not questioning God's decision to ask angels and *Jinn* (see Chapter 9) to bow to Adam, but rather Satan's rejection of this command out of pride and arrogance:

"(God) said: 'O! Iblis (Satan), What is your reason for not being among those who prostrated themselves?' (Satan) replied: 'It is not for me to prostrate myself to man, whom You created from sounding clay, from mud molded into shape'" (15:32–33).

The Koran, therefore, identifies arrogance as the root cause of rejecting faith. Linguistically, *Kafir* comes from the root word meaning "a farmer who covers his seed with soil." Similarly, a soul that covers up the truth after it has been made clear is in a *Kafir* state.

Chapter 14

Achieving Koranic Ethics and Morality

In This Chapter

▶ Understanding the five ethical principles in the Koran

▶ Zooming into the Koranic perspective of good morals and values

▶ Purifying the heart and soul towards morality

T he Koran places heavy emphasis on building personal lives and societies that resonate with divinely-inspired ethics and morals.

In this chapter, I focus on what ethics and morals mean from the Koranic perspective, and how the Scripture teaches its followers to attain the moral ideal.

Discovering Ethical Principles in the Koran

Ethical principles in the Koran focus on preserving five essential elements. Every single law in Islam (see Chapter 17) finds its roots in one or more of these five principles.

Those entities that protect and preserve a healthy Islamic lifestyle are considered beneficial ethical engagements at the individual and societal level. However, those that violate Islamic laws and principles lead to unethical practices.

Preserving religion

The Koran requires Muslims to submit to God's Will completely and whole-heartedly (2:208). As such, preservation of Islam as a way of life and worship to God alone is among the foremost ethical principles. This ethical principle serves as the head of all other ethical laws and understandings in the Koran.

"Religion" refers not only to formal worship, but to the entire comprehensive system of living, including the five-pillars of Islam.

From the Koranic perspective, every individual in society has the obligation and right to worship the Divine. This obligation must be facilitated, honored, and protected by an Islamic society in order to live by the ethical teachings of the Koran (2:256; 22:40).

This principle also protects all other forms of worship, including the prayer offered in monasteries, synagogues, and churches. The Koran describes these houses of worship as places where God's name is exalted (22:40).

Also, included in the ethics of preserving religion is the obligation to defend Islam from destruction, corruption, and inner and outer threats, by armed struggle if necessary.

Preserving life

To save and preserve human life is ethical, and anything that unjustly takes life away is considered unethical. This tenet comes from the Koranic teaching that God made all life sacred (4:29; 6:151) regardless of religion, race, class, or any other characteristic that distinguishes people in the worldly sense. (See Chapter 9 for details on the Koranic perspective on the treatment of animals.)

Like the Torah, the Koran says that killing one person without just cause is like killing all of humanity; saving one life is equivalent to saving all of humanity (5:32). Killing innocents is regarded as one of the gravest sins a person can commit (25:68–69).

However, in order to save a life, sometimes the life of another needs to be taken away. The Koran says that in the law of just retribution there is life (2:179). For example, putting a murderous tyrant to death saves the lives of other people. Taking the life of such a person who threatens the life of others is, generally speaking, considered an ethical act.

Preservation of life must also take precedence over certain religious laws in the Koran. For example, the Koran prohibits eating pork, but if you are dying of starvation and the only thing available to eat is pork, then the ethical choice becomes eating pork in order to preserve human life. Similarly, alcohol is strictly forbidden by the Koran, but if alcohol is absolutely necessary for use as a medication to preserve human life, then alcohol is permitted, according to a majority of the scholars on Islamic law.

The ethics of abortion

Because it is clear, according to the Koran and prophetic sayings, that life begins in the womb (39:6, for example), abortion is viewed as unethical because it takes away an innocent life.

However, the mother's life takes precedence over the life of the fetus, because she is a full-fledged human being with relationships and responsibilities. If a doctor says that the mother's life is in danger because of her pregnancy, then a majority of Islamic scholars say that abortion is allowed in order to save the mother's life.

In 6:151 and 17:31, the Koran condemns and strictly prohibits taking a child's life due to fear of poverty. Also, female infanticide, which was very common in pre-Islamic Arabia, and unfortunately still is in some parts of the world, is also strictly forbidden in many passages throughout the Scripture (16:58–59, for example).

Preserving lineage

The Koran considers it one of the worst possible sins to cut sacred kinship bonds (4:1). Lineage preserves the identity of individuals within society; lineage also emboldens the family structure that is so essential to the development of a society based on Koranic ethics (see Chapter 15). (Among other reasons, the Koran prohibits fornication and adultery because these activities threaten the very foundation of family and destroy the lineage of children born out of wedlock.)

According to this ethic, last names that carry family lineage can't be changed; however, you see many cases in Muslim culture that violate this ethic. For example, many people who convert to Islam change their last names to more Arab-sounding names. According to a majority of scholars, they should not change their last names, because doing so violates preservation of lineage. Also, according to a majority of scholars, it's wrong for a woman to change her last name after marriage, because she remains a part of her own family heritage, even after marriage. However, scholars say that a woman should be allowed to add her husband's last name to her last name.

Enslaving another human being and changing his or her name and identity also violates this ethic of lineage preservation.

The Koran is so adamant about preserving lineage that it doesn't even allow adoption, at least not as it is commonly practiced in Western countries. Caring for an orphan qualifies as one of the highest acts of charity and responsibility, according to the Koran. (The Prophet even said that anyone who cares for an orphan will be as close to Him as middle and index fingers are on the Day of Judgment.) However, an orphan also has the right to preserve his or her heritage and lineage. Therefore, an orphan's last name should not be changed, and adoptive parents or caretakers should tell their adopted children where they come from (33:4–5). Adoption is permissible as long as the child's last name is preserved.

Preserving property

The Koran considers property sacred (2:188, for instance). Violating someone's property or wealth qualifies as unethical.

As such, taking another persons property by force, without just cause, is a major sin according to the Book. Doing so carries a heavy penalty. (See Chapter 17 for information on penal laws in the Koran.)

The Koran says, "O you who believe! Do not devour one another's possessions wrongfully — except by trade based on mutual agreement — and do not destroy one another: For behold, God is indeed compassionate towards you" (4:29).

Protecting property and enjoining in fair and beneficial business practices make up a major part of ethical principles in the Koran. Business ethics and laws count among the most important subjects for a healthy Islamic society.

Prophet Muhammad emphasized the sacredness of protecting property when he said that one who dies in the pursuit of defending his property or the property of others is a martyr in the sight of God.

Preserving honor

The Book says that God has honored and favored the children of Adam (all human beings) over any other of His creations (17:70).

Preserving, protecting, and nurturing this honorable status is a foremost concern of ethical teachings in the Koran. In fact, most actions prohibited by the Koran, such as public indecency, are prohibited in an effort to save the honor of human beings. Similarly, most actions encouraged by the Koran, such as modesty, are meant to raise the honor of human beings.

The Koran strongly warns against engaging in slandering, backbiting, and all other deeds that expose the faults of people in society (49: 12). According to Prophet Muhammad, one of the worst sins a person can commit is falsely accusing a chaste woman of sexual indecency. The Koran calls for the public flogging of those who accuse others of sexual immorality without any proof (24:23).

Ethics of human interaction also comprise a major part of preserving honor. The Koran commands Muslims to speak to one another only in the most kind and just manner. Therefore, making fun of people is completely prohibited in Islam (49:11).

The Koran also teaches that even those who speak or act towards Muslims in an unjust and ignorant manner should not be treated with the same dishonor. Rather, Muslims are instructed to respond with words of peace (25:63), and to repel evil with good, so that friendship replaces hatred (41:34; 25:72). From the Koran's perspective, treating even your personal enemies with respect eventually leads to good relations with that person.

Leading the Life of Good Virtue and Character

In the case of each quality that is undesirable and prohibited, the Koran encourages and enjoins the opposite behavior. For example, with the rejection of falsehood, the Koran enjoins speaking and acting on the truth. (To understand the full nature of what the Koran allows and disallows, see the previous section in this chapter.)

In the following sections, I look at morals and virtues that the Koran encourages and the immorality and vice it discourages its followers from practicing in their daily lives.

Discouraged behaviors

The Koran discourages Muslims from engaging in the following activities.

Falsehood and deception

The Koran shows great disdain for speaking or enjoining in falsehood of any type (26:222). The greatest falsehood, according to the Scripture, is joining partners with God (25:68). Those who try to deceive God through hypocrisy only deceive themselves (2:9). Also, the Book condemns those who try to deceive their fellow human beings (16:92).

The Book also strongly warns against bearing false testimony, and says that participating in falsehood makes people lose their dignity in society and in the sight of God (25:72).

Arrogance

The Scripture says that arrogance leads to disbelief in God, and the worst type of arrogance is to deny the Creator (4:172).

Arrogance is described as the way of tyrants and oppressors, all of whom will be doomed in the Hereafter (46:20). As such, Prophet Muhammad said, "He who has in his heart an atom of arrogance will not enter paradise."

Pretension

Sometimes the soul sinks into a constant desire to gain the praise and pleasure of other people instead of aspiring to please God. The Koran argues that when this happens, people have a hard time making good moral choices when they face difficult issues.

Prophet Muhammad described this insincerity towards working for the sake of God alone as a type of association with God *(Shirk)* that is as subtle as a black ant in the dark night.

But, by doing good deeds only for the sake of God, people can practice excellent morals and ethics, even if doing so draws the criticism and displeasure of those who seek worldly gain over what is right.

Hypocrisy

The Book gives special criticism of hypocrites who say that they believe in God, but all their actions, especially outside of the social eye, suggest otherwise (61:2–3). The Koran warns that such people think that they are deceiving other believers and God, but in fact they are only deceiving their own souls (4:142–143; 2:810).

Tyranny and injustice

The Koran speaks strongly against those who oppress others and spread fear and devastation on earth (2:204–206 for instance).

For example, the Koran condemns unjust rulers, such as the Pharaoh who fought Prophet Moses, and also those who treat their families with injustice and tyranny (16:90).

Prophet Muhammad said that such tyrants face severe punishment on the Day of Judgment (see Chapter 9), and any good action that they may have committed will transfer to the people they oppressed. Muhammad also said that the greatest form of *Jihad* (struggle in the path of God) is to speak the truth in front of a tyrant.

Transgression

According to the Scripture, *transgression* means explicitly violating God's laws. For example, God's law in the Koran states that a man and a woman must express sexual relations only within the institution of marriage. Therefore, fornication or adultery qualifies as a transgression of that law.

Secondly, transgression means going beyond the limits set by God. The Koran especially warns against exceeding the due limits that the Koran places in war: "Fight for the sake of God those who fight against you, but do not be aggressive. God does not love the aggressors."

The Koran also warns against being excessive in matters of law and theology. For example, forbidding things for yourself that God has not forbidden counts as excessive (5:87). From a theological perspective, in loving and respecting a prophet of God so much that you begin to attribute divinity to that prophet, you commit the worst sin by joining partners with God *(Shirk)*.

Wastefulness

The Koran says that God doesn't love those who waste the resources He provides (6:141). As such, Prophet Muhammad has said that men and women will be questioned on the Day of Judgment about how they spent every single penny of their wealth.

On the other hand, those who give money to charity only reluctantly fall into the materialism and hoarding of wealth that the Koran strongly condemns (104:2–3, for example).

Alcohol

Alcohol is completely prohibited in the Koran. Consuming alcohol leads to an unclear mind that can't exist in the state of God-consciousness required at every moment in a believer's life.

Also, alcohol and intoxicants in general open the harmful path of addiction and slavery to lower desires. Furthermore, the Koran warns that alcohol stirs up animosity between people in society because of the unintended actions and consequences brought on by drunkenness (5:91).

By prohibiting alcohol, the Koran seeks to protect both the individual and society from harm.

Gambling

Like alcohol, the Koran warns against games of chance because they can cause unintended animosity between people (5:91). Also, gambling can become so addictive, forcing people to fall into debt. To protect people against these ill consequences, the Scripture prohibits gambling.

Encouraged behaviors

The Koran encourages the opposite behavior of all the undesirable values and qualities mentioned in the previous section. In this section, I tell you about some additional morals and values taught by the Koran.

Sincerity

Doing righteous deeds only for the sake and pleasure of God should be a foremost concern for any believer, according to the Koran.

The Scripture also says that God judges intention as well as actions on the day of accountability (3:29). As such, Prophet Muhammad said, "God looks not at your figures, nor at your outward appearance, but He looks at your hearts and deeds." Muslims strive to abandon mundane concerns for the Real (the Divine).

Self reflection

The Koran urges its followers to reflect within themselves and on their deeds as a means of taking account before God does (3:190–194). Prophet Muhammad said, "A wise man is one who calls himself to account and does noble deeds to benefit him after death; and the foolish person is the one who submits himself to his temptations and desires and seeks from God the fulfillment of his vain desires."

Patience

Perhaps the most oft-mentioned of all qualities, the Koran repeatedly says that every Muslim must possess patience. In the name of patience, the Koran advises believers to say, "To God we belong, and to Him is our return" (2:153–157) in times of hardship, instead of expressing grief or animosity.

Secondly, the Book tells its followers to be patient when seeking help and aid from God. In other words, don't expect immediate results, because God will deliver His help at the best time, according to His Wisdom and Knowledge (2:214).

Thirdly, the Koran asks its followers to be steadfast and patient in controlling themselves against sin and their lower desires. As such, the Scripture says the righteous are those who pardon and forgive even when they are in a state of anger (3:134; 42:37). Also, Prophet Muhammad said, "The strong man is not the one who wrestles, but the one who controls himself when he is angry."

Forgiveness

The Book teaches believers to "show forgiveness, enjoin what is good, and turn away from the foolish" (7:199). The Koran says that God forgives those who forgive others for their shortcomings (24:22).

Prophet Muhammad said that all the prophets who came throughout history were persecuted by their people because people hated to hear the truth. But, each prophet always prayed to God for the forgiveness of his people by saying, "O God! Forgive my people, because they know not."

Practicing forgiveness is following in the moral footsteps of all the prophets.

Modesty

The Koran enjoins modesty on both men and women (23:5; 24:30–31) as a way of preserving the respect, dignity, and honor that God built into every human being (17:70). (See Chapter 15 for more on modest and sexuality.)

Modesty isn't limited only to the way someone dresses. Modesty also applies in showing humility when meeting other people (53:32) and talking in a balanced voice. For this reason, the Koran also teaches believers to lower their voices in modesty (31:19).

Simple living

The Book encourages its followers not to get bogged down in the short life of this world at the expense of an everlasting Hereafter. As such, the Koran discourages materialism and any type of overindulgence in worldly affairs (3:14; 35:5; 29:64; 57:20).

Prophet Muhammad warned about wealth and fame by saying that "Two hungry wolves sent into a flock of sheep are not more destructive to them than a man's greed for wealth and fame is to his religion."

Contentment

The Koran says that people should be happy with what God has blessed them with, and that they should never complain about the lack of anything. Nor should they go out and beg of others (2:273). Instead, believers should work hard and seek trust in God's sustenance (11:6).

Prophet Muhammad taught his companions, "Richness is not in plenty of provisions; the real richness is the richness of the soul." Muhammad also advised his followers that if their souls desired something, they should look to people less fortunate than themselves and praise God for His blessings.

Charity

The Scripture teaches that whatever you spend in charity, God will replace it with something even better (34:39). Also, generosity provides a means of purifying and benefiting the soul (2:272).

Using talents or energy for good causes also count as charity — not just giving money.

Prophet Muhammad said that even meeting your fellow brother (in humanity) with a smile is an act of charity. Muhammad also narrated a story of a man who came upon a thorny branch on the road. The man removed the branch in order to protect others from harm, and for this act, God forgave the man of his sins.

Purifying the Heart

Achieving a moral state of being that lives in constant remembrance of God (in word and deed) requires a pure heart, which directs human consciousness towards the "straight path" of excellent moral and ethical behavior. According to the Koran, someone who nurtures his soul has success, and someone who stunts its growth is destroyed (91:7–10).

In this section, I talk about some of the active measures that the Koran asks its followers to take, outside of the formal rituals, to attain a pure heart and soul.

This purity prepares the individual and society for actively enjoining in the morals and ethics of the Koran, and should, therefore, not be seen as an end in itself.

Remembering the Divine: Dhikr

The Koran says that God guides to His path, "Those who believe, and whose hearts find peacefulness in the remembrance of God: for without doubt in the remembrance of God do hearts find peacefulness" (13:28). This state of remembrance is called *Dhikr* in Arabic, which means several things, including to remember, to commemorate, to make mention of, to praise, and to give honor.

Devout Muslims purify their hearts by mentioning God and honoring Him in their daily lives (30:17). They remember God through ritual prayer, and also after the prayer, when Muslims sit quietly and mention God's attributes by three of His Names:

- *Subhan Allah* (God is most Perfect)
- *Allhamdulillah* (All praise is due to God)
- *Allahu'Akbar* (God is the greatest)

Worshippers mention each name about thirty-three times, while they reflect on God's attributes.

Following in this tradition, Muslims mention God at the beginning of every action by saying, "In the name of God, the most Merciful, the most Compassionate." When Muslims want to praise someone else or mention something good that happened in their own lives, they say, "By the will of God *(Mash'Allah)."* When hoping or promising for something good in the future, Muslims are required to say, "If God wills *(Insh'Allah)"* (18:23–24).

Mentioning God dispels thoughts and feelings that take a person away from God-consciousness. *Dhikr,* then, stems from *Tawbah,* or returning to God, in which an individual seeks to replace the mundane with the Real so that the soul remembers God's presence even during the most difficult or tempting of times.

Many Muslims and students of Islam mistakenly believe that *Dhikr* means simply sitting in a corner and mentioning God's name. While doing so can lead to deep reflection, it alone does not fulfill the purpose of *Dhikr.* Actions contribute to *Dhikr,* as well. When you praise and honor God in your life through pious and righteous deeds, you complete the process of *Dhikr.*

Following God's laws

Some people mistakenly believe that *Shariah,* or Islamic law, is a set of penal codes that an Islamic government applies over its citizens. In truth, *Shariah* (see Chapter 17) is a comprehensive system of laws that governs individual life as well as state affairs.

Islamic law benefits the individual soul and society at large. In doing so, Islamic law also protects individuals and society from spiritual and physical destruction. The sacred law establishes certain behavior, such as murder, adultery, and stealing, as the worst of social evils. In order to prevent such immorality from existing, Islamic law prescribes rules and regulations that act as a protecting border against the major sins. So, generally speaking, actions that can reasonably lead to major sins are also considered unlawful.

For example, Islamic law prohibits a man and woman who are not related or married to each other from meeting in complete seclusion. This law protects both man and woman from pursuing a course of action that violates the limits of sexual relations outlined in the Koran. By following this Islamic law, Muslims avoid falling into the major sin of fornication and adultery.

Also, this law preserves the sanctity of honor that forms one of the five elements of Islamic law and ethics (see "Discovering Ethical Principles in the Koran," earlier in this chapter); neither man nor woman can falsely accuse the other of any type of indecency since they are in the presence of witnesses in the public eye.

Ultimately, obedience to God's laws protects the individual, and society, from sins that lead to major harm and corruption. These divine laws nurture the soul towards purification and away from evil.

Keeping company with pious people

To help motivate the heart and soul towards the path of purification, the Koran advises believers to seek the gathering of righteous people (18:28) who engage themselves in God-conscious ways — both in speech and deed.

Prophet Muhammad provides an analogy to describe the influence of good company and bad company in one's life. He says that the influence of good company is like the presence of good smelling musk that also gives you a nice smell. Similarly, the influence of bad company is like the presence of a bad odor.

Controlling passion and struggling for good

Devout Muslims practice *Jihad* every single day by struggling against their lower passions and emotions. For example, when a Muslim gets angry, but holds back his or her anger, that person practices *Jihad.*

Practicing *Jihad* in this manner helps Muslims attain the ideal personality based on Koranic ethics and morals; every individual has inner and outer temptations that can lead to impurity in the heart and mind.

Practicing self-restraint and struggling for good, both in individual and social contexts, purifies the soul by turning the heart's attention and desire to the path of God (29:69).

See Chapter 18 for more information about *Jihad.*

Chapter 15
Raising a Family the Koranic Way

In This Chapter

▶ Building a moral society through the family

▶ Becoming husband and wife

▶ Raising children

▶ Dealing with issues of inheritance and divorce

The institution of family represents the cornerstone of a Muslim community that centers around Koranic ideals. The Book describes the truly Islamic household as one that represents and spreads divine light to society at large. As such, the relationship between a man and a woman in marriage, according to Scriptural teachings, is a sign of divine Tranquility, Love, and Mercy. The relationships between members of a family represent the highest acts of kindness in the Koran.

In this chapter, I focus on specific passages that define the institution of family in the Koran and take a look at various relationships within the family unit. Also, I discuss some controversies regarding family ethics and what the Scripture has to say about those issues.

Healthy Family Equals Healthy Society

The Koran espouses a family built around God-consciousness, out of which emerges mutual rights and responsibilities.

Through the family, God's creation continues to grow and spread on earth, or not. If the institution of family is corrupt, then corruption spreads throughout the world; if the family institution is pure, it, in turn, produces a highly moral and ethical society based on divine values. Through marriage, human populations spread throughout the earth, along with values that either give rise or fall to human dignity, depending on the ethical and moral practices of the family.

Prophet Muhammad said that "Ties of blood-relation *(Rahem)* are derived from the most-Merciful *(Al-Rahman),* and God says to it: 'Whoever keeps you, I shall join him. And whoever severs you, I shall sever connection with him.'" Whoever acts to preserve and strengthen the family receives God's Mercy. But, whoever cuts family ties and weakens the group loses God's Mercy in his or her life.

This and other strongly worded teachings stress the sanctity of the family institution. Islamic scholars also point out that the family relationship is so naturally close that if patience, mercy, forgiveness, and other qualities of healthy coexistence can't be practiced within the family, then society has little hope of achieving those qualities.

Looking for a Spouse: Let the Search Begin

Searching for a suitable spouse is probably one of the most interesting aspects of Muslim culture. Generally speaking, Islam forbids dating, or at least "dating" as understood in most Western cultures. Usually, Muslim marriages become a family project in which parents, uncles, aunts, siblings, and close friends take a dip into the complex sea of matchmaking. As such, Muslims often joke that the "Auntie-net is faster than the Internet" if you are looking to get married.

Sometimes Muslim parents arrange marriage for their sons and daughters with extended relatives and close family friends, and other times, spouses meet through mutual friends. Even when a Muslim man and woman know each other personally and decide to pursue marriage, the man usually asks his parents to approach the woman's family for her hand in marriage.

Forced marriage is completely forbidden in Islamic law, as alluded to in 4:19. Both the man and woman must agree and consent to the marriage in order for it to be considered legitimate by Islamic courts. A few Muslim cultures practice forced marriage, particularly poor societies, but such marriages violate Islamic teachings, rather than fulfill them, as some would have you believe.

Looking beyond the surface

The Koran advises Muslim men and women to marry those who are virtuous believers of God, even if the virtuous may not be as physically attractive or economically rich as those who disbelieve in God and don't practice good morals.

In fact, the Scripture says that it is better to marry a virtuous slave rather than an amoral free man or woman (2:221). For pre-Islamic Arabs, it was inconceivable that a free rich man or woman would marry a slave, and the Scripture seeks to remove this baseless stigma. This passage is a revolutionary concept in many societies, even today, where people base marriage on socioeconomic class and looks, rather than virtue and good morals.

Muhammad taught his companions that although some men marry some women for their status, money, and beauty, the only man who will be happy and successful is the one who marries a woman for her virtue and piety. Once Muhammad advised his closest companion, Abu Bakr, that the most treasured things in life are "the tongue in remembrance of God, the heart filled with thanks to God, and a pious wife who helps in virtuous deeds."

Whatever advice the Koran gives to men about a wife also applies to women in search of a husband, because the term *Aawj* can be translated as either "wife" or "spouse." Also, the Koran addresses both men and women, unless specifically stated otherwise.

Prophet Muhammad advised women that if they are satisfied with a prospective husband's piety and character, they should marry him. Muhammad further added that "If you do not do so, there will be trials on earth and a great deal of evil." Scholars have interpreted this remark as commentary on how the individual family unit can impact society; if the husband is corrupt, then the family is easily corruptible, which can, in turn, lead to corruption in society (see the section "Healthy Family Equals Healthy Society," earlier in this chapter, for more information on the Koranic view of the importance of family).

Islam prides itself as a religion that combines the idealistic with the practical. As such, it isn't forbidden to marry based on beauty, wealth, status, and other such considerations, but both Scripture and prophetic tradition highly recommend marriage first and foremost based on good virtue and character.

Making sure the marriage is legal

The Koran allows for the marriage of any man or woman regardless of race, cultural background, or status. However, the Koran does impose some restrictions on marriage partners, including the following:

- **Divorced wives of your father (4:22):** Prohibits a common practice found in pre-Islamic Arabia.

- **All immediate relatives (4:23):** Prohibits marriage to parents, children, siblings, aunts, uncles, nieces, nephews, milk-mothers (those who fed you milk as a child, such as a wet nurse) and their children, daughters- and sons-in-law, and brothers- and sisters-in-law.

✔ **Women who are already married (4:24):** Women who are already married can't marry other men (see the following section to see how this issue plays out for men in the Koran).

Giving equal time: Polygamy for men

Some people unfamiliar with Islam and the Koran say that the Book encourages polygamy for men. In truth, the Scripture seeks to limit polygamy, which was uncontrolled and widely practiced in pre-Islamic times across Arabia and other parts of the world. So, to say that the Scripture advocates polygamy is both factually and historically incorrect.

According to the Koran, a man is allowed, in principal, to marry up to four women at one time as long as he can deal with all his wives justly. The man must provide economical, physical, and emotional care equally to all his wives if he chooses to have more than one. If a man can't do justice to all his wives, he can't marry more than one (4:3). In traditional Islamic law, scholars have said that a man can't marry even one woman if he or his family can't support her with proper care (24:33).

The Koran also warns that men will "never be able to do justice between wives no matter how sincerely they try" (4:129). Some scholars interpret this passage as allowing men to have more feelings for one wife over another, because it is impossible to control that aspect of human nature. However, other scholars have understood this verse to mean that polygamy is highly discouraged, because it is nearly impossible to deal justly with more than one wife. These scholars also argue that polygamy should only be practiced in times of necessity, such as during times of war, when typically the ratio of women to men dramatically increases. In such situations, these scholars argue, polygamy can be used so that women aren't forced to remain single if they want to marry.

Also, Muslims often point out that polygamy, in which marriage is sanctified by love and certain rights and responsibilities, is much better from a moral standpoint than adultery. As such, instead of becoming involved in a secret love affair, it is much better to honor the family system by committing to the sacred institution of marriage.

Forced marriage is completely forbidden by the Koran (see "Looking for a Spouse: Let the Search Begin," earlier in this chapter, for more information), which has some implications on the issue of polygamy. The first wife must consent in order for a polygamous arrangement to be considered acceptable in an Islamic court. Also, according to a majority of Islamic jurists, the first wife can stipulate in her marriage contract that she will not accept her husband taking another wife, and by Islamic law, the man then has to honor that contract.

Explaining the bridal gift *(Mahr)*

The bridal gift *(Mahr)* is sometimes wrongly described as "buying a woman from her family." This major misconception has no basis in the Islamic tradition. The woman isn't considered a possession that can be purchased. Also, every single penny of the bridal gift goes to the woman, and not to her family, so it would make no sense to describe the bridal gift as "buying the woman" or anything else like that.

The bridal gift provides a means of creating good will between the couple, and also serves to provide some sort of financial independence to the woman so that she can maintain her own wealth. No one can take a single penny from the woman's bridal gift unless she gives it out of her own good will.

The *Mahr* can be given all at once up front, or in installments over time, depending on mutual agreement of those involved. Also, a wife may remit some part of her bridal gift from the goodness of her heart if she so wishes even after the contract has been agreed upon (4:4; 4:24). However, Islamic law forbids forcing a woman to give up any part of her dowry.

The couple decides the form of the gift before the marriage. It can consist of a large sum of money or can be as little as a small gift. For example, I knew a man during my stay in the Middle East whose bridal gift for his wife was $50,000! On the other hand, I have a friend whose bridal gift to his wife consisted of a copy of the Koran and a prayer rug.

Prophet Muhammad even allowed a man to teach his wife chapters of the Koran that he had memorized to fulfill his dowry requirement. The form of the dowry really depends on what the couples want to do.

Celebrating Marriage as the Basis of Family

The Koran considers marriage as a divine institution through which the greatest acts of tranquility, love, and mercy are displayed in society as a manifestation of divine qualities on earth. According to the Book, the deep and intimate relationship between a man and a woman in marriage qualifies as a sign of God's existence and creation (30:21).

Scholars say that putting love and mercy into a relationship results in tranquility for both husband and wife. That sense of peace and calm then spreads to the family, which in turn, disperses it to the entire society.

The Koran also says, "They (women) are a garment for you (men), and you (men) are a garment for them (women) . . ." (2:187). This passage describes the marriage relationship as one built on mutual cooperation and trust that brings comfort, completeness, and beauty to the soul, just as a good garment does for the body. Also, the Koran says that husband and wife should live together on "a footing of kindness and equity . . ." (4:19). In another passage, the Koran describes the relationship between men and women (in general as well as in marriage) as "friends and protectors of one another" (9:71) in righteous actions that establish good in society. So, the Koran really sees the overall spirit between couples as one of cooperation — not competition.

Practically speaking: Basic functions within a marriage

Before I take a deeper look into this subject, I must point out that you have to look at Koranic laws and teachings regarding the rights and responsibilities of marriage under the broad light of the cooperative spirit of marriage.

Rights are based on responsibilities. Rights are sacredly bestowed by divine will, and not given to prefer the man over the woman, or the other way around. Rights make the fulfillment of responsibilities easier and more accessible.

Since the marital roles of man and woman complement each other, Islamic law stipulates that a husband's responsibilities are his wife's rights, and a wife's responsibilities are her husband's rights. Therefore, I focus on the responsibilities, with the understanding that those responsibilities correspond to the rights of the other spouse.

Providing for the family

The Koran teaches that a man must bear the responsibility of taking care of all the financial needs of his wife and family (4:34). He must provide for their food, clothing, housing, and all other necessities (65:6–7).

The Koran places this responsibility on the man's shoulders because, traditionally, men had more access to work. Because of the physical limitations presented by such realities as childbirth, placing the responsibility of providing for the family on the woman was thought to be unfair. This doesn't, however, mean that women aren't allowed to work outside the home. (See Chapter 19 for more on women in the Koran.)

Leading the family

Prophet Muhammad said that "a man is a guardian and responsible for his family." The Koran also places the responsibility of leadership on the man in providing for the family (4:34) and steering it towards a morally good life.

Many men misunderstand familial leadership as a right, a sign of how badly the concept of leadership is understood today. Leadership, in fact, entails a very heavy responsibility in the Koran and prophetic teachings. Leadership requires a great deal of justice, patience, and kind treatment. Leadership is abused when it takes the form of oppression and tyranny; leadership is fulfilled when it takes the form of justice and mercy.

Some people think that this leadership responsibility gives the husband unilateral authority to make and enforce decisions on behalf of the family. Actually, men, and all leaders for that matter, must practice *Shura,* or mutual consultation that encourages consent, according to Scriptural teachings (2:233; 42:38). If some disagreement on any issue arises, the man doesn't have the right to make a decision based on his own whims and desires. Rather, he must resolve the dispute based on Koranic and prophetic teachings, and the resultant decision must benefit family and society alike.

Protecting the family

The mother bears the responsibility to look after the house and actively raise the children into righteous, pious, ethical, and moral men and women. The Koran honors the mother as the teacher of society, without whom the moral stability of civilization would crumble (46:15–18).

According to some scholars, looking after the house means protecting her family's property with honor. It doesn't mean that she is obligated to do house chores, such as cooking and cleaning. Rather, this work must happen in mutual support by husband, wife, and children. (Even Prophet Muhammad helped his wife in the home, and washed and mended his own clothes.) If a wife takes on these household chores as her responsibility, she does an act of charity for which she will be greatly rewarded, but such work is not considered part of her obligatory responsibility. However, other scholars believe that house chores do constitute a part of a woman's responsibility to her family; these scholars also believe that, in the example of Prophet Muhammad, the husband should help with these chores.

Obeying and rebelling within the family

Since the Koran says that the husband has been placed in a leadership position within the family unit (see the section, "Leading the family," earlier in this chapter), the wife and children have the responsibility to "obey" him (4:34), rather than to rebel against his decisions simply for the sake of rebellion. Of course, this obedience is not absolute or unqualified. A husband's leadership must fall within the guidelines of permissible actions in Islamic law, must remain within his rights, and must not transgress the laws of God.

For example, if a husband asks his wife not to make the intention for voluntary fast on a specific day so that he may experience sexual intimacy with her (which is impermissible during a fast), then she should, generally speaking, grant permission for that request. But, if a man asks his wife not to fast during Ramadan (when fasting is obligatory), then she must not obey her husband, because he would be asking her to do something which violates the laws of God.

At times, it even becomes obligatory for a wife to rebel against her husband. For example, Pharaoh's wife, who is praised in the Koran for opposing her husband's tyranny and oppression, did just that. Sometimes justice necessitates rebellion in order to preserve the family unit.

But, as mentioned in the previous section, the family unit works in mutual consultation and sincere leadership, not with dictatorial or oppressive ways.

Intimacy: Both spiritual and physical

Both spouses enjoy the right to experience sexual intimacy with one another. The Koran views sex within marriage as a healthy and sacred act that merits divine rewards and blessings. In fact, the Koran encourages couples to perform some good actions that bring purity to the souls, such as remembering God by mentioning His Names, before engaging in sexual intimacy (2:223). The Koran regards the sexual experience between a couple as both a spiritual act and a physical one.

According to the Koran, both husband and wife have the responsibility to make themselves sexually available and attractive for each other. Often times, sexual intimacy is seen only as a right of a husband over his wife, and there is no doubt that that right is stressed more in the teachings of Prophet Muhammad. But the husband must also fulfill the physical and spiritual need of the wife. In fact, some jurists were so concerned with preserving this right for women that some schools of law even say that a man must not abandon his wife sexually for more than four days at a time. All scholars agree that a husband abandoning his wife without cause is completely impermissible.

However, a man must also take his wife's mood and health into account before engaging in sexual activity. In order to regulate the man's sexual nature that may neglect the condition of his wife, the Koran forbids the man to have sexual intercourse with his wife during her period (2:222), and Islamic law has made other similar regulations in order to safeguard the woman's health and wellbeing.

Also, Prophet Muhammad taught his companions to approach their wives in a way that takes her feelings into account as much as their own, by saying: "Let none of you fall upon his wife like a donkey falls upon a she donkey." In other words, sexual intimacy should consist of human compassion and love, rather than animalistic drive.

Also, anal intercourse is strictly prohibited as an unhealthy practice, and one that resembles animal behavior, rather than dignified human intimacy. But, all positions of vaginal intercourse are permitted by the Koran (2:223).

Preserving modesty through Scriptural teaching

Sexuality is considered sacred, and not shameful, only if it surfaces within the institution of legal marriage. As such, Islamic law seeks to guard modesty outside of the sacred relationship of marriage. Guarding chastity and modesty is one of the most oft repeated ethical teachings in the Koran. Prophet Muhammad even said that the defining characteristic of Islam is modesty.

The Koran speaks about public modesty in the definitive passage 24:30–31. This passage begins by urging Muslim men "to lower their gaze and to be mindful of their chastity" so that they may attain a pure state of God-consciousness (24:30).

The sayings of Prophet Muhammad state that the physical modesty of a man consists of covering at the very least his body from the navel to the knees. However, if the man can afford to purchase enough cloth, and he doesn't work in the fields, then he is encouraged to also cover his chest and abdomen area. Also, men must wear loose clothes so as to not define the shapes of the body. Shirts that display muscles are a no-no in the Islamic tradition of modesty, as an example.

The passage continues in 24:31 to tell Muslim women that they should also "lower their gaze and to be mindful of their chastity." The passage continues to describe the woman's modesty in more detail: "and not to display their charms beyond what may be apparent thereof. Hence, let them draw their head-coverings over their bosoms."

Classical interpretations take this passage to mean that women should cover their entire bodies, except for their faces, hands, and feet in public — most Muslim women around the world follow this practice. However, a stricter interpretation takes this passage to mean that the woman's entire body, including the face, hands, and feet, should be covered.

A more liberal rendering — found in modernist interpretations — of this verse says that this passage obligates women to cover their chests and dress modestly, something that wasn't practiced by pre-Islamic Arabian women. Women who follow this interpretation believe that the covering doesn't include the hair and arms, both of which are covered under traditional Islamic dresses for women. However, this is a weak opinion because the verse specifically talks about extending the *Hijab* over the chest, but not to the exclusion of the head.

The dress, like the male's dress, must also be loose and must not define the shape of the woman's body, especially her chest area. In certain cultures, such as in Saudi Arabia, women dress in all black. Yet, in other cultures, such as in West Africa, women actually dress in very bright colors, such as yellow and blue. This is more of a cultural preference then a religious one.

Also, the woman doesn't have to dress with this level of modesty within the privacy of her home in front of other women, her immediate male relatives, male servants who are beyond an age of sexual desire, and unrelated children who are innocent of sexual conceptualizations (24:31).

Public modesty sanctifies the honor of both men and women, so that they may function honorably in society without being glorified or condemned for their physical appearance. In other words, the "dress code" seeks to protect both men and women from looking at each other through the lens of sexuality, and encourages a relationship of mutual dignity and respect.

As such, the Koran also encourages men and women to lower their eyes when they meet each other, rather than stare each other in the face (24:30–31). If you meet a Muslim of the opposite sex and he or she doesn't look you in the eye, don't misunderstand that as a sign of disrespect. Rather, it is an expression of respect for the opposite gender in Islamic culture.

Bringing Up Children

A supplication that Muslims are encouraged to recite every day says, "O our Sustainer! Grant that our spouses and our offspring be a joy to our eyes, and cause us to be foremost among those who are conscious of You." This beautiful prayer must also be backed up by beautiful actions in raising children and the family as a whole.

Raising righteous children qualifies as one of the greatest acts of charity for society. Prophet Muhammad said that he guaranteed paradise for anyone who raised three righteous daughters, as they become the first teachers of God-consciousness and set high moral standards for their children. These children, then, spread these qualities of righteousness all across the earth wherever they go.

The following sections examine the intimate relationship between parents and their children.

Treating parents well: The best act of piety

The Koran calls on Muslims to treat their parents in the most beautiful manner *(Al-Ihsan)* with the highest acts of kindness, mercy, and love *(Al-Birr)*. The Scripture even forbids a child to show a sign of disrespect to his or her parents by sighing in frustration, and instead calls on children to speak to their parents with kindness, reverence, and humility (17:23–24). Other than Prophet Muhammad, parents are the only other characters in the Koran that are mentioned side-by-side with God in the same verse to indicate the respect and thanks that is owed to them (31:14).

The Koran especially asks for respect and kindness towards the mother, who goes through much pain and hardship to give birth and provide complete sustenance after birth (46:15). As such, Muhammad said that the garden of paradise lies beneath the feet of a mother. So, as you can see, the position of mother is the most prestigious position in an Islamic society.

According to the Koran, children have the following responsibilities towards their parents:

- **Showing obedience to the parents (31:14–15):** Part of the concept of *Ihsan,* or beautiful treatment of your parents, is to hold them in such honor that you obey them when they ask you to do something, unless they ask you to do something that violates the laws of God. However, the parents too have the responsibility to give respect to the wishes of their children, and must not act like tyrant dictators.

- **Supporting parents in old age (17:23):** Just as your parents support and maintain you when you are young, you also have the responsibility to support and maintain them when they reach old age. You must provide for their food, home, and clothing if they can't do so for themselves. Muslim families often enjoy joint-family situations where parents and children live together in one house even after the children marry.

- **Providing sincere advice:** Despite the high respect that is to be shown to your parents, it is also your responsibility to advise and remind them if they err in the path of wrongdoing. For example, in the Koran, Prophet Abraham calls on his father with the highest words of love and respect *(Ya Abati),* "O my father!" Abraham advises his father to turn away from the pagan practices of his people and to worship One God alone without associating any partners (19:42–44).

> Even when Abraham's father rejects him, and threatens to stone him to death because of his preaching, Abraham responds to his father with utmost kindness by saying, "Peace be upon you!" And, Abraham continues to pray for his father's guidance and forgiveness (19:47–48).

Raising children with wisdom

Passage 31:13–19, named after Luqman, a sage known for his great wisdom in the Koran, contains the most detailed passage regarding the rearing of children. Luqman addresses his son in the kindest and most loving manner, by saying: "*Ya Bunayya*" or "O my (dear) son!"

Luqman offers the following advice to his beloved son, which serves as a five-step guideline for Muslim parents even today:

✔ **Do not ascribe partners with God** *(Tawhid)* **(31:13):** The first aspect of wisdom that parents teach their children is the oneness of God without associating any partners with Him whatsoever, known as *Tawhid*. From this teaching emanates all other religious guidance on virtue, ethics, and morality.

✔ **God is all aware of your actions** *(Taqwa)* **(31:16):** The second aspect of wisdom parents should teach children is that God is all-knowing, and will bring forth even "a mustard seed" that is hidden "in a rock." In other words, after teaching your children *Tawhid* (oneness of God), you have the responsibility to teach them that God is near to them and watches over every action and word that a child may utter *(Taqwa)*. This instills a state of constant divine awareness within the child that prevents him or her from evil deeds even in the privacy of his or her own home. *Taqwa* also motivates the child towards good even under the most difficult circumstances.

✔ **The ways of righteous actions (31:17):** The story of Luqman says that parents need to show their children the paths of righteous actions by "establishing prayer, and enjoining the doing of what is right and forbid the doing of what is wrong, and bear in patience all hardship." The parents instruct their children in spiritual practices (prayer) and show them how to become active members of society in struggling for justice in all its forms. The underlying principal says to bear the struggle for spiritual growth and societal development with a patient heart that is at peace and not in turmoil. In other words, the inner state of the child directly affects his outward state and behavior.

✔ **Teaching the child humility (31:18):** Parents must teach the child to speak and act towards all of God's creation with humility, and to walk on the earth in a gentle manner, rather than with pride. The basics of morality can never live side-by-side with false pride.

✔ **Teaching the child modesty (31:19):** Raising your children with wisdom requires that you teach them nice manners, which are defined most of all by modesty and gentle speech. Scholars say that Luqman teaches these two qualities in particular because in Islamic spirituality the tongue is known as the interpreter of the heart. If the heart is corrupt, then this corruption comes out in foul and harsh language. And, if the heart is pure, then it comes out in kind, modest, and soft speech as the tongue mirrors a pure soul.

Parental responsibilities to their children

Aside from the responsibilities mentioned in the previous section, the Koran says that parents also bear the following responsibilities towards their children:

✔ **Providing a good name:** Parents must choose good names for their children that recognize their dignity as human beings. These names often take the form of a nice meaning (such as *Sabira,* meaning the patient one) or the remembrance of an honorable man or woman. For example, my parents named my sister Sohaira after a companion of Prophet Muhammad who traveled great distances each day in the pursuit of knowledge.

Prophet Muhammad said that the most loved names by God are Abdullah (servant of God) and Abdul-Rahman (servant of the most Merciful).

✔ **Providing maintenance and sustenance:** The parents must provide utmost love, compassion, mercy, forgiveness, and all other qualities that nurture a spiritually and physically healthy child who can become an active and positive influence in his or her community. This responsibility entails clothing, feeding, and housing your children to the best of your ability.

✔ **Providing children with an education:** Parents must provide their children with a good education, so that they may function to the best of their abilities in society. Prophet Muhammad said that "the seeking of knowledge is incumbent upon all Muslim men and Muslim women." So, according to Muhammad's teachings, it is wrong to discriminate against good education for women. This is why some of the greatest teachers of the Islamic tradition, including the Prophet's wives, were women. Education here transcends formal schooling. It is the proper physical, psychological, worldly, and spiritual nurturing that is obligated here.

A Matter of Inheritance: Who Gets What

The Koran lays out extremely detailed laws of inheritance, which promote equitable distribution of wealth among family members. These very complex inheritance laws count among the most detailed subjects in the books of Islamic law.

The following breakdown tells you who gets what according to the Koranic passage 4:11–12:

- **Children's inheritance:** Sons inherit the equivalent of two sisters' shares. If the family has more than two daughters, then each daughter receives a two-thirds share. If the family has only one daughter, she receives one-half of the inheritance.

- **Parent's inheritance:** If a man or woman dies leaving children behind, then his or her parents receive one-sixth of the inheritance. But, if he or she dies without any children, with the parents the only heirs, then the mother receives a one-third share. If the man has brothers and sisters, then the mother receives one-sixth of the inheritance.

- **Spouse's inheritance:** If a woman leaves behind no children, her husband receives one-half. But, if she leaves behind children, then her husband receives one-quarter of her wealth.

  If a man dies without leaving behind any children, then his wife receives one-quarter of his wealth. But, if the man leaves behind children, then the wife receives one-eighth of his inheritance.

- **Sibling's inheritance:** If a man or woman has no direct heir in the form of children, then both his brother and sister receive one-sixth. But, if more than one brother or sister exists, then each sibling inherits one-third.

In all cases, the inheritance is given out only after all contractual agreements and debts have been paid off in behalf of the deceased.

However, inheritance laws in Islamic law are not as simple as they appear to be at first. In reality, the books of classical Islamic law spend hundreds of pages explaining the inheritance laws — of which there are 40 branches — in detail. The verse of the Koran only provides an established framework. The application of these laws proves quite sophisticated and complex.

You may have noticed that in most cases of inheritance, the woman receives about half of what the male receives. Islamic scholars point out that this isn't because the woman is worth half of a man, as is wrongly believed by some. Rather, the man, within Islam's family structure, has much greater financial responsibility than the woman. Islamic law obligates the man to financially provide for his wife, children, and other dependents, such as parents and siblings, who can't sustain themselves. The woman, on the other hand, isn't obligated to spend a single penny of her wealth on anyone, including her family, unless she does so from the kindness of her own heart. The laws of inheritance are not equal between genders, but they are equitable based on the financial responsibility that each bears within the family unit. As such, Muslim women often jokingly tell their husbands, "What is yours is mine, and what is mine is mine."

Tackling Divorce in the Koran

Divorce is known as the "most hated, permissible act in the site of God," according to Prophet Muhammad. Divorce is highly discouraged, but permissible in order to deal with the realities of life. To make peace and reconciliation is by far the better path to take (4:19–21). However, the Koran strongly forbids men from holding their wives in marriage against their will.

If a major dispute exists between man and wife, the Koran advises that an arbitrator from the woman's side and an arbitrator from the man's side should come together and try to resolve the marital dispute in fairness (4:35).

Once a man declares divorce to his wife verbally, the couple separates for four months to think things over (2:226). If the couple still wants divorce after this period, then the woman must undergo a "waiting period of three monthly courses" before remarrying (2:228). This waiting period avoids any confusion regarding paternity in the case of pregnancy.

Also, during this period, the Koran gives the couple yet another chance to reconcile and put things right by recommitting themselves in marriage (2:228). After this period expires, then either the couple should get back together or peacefully separate on equitable and fair terms (2:229).

Scholars differ on whether a woman can initiate divorce (4:128). A majority of scholars believe that a woman can indeed initiate divorce with generally the same rights as a man. If the man initiates divorce, then he must fulfill his obligation to pay the bridal gift (see the sidebar "Explaining the bridal gift (*Mahr*)," earlier in this chapter) before he can divorce his wife, unless the woman forgoes this right. The Koran encourages "an amicable settlement between the husband and wife" (4:128) in all such cases.

For more information on the Koran's laws regarding care of the children and other aspects of divorce, read passage 2:224–233.

Part V
Relating the Koran to the World

The 5th Wave · By Rich Tennant

"Maybe we should read the Koran to help us interpret this event."

In this part . . .

This part examines the Koranic perspective on social change, law, war and peace, women's rights, and Islam in relation to modernity. The diversity of voices on these topics is too great to present in single chapters. As such, not all Muslims share the same views that I offer on these global debates.

Chapter 16

Connecting the Koran to Society

In This Chapter

▶ Taking middle ground in faith and society

▶ Bearing witness to the truth

▶ Doing battle with evil and fostering good

▶ Making brothers of all men and women

▶ Fighting against oppression for the sake of God

Muslims believe that the Koran was sent to provide moral guidelines for both individuals and society. The Koran and *Hadith* discourage a hermit-type lifestyle devoid of any social rights and responsibilities. The Koran sees the body of Muslims, known as *Ummah* in Arabic, as the vehicle of God's justice that should establish divine laws and teachings on earth.

In this chapter, I explore the characteristics and mission of a divinely-organized community according to the Koran. I also look into the divine rights that God gave humanity in the Koranic worldview. Finally, I provide insight into Muslim and non-Muslim relations as well as the concept of *Jihad*.

Divining a Community of the Middle Path

The Koran says, "And thus have We made you to be a community of the middle path, so that you might be witnesses to the truth before all mankind, and that the Messenger might bear witness to it before you . . ." (2:143).

This verse has caused a lot of discussion and disagreement between commentators of the Koran, who point out various aspects of this verse in its textual and historical context. I focus on those commentaries and understandings that deal with the subject of how the Koran relates to society.

The path of moderation, or balance, comes forth in four fundamental ways that define an ideal society as envisioned by the Koran.

Having a balanced approach to the Divine

Theologically, the Koran presents a balanced approach to the relationship between God and humans. At once, God is both intimately near (2:186, 50:16), like a friend, and at the same time, above and unlike His creation, like a king (10:3).

Scholars of Islamic theology account for this contrast in imagery by pointing out that God is so Great and Omnipresent that He needs no intercessor to hear the prayers and cries of his servants; God is with every human being regardless of where he or she is. However, at the same time, the Koran says that He is the Creator and Sustainer of the universe, and therefore all worship and service is due to Him alone.

The Koran strikes a balance between the two extremes of God's friendship and Lordship with humanity. Both are necessary for the proper function of the human soul. If a person has an idea of God as friend without understanding God as Creator, then the soul and body can stray away from worship and servitude to the Divine. At the same time, if a person, or society, believes that God exists only above and beyond creation as the Creator, then feelings of loss and despair can develop, without the knowledge and understanding that God and His help are near (2:214).

Similarly, the Koran and prophetic tradition call for a balance between fear of divine Justice and hope in divine Mercy. Prophet Muhammad described fear and hope in God as the two sandals of a spiritual traveler. Scholars have likened hope and fear as the two wings of a bird that give a creature strength and straightness in flight.

The Koran warns against extremes in hope for God's mercy and fear of God. Having excessive hope in God's mercy can lead the soul and society to neglect responsibilities before God and transgress the boundaries of God's laws. At the other extreme, having too much fear of God's wrath can make an individual or society extremely rigid, without the understanding that God is Merciful and loves to Forgive.

Balancing the worldly and the spiritual in society

The balanced, middle path described in Koranic teachings takes both human strengths and weaknesses into account. The middle path recognizes the need for a balance between the two extremes of the worldly (*Dunya*) and the spirit

(Ruh) found in the human experience. The middle way negates the conflict between flesh and spirit, which join together in an interdependent marriage under the middle path.

Two commandments, which the Koran almost always mentions together, create this balance: prayer *(Salat)* and the payment of purifying alms *(Zakat)*. Prayer provides the freedom of worship and grounds for a healthy spiritual community that lives in a constant state of God-consciousness. Purifying alms uplift the status of the poor and institute socioeconomic justice in society. With these two institutions, the Koran calls for the middle path between the needs of the self and of society.

An example of this middle way between spiritual and worldly is found in Prophet Muhammad's advice to the prayer leaders (known as *Imam* in Arabic) of his community: "When anyone of you leads the prayer, he should not prolong it because the congregation includes those who are weak, ill, old, and those who have to attend to work."

Managing justice and mercy in society

While justice must be a central part of any functioning society, in order to preserve morality, a culture of values, and socioeconomic security, justice must be balanced with mercy and forgiveness.

For example, under the law of just retribution, the Koran calls for the death penalty in the case of murder. However, in the same passage, the Scripture encourages the victim's family to ask for something else other than the life of the murderer (such as monetary compensation), so that society can practice mercy and forgiveness over revenge. Furthermore, the Koran forbids the victim's family from transgressing the boundaries of law (such as causing injury to the murderer's family — which was a common practice in pre-Islamic Arabia) (2:178).

The Book encourages believers to practice the middle way of mercy and justice in all relationships. Muslims are called to treat each other with kindness and respect, but at the same time, this mercy should not violate the principles of justice. For example, a Muslim can't hide a murderer, whether family or friend, in his or her home to protect them from the justice of law. Even within the sacred family institution, where the Koran commands the highest level of kindness *(Al-Birr)*, the Koran says that a Muslim citizen must stand up for justice, even if it is "against your own selves or your parents and relatives" (4:135).

Avoiding extremes in religious practice and manners

The Koran says, "O you who believe! Do not deprive yourselves of the good things of life which God has made lawful to you, but do not transgress the bounds of what is right: Verily, God does not love those who transgress the bounds of what is right" (5:87–88).

Scripture teaches its followers not to go into the extreme paths of depriving the soul and body of those things that God has permitted. For example, depriving the body of food for an extended period of time on a consistent basis in an attempt to reach spiritual heights actually can lead to an unhealthy path, both spiritually and physically. Instead, the Scripture says that you should eat and drink with God's blessings, while also taking care not to waste food or overindulge in eating, because God "does not love the wasteful" (6:141).

The Koran argues that God is always accessible and present in every individual's life, and therefore it is not necessary to go through extreme hardship to reach the Divine (2:186). Rather, the Koran advises that "God intends for you ease, and He does not want to make things difficult for you" (2:185).

According to Prophet Muhammad, going to excess in matters of religion creates great danger: "Ruined are those who insist on hardship in matters of the Faith," is a caution that he repeated three times. Muhammad advised the Muslim community by saying, "The religion of Islam is easy, and whoever makes the religion a rigor, it will overpower him. So, follow a middle course." Following this advice, Muhammad taught his companions that "When one of you feels drowsy during prayer, let him lie down till drowsiness goes away for him, because when one of you offers prayers while feeling sleepy, he does not know whether he seeks forgiveness or abuses himself."

These Koranic and prophetic teachings make the middle path a necessary element for the survival of a healthy soul and society; therefore, those in positions of authority who demand unnecessary hardships from their citizens act wrongly.

In many ways, I think that this kind of extremism contributed to the downfall of the Taliban in Afghanistan (who were themselves reacting to extremist secular forces). Instead of following a middle course, the Taliban insisted on things — such as growing a beard and banning women from schools and the workplace — that should be left to individual choice rather than harsh, state-sanctioned policy (see Chapter 17 for a complete understanding of Islamic law). Muhammad said that extremes destroy religion by making it difficult for the soul and society to maintain religious life consistently, over time. If society starts following extreme ways, then people turn away from religious gatherings and a communal atmosphere where religion plays a central role in uniting citizens.

Following a middle path of moderation, rather than difficulty, is an important concept of Islamic law. For example, although saying prayers at the right time and making the full number of cycles are obligatory, when you are travelling, you can combine prayers and shorten their cycles (Rakat) in order to make prayer a joy, rather than a hardship. Similarly, fasting during the month of Ramadan is also obligatory, but if you are sick or on a journey, you can make up the fast at a later date.

Even in individual matters and mannerisms, the Koran calls for moderation. For example, the Scripture says that those who are "servants of the most Merciful (25:63) are those who are neither 'wasteful' nor 'niggardly' in spending upon others, recognizing that there is a just balance between the two extremes" (25:67). Similarly, the Koran teaches moderation even in the way you walk and talk, encouraging humbleness in your steps and lowering your voice, instead of arrogance and speaking loudly (31:18–19).

Most Muslims agree that extremism and moderation are not subjective concepts. Rather, the Koran and prophetic tradition (Sunnah) describe the balanced way, which should not be left to individual preferences. For example, a Muslim can't just decide one day that praying five times a day is too much; doing so would mean following lower desires that contradict God's laws and commands as spelled out in the Koran.

Witnessing the Truth

The second part of verse 2:143 says that the middle path (see the section "Divining a Community of the Middle Path," earlier in this chapter) adopted by the Muslim society must, by its very nature, "bear witness to the truth before all mankind."

Commentators of the Koran say that this bearing of witness takes place through both words and actions. Bearing witness to the truth of the Koran creates a model community that represents the best ethics and morals of the Koran (see Chapter 14). The ideal Muslim community envisioned by the Scripture exhibits all the qualities of a great moral and ethical civilization, such as belief in One God, mercy, compassion, justice, and other such teachings.

Some scholars say that the middle path and the bearing of witness to the truth are mentioned together in verse 2:143 because they go hand in hand. A model community, these scholars argue, needs to hold on to the balanced path that serves both individual needs and societal needs, and nurtures both the spirit and civilization. When a society walks on the path of both mercy and justice, it can be a fair peacemaker that practices and promotes the truth.

From the Koranic perspective, Muslims form a social movement dedicated to spreading and implementing divine teachings and laws on earth. In essence, the Koran envisions its community of believers as the inheritors of the prophetic tradition that is responsible for teaching humanity about God's Oneness and the ways of righteous actions that manifest divine will.

Enjoining Good and Forbidding Evil

The Koran says, "You are indeed the best community that has ever been brought forth for mankind: You enjoin the doing of what is right and forbid the doing of what is wrong, and you believe in God . . ." (3:110).

Various interpretations of this verse exist, with some saying that "the best community" refers only to the generation of Prophet Muhammad whose companions were in a sense the ideal Muslims in belief and worship. However, others argue that this community is the broader Muslim community who practice good and forbid evil throughout time. In any case, no one can question that this verse describes the ideal community.

The Scripture calls its community of believers to be the best of humanity, not because they belong to a specific race or economic status, but because they actively participate and encourage the doing of good, and actively participate and discourage against evil.

Scholars have almost unanimously agreed that when the Muslim community strictly adheres to this concept of "enjoining good and forbidding evil," then it is given leadership as an exemplary community on earth. But, if the Muslim community leaves behind the practice of good, fails to prevent evil, and abandons sincere belief in One God, then it can no longer be considered the "best community."

The Koran calls the Muslim community to become the torchbearers of the Koranic way of life in promoting the Scripture's theology, ethics, and morality. Most commentators warn Muslims not to view the title of "best community" with false pride or wrongly understand it as "God's chosen people." Rather, this verse places a heavy responsibility on the Muslim community as the moral leaders of humanity.

Prophet Muhammad called upon each one of his followers to become active citizens of society who do not stand idle in the presence of wrongdoing. Muhammad said, "Whoever amongst you sees an evil, he must change it with his hand. If he is not able to do so, then with his tongue. And if he is not able to do so, then with his heart, and that is the weakest form of faith."

With this understanding, Prophet Muhammad also warned his community that if righteous people allowed evildoers to continue their actions unopposed, inaction would result in the destruction of society. Muhammad said, "The likeness of the man who observes the limits prescribed by God and that of the man who transgresses them is like the people who get on board a ship after casting lots. Some of them are in its lower deck and some of them in its upper deck. Those who are in its lower deck, when they require water, go to the occupants of the upper deck, and say to them: 'If we make a hole in the bottom of the ship, we shall not harm you.' If the occupants of the upper deck leave them to carry out their design they all will be drowned. But, if they do not let them go ahead (with their plans), all of them will remain safe."

The Koran views striving for the application of God's laws as a requirement for the social and moral preservation of the entire community. Many commentators, from the post-Islamic civilization period in particular, argue that abandoning this responsibility causes the downfall of Muslim nations, which in their eyes have become subservient to the rest of the world instead of becoming its leaders.

Muslim reformers involved in sociopolitical movements, such as the Islamic Brotherhood in Egypt or the Party of Islam in Pakistan, argue that to realize this Koranic ideal, an Islamic state must be formed. Without an Islamic state, these reformers argue, Muslims can't implement the comprehensive system of rights and responsibilities established by divine laws.

However, some people, usually modernist or secularly oriented Muslims, remain skeptical of the role of government in religion, because governments are vulnerable to corruption and can therefore use Islam for propaganda purposes rather than for the just cause of enjoining good and forbidding evil. Instead, this school of thought argues that government should only run the basic affairs of the community, and the leadership of society should fall to Islamic scholars who stay untethered by special interest politics. This Koranic concept causes a lot of debate about the method of its application in a Muslim society today.

The last part of passage 3:110 describes the ideal community as one that "believes in God." Without the belief in God and His message, the notion of good and evil can easily become subjective with the trends of time and culture. Belief in God mandates that good and evil be defined by divine words and laws, rather than corruptible human intuitions.

Policing good and evil

How to go about enjoining good and forbidding evil? Does this concept require a religious police force that carries a stick around to stop evil, or should this responsibility fall to means such as sincere advice? Perhaps the answer lies somewhere in the middle.

Clearly, the Koran argues that forbidding evil sometimes calls for armed struggle, such as stopping a tyrant from his or her oppression. The Koran says, "And why should you not fight for the cause of God and of the weak among men and of the women and the children who are crying, 'Our Lord! Rescue us from this town of which the people are oppressors! O, give us from Your presence some protecting friend! O, give us from Your presence some defender!'" (4:75).

But, at other times, armed struggle and punishment is unadvisable, and should instead give way to advice with kind words or other helpful actions. For example, in the Koran, God sends Prophet Moses to the tyrant Pharaoh not to declare war, but rather to preach God's message and to warn Pharaoh against his oppressive rule (7:104–105). So, encouraging good requires a combination of methods that fit the time and situation Muslims find themselves in.

Uniting a Community with the Rope of God

The Koran urges its followers, "And hold fast, all together, unto the rope of God, and do not draw apart from one another. And remember the blessings which God bestowed upon you: How, when you were enemies, He brought your hearts together, so that through His blessing you became brothers (and sisters) . . ." (3:103).

The rope of God is traditionally understood as the Koran itself, because Prophet Muhammad said, 'The Book of God is God's rope stretched from the heaven to earth." As such, this passage calls for the unity of mankind under the theological, ethical, and moral teachings of the Koran. The scripture teaches that ideological unity, rather than unity based on race, language, and other factors, is so powerful that it can bring together even those who were once at war, such as the tribes of pre-Islamic Arabia.

Equality of mankind before God

The entire notion of unity and brotherhood can't exist if prejudices exist in the form of tribes, nations, race, language, or even religion. The Scripture, therefore, states that all human beings are equal before God:

"O humanity! Behold, We have created you all out of a male and a female, and have made you into nations and tribes, so that you might come to know one another. Verily, the noblest of you in the sight of God is the one who is most deeply conscious of Him. Behold, God is all-knowing, all-aware" (49:13).

Notice that this passage addresses all of humanity and not only the Muslim community. This passage describes the nature of a true Islamic society, which must be built on equality, dialogue, and virtue.

This verse becomes the foundation of respect for diversity as the will of divine creation and design. In another passage, the Koran says that "Among His signs is the . . . diversity of your tongues and colors: for in this, behold, there are messages indeed for people who think" (30:22).

Prophet Muhammad, in his famous "Farewell Sermon" shortly before his death, called for equality in all affairs: "All mankind is from Adam. An Arab has no superiority over a non-Arab, nor does a non-Arab have any superiority over an Arab. A white has no superiority over a black, nor does a black have any superiority over a white — except by piety and good action. Learn that every Muslim is a brother to every Muslim and that Muslims constitute one brotherhood." In this sermon, the Prophet also preached a universal brotherhood by reminding his followers that all men and women are from Adam (and Eve).

The brotherhood of man

Teachers of the Islamic tradition warn against simply using the Koranic concepts of unity and brotherhood (49:10) in rhetoric without any concrete action. Muhammad spoke extensively about the rights and responsibilities of brotherhood.

Muhammad underlined the principal of brotherhood by saying, "No one of you becomes a true believer until he likes for his brother what he likes for himself." Imam al-Nawawi, a famous scholar of Islamic law, believed that the brotherhood related in this *Hadith* refers to the brotherhood of all humanity as children of Adam, and not only faith-based brotherhood.

In describing the treatment of mercy that brotherhood entails, Muhammad said, "The believers in their mutual kindness, compassion, and sympathy are just like one body. When one of the limbs is afflicted, the whole body responds to it with wakefulness and fever."

The responsibilities of brotherhood

The *Hadith* obligate seven primary duties that citizens of a Muslim community must confer upon one another:

- ✔ **Visiting the ill:** Scholars of Islam point out that this *Hadith* applies to physical ailments, as well as cases of distress, tragedy, and other mental hardships. Also, "visit" implies offering your complete help and support for the one in hardship.

- ✔ **Attending the funeral prayer of another Muslim:** You pay your final respects to the deceased and beg God for your brother or sister's soul at a time when the soul most needs God's forgiveness and mercy.

- ✔ **Showing gratitude for a favor:** When a Muslim sneezes and says, "Praise be to God," then you are obligated to respond by saying, "May God have Mercy on you." This is basically an act of praying for your brother- or sister-in-faith by asking for God's blessings and continued sustenance in their lives. This concept is extended in showing gratitude to another Muslim when he or she does something for you, by saying "May God Bless you." By logic this rule extends to showing gratitude for all the favors one receives from his fellow brother or sister.

- ✔ **Helping an oppressed brother or sister:** This applies to state-sanctioned oppression as well as cases of social oppression, such as domestic abuse, social injustice, poverty, and so on. Basically, Muslims must relieve one another of hardship whenever possible.

- ✔ **Helping to fulfill oaths made by others:** Applies to financial transactions as well as social contracts. For example, if your brother- or sister-in-faith owes somebody money, but can't repay the money due to financial hardship, then you must help pay off the debt if you can.

- ✔ **Accepting the invitation of your brother or sister:** Of course, this applies only if you aren't bound to any other obligation or invitation. The basic concept here is to strengthen, preserve, and, at times, repair the relationship between people by eating and spending time together. In Muslim culture, it is common that if two people fall into a fight or argument, then one of them will invite the other over for tea as a sort of peace offering (49:10).

In Muslim cultures, it is considered offensive to turn down an invitation to someone's home or food.

Many people who have traveled to Muslim countries for the first time are often surprised at the hospitality they encounter, even in times of hostility. For example, many journalists who reported from Afghanistan and Iraq during conflicts there have said that despite the war, they were generally treated very hospitably by the people.

- ✔ **Responding in kind:** When a Muslim greets you with the traditional "Peace be upon you," you must respond to that peace with the same or something even better, by adding "And may God's Mercy and Blessing be upon you." In doing so, you give due and proper respect to your fellow brother or sister. This is also another way for two Muslims to renew and reconcile their relationship even if they may have fallen into a fight or argument. Also, the concept extends into responding to kindness with equal or preferably even more kindness.

All these laws and teachings safeguard Muslims from disunity and ill feeling towards one another by creating a foundation for human interaction embodied in the language of kindness, love, utmost care, mercy, and forgiveness.

Special treatment towards neighbors

The Koran gives special emphasis under the notion of brotherhood for neighbors in a Muslim society (4:36 for example). To underline the importance of neighbors in the Islamic tradition, Prophet Muhammad told his companions that Angel Gabriel emphasized the rights and kind treatment of neighbors to such an extent that he started to think that God would give neighbors the right of inheritance.

As such, Muhammad also told his followers to share their food on a consistent basis with their neighbors. He advised one of his companions, "O Abu Dharr! Whenever you prepare broth, put plenty of water in it, and have in your mind the members of the household of your neighbors and then give them out of this with courtesy." Muhammad also advised the believing women of his community to share their food regardless of how little it was, saying that no gift is insignificant. Muhammad advised his wife, Aisha, that if she is unable to present a gift to all her neighbors, then the one whose door is closest has the greater right to her gift.

Living in close spaces places an even greater duty on Muslims to think about the physical and moral security of their neighbors. Muhammad repeated three times that those who threaten the security of their neighbors are not believers. The relationship with neighbors in a God-conscious society is stated in a *Hadith* where Muhammad said, "The best of companion with God is the one who is best to his companions; and the best of neighbors to God is the one who is the best of them to his neighbor."

Leadership and Citizenship in the Koran

Islam isn't a rigid system of fixed laws that govern every aspect of life. Rather, Islamic tradition lays out solid principles from which human intellectual thought grows to give structure to society.

An Islamic government must by its very nature center its constitution and laws around the guidance of the Koran and the example of Prophet Muhammad, known as *Sunnah*.

Forming a political identity

The Koran says, "O you who believe! Pay heed unto God, and pay heed unto the Messenger and unto those from among you who have been entrusted with authority. And if you have a dispute over any matter, refer it unto God and the Messenger, if you truly believe in God and the Last Day. This is best for you, and best in the end" (4:59).

Scholars stress the following essential elements of this verse in forming a political identity for an Islamic state:

- **Following divine law:** The constitution and principles of government must be based on divine teachings of ethics and morality as laid out by the Koran and the example of Prophet Muhammad *(Sunnah)*.

- **Leading by the law:** A leader, known as a *Caliph,* gains legitimacy by sincerely following the Koran and the Prophet's example. Muslims must follow their leaders only if those leaders base their actions and policies on the ethical and moral foundations of the Koran and *Sunnah.* If a leader violates the ethics of these two divine sources, then Muslim citizens are under no obligation to follow that leader.

  In their inaugural speeches, both Caliph Abu Bakr and his successor, Umar, said: "Help me if I am right. Set me right if I am wrong. . . . Obey me as long as I obey God and His Prophet. When I disobey God and His Prophet, then obey me not."

  Citizens have the right, and at times even the responsibility, to challenge the government on any policy that seems unjustified in the light of the Koran and *Sunnah.*

- **Selecting leaders:** This passage says "and unto those from among you who have been entrusted with authority." Muslim political activists in particular argue that "from among you" means that leaders must be chosen by the people, and not imposed upon them in a dictatorial fashion.

  This position is strengthened by the concept of mutual consultation, known as *Shura* in Arabic (42:38), which is the basis for calls to democratic reform in the Muslim world (see Chapter 20 for more about the Koran and democracy).

- **Espousing justice:** When disagreements among leaders, or between leadership and citizens, arise, experts of the Islamic tradition should resolve these disagreements in consultation of the Koran and *Sunnah.* These experts (who are likened to the Supreme Court in the United States) must judge based on justice and not self-interest politics (16:90, 49:9).

The leader and government in an Islamic society establish justice by applying God's laws and teachings. Divine laws don't simply require applying the criminal penal code (see Chapter 17), but insist on a path of social and economical equity that honors human life and provides a secure society in which human morals and economies can flourish.

Governing by the Book

An Islamic government has the following responsibilities towards its citizens, according to interpreters of the Koran:

- **Uplifting the spiritual and moral standards of society:** This applies specifically to the establishment of prayer and purifying alms (see Chapter 12 for more on prayer and almsgiving). The government makes it as easy as possible for citizens to practice that which is good, and makes it as difficult as possible to practice that which is evil.

- **Securing the nation from all internal or external threats:** The Koran provides various laws (see Chapter 17) that the government must implement in order for physical, moral, and economic security to prevail. Part of this obligation is to organize an army to protect against any attacks or threats.

- **Pursuing freedom for all citizens:** The government must pursue freedom for all its citizens so that each man and woman serves only the Divine. As such, an Islamic government must work towards the abolishment of slavery, and against unfair labor practices, such as child labor and cheap labor. Also, the government must help those enslaved by tyrants, even if they are in other lands (4:75).

- **Setting up institutions of just law to maintain the rights of citizens:** These institutions judge in matters of dispute, whether it concerns business transactions, divorce (see Chapter 15), or any other communal issues.

- **Providing citizens with equity:** A government's policies should allow even the poorest of the poor the ability to rise up in society by fair and just means. Leaders should create the environment necessary for free trade to flourish (such as security), with the condition that this environment doesn't harm society physically or morally. Therefore, selling drugs or pornography, for example, would be completely unacceptable even if it were for "mature" audiences only.

- **Providing education to all its citizens, both male and female:** Prophet Muhammad said, "The seeking of knowledge is obligatory upon all Muslims (which includes male and female)." Also, Muhammad advised his companions, "Seek knowledge from the cradle to the grave." Religious knowledge has been categorized as obligatory on every single individual; some members of society must gain knowledge of other sciences for the proper development of civilization.

Seeing rulers through prophetic eyes

Once Muhammad asked his companions, "Do you know who is the bankrupt?" They said, "The bankrupt among us is one who has neither money with him nor any property."

Muhammad replied, "The real bankrupt of my community would be he who would come on the Day of Judgment with prayers, fasting, and charity, but finds himself bankrupt because he reviled others, brought slander against others, unlawfully devoured the wealth of others, shed the blood of others, and beat others. So, his virtues would be credited to the account of those (who suffered at his hands)."

Tyrannical, dictatorial, or corrupt leadership contradicts the teachings of the Islamic tradition. The description of a truly Muslim ruler lies in Muhammad's saying that "The best of your rulers are those whom you love and who love you, and those who invoke God's blessings upon you, and you invoke God's blessings upon them."

Living up to citizenship

Citizens play a very important role in any Islamic society. Any good government needs the support of its citizens in order to work for the betterment of society.

The Koran spells out the following obligations for citizens:

- **Enjoining good and forbidding evil:** Citizens have the obligation to apply this principle to greater society (see the section "Enjoining Good and Forbidding Evil," earlier in this chapter, for more information on this concept). For example, someone who is intellectually gifted should use his or her talents for good causes, such as creating policies against poverty. Someone who is physically very strong should enjoin in good causes, such as building places of residence or worship.

- **Following just leaders:** Even if you have a personal disagreement with the ruler, it should not stop you from enjoining with the government in good practices and projects, as long as the government follows divine law.

  A citizen must not abandon following his ruler just because the ruler doesn't belong to his tribe or race, as has been very common both in past and present history.

- **Advising the government against unjust ways:** If Muslims have a tyrant ruler, they must oppose the tyrant. As such, Prophet Muhammad said that the greatest Jihad (struggle in the path of God) is "to speak the truth in front of an unjust ruler." If a person dies in the process of opposing a tyrant ruler, then he or she is considered a martyr in the sight of God. This martyrdom encourages equality, justice, and freedom in society.

Receiving the rights of citizenship

The Koran gives equal attention to rights and responsibilities that work inter-dependent of one another. One person's right becomes another person's responsibility. For example, every human being has the right to own property. Therefore, the government and citizen has the responsibility to protect the property of human beings. Similarly, honor is every citizen's divine right, and therefore it is the responsibility of both government and citizen to protect the honor of all members in society.

The rights of all citizens under Islamic rule are based on the Arabic word *Huqquq,* meaning "that which is firm, well-established." Interestingly, the term comes from the root word *Haq,* which means Real, one of God's attributes. The traditional understanding is that the rights of men and women derive from the divine gifts of God; therefore, no one has the right to violate these rights unless it be for a just cause that is mentioned in the divinely-inspired texts of either the Koran or *Sunnah.*

Traditional scholars of the Koran say that all human rights emanate from two fundamental, universal principles: dignity and equality. Dignity gives humans their humanity according to Koranic teachings (17:70), and equality is a fundamental Scriptural teaching (49:13) as well as a prophetic teaching.

Vast rights emerge from these two principals. In the following sections, I tell you about these rights by classifying them into two basic categories.

Honorable rights

The Koran states that God instills honor as the virtue of every human being (17:70). In order to nurture and preserve human honor, the Koran prescribes the following rights:

- ✔ **No compulsion in religion:** The Koran clearly says that forced religion contradicts the very nature of faith that requires freedom in order to be considered true (2:256). To force someone into religion violates their human dignity as free, thinking individuals. In fact, Islamic law states that if someone comes to the courts saying that they were forced to change their religion to Islam, then the court must allow them to revert back to their previous faith if the individual so chooses.

- ✔ **Freedom:** Preserving human dignity requires preserving human freedom. Enslaving a person degrades that individual, and therefore violates human dignity. Freeing a slave is one of the highest acts of charity in the Koran (2:177, 90:13) and is regularly obligated for the purification of specific sins (4:92, for example).

Caliph Umar said it best when he admonished one of his companions who had taken a slave: "When were you able to enslave those whose mothers bore them as free men?"

However, this freedom can't infringe upon the rights of others, and must not adversely affect the public. For example, Islam recognizes freedom of speech, but that speech can't violate the sanctity of another human being's honor by use of backbiting and slandering. Tabloids, for example, would be a big no-no in an Islamic society.

✔ **Privacy:** Human dignity necessitates privacy regarding life within the confines of the home. The Koran clearly affords all human beings the right to privacy: The Book forbids Muslims from spying on one another (49:12) and entering houses without permission (24:27–28). The Koran even provides laws for privacy within the family unit by specifying permission that must be granted in order to enter private quarters (24:58–59).

Of course, privacy laws have conditions, which can be violated in order to benefit or secure the society. For example, if the government learns that someone is making bombs at home in order to cause injury to society, then the government not only has the right, but also the responsibility, to invade that person's home to avert evil action.

✔ **No collective punishment:** One person can't be held responsible for the crimes of another person (6:164). If a person belonging to a specific group commits a wrong action, the entire group can't be punished.

From an ethical standpoint, modern warfare presents many issues. Bombs and missiles may be sent to kill one person or group, but they may end up killing several others. The Islamic tradition understands no such thing as collateral damage, which many Muslims see as a dishonorable way of describing the violation of innocent human life.

✔ **Innocent until proven guilty:** This important concept of Islamic law protects those accused of crimes.

✔ **Honoring the disabled:** The Koran speaks out against people, especially among the pre-Islamic Arabs, who disrespect those with physical or mental disabilities. Towards the end of *Surah* 24 in the Koran, the Scripture stands up for the respect of the disabled by saying that all believers are brothers one to another, and there should be no stigma attached to those who are blind, lame, or sick, and in no way should the disabled be excluded from the community (24:61).

Showing dishonor towards the disabled and sick is so serious that the Koran even rebukes Prophet Muhammad, who frowned and turned his face away from a blind man who had come to ask a question while the Messenger preached to a group of tribe leaders in Mecca (80:1–10). The entire chapter (*Surah* 80) goes on to warn man against arrogance, which is the only way a person can have dishonorable attitudes towards any other human being.

Equality rights

The Koran believes in the equality of all humanity, and has therefore established certain social rights based on this conviction (4:1):

- **Right to own property:** No citizen, regardless of race, gender, or religion, can be denied the right to own property in an Islamic society. This also includes the right to "access of commons," which entails the right to take benefit from public lands and resources, such as rivers.

  Of course, with this right comes responsibility. For example, if someone violates the rights of the earth by polluting the river, then he or she loses his or her rights to that access of commons.

- **Poor and rich are equal:** Any discrimination between a poor person and a rich person is a severe violation of Islamic ethics. Citizens in an Islamic system have the right to fair institutions of justice that don't discriminate based on economic status.

  Unfortunately, the poor and rich often receive different treatment before the law, both in Muslim countries and elsewhere. Rich people often can bribe their way out of a crime, or hire the most expensive lawyer in order to be freed from the legal system. Innocent poor people often don't have the means to fight their cases in the legal system, and end up unjustly incarcerated. Such treatment does not manifest the Koranic ideal of justice.

- **Race equality:** Racism is completely outlawed in the Koran (49:13).

- **Equality of men and women:** While society sometimes dictates different primary roles between the genders, the Koran views women as completely equal to men in the sight of God. The Koran says, "Whosoever does a righteous deed, whether male or female, and is a believer" (16:97).

  The Koran calls for an interdependent relationship based on good works between males and females, rather than male superiority or female superiority: "And the believers, men and women, are friends to each other; they enjoin what is good and forbid what is evil, and they establish the prayer and pay the purifying alms and obey God and His Messenger . . ." (9:71).

  See Chapter 19 for more on women and the Koran.

Non-Muslims living in Muslim lands

The relationship of an Islamic government with its non-Muslim populace is perhaps one of the most misunderstood concepts among radical Muslims and some Orientalists (Western academics who study Islam) who study Islam from the outside. These critics of the Koran often point to 5:51 as their proof that Islam is inherently hostile to non-Muslims and does not permit friendship with them (see Chapter 10). However, this verse doesn't present a complete picture of this complex issue.

Passage 60:8–9 qualifies 5:51 by saying that "God does not forbid you, with regard to those who do not fight you on account of your religion nor drive you out of your homes, to treat them with goodness and to be just to them. Truly, God loves those who are just." The passage goes on to explain that "Indeed, God forbids you only with regard to those who fight you on account of your religion and drive you out of your homes, and assist others in driving you out, that you turn to them (in friendship), they are wrongdoers."

This passage calls for Muslims to deal with non-Muslims in a just manner; it also calls on the relationship to be built on *Birr,* an Arabic word that is very comprehensive in meaning, but basically means "extreme kindness or goodness." Interestingly, the same word *(Birr)* describes the honorable treatment that parents deserve from their children. The Koran uses the word *Birr* to describe the most excellent form of kindness, justice, and generosity. So, Muslim and non-Muslim relations aren't built on war or hatred, as some would like to believe. Koranic teachings say that believers should pursue such relations with mutual kindness and justice.

As such, the concept of a "Clash of Civilizations" stands out as completely alien to the Islamic ethic. A more appropriate terminology for the Islamic approach is a "Dialogue of Civilizations," which you can find in verses such as 49:13.

Relations with People of the Book

While the Koran clearly articulates some serious theological and legal disagreements with both Jews and Christians, the Scripture reminds Muslims that both these religions are part of the Islamic legacy of prophets, and are also recipients of divine revelation.

However, theological and legal disputes should not prevent Muslims from enjoying good relationships with non-Muslims. As such, the Koran says, "Today, all the good things of life have been made lawful to you. And the food of those who have received earlier revelations (People of the Book) is lawful to you, and your food is lawful to them. And, (lawful to you are) in wedlock, women from among the Believers, and in wedlock women from among those who have received earlier revelation — provided that you give them their dowers, taking them in honest wedlock, not in fornication, nor as secret love-companions . . ." (5:5).

The Koran enjoins two social constructs (eating food together and marriage) that encourage healthy coexistence. The permissibility of marriage, which is described as an institution of love and mercy between the hearts of a man and woman in the Koran (30:21), provides proof of the Koran's call for living in harmony with non-Muslim citizens in an Islamic society.

Even on disagreements about religion, the Koran urges Muslims to have dialogue in the best manner: "And do not argue with the followers of earlier revelation other than in a most kindly manner . . ." (29:46).

Rights of non-Muslims under Islamic rule

Non-Muslims living in Muslim lands are called *Ahl al-dhimmah* or *Dhimmies,* meaning "Protected People." The Muslim community has made a covenant with non-Muslims so that they may live in safety and security under an Islamic government:

- ✔ **Violating the rights of any non-Muslim citizen is a grave injustice.** Prophet Muhammad said that "On the Day of Judgment I shall dispute with anyone who oppresses a person from among the People of the Covenant, or infringes on his right, or puts a responsibility on him which is beyond his strength, or takes something from him against his will."

- ✔ **The Islamic legal system must not discriminate against non-Muslims in the court of law, and must base its decision solely on the basis of justice.** Even when the fourth *Caliph* of Islam, Ali, fell into a dispute with a non-Muslim about a certain matter, the Islamic courts ruled in favor of the non-Muslim over the *Caliph* himself.

  In another well-known incident, the Islamic courts ruled in favor of the non-Muslim populace over the Islamic government when the Islamic government captured the city of Samarqand. The non-Muslims produced a document that detailed a truce made during a previous time between the city's people and other Muslims. The Islamic courts honored that agreement and ruled against the Islamic government. Of course, examples surface in history when this covenant has not been fulfilled, but these are violations of the law and not a fulfillment of it.

- ✔ **Scholars of Islam all agree that non-Muslim citizens must be afforded the same rights as Muslims, namely the sanctity of life, honor, and property.**

- ✔ **Non-Muslims can never, any under circumstance, be forced to convert to Islam under the Koranic teaching.** The Koran says, "Let there be no compulsion in religion" (2:256). Islamic government must protect the freedom of worship for all citizens.

Non-Muslims have the right to set up their own communal laws according to the principles of their religion, as long as their laws don't violate any major state law, such as the sanctity of honor and life. Critics of Islam feel that this creates a barrier between the Muslim and non-Muslim communities that could lead to ill feelings through a lack of communication. Islamic scholars and activists argue that giving non-Muslims jurisdiction over their own communal laws is the only way to truly protect the freedom of worship.

Paying the *Jizya* tax

Non-Muslims must pay a tax, called *Jizya,* in return for guarantee for their security. An Islamic government has the right to fight against the non-Muslim populace if they refuse to pay this tax, granted that the government fulfills its responsibilities in securing the rights of the non-Muslims. However, with a change in the sociopolitical culture of the modern era, this tax is no longer levied on non-Muslims anywhere in the Muslim world.

Some have complained against this system, believing that it discriminates against non-Muslim citizens, because the Muslim population doesn't have to pay this tax. However, these critics fail to realize that Muslim citizens must pay the purifying alms *(Zakat),* and the Islamic government can fight any Muslim who refuses to pay them. However, applying the purifying alms to non-Muslims would be unfair because the *Zakat* is a religious institution, and therefore only Muslims should be forced to pay it. The *Jizya* tax supports society, just as *Zakat* does, and both are rights that an Islamic government has over its population.

Jihad: Struggling in the Path of God

The term *Jihad* is probably the most misunderstood and abused term in the world today. It is often wrongly translated as "Holy War," which is a concept that emerges from the time of the Crusades in Europe. *Jihad* means "to struggle in the path of God." Even within the context of armed struggle, a more appropriate translation would be "Just War," rather than "Holy War," to borrow terminology from the Christian experience of understanding war. War is in fact never Holy, but at times it is necessary for the benefit of human beings.

Struggling against evil

Understanding the path of God is essential to understanding *Jihad.* The Koran defines the "path of God" by notions of justice and mercy, which directly oppose the notions of tyranny, oppression, and evil. Merely claiming to struggle in the path of God, or merely claiming to be a martyr, does not truly make one's struggle for God or make one a martyr. Rather, the claim must be backed by actions. If a struggle is based on the establishment of justice and mercy, and the removal of all that is opposite to the path of God, it is truly a struggle for God. However, if the struggle results in unnecessary violence, tyranny, injustice, and works against the path of God, then it can in no way, from the Koranic standpoint, be considered a struggle in the path of God.

Struggle does not only mean armed struggle, although that too is part of *Jihad.* Struggle means to actively engage and work towards a goal using various means and methods that may even call for the sacrifice of one's own life and wealth. Struggle in the path of God must be for causes that are esteemed to be righteous, ethical, and moral by the Koran. Therefore, struggling against poverty, intoxicants, pornography, and all other elements that bring moral, economical, or physical harm to a society can be considered a part and parcel of *Jihad.* Every Muslim individual and society has a responsibility, as inheritors of the earth and representatives of God (see Chapter 8), to engage actively in *Jihad,* struggling for what is good, and struggling against what is evil (2:148).

Jihad can best be described as the struggle (uphill road) to free men and women from servitude and lordship of anything or anyone other than the Divine, so that he or she can choose and practice submission to God (Islam) without any restrictions (90:8–18). Elements, such as intoxicants and pornography, must be struggled against because they enslave men and women to their lower desires in a way that they are no longer able to function as servants and representatives of God on earth. Similarly, elements, such as a tyrant ruler, must be struggled against because they impose their will above God's Will on the people who lose their ability to worship and submit to divine teachings.

Jihad as armed struggle

When the Koran uses the term *Jihad* alone, it denotes a broad struggle that can take several forms, such as speaking out for human rights. When the Koran addresses the issue of armed struggle, it uses the word *Kital,* meaning "fighting." This in itself clearly shows that *Jihad* does not mean war, because if it did, then there would be no need to use another term (*Kital*) to describe fighting and war in the path of God.

The Koran permits armed struggle under the following three circumstances:

- **War of self defense:** The Koran allows Muslims to fight in armed struggle against "those who wage war against you . . ." (2:190). In this circumstance, Muslims are allowed to kill their aggressors and drive them out of their land in order to protect the Islamic state (2:191).

  Islam is not a pacifist religion. Rather, the Koran believes in self-defense in the form of war, if necessary, and with appropriate force. Once this battle begins, the Muslims are told to "fight against them until there is no more oppression and all worship is devoted to God alone" (2:193).

  The two objectives of armed struggle in defense are to protect the community from oppression and preserve the community's ability to worship freely.

An Islamic state is not allowed to attack another nation unless it perceives some sort of threat or is actually attacked. The Koran says within the same passage of 2:190, "but do not commit aggression — for, verily, God does not love aggressors." And, in 2:192, the Scripture also says, "But if they desist — behold, God is much Forgiving, most Merciful," a sentiment that is reinforced in 2:193. The Koran teaches its followers not to continue fighting the aggressors if they surrender or cease fighting.

The Koran argues that this armed struggle becomes necessary because if self-defense were disallowed then "all monasteries and churches and synagogues and mosques — all in which God's name is abundantly extolled — would surely have been destroyed" (22:39) by those people who incline towards evil and destruction on the earth.

Also, self-defense includes perceived threats, such as the breaking of a treaty or killing of a diplomat. *Surahs* 8 and 9 of the Koran speak of how Muslims should treat those Pagan Arabs who had broken the treaty with the Muslim community and began aiding the destruction of the Muslim community with other such aggressors.

✔ **War of liberation for the weak and oppressed:** In passage 2:191, the Koran says that "oppression is even worse than killing." This belief is strengthened by the Koran's call for Muslims to fight against oppression in all its form with the use of armed struggle, if necessary.

The Koran asks those who are inclined against fighting in the path of God, "And why should you not fight for the cause of God and of the weak among men and of the women and the children who are crying, 'Our Lord! Rescue us from this town of which the people are oppressors! O, give us from Your presence some protecting friend! O, give us from your presence some defender!'" (4:75).

✔ **War for the freedom of faith:** This war is fought in lands where the Islamic faith is suppressed and the message of the Koran is not allowed to be preached and taught to the inhabitants of a place. This war can take place only to allow for the free thinking and preaching of Islam, but can't be used to force conversion to Islam (2:256).

See Chapter 18 to understand how *Jihad* does not equal terrorism, and for more information on contemporary issues, such as suicide bombing, that define *Jihad* in the world today. Also, in Chapter 18, I talk about the limits and ethics of war in the Islamic tradition.

Chapter 17

Purifying Society through Islamic Law

In This Chapter

▶ Identifying the sources of Islamic law

▶ Knowing how scholars arrive at judicial rulings and opinions

▶ Understanding the content of Islamic law

▶ Reasoning with Islamic law's penal codes

*I*slam is a way of life built on the notion of submitting to the Will of God. Islamic law, known as *Shariah* in Arabic, provides answers to the daunting question "What is the Will of God?" The Koran contains several passages that give clear legal injunctions, and also serves as the primary source from which Islamic law is derived.

Islamic law deals with the most mundane aspects of life, as well as the most complex ethical and moral questions that face society.

Many Muslims would agree that not a single country in the Muslim world today actually functions according to the authentic teachings of Islamic law. As such, this chapter reflects the classical tradition of *Shariah*, and not the practice or laws of any Muslim country — even those that claim to follow Islamic law.

In this chapter, I examine the meaning of *Shariah* and look at how scholars derive its rulings. I also tell you about what Islamic law covers and how it shapes everyday life. Finally, I explain the seemingly controversial penal codes of Islam and their purpose in an Islamic society.

Defining Shariah

Unfortunately, many non-Muslims today often associate the term *Shariah* exclusively with the Islamic penal code, which constitutes only a small part of Islamic law. In reality, *Shariah* lays out a spiritual and moral path that covers all aspects of life — individual and societal — and continues to play an important and dynamic role in the everyday lives of Muslims.

The word *Shariah* sheds light on the purpose and basic philosophy of Islamic law. (In Chapter 4, I discuss the importance of the Arabic language in searching for the philosophical roots of Koranic concepts.)

The root of the word *Shariah, Shar',* evokes the following six meanings, among others. While the first four do not form the basis of Islamic law, they point to important and interesting aspects of Islamic law as a living path:

- ✔ **To begin:** Islamic law serves as the foundational, beginning code of living in a Muslim society.

- ✔ **A sailboat:** A sailboat allows people to move forward and progress towards their ultimate goal. *Shariah* acts like a sailboat in moving forward the development of a spiritual, moral, ethical, and intellectual community.

- ✔ **A tent:** Like a tent, *Shariah* protects people from physical, spiritual, and moral destruction.

- ✔ **To legislate:** This meaning points to the literal judicial process of codifying Islamic law for purposes of governance. Also, *Shariah* codifies social behavior based on certain rights and responsibilities afforded to each citizen.

- ✔ **A path to the well of water:** Water, especially in the dry lands of Arabia, offers the primary source of life for all creation. In this sense, Islamic law serves as the spiritual, moral, and physical life of an Islamic community. The path rightly suggests that *Shariah* is not only an end, but also the means to an end rooted in submission to the Will of God. Islamic law creates an environment in which moral good flourishes, and moral evil subsides.

- ✔ **A source of water that never runs dry:** This form represents the actual word *Shariah* and not only its roots. Continuing with the theme of water, this meaning points to the Islamic philosophy that *Shariah* is a universal wisdom whose benefit for humanity will never end. This law, then, applies not to a single tribe, nation, or time period. Rather, it applies to all who accept the Islamic faith regardless of national origin.

Shariah, the source of a divine ethic, seeks to build a civilization of progress and protection.

Extracting and Interpreting Sacred Law

The laws that make up *Shariah* come from several sources (see the following section). The laws extracted from these sources are shaped into a formal code through a sophisticated science, known as *Fiqh,* or jurisprudence. This science seeks to interpret the Will of God.

Those who undertake the scholarly pursuit of jurisprudence *(Fiqh)* are known as *Fuqaha'* (singular, *Faqih*). These scholars usually work independently of the government. They have the authority to issue legal opinions from other established *Fuqaha'* in the form of a "permission" called *'Ijaza.*

This study takes serious dedication that lasts a lifetime. Many of the teachers I have learned from over the years have said that they are only beginners in this science, despite studying the tradition for over 20 years. Because of the complexity of this science, this chapter covers less than one week's worth of the knowledge that *Fuqaha'* receive over their lifetimes.

Islam, at least in the majority Sunni tradition, does not believe in a hierarchical structure of priesthood that interprets God's Will and then conveys it to the masses. Also, Islam in the Sunni tradition does not believe in a Pope sort of figure who directly communicates with God. Interpreting the Will of God is a deeply human, intellectual, and spiritual effort. (See *Islam For Dummies,* by Malcolm Clark, for more information on the Sunni tradition.)

According to the Islamic tradition, the interpretation and application of divine guidance takes place through human beings who have thorough knowledge of jurisprudence. These highly-respected jurists are also checked by other intellectuals in the community of jurists, because no one person has direct access to divine revelation. This process of checks and balances allows for differences of opinion and open debate in society, known as *Ikhtilaf.* This then opens the way to *Ijtihad* — an intellectual struggle undertaken to know the will of God. The result is either agreeing to disagree *(Ikhtilaf)* or consensus on a certain issue *(Itifaq).*

Differences of opinion give rise to diversity of practice on matters that the Koran and *Sunnah* leave gray. Muslims can accept the opinions of different scholars on these matters so long as those opinions don't violate the teachings in the Koran and *Sunnah.*

Juristic opinions are known as *Fawah* (plural, *Fatawah*). Trained scholars, not laypeople, have the authority to issue these usually non-binding legal opinions. *Fatawah* issued by those who are not trained in the classical science of jurisprudence cannot be considered authoritative or authentic, in classical Islamic thought.

Searching for Rulings and Principals

Islamic jurists use four basic sources to extract the laws that form *Shariah:*

- ✔ The Koran
- ✔ The prophetic tradition *(Sunnah)*
- ✔ The consensus of the Scholars *(Ijma')*
- ✔ Juristic analogy *(Qiyas)*

These sources provide the building blocks of reform and renewal for each generation that faces new opportunities and challenges. In the following sections, I explain the role of each source in developing Islamic law.

In the Koran

The Koran says about itself, "Here is a plain statement to men, a guidance and instruction to those who are conscious of God" (3:138). This passage describes the laws of the Book, which tend to be laid out in concise and clear language, leaving little doubt about their meaning. However, some laws progress and flesh out over the course of revelation, which means that clearly defined laws can be further explained or limited in other passages of the Book.

The Koran was revealed in stages — not all at once. As such, Islamic laws developed with the moral and social progress of the Muslim community. Take, for example, the prohibition of intoxicants and gambling, which were common pastime activities in pre-Islamic Arabian culture. First, the Koran discourages intoxicants as the opposite of "goodly provision" (16:67). Then, the Book discourages intoxicants and gambling as major sins with little benefit (2:219). Thirdly, the Koran goes one step further by prohibiting prayer under the influence of intoxicants (4:43). Since Muslims pray five times a day, this law seriously limited the use of intoxicants in order to prepare the Muslim community for the last stage. Finally, in the fourth stage, the Koran prohibits the use of intoxicants and gambling altogether (5:90–91).

The Koran actually lays down very few laws in detail. The Scripture contains general, broad moral directives that form the basis of principles in Islamic law. *Fuqaha* (see "Extracting and Interpreting Sacred Law," earlier in this chapter) sometimes derive several principles from a single verse. The wisdom *(Illah)* or reasoning behind specific laws then provides the basis for additional legal ruling as new situations arise.

Most laws in the Koran derive from the concept of public benefit, which concerns itself with the physical, intellectual, moral, and spiritual well-being of individuals and society. The idea of public benefit extends into a principal of Islamic law that can be applied to new cultures and modern situations. In the modern age, traffic laws, for example, become a part of the sacred law *(Shariah),* and violating traffic laws is considered a sin before God. These traffic laws seek to bring physical protection to society, and are therefore an extension of one of the purposes of Islamic law.

Another example of a Koranic principal is the law of ease, which is derived from the Koranic saying, "God intends every ease for you. He does not want to put you to difficulties . . ." (2:185). From this principle, jurists concluded that piety does not come from undue hardship (like causing pain to the body), but rather from the ease of sincerely following God's laws. Islamic law understands this principle as the path of "moderation," known as *Wasatiyyah,* which encourages making things easy for people when issuing *Fatawah* and giving glad tidings when inviting people to Islam. It also encourages firmness in applying the fundamentals and in strengthening the objectives of Islam, while taking it easy on the details and being flexible on the ways and means of achieving Koranic objectives.

All the laws of the Koran can be broadly categorized into six main principles that form the basis of the *Shariah.* All laws found in the Islamic tradition find their roots in these six principles:

- ✔ **Preservation of religion:** These laws seek to establish the Oneness of God in society and the practice of Islamic faith. This principal also protects the free worship of all religions in society.

- ✔ **Preservation of life:** These laws sanctify the life of every human being and establish laws that protect life in society.

- ✔ **Preservation of lineage:** These laws preserve and strengthen family ties — the foundation of a healthy Islamic society. Also, laws that punish fornication and adultery fall into this category.

- ✔ **Preservation of property:** These laws preserve the rights of citizens to own property and seek wealth. Also, these laws protect society from theft in all its forms.

- ✔ **Preservation of honor:** Honor is the basis of human rights and dignity in the Islamic tradition. As such, these laws preserve the honor of citizens in society.

- ✔ **Preservation of intellect:** The Islamic tradition considers intellect and human reason sacred. As such, the *Shariah* seeks to protect the human intellect from any sort of physical or psychological harm. The laws prohibit things like alcohol, which impairs the use of intellect and judgment.

Muslims base their beliefs and actions on these principles of Islamic law that are found in the Koran.

Religious practices

The Islamic tradition considers every single moment of life sacred. Each act in life constitutes pious religious practice if done under divine guidance.

The four active pillars of faith constitute religious practice in the context of Islamic law:

- Prayer *(Salat)* five times a day (2:3)
- Fasting *(Sawm)* from dawn to sunset every day during the month of Ramadan (2:183–185)
- Purification of wealth through almsgiving *(Zakat)* (9:60)
- Pilgrimage to the House of God in Mecca once in a lifetime if you are financially and physically able *(Hajj)* (2:196–200)

See Chapter 12 for more information on what the Koran says about each pillar.

Social behavior

These laws deal with the rights and responsibilities that Muslims have over each other. This also includes proper social interaction, peaceful coexistence, and ethical economic transaction. Social behavioral laws also determine punishments for major crimes, such as murder and theft. See the section "Understanding the Islamic Penal Code," later in this chapter, for more information on the Islamic penal code.

Family law

Family laws in the Koran deal with healthy conduct in familial relationships, marriage, sexuality, divorce, and inheritance. Women's rights and responsibilities also play a large role in family law. See Chapter 15 for more information about Koranic laws and the family.

Dietary laws

Laws on eating and drinking form a small, yet important topic under Islamic law. What goes into your body directly affects your spiritual state of God-consciousness. As such, these laws form an essential part of the *Shariah*.

Laws of warfare

The Koran lays down specific conditions in which war is permissible. The Book also touches on the basic ethics during the time of war, including the distribution of war booty.

In the prophetic tradition

The Koran says about Muhammad, "You have indeed in the Messenger of God an excellent example for him who hopes in God and the Last Day, and who remember God much" (33:21). The Koran clearly points to Muhammad as the second source of authority in religious matters by calling on Muslims to "obey God and obey the Messenger," and if an argument arises to "refer it to God and the Messenger" (4:59).

The life example of Prophet Muhammad, known as the *Sunnah,* constitutes the second source of Islamic law. The *Sunnah* are narratives on Muhammad's life from his companions in the form of detailed events and quotes. The *Sunnah* includes the actions, sayings, and those things that Muhammad permitted or allowed by way of silence (known as approval) where the Prophet neither encouraged nor discouraged an act that took place in his presence. The *Sunnah* is historically preserved as reports, or *Hadith.*

The *Sunnah* explain and expand upon teachings of the Koran. The *Sunnah* also help clarify how to apply Koranic principles in life. For example, the Koran calls on Muslims to establish the daily prayers in their lives, but the Book never lays out the exact steps of how to pray. So, the *Sunnah* provides all the details of how to perform the prayers and detailed laws concerning the ritual.

Similarly, the Koran instructs Muslims to pay purifying alms, but the Book never says how much to pay. Muslims turn to the *Hadith* to find out how much purifying alms they must pay annually.

When Muslims seek to know the Will of God, they first begin with the Koran and then turn to the *Hadith* as their two primary sources of sacred knowledge. The life example of Prophet Muhammad plays a very important role in the development of Islamic law.

A *Hadith* consists of two parts: the chain of narrators (*Isnad;* see the following section) and then the body or content *(Matn).* A typical *Hadith* looks something like this:

> Malik bin Anas relates from Abu al-Zinnad and Muhammad bin Yahya bin Habban from Al-A'raj from Abu Hurayra that the Messenger said:

> "Let none of you seek a woman in marriage if his brother (in faith) already is seeking her."

Over time, collectors of *Hadith* traveled all across the Muslim world to find *Hadith.* Six collections of *Hadith* have particular authority and authenticity in the Islamic tradition: Ismail al-Bukhari, Muslim ibn al-Hajjaj, Abu Dawud, al-Nisai, al-Tirmidhi, and Ibn Majah. Al-Bukhari and Muslim enjoy the greatest authenticity in transmitting *Hadith.*

During the collection of the *Hadith*, obvious problems occurred with false or inaccurate reporting of what Muhammad did in fact say and do. To face this challenge, a tradition of *Hadith* criticism *(Mustalah al-hadith)* was developed to discern authentic reportings from unauthentic ones.

The science of *Hadith* collection examines both the *Isnad* and the *Matn* of a *Hadith*.

Isnad: Examining the chain of narration

For a *Hadith* to qualify as authentic, scholars must be able to trace it directly to someone who was present at the time Muhammad spoke or acted on the contents in the *Hadith*. The *Isnad* thoroughly examines the lives, character (trustworthiness), and memory of each person on a chain of narration that relates a saying or action of the Prophet. Doing so ensures that the *Hadith* truly represents the Will of God as spoken or acted by Prophet Muhammad.

The words of each narrator in the chain for a specific *Hadith* narration must match exactly in order to fully authenticate a *Hadith*. However, at times, two or three versions of a *Hadith* may exist as long as the wordings closely match and the meaning remains the same, but these *Hadith* have a slightly lesser degree of authentication.

Matn: Examining contents of the Hadith

Along with the chain of narrators, scholars also examine the actual contents of the *Hadith*. The contents must agree with the teachings and spirit of the Koran, since Muhammad's primary role was to convey the teachings of the Book. If a *Hadith* contradicts the Koran, then it is rejected as unauthentic. Similarly, if a *Hadith* under question directly contradicts a *Hadith* that has already been authenticated, then the *Hadith* is usually also rejected.

However, the teachings of Muhammad, like the Koran, evolved over time as the experiences of his community progressed. As such, two *Hadith* may offer different courses of action regarding a particular subject. These are not contradictory *Hadith*. Instead, there may be more than one way to do something, or a specific law develops after the complete development of the Muslim community. In such cases, the *Hadith* that is recorded later in history takes precedence over the *Hadith* related earlier in time.

Examining the contents of a *Hadith* ensures that the message remains consistent with the Koranic spirit and with those *Hadith* that have already been authenticated.

Levels of authentication

After examination of the *Isnad* and *Matn*, a *Hadith* may receive any one of the following levels of authenticity:

✔ **Sound *(sahih)*:** This is the best level of authenticity, where the chain of narrators and contents of the *Hadith* are impeccable. These *Hadith* become authoritative in the coding of Islamic law.

✔ **Good or acceptable *(hasan)*:** This level of authenticity usually applies to *Hadith* where some slight doubt about the chain of narration exists. For example, one of the narrators may have had a weak memory or some other weakness, but the other narrators passed the test of authenticity. These *Hadith* can also be used in the coding of Islamic law, but *sahih Hadith* are preferred over *hasan Hadith.*

✔ **Weak *(daif)*:** These *Hadith* are considered unauthentic either because a serious break in the narration exists or because the content of the *Hadith* is not acceptable.

However, the *Hadith* can still be used if it doesn't contradict the Koran or an authentic *Hadith* in spirit. For example, a famous saying of Muhammad reads, "Seek knowledge even if it is in China." This *Hadith* is in fact considered weak *(daif)* because of its chain of narration. However, its spirit is consistent with an authentic *Hadith* that says, "Seeking knowledge is incumbent on all Muslim men and Muslim women." And, it is certainly encouraged that Muslims use those *Hadith* that have been fully authenticated.

In the consensus of the scholars

Prophet Muhammad said that "The scholars of my community will never agree on a wrong." As such, in the development of Islamic law, consensus of the scholars, known as *Ijma'*, became the third source of sacred law. The basic idea of *Ijma'* is that if the scholars of a particular generation unanimously agree on a religious matter, then that ruling is codified into Islamic law.

Ijma' only comes into play when scholars can't find a clear directive on a particular matter in either the Koran or *Sunnah*. Scholars with a deep knowledge of Islamic sciences must make these rulings. They base their opinions on the spirit and reasoning of the Koran and *Sunnah,* and not on their own ideas.

As an example, take the following issue. When Islamic civilization grew outside the borders of Arabia, the Muslim community faced the new challenge of whether or not it was acceptable to make treaties with non-Muslim nations that opposed the Islamic state. Since no clear-cut directive existed in the Koran and *Sunnah* regarding this issue, scholars examined the spirit of the Scripture. The Koran says, "But if the enemy incline towards peace, you also incline towards peace" (8:61). From this verse, the scholars came to a consensus that it was in fact permissible to make treaties with those states that were belligerent towards the Muslim community as long as they ceased all hostilities.

In juristic analogy

Jurists in the Islamic tradition developed an institution of *Jtihad,* or an intellectual struggle to know the Will of God, to arrive at legal rulings in new cultures and times. At first this intellectual struggle was based on reasonable opinions *(Ra'y)* that were rooted in the Islamic tradition. However, over time, scholars felt that this methodology was too lose and feared that all sorts of unauthentic opinions could arise from this practice.

Under the leadership of the famous and influential jurist, Shafi', scholars of Islamic law institutionalized reason into a process of juristic analogy, known as *Qiyas.* If no clear ruling in the Koran, *Sunnah,* or *Ijma'* exists on a particular subject, then scholars seek a solution based on analogous situations found in the three sources.

Exploring the Contents of the Sacred Law

Scholars categorize the laws of *Shariah* into five ethical standards:

- **Obligatory *(Fard)*:** These laws are mentioned as explicit commands in the Koran and *Sunnah,* and can be derived from their wisdom and reasoning. These laws derive from the concept of benefit for individual and society alike. Acting on these obligations merits great reward from God. Avoiding or neglecting these duties constitutes a sin, punishable by God in the Hereafter and in some cases in this world as well.

  Personal obligations include the knowledge and practice of those things that every Muslim must do in their life as a Muslim. This includes things like practicing the pillars of Islam.

  Communal obligations include those duties that are obligatory on the community, but not necessary for every single Muslim. For example, not everyone must defend the community, but it is a communal obligation to secure the homeland.

- **Recommended *(Mandub)*:** These laws supplement the obligatory laws. These actions merit reward for their doing, but no sin for their neglect.

  For example, it is obligatory to pray five times a day. It is *recommended* that you add supplemental prayers onto those five prayers throughout the day in order to draw a closer connection with God.

- **Permitted *(Mubah)*:** These actions are simply allowed, without any moral quality of good or evil. For example, the Koran allows eating meat prepared by people of other monotheistic faiths and also marrying women of monotheistic faiths (5:5). These two actions are neither morally good nor morally evil; they are simply permitted with no reward or punishment attached.

Unless the Koran or *Sunnah* place a restriction on an action, it is usually permissible in its natural state, which means that everything is permissible unless it is specifically prohibited or contradicts the spirit of Islamic teachings. This is the most fundamental rule on dealings of daily life in the Islamic ethic.

✔ **Disliked *(Makruh)*:** These actions aren't forbidden, but are disliked or reprehensible. There is no punishment or sin for doing these actions, but there is reward in avoiding them. An excellent example of this concept is divorce. Divorce is considered "the most hateful of permissible things in the sight of God."

✔ **Forbidden *(Haram)*:** These actions are clearly prohibited. Forbidden actions are prohibited because they bring harm to the individual and to the community. Committing these actions is considered a sin, and in some cases is punishable. Avoiding these actions merits reward from God. Examples of Haram are murder, theft, adultery, drinking alcohol, and gambling. Generally speaking, those actions that lead to forbidden actions are also considered forbidden.

There are two types of forbidden actions: Those that are in themselves harmful, and those that are permissible, but become unlawful under certain circumstances. For example, giving charity qualifies as a morally good action, but giving charity from unlawful wealth (such as stealing money or unfair business practices) is forbidden.

Not all scholars agree on the categorization of every single ethical action. For example, some scholars feel that growing a beard is obligatory, while others say it is only recommended.

Also, the categorization of an ethical action can change over time with changing circumstances. For example, when the issue of smoking first came up, many Islamic scholars categorized it as disliked, because of the bad smell that comes from smoking. However, as medical discoveries made it clear that smoking in fact caused serious bodily harm, such as cancer and other diseases, then many scholars categorized smoking as prohibited, because it harms the preservation of life, which the *Shariah* seeks to protect. However, some legal opinions maintain that the ruling on smoking is a case-by-case basis, and depends on how smoking affects the individual's health.

Understanding the Islamic Penal Code

The Islamic penal code acts as a deterrent to evil. By setting strict standards on the most evil practices, people have to think ten times more before doing something they know they shouldn't do.

In Islamic courts that run on true Islamic teachings, penal laws have very high standards for conviction. Jurists rule each issue case-by-case, and the evidence presented before the court must be very solid.

The penal code also provides important exceptions. For example, according to the *Sunnah,* you can't convict those who are below the age of maturity or those who are not mentally fit to make ethically conscious choices.

In addition, when conditions make it humanely impossible or extremely difficult to abide by certain laws, then the Islamic courts can temporarily suspend those laws. For example, during the time of *Caliph* Umar, a major famine took place in an area that was under Islamic rule. In this situation, Umar applied a moratorium on the punishment of theft, since people were driven by severe need for basic necessities.

The penal code is built on the rule of law; Muslims can't just take the law into their own hands. As such, in the absence of an Islamic government, the penal code can't be applied. Islamic law can't be applied without the due process of law and right of appeal that can only take place in an Islamic state and Islamic courts.

In the following sections, I give you a quick rundown of each penal code and explain the Koran's reasoning behind each code.

Punishing murder

The Koran says that the penalty of unjustly taking another's life is the death penalty (2:178). This law applies equally, regardless of social or economic class.

However, the Koran also offers a second option out of the death penalty, called *Qisas,* or the law of remission. If the victim's family so wishes, they can forgive the murderer by asking for a reasonable compensation. The family and judge of the Islamic court decide the form of this compensation. The Koran strongly encourages this second option as "a concession and a Mercy from your Sustainer" (2:178). Also, in classical Islamic law, there must be four witnesses to the murder in order for the punishment of the death penalty to apply. Otherwise, some other penalty is given, such as life in prison.

However, the law of remission doesn't apply to a mass murderer or a serial killer. *Qisas* only applies for the murder of one person against another.

The Koran gives a very interesting explanation of this law by saying, "In the law of just retribution, o you men of understanding, there is life for you, so that you may restrain yourselves" (2:179). The Koran views the law of just retribution as a way of protecting life in society by encouraging patience rather than bloodshed, and by removing from society a person (the murderer) who has no regard for the sanctity of life. The law serves as both a deterrent and a way of preserving life in society.

Punishing the spreading of violence

The word for this penal code in Arabic is *Hirabah.* The Western tradition of Islamic Studies translates this word as "highway robbery" or "banditry." However, those crimes are only a part of a broader concept that seeks to prevent the instability in society caused by violence and fear. Indeed, in the Islamic tradition, jurists rarely ever limited the definition of *Hirabah* to armed robbery or its like. For example, a famous Spanish jurist by the name of Ibn 'Abd al-Barr defined *Hirabah* in this way:

> "Anyone who disturbs free passage in the streets and renders them unsafe to travel, striving to spread corruption in the land by taking money, killing people or violating what God has made unlawful to violate is guilty of Hirabah . . . be he a Muslim or a non-Muslim, free or slave, and whether he actually realizes his goal of taking money or killing or not."

The punishment for *Hirabah* is very severe. One found guilty of committing such a crime is to be "executed or crucified, or that their hands and feet be cut off from opposite sides, or that they be exiled from the land . . . except for those who repent before you are able to subdue them" (5:33–34).

Jurists can choose from among these four punishments for this crime based upon its severity. Jurists disagree on what level of crime merits what punishment.

Punishing high treason

Islamic jurists categorize high treason as a part of the spread of violence. This law applies to those who turn against Islam and assist the enemy in destroying the Islamic State.

Treason has different levels; the highest form of treason warrants the death penalty. Most non-Muslim countries, including the United States, have similar laws that apply to citizens found guilty of spying and other activities that harm national security.

The penal code deals very harshly with the spread of violence because it destabilizes society and inhibits human progress. This is one of those crimes that violates almost everything that *Shariah* wants to protect. Since Islamic law strives to bring benefit to society, it must strictly clamp down on those elements that bring utmost harm to society.

I strongly suggest that you read the article, "Domestic Terrorism in the Islamic Legal Tradition," by Professor Sherman Jackson, which compares and contrasts *Hirabah* with terrorism. You can find this article in the Fall 2001 edition of *The Muslim World*. You can read more about this journal at: www. blackwellpublishing.com/journal.asp?ref=0027-4909.

Punishing theft

The Koran lays down the law of robbery in the following passage: "As to the thief, male or female, cut off his or her hands: A retribution for their deed and exemplary punishment from God . . . But if the thief repents after his crime, and amends his conduct, God turns to him in forgiveness, for God is oft-Forgiving, most Merciful" (5:38–39). However, a majority of jurists say that, in light of the *Sunnah,* only the right hand should be cut off, and not both hands.

This law has three strict conditions placed on it, which prevent the punishment from taking place:

✔ **Unguarded objects:** If someone steals an unguarded object, then an Islamic court decides the punishment; cutting off the hand does not automatically apply. The judge may decide to apply a softer punishment.

✔ **Amount of stolen goods:** Jurists disagree on how much stolen goods warrant this punishment. The majority of jurists agree that petty thefts are exempt from this cutting off the hands, especially for first-time offenders.

✔ **Stealing necessities:** This punishment doesn't apply to those who steal out of the desperate need for survival. As such, this law does not apply to stealing food. Also, for example, if a homeless man or woman suffers from extreme cold and steals a coat, then this law does not apply to them. This restriction takes into account the obligation of the Islamic government to provide basic needs for survival, such as food and shelter, to each of its citizens.

This strict law seeks to strongly discourage and deter the theft of property, which is sacred in Islamic law. Those who violate this sacred law receive severe punishment in order to safeguard the rights of society as a whole.

Preventing unlawful sexual relations

The Koran says a man and woman that are found guilty of fornication should be flogged 100 times (24:2). According to the *Sunnah,* those who commit adultery should be lashed 100 times as well as stoned to death.

However, the proof for fornication or adultery is extremely strict. Basically, in order to convict a man or woman of unlawful intercourse, four male witnesses with a clean record of trustworthiness must have witnessed the act of sexual intercourse (24:4). Only the actual witnessing of the act — not just suspicion — can stand in an Islamic court.

Also, spying is completely forbidden in the Koran (49:12). As such, the testimony of someone who peeks or invades the privacy of another person's home can't be accepted. So, quite obviously, fornication or adultery is nearly impossible to prove, unless a man and woman commit a lewd sexual act in public.

Many people have a major misconception that this law applies only to women. In reality, the Koran makes it crystal clear that the law applies to both "the woman and the man" (24:2). Also, some courts, such as in Nigeria, have wrongly convicted women of fornication or adultery because they became pregnant outside of marriage. This is a misapplication of the law; neither the Koran nor the *Sunnah* allows pregnancy as proof of the crime.

In the following situations, the law does not require four witnesses for proof:

- **Husband witnesses his wife in adultery:** A man who witnesses his wife commit adultery with another man without any witnesses is required to come before the Islamic court and swear four times by God that he is speaking the truth. He takes a fifth oath that says that "he solemnly invokes the curse of God on himself if he tells a lie" (24:6–7). Then, the wife responds to the allegation in court. The wife also swears by God four times that she is not telling a lie. Her fifth time she, like her husband, invokes the wrath of God on herself if her husband is telling the truth (24:8–9).

  After the oaths, no penalty applies on the woman or the man since it is his word against hers. However, the marriage is dissolved in such a situation.

- **In the case of rape:** According to the *Sunnah,* in the case of rape, the testimony of the raped victim suffices to accuse the rapist, provided due process of law exists. If found guilty, the man faces death by stoning. The woman goes free without any punishment whatsoever.

Punishing false testimony of adultery

The Koran says, "And those who launch a charge against chaste women (or men), and produce not four witnesses (to support their allegations) — flog them with 80 stripes, and reject their evidence ever after: for such men are wicked transgressors" (24:4).

Making false charges of adultery is considered a grave sin in *Shariah.* This applies to those who make charges without four witnesses, and to those who produce four witnesses but through due process are found to have fabricated the event.

✔ **Admission of guilt:** If a person comes to the court saying that he or she committed fornication or adultery, he or she doesn't have to produce any witnesses. However, Islamic law generally discourages exposing that which God has kept hidden for you.

Also, according to the *Sunnah,* if a person comes to the judge with an admission of guilt, the judge should turn the person away three times to discourage self-indictment. Only if the person pursues the matter further should the judge also pursue the admission of guilt. You may be thinking, "What insane person would admit to committing adultery?" Pious Muslims believe that if one has accounted for a sin in this life, then he or she will not be punished for it in the hereafter.

Shariah seeks to preserve lineage and family. The institution of family serves as the moral and ethical foundation of the entire society. As such, harming the institution of marriage is a grave sin, one that *Shariah* seeks to stop at its roots.

Looking at the Four Schools of Law

Over time, four primary classical schools of Islamic law developed to interpret God's Will in the Koran and prophetic tradition. The four *Imams* don't have any major disagreements between them, but the principles that they derive for legal rulings differ widely. Most Muslims, either consciously or subconsciously, follow one of these four legal schools of thought.

The Hanafi School of Law

This school of law gets its name from An-Nu'man Ibn Thabit Abu Hanifa (700–767), originally from Afghanistan and the grandson of a freed slave. His work established a set of principles by which scholars could extract Islamic law from the Koran.

Abu Hanifa placed a lot of emphasis on *Qiyas,* or juristic analogy in order to gain flexibility in his legal opinions. Abu Hanifa also relied heavily on juristic preference *(Istihsan),* in which a jurist can choose between two options in order to promote the common good. As such, Hanafi law is considered one of the most flexible or lenient schools that exist today.

Hanafi law has the largest number of adherents. Its laws prevail in Central Asia and South Asia, where the largest numbers of Muslims live. Also, Hanafi law is very common in the South-Asian community of American Muslims.

The Maliki School of Law

Malik ibn Anas (716–795) was the first to publish a book on Islamic law, known as *al-Muwatta.* This *Madhhab* uses the narratives of the people of Medina (Prophet Muhammad's companions) as a source for Islamic law. Malik believed that since this generation of believers formed the original Muslim community, they would not create laws or practices that would differ from the prophetic guidance.

Malik also advocated making exceptions in Islamic law based on local custom *(Urf)* so long as that custom doesn't contradict the spirit of an established Islamic law. Malik also argued that development of law and legal rulings about modern concerns should favor the public good and the general welfare *(Istislah).* In such cases, the spirit of the law can sometimes override the letter of the law.

The Maliki School has the greatest number of followers in West Africa and North Africa; it is also commonly found in Egypt, the Sudan, Bahrain, and Kuwait. Also, this school is gaining popularity in the United States as some influential scholars advocate its practice for American Muslims.

The Shafi'i School of Law

Muhammad bin Idris al-Shafi'i (767–820) is considered among the most brilliant jurists in Islamic history. He codified the sources of Islamic law strictly into the Koran, *Sunnah* (prophetic tradition), *Ijma'* (consensus of the scholars), and *Qiyas* (juristic analogy). Shafi'i also rejected the Hanafi use of juristic preference *(Istihsan)* and the Maliki use of the Medina community as a source for Islamic law.

This school of law dominates in Southern Egypt, Southern Arabia, East Africa, Malaysia, Indonesia, and in some parts of Central Asia. American Muslims also commonly follow this school.

The Hanbali School

The school of law named after Ahmad Ibn Hanbal (780–855) is considered the most conservative of the four schools. Ibn Hanbal grew weary of using reason and analogy in the legal coding of Islamic law. However, he also developed the theory of permissibility *(Ibaha),* where any action that doesn't contradict the Koran and *Sunnah* is presumed lawful or legal. This created flexibility in an otherwise conservative tradition.

Muslims in Saudi Arabia, Oman, and Qatar mostly follow Hanbali law. This school also has a growing trend among converts to Islam in the United States.

Chapter 18

Struggling for God: Jihad

. . . .

In This Chapter

▶ Examining passages in the Koran about *Jihad*

▶ Knowing the ethics of *Jihad*

▶ Understanding the relationship between *Jihad* and Islamic law

▶ Finding out about martyrdom in Islam

▶ Analyzing contemporary *Jihad*

. . . .

irst things first: *Jihad* does not mean "Holy War." *Jihad* simply means to
struggle against evil for the sake of good. It forms an essential component of the Koran's message.

Jihad takes many forms. Prophet Muhammad told his companions that
"the greatest *Jihad* is to speak the truth in front of a tyrant ruler." Once a
young man came to the Prophet desiring to go with him on the battlefield
to defend the Muslims. Muhammad asked him if his parents were alive.
When he responded in the affirmative, Muhammad told the young man that
taking care of his parents was his *Jihad*. In the books of Islamic law, *Jihad*
encompasses non-military struggle, such as defending your property or the
property of another person or defending your family or another person's
family.

However, in the context of this chapter, I talk about a branch of *Jihad*, known
as *Qital* or "armed struggle." First, I begin by looking at a few verses in the
Koran that speak about *Jihad*. I also explain the ethics of armed struggle in
Islamic law. Next, I examine the relationship between the ideals of *Jihad* and
the ideals of Islamic law that shape *Jihad's* purpose. Finally, I analyze the concept of martyrdom in the Islamic tradition, and how this topic relates to the
modern world.

Finding the Spirit of Jihad

Islam is a proactive faith. *Jihad* gives Muslims a mechanism through which they can defend the sanctity of life, human rights, and freedom of religion.

In the following sections, I look at passages in the Koran that talk about the purpose and spirit of a branch of *Jihad,* known as *Qital* or armed struggle.

Defending life and religion

The first passage that speaks about *Qital* (armed struggle, a branch of *Jihad*) in the Koran begins by saying, "Fight in the cause of God those who fight you, but do not transgress limits, for God loves not transgressors" (2:190).

The Koran's very first clause about *Qital* establishes the purpose of armed struggle as self-defense, and explicitly prohibits excessive force.

The passage goes on to say, "And slay them wherever you catch them, and turn them out from where they turn you out. For oppression is worse than killing. But fight them not at the Sacred Mosque, unless they fight you there. But if they fight you, slay them. Such is the reward of those who oppose faith" (2:191).

Some critics of the Koran like to take the "them" in 2:191 out of context and then claim that Islam teaches the killing of all non-Muslims. In truth, the "them" comes from the previous passage (191) and refers specifically to "those who fight you."

Sharing the fight

You can find this concept of good fighting evil in Islam, Christianity, and Judaism. For example, all three faith traditions celebrate the story of Prophet David's heroic defeat of the tyrant Goliath as a way to inspire the weak over the strong. Even outside the Abrahamic faiths, *Jihad* often surfaces in one form or the other. For example, Zoroastrians believed that wars would always exist between the forces of light and darkness, between good and evil.

Jihad is not this new, wild concept that Muhammad suddenly came up with. Rather, most of the world's religions share this struggle of good against evil.

Verse 2:191 advises that once the battle for self-defense has begun, then it should be pursued with full vigor and not half-heartedly, so that oppression may end. The verse also says that Muslims should not fight their enemies near the Sacred Mosque unless the enemies attack first.

Next, the passages says, "But, if they cease, God is oft-Forgiving, most Merciful" (2:192). This clause introduces a further ethical limitation that tells Muslims to forgive their enemies if they end their war of aggression, in order to reflect God's Forgiveness and Mercy.

Then, the passage teaches to "Fight them on until there is no more oppression and religion belongs to God alone. But, if they cease, let there be no hostility except to those who practice oppression" (2:193). This passage outlines *Qital's* objectives against those who continue their war of aggression: Fight to end oppression; fight to secure the freedom of religious worship — of both belief and practice of faith. Like the ethical limitation found in 2:192, this passage calls for the end of all hostilities if the enemy ceases to fight. But, the war must continue against those who continue to oppress.

Ayah 2:194 introduces the final ethical limitation to this first passage about armed struggle. (See Chapter 3 for more information about the *Ayah*.) The *Ayah* says that no fighting should take place in the last four months of the year, known as the "prohibited months," unless the Muslims are attacked first. (This was actually a pre-Islamic Arab custom and the Koran honors it as a means to achieve peace.) As such, Muslims are only allowed to break the custom if they are "transgressed" against first.

This important law shows that the ethics of *Jihad* do accept institutions and customs that seek peaceful resolutions to conflicts or provide an alternative to war even in times when enemies create conflict.

This passage, in relation to *Jihad* as armed struggle, seeks to defend the sanctity of life and freedom of worship.

Defending human rights and freedom of worship

Passage 22:39–41 provides clear objectives for *Qital.*

Ayah 22:39 reinforces the notion of self-defense (see the previous section) by giving Muslims permission to fight against those who wage war on them.

Ayah 22:40 establishes a clear-cut reason to pursue *Qital:* "They are those who have been expelled from their homes in defiance of right (for no cause), except that they say, 'Our Sustainer is God.'" This *Ayah* allows *Qital* for the purpose of defending human rights and the freedom of religion.

The same *Ayah* goes on to say, "Did not God check one set of people by means of another, there would have surely been pulled down monasteries, churches, synagogues, and mosques, in which the name of God is commemorated in abundant measure. God will certainly aid those who aid his cause. . . ." This incredible *Ayah* speaks of defending the freedom of worship for Muslims *and* for other faiths!

Ayah 22:41 describes how Muslims should behave if they win against their enemies and assume leadership of the land: "Those who if We establish them in the land, establish regular prayers and give purifying alms. Enjoin what is right and forbid wrong. . . ." In victorious *Jihad,* Muslims should avoid arrogant displays of rampage and oppression against former enemies. Rather, they should establish freedom of worship, uplift the economic condition of the poor and needy, and implement public benefits while struggling against public harm. In essence, *Jihad* establishes human rights for people in the land.

Dispelling the myths behind passage 9:5

A few passages about *Qital,* when read out of Scriptural and historical context, give rise to misunderstandings about the objectives and ethics of armed struggle in Islam. Of course, I can't go over all of them in this book, but I want to tell you about one passage in particular that both Muslim radicals and non-Muslim critics love to quote in pursuit of their specific agendas.

This passage is 9:5, which in part says, "And so, when the sacred months are over, then fight and slay those who associate divinity with other than God wherever you find them, and seize them, beleaguer them, and lie in wait for them in every conceivable place. . . ."

Radicals wrongly use this passage to argue that Muslims must fight and kill the unbelievers, or at the very least, to justify the killing of innocent non-Muslims in terrorist attacks. Critics of the Islamic tradition misuse this verse to try and "prove" that Islam is an inherently violent religion that encourages the killing of "infidels."

The beginning of this passage points to one of the major mistakes that people make when they misuse this verse. The *Ayah* begins with "And so." From a grammatical standpoint, obviously, "And so" refers to important, related text — its *context* — that precedes this *Ayah.* If you start backtracking, you find four essential verses that precede 9:5. Looking at these four *Ayat,* you find the context of the entire *Surah,* even if you don't know anything about Islamic history.

Fighting ethically

The teachings of Abu Bakr, the first *Caliph* of Islam and close companion of Prophet Muhammad, clarify the ethics of armed struggle. He taught his companions the following ethics:

- **Do not commit treachery or deviate from the right path:** This teaching calls believers not to abandon the Muslim army during conflict, to fight in battle with a God-conscious mind, and to avoid becoming the oppressor in the fighting against oppression.

- **Do not mutilate dead bodies:** This teaching seeks to end oppression and bring freedom, not to dishonor those who have died and those who are alive.

- **Do not kill women, children, or aged men:** Scholars also include non-combatant men in this teaching.

- **Do not harm fruit-bearing trees:** *Jihad* seeks to end oppression. As such, Muslims must protect the environment and food stocks so that inhabitants of the land do not suffer hunger or disease.

- **Do not steal the enemy's food:** Stealing is prohibited as an unethical act, and war does not legitimize stealing.

- **Protect rabbis, priests, and monks:** Muslims must protect religious people and institutions because *Qital* seeks to establish the freedom of worship.

Scholars of Islamic law have identified other war ethics from the practice of Prophet Muhammad and early generations of pious Muslim leaders:

- **Do not wage wars of hostilities:** Muslims can't start wars unless they have justification of self-defense, stopping of oppression, or freedom of religion.

- **Only a state leader can declare war:** Islamic scholars agree that offensive armed struggle can't take place unless the leader of an Islamic state officially declares war. Surprise attacks and unofficial wars are completely forbidden. However, defensive armed struggle to resist oppression and tyranny is generally permitted even without a legitimate state leader.

- **Invite enemies to Islam:** Before any hostility takes place, the Islamic state must invite its enemies to Islam. If they accept, then all hostilities must end, and former enemies become brothers in faith. According to several Islamic jurists, the state must also issue this invitation throughout the war in an effort to end hostilities.

- **Struggle only for good purposes:** *Qital* may only occur to serve the public good. Any other type of war, such as one fought to acquire resources, is completely forbidden. Resources can only be acquired through trade that is by mutual goodwill — that benefits public good of both the seller and the buyer. Killing and destruction for resources is not an ethical act, even if it may benefit some in the short term (4:29–30).

- **Do not wage war to seize land or expand territory:** Muslims are allowed to fight for just reasons, but simply conquering land without establishing justice is impermissible.

- **Do not poison wells or food stocks:** Many contemporary scholars of Islamic law believe that this rule also forbids the use of modern warfare with chemical and biological weapons.

Ayah 9:1 announces the annulment of a treaty from God and His Messenger with the Pagans. Historically, this treaty, known as the Treaty of Hudabiyya, guaranteed mutual peace for ten years. *Ayah* 9:2–3 gives a period of four months for the Pagans of Mecca to travel freely and time to repent. *Ayah* 9:4 then clarifies the reason for this announcement of war. It says that treaties are "not dissolved with those Pagans with whom you have entered into alliance and who have subsequently not failed you in anything, nor aided anyone against you. . . ."

The *Ayat* that precede 9:5 identify a very specific foe on which *Jihad* should be waged: those Pagans (by logic of 9:4) who broke the treaty by showing hostility, and aided the enemies of the Muslim community. As such, it is a severe distortion to depict 9:5 as an absolute, eternal war of Muslims against all Pagans (peaceful or hostile) for all times to come. Rather, 9:5 only justifies war against those who violate mutually agreed upon treaties, wage violent attacks against the Muslim community, and aid others in destroying the Muslims.

As you read further on, the passage tells Muslims to honor their treaties with Pagans who stand true to their pledges. Even those Pagans who break a treaty are given ample time to mend their ways, and are even guaranteed asylum if they come to the Muslims seeking protection (9:6–16).

Giving Ayah 9:29 its proper context

Ayah 9:29 says that Muslims should fight those who deny God and the Last Day, and deny the laws of moral law, and refuse to acknowledge the Truth from among the People of the Book, until they pay the exemption tax *(Jizya)* willingly after being subdued or humbled in war.

Some people mistakenly take this *Ayah* to mean that Muslims should fight Jews and Christians living in Muslim lands unless they pay the *Jizya* tax. In truth, the *Hadith* (see Chapter 17) clearly outlines the true purpose of the tax: to exempt non-Muslim men from service in the Muslim army. (Non-Muslims shouldn't be required to participate in armed struggle for a faith they don't believe in.) The money of this tax then goes into supporting the Islamic state's army, which guarantees protection of all non-Muslim communities living under the Islamic state. However, non-Muslim men who are not income providers for their families do not have to pay the *Jizya* tax.

This passage appears in the context of a *Surah* that discusses the hostilities of war during the time of revelation — a time when Jews and Christians aided the Pagans against the Muslim community. However, *Ayah* 9:29 in no way diminishes other passages found throughout the Koran that call for peaceful coexistence between faiths, such as 60:8.

Connecting Qital with Islamic Law

When discussing the purpose and ethics of *Qital* in the Islamic tradition, you must understand that *Qital* does not exist as an independent institution. Rather, *Qital* exists under the objectives of Islamic law (*Shariah;* see Chapter 17).

Keep the following points of Islamic law in mind when considering the role of *Jihad:*

- **Having rationale *(Ma'aillah)*:** Some Islamic laws have a clear rationale behind them, and some laws don't, such as the prohibition on eating pork. *Qital* as law has a clear rationale of pursuing justice. *Qital* can't take place without distinct objectives and proper rationale.

- **Promoting public policy for good:** Islamic law fosters public benefit for good, such as protecting the sanctity of religion, life, family, property, honor, and intellect. As such, *Qital* must serve these purposes and not harm them in the least.

- **Measuring good and evil:** Islamic law dictates that if you face an evil choice that may lead to some good, then you must still choose to avoid the evil. *Qital* must operate under the same principle. Protection from harm takes precedence over acquisition of benefit.

- **Protecting public security:** Islamic law protects society from fear, terror, and a sense of helplessness. Violating public security entails heavy penalties (see Chapter 17). *Qital* should never include actions, such as random murder or hijackings, which create public insecurity.

- **Reflecting the realities of time and place:** Islamic law functions through a systematic process that must take into consideration the realities of modern life. *Qital,* too, must reflect the social, economic, and political realities of the modern world.

Understanding Martyrdom

Those who die fighting in a just war, living by the ethical principles of *Qital,* receive the honorary title of *Shaheed,* loosely translated as "martyrdom." However, the Arabic translates better as "to have witnessed." A martyr witnesses the Truth by sacrificing his or her own life for the greater good of society.

Elevating justice over revenge

Caliph Ali was once in a battle where he wrestled his enemy to the ground. As Ali lifted his sword to kill the enemy, the man spat in his face. Ali paused, dropped the sword, and let the man go, because he was afraid that his heart had become impure with a sense of anger and revenge, rather than justice — the true pursuit of the Muslim warrior during *Qital.*

Many such stories in the Islamic tradition emphasize inner consciousness over ego on the battlefield.

Like *Qital,* martyrdom can take place anywhere, not just on the battlefield. Any Muslim who dies in a sincere effort to bring good to the world becomes a martyr. As such, the *Hadith* teach that a mother who dies in childbirth achieves the status of a martyr. Similarly, someone who defends a life, or property, or any other sacred aspect of life, and dies in the process is honored as a *Shaheed al-akhira.*

However, the *Hadith* also clearly state that martyrdom comes only to those whose hearts fight sincerely for the sake of God, and not to those who seek worldly admiration. In fact, such people will go to the hellfire, instead of paradise, on the Day of Judgment.

The true martyr receives high rewards in the Hereafter for putting down his or her life for the greater good. God forgives the sins of a martyr, and grants him or her the highest levels of paradise and right to intercede.

Prophet Muhammad and his companions gave greater attention to the inner *Jihad* (struggle) of elevating the soul over the ego than they gave to armed struggle. A warrior must be brave and steadfast; he or she must also possess disciplined piety, with the awareness that God watches his or her every move.

Looking at Jihad in Today's World

The world faces some serious uphill battles today as activists and academics try to bridge the gap between the Muslim world and the West. *Jihad* in the modern era plays a major role in shaping this debate.

It goes without saying that this subject is more complex than a single section can cover fully. The following basic concepts can help you begin your understanding of this topic.

Radical readings of the sacred Scripture have turned the justice of *Jihad* into fear of *Jihad*. Some violent groups try to achieve legitimacy by distorting passages from the Koran to fuel their campaigns (see the section "Finding the Spirit of *Jihad*," earlier in this chapter).

Such groups often use an element in the science of Koranic interpretation *(Tafsir)* to justify their beliefs and cause. This element of *Tafsir* is known as "Abrogation," whereby earlier injunctions are replaced by later injunctions that were revealed after the full development of the Muslim community. For example, if two different teachings on one subject exist, then the *Ayah* revealed historically later cancels out the historically earlier *Ayah*.

Abrogation facilitates the process of gradual teaching, such as the prohibition of alcohol in three different steps. But, classical interpreters never used this method to replace verses based on their whims and desires. However, radical interpreters began arguing that passages, such as 9:5 and 9:29, which call Muslims to arms against non-Muslims, abrogate all other passages in the Koran that call for mutual cooperation and kindness — without any credence to the context of the *Ayat* and its scientific interpretation. So, these radicals also abrogate the just war teachings that place ethical limitations on *Qital*.

Such groups also take advantage of the fact that some historical understandings of *Jihad* are also difficult to translate into the modern era. During the time of Prophet Muhammad, and in the generations that followed, Muslims lived in extremely dangerous times and places. Imperial civilizations that constantly sought to expand their territory dominated the world; Muslims lived in a world that primarily espoused a "conquer or be conquered" philosophy.

Muslims reacted to this historical reality by expanding their civilizations. They did so as proactive self-defense and also with a belief that freedom of worship could only occur with Islamic rule. Some scholars of Islam (certainly not a majority), living in this political fear, also developed a theory that said that all of Islamic civilization was the "Abode of Peace *(Dar-al-Islam)*" and territory outside of Islamic civilization was the "Abode of War *(Dar-al-Harb).*" This was not a prophetic teaching, but rather a worldview that reflected the political climate of the time. Other scholars living in the same period disagreed with this categorization. Instead, they argued that Islamic civilization was *Dar-al-Istijaba* (Abode of the people who answer the call of Islam) and *Dar-ad-Dawah* (Abode of people who should be invited to Islam).

Most Muslims today realize that humanity lives now in a new social and political order where such a worldview no longer applies. But some radical groups cling to this theory. They see the entire world as an Abode of War, because not a single country functions according to their interpretation of Islam. Rhetoric by some politicians in the West that says, "either you're with us or with the terrorists" helps fuel this thought.

Many living in the Muslim world often view the world through the lens of their lives, which are often full of despair, lack of purpose, and feelings of humility. Poverty plays a role, but not the primary one.

More so, from my observations, Muslims, poor and rich alike, are frustrated by the failed regimes that rule over them. The citizens of these countries feel that their governments have allowed world powers to exploit their resources, while Muslims are left without jobs and other public benefits.

Also, many Muslims are angered by the perception that while world leaders talk about democracy and freedom, they sometime support the very regimes that have crushed true Islamic movements based on democracy, freedom, and justice in the Muslim world. This is why the Koran warns: " . . . O mankind! All your transgressions are bound to fall back upon your own selves. . . . "(10:23).

So, all these elements (and more) are exploited by radical groups for their political agenda by using unjust or unethical means of violence.

However, it is not fair or accurate to classify all Muslim revolutionaries and reformers with a broad paintbrush. In many countries, Muslims fight for their freedom and right to be governed by justice. Many Muslims engage in just struggles against oppression, and are wrongly called "radicals" or "terrorists" — politically loaded words often used to discredit the opponent, their reforms, and their ideas. But, as President Kennedy once said, "Those who make peaceful revolution impossible, make violent revolutions inevitable."

In order to sideline the radical, politically violent interpretations of _Jihad,_ the West needs to work with Muslims to eliminate the political and social realities that feed radical thought. Doing so entails much more than sheriff-style military occupations; it requires working with Muslim intellectuals, reformers, and activists both in the Muslim world and in the West to bring just reforms

Ultimately, change must come from within. The Koran reminds believers of a spiritual truth: "Verily, never will God change the condition of a people until they change what is in themselves . . ." (13:11).

If you want to read more about _Jihad_ in the modern world, I recommend _Unholy War: Terror in the Name of Islam,_ by John L. Esposito, published by Oxford University Press.

Chapter 19

Discussing Women in the Koran

In This Chapter

▶ Looking at stories that relate to the Koranic worldview on women

▶ Examining verses that speak of women's rights and roles in society

▶ Clearing up misconceptions about women in the Scripture

The topic of women in the Islamic tradition inspires a great deal of passionate debate. All too often, this debate disintegrates into sweeping generalizations about the traditional Muslim woman and the Western woman: The Muslim woman is called oppressed and old-fashioned; the Western woman is accused of being a commercial product who uses her body to sell everything from cars to beer.

The roots of this impasse lie in a lack of education about the Islamic tradition by the West, and a lack of education about Western society in the Muslim world. In reality, as this chapter demonstrates, the two worldviews about women's rights and liberation are quite similar, even if those views are expressed outwardly in different ways.

In this chapter, I offer a look at women in the Koran that counters many popular notions about the Muslim woman. First, I discuss the Koranic worldview about women through stories in the Scripture. Then, I tell you what rights the Koran gives women.

Finding Equality in the Scripture

Every religious tradition transmits stories from one generation to another. These stories convey ethical and moral values to inspire young and old towards greatness.

In this section, I point out stories in the Koran about women with an eye on how these narratives form a unique worldview in the Islamic tradition.

Eve: A model for gender equality

The story of Eve in the Koran serves as the basis for the spiritual equality of both genders, and as the foundation for cooperation between both sexes.

Eve's story in the Koran stands in stark contrast with the Biblical narrative of creation. Feminists might find these differences between the Biblical and Koranic narratives quite interesting.

In the Garden

Consistent with the overall literary style of the Koran, which presents its stories in a moral narrative rather than a historical narrative, Eve doesn't appear until passage 7:19 as Adam's wife. Here, God tells Adam to dwell with his wife in the Garden while enjoying its fruits, except for a specific tree known as the Forbidden Tree.

Unlike the Bible, the Koran presents Eve as being created independent of Adam (not from his rib), and also as having equal knowledge of the Forbidden Tree.

In passage 7:20–22, the Koran says that Satan, in the guise of a sincere advisor, begins whispering temptations into the hearts of both Adam and Eve to eat from the Forbidden Tree. Adam and Eve fall into Satan's temptation by eating from the tree, which causes their fall from heavenly bliss. As the couple struggle to hide their shame as a result of sinning, God reminds both Adam and Eve that he warned them about Satan's deceptions.

The Koran offers a story that absolves Eve, and thus woman, from tempting Adam into sin. Rather, the Koran identifies Satan as the enemy of both sexes. Satan plays tempter while Adam and Eve together represent the tempted.

Before Adam and Eve are sent down from the Garden, they offer a supplication together, saying to God: "Our Sustainer! We have wronged our own souls. If you forgive us not and bestow not upon us Your Mercy, we shall certainly be among the losers" (7:23). This supplication recognizes both Adam's and Eve's ability to understand the nature of good and evil at the spiritual and intellectual level. Furthermore, Adam and Eve mutually agree that their own souls caused their fall, rather than Eve blaming the Serpent and Adam blaming the woman for the cause of sinning, like in the Biblical narrative.

Finally, both Adam and Eve are forgiven for their sin, because they acknowledge their wrongdoing and repent to God. Adam and Eve go to earth not as a punishment, but as the next step in their spiritual and moral development. More importantly, in the context of this chapter, Eve doesn't receive the punishment of pregnancy and serving under her husband's rule, as is assigned to her in the Bible. Rather, as the supplication to God shows, Eve goes with Adam to earth as a spiritual companion who turns to God seeking His forgiveness and guidance.

Beyond the Garden

The story of Eve serves as the foundation of the Koranic worldview on women in six ways:

- ✔ Woman is created from a single soul, just like man.

- ✔ Women and men have equal knowledge and ability to comprehend divine injunctions.

- ✔ Men and women are spiritual partners who have the ability to enjoy God's presence and are equally susceptible to Satan's temptations.

- ✔ Both men and women are inherently modest in covering their sexuality in front of each other.

- ✔ Both men and women equally posses the spiritual awareness *(Taqwa)* to return to God *(Tawba)* after oppressing their own souls through sin.

- ✔ Both men and women equally deserve and equally receive God's Mercy and Forgiveness after repenting for their sins.

Respecting woman as childbearer

The Koran views Eve's ability to bare children not a punishment, but as a deeply spiritual experience. The Koran says that the parents, and especially the mother, deserve almost the same respect and gratitude as God Himself for upholding hardship and nurturing their child during pregnancy and afterwards (31:14, 46:15).

God has also said, through Prophet Muhammad, that the womb *(Rahm)* derives its name from divine Mercy *(Rahman)* and serves as the source of mercy for humanity. Also, Prophet Muhammad said that a pregnant woman's spiritual experience is like someone who spends all night in prayer, and all day fasting. Muhammad also said that the status of anyone who dies in childbirth is the same status as a martyr in the sight of God.

The Scripture presents this worldview of gender cooperation most articulately with passage 9:71, which describes men and women as friends who together enjoin good and forbid evil in society. Also, the cooperative relationship between Adam and Eve as husband and wife is defined by tranquility in mutual love and mercy (30:21).

The Virgin Mary: A divinely inspired woman

Mary (*Maryam* in Arabic) is known as the one who has been chosen and raised in stature by God as the role model for all of humanity (3:42). As such, looking at how the Koran describes Mary can help you understand the overall Koranic worldview on women.

Woman as equal to man

Mary's story begins with her mother, who the Koran calls the wife of Imran. Mary's mother pledges the fruit of her womb to the service of God (3:35). By making this pledge, Mary's mother assumed that God would bless her with a son who would devote himself to the Temple. But, to her surprise, she bears a female child, who, according to traditional Judaic law, couldn't be devoted to the Temple. To this surprise, God says "The male is not like the female" (3:36).

Those with false pride of male superiority wrongly take this verse to mean that the male is better than the female. However, the Scriptural context of this verse proves the falsity of such a claim. Rather, God says that this child, by virtue of being woman, possesses the spiritual and physical ability to give birth to one of the greatest gifts to humanity — namely the birth of Jesus. The honor for Mary is so great in the Koran, that whenever Jesus is mentioned, he is described as the "son of Mary." In other words, Jesus, with his own prophetic greatness, is honored through Mary.

In service to God

People sometimes mistakenly say that truly righteous women dedicate themselves to obeying their husbands. However, as the role model for humanity, Mary is honored in the Koran not for her service to her husband, but rather for her service of God. This does not mean that Muslim women should avoid marriage and nurturing the family into a God-conscious unit of society. Rather, "obedience" (see Chapter 15 about women's role in family life) to the husband within the family unit depends on obedience to God and His laws first and foremost.

The Book describes Mary as prostrating humbly before God, and describes her soul as divinely inspired purity and beauty (3:37). When the angels come to Mary in 3:42–43, they teach her that in order to achieve purity, she should worship her Lord devoutly, prostrate herself in humility, and bow in respect with all those who prostrate and bow before God.

In the Koran, Mary doesn't confine herself to the home in order to reach purity, but rather joins a group of God's devotees who also submit to God through worship.

A birth in purity

In 3:45, the angels give Mary the good news of baring in her womb a Prophet of God, known as Jesus Christ, who is to be honored in this world and in the Hereafter. Mary is shocked to hear the news, because no man had ever touched her. To this God says, "Even so, God creates what He wills. When He has decreed a matter, He but says to it, 'Be,' and it is" (3:47).

When Mary becomes pregnant, she retires to a remote place where the pains of childbirth drive her to anguish. During this time of distress, an angel calls out to her to shake the tree that gives her refuge. Upon doing this, Mary receives the gifts of fresh ripe dates and cool water.

Of course, as is the nature of people, false rumors start spreading about Mary when she brings baby Jesus to her people (19:27–28). The Koran vehemently defends Mary from all false accusations of being unchaste, and categorizes her accusers as among those who have rejected faith (4:156). The Koran also says that Jesus performs the miracle of speaking from the cradle in defense of Mary's chastity. As such, one of Jesus' main duties is to honor and treat his mother, Mary, with utmost kindness (19:32).

For womanhood

Mary's story represents some very important teachings about women according to the Koranic worldview:

✔ People should treat the birth of a female child with the same joy as that of a male, because both sexes have the ability to devote themselves fully to God.

✔ Purity of the soul for both sexes comes from their worship and obedience to God alone, from which all other social rights and responsibilities emanate.

The Koran dismisses the false notion that women were created to serve their husbands. Rather, just like men, women were created for the purpose of serving God.

- ✔ Women have the ability and human purity to receive divine inspiration. As such, a minority of Islamic scholars believe that Mary was actually a prophet, and all agree that she was at the very least an honored and pious sage.

- ✔ Childbirth is not a means of punishment, rather a means of purification that earns utmost honor and kindness from society, and from children in particular.

The Koran articulates complete moral and spiritual equality between the sexes in a beautifully rhyming verse, 33:35–36, which describes the righteous qualities and responsibilities of men and women as being exactly the same.

Other famous and infamous women in the Koran

In this section, I look at other stories in the Koran with female characters, in order to show the Koranic worldview that women, like men, are capable of great spiritual and moral achievements, as well as evil actions.

The mother of Moses and wife of Pharaoh

Passage 28:7 introduces Moses' mother, where God inspires her to give suckle to Moses. Fearing for his safety (because Pharaoh ordered the killing of all children born to the Israelites), she casts baby Moses into the river with the promise that God would return her beloved son back to her.

The people of Pharaoh find baby Moses in the river and take him to be killed. Pharaoh's wife shows mercy to the child and begs Pharaoh not to harm him (28:9). In the meantime, Moses' mother feels such anguish that she begins to lose faith; the Koran says that God strengthens her heart with faith (28:10). In the following passages, Moses is restored to his mother as a sign that God's promise always holds true (28:12–13).

In both of these stories, women receive divine inspiration and perform acts of great spiritual strength and truth. Pharaoh's wife is only briefly mentioned, but her role is significant because part of her piety is to struggle against her unjust and tyrant husband. For this, the Koran honors her as a role model for all believers in God. As such, the Koranic worldview discredits the portrayal of women as submissive and weak beings. Rather, the Koran tells the story of brave women who show great strength of faith at times when they could succumb to despair.

The queen of Sheba

The story of Sheba, Bilquis in the Arabic tradition, comes up in the context of Prophet Solomon's story and his ability to communicate with animals. A Hoopoe (a type of bird, known for its beautiful chest) reports to Solomon that he has found a woman ruling over Sheba with a great kingdom (27:23). The Hoopoe tells Solomon that the queen of Sheba's kingdom associates partners with God by worshipping the sun.

Solomon sends a letter to the queen of Sheba that calls her in the name of God, most Gracious, most Merciful, to turn away from all arrogance and to submit to God alone (27:28–31). The queen of Sheba then seeks the advice of her counsel who advise her to declare war on Solomon. The queen rejects the counsel's advice and says that only kings invade lands and distort the nature of noble people. Instead, she sends Solomon a monetary gift through her ambassador (27:35).

Prophet Solomon tells the ambassador that what he really wants from the queen is not her money, but rather for her to submit to God (27:36–37). The queen of Sheba herself comes before Solomon, and, after hearing the teachings of God, she turns away from her association with other gods. The queen then turns in repentance to God saying, "O my Sustainer! I have indeed wronged my own soul: I do submit, with Solomon, to the Sustainer of the worlds" (27:44).

This story represents a very intriguing worldview about women in the Koran. First, the queen of Sheba serves as a leader who possesses the intellectual strength to go against the advice of her mostly-male counsel. Also, the queen has the moral consciousness of knowing the true nature of unjustified invasions into other lands. Finally, the queen of Sheba possesses the spiritual awareness to reject false worship and to turn to God in repentance and submission. In short, the queen of Sheba represents woman's ability to serve as an effective leader with the courage, moral consciousness, and spiritual awareness necessary to make just decisions on behalf of her people.

The wives of Aziz, Noah, Lot, and Lahab

These four wives represent the dark side of human consciousness in the Koran.

The wife of Aziz is Prophet Joseph's master. The Koran condemns her for following her passionate desires and trying to tempt the handsome Joseph into committing adultery. When Joseph rejects her temptations by remembering God, the wife of Aziz seeks to punish him by accusing Joseph of tempting her. Joseph is found not guilty because his shirt was torn from the back, which proved that he was trying to escape the woman's temptation. Aziz's wife, still driven by her lower passions, forces Joseph to either sleep with her or to live in prison. Joseph, as a truly righteous servant of God, chooses prison rather than sexual immorality (12:21–33).

The wife of Aziz is the first woman to be condemned in the Koran, because her lower passions make her commit injustice against Prophet Joseph.

The Koran condemns the wives of Prophets Lot and Noah in separate passages for rejecting, out of arrogance, their husbands' divinely inspired call to serve God (66:10). Both are condemned not for disobeying their husband, but for rejecting God's divine injunctions.

Finally, the wife of Abu Lahab, who was Prophet Muhammad's worst enemy, is also condemned in the Koran because of her persecution and acts of cruelty against the Muslims of Mecca (111:4).

The only time women are condemned in the Koranic worldview is when they, just like men, follow their lower passions, reject God in arrogance, and practice cruelty towards others. Otherwise, the stories that represent women in the Koran give narratives of piety, nobility, compassion, courage, and intellectual greatness. These righteous stories have inspired women throughout Islamic history and continue to do so. Perhaps the treatment of women in many Muslim cultures today provides a sign of how much Muslims can forget and ignore their own tradition's teachings.

Discerning Women's Rights in Divine Law

Many of the rights granted to women in the Koran are the same rights that women had to fight for in the United States and were not granted until the early 1960s. Many of these laws are even more startling when you consider that they were revealed over 1,400 years ago in a society that by all historical accounts simply treated women as tools for sexual gratification.

Divine law presents the rights of women as supplemental to the broader context of human rights. In other words, women receive all the same rights as the rest of society in Islamic law (see Chapter 17).

Some of the laws regarding women, such as modesty rules, inheritance, marriage, and so on, are discussed briefly in passages of the Koran. More laws regarding women are found in the *Sunnah*. Laws on women's rights and responsibilities are a major focus of books on jurisprudence, with hundreds of pages dedicated solely to women in relation to Islamic law.

Having full rights under the law

Because the Koran makes it crystal clear that women are spiritually equal to men (4:1; 4:124; 33:35; 57:12; 49:13), society and Islamic law must treat them as equals. As such, women have the same moral duties and responsibilities (with a few exceptions) as men, and are held accountable for their deeds in the same way as men.

Right to inheritance

The Koran affords women rights to the inheritance of their relatives (4:11–13). Generally, the inheritance of the woman is half that of men.

Some erroneously argue that this inheritance law proves that Islam values men more than women. However, you must remember that under Islamic law, women bear absolutely no responsibility to financially maintain their families. Women can spend their wealth in any way they see fit (of course, within moral boundaries). On the other hand, Islamic law gives men the responsibility of financial caretakers for their families. Men must spend their wealth in housing, feeding, and fulfilling all other legitimate requirements for their families, including their parents and siblings if the need occurs (4:34). Inheritance laws are not meant to show preference for one gender over the other, but rather to facilitate the fulfillment of social responsibilities.

As further proof that inheritance laws are not intended to discriminate between genders, remember that under certain categories, such as the inheritance of siblings, both men and women get exactly the same fraction of wealth. Also, note that some modernist interpretations say the spirit of the law is based on facilitating justice; according to these interpretations, women who find themselves in the role of caretakers for their families should receive the same inheritance as men.

See Chapter 15 for more information on inheritance rights.

Right to own property, manage business, and control wealth

Women have the full right to own property (4:32–33). Even after marriage, their property remains fully in their hands and does not in any way transfer to the husband in case of divorce. For this reason, there is no need for pre-nuptial agreements in matters relating to a woman's wealth prior to her marriage.

Women can manage their own businesses if they so choose. In fact, Prophet Muhammad's first wife, Khadija, was a wealthy businesswoman, and Muhammad actually worked for her.

Also, women have full control over their money, which they can use for any purpose they deem fit. You find many examples of wealthy Muslim women in history who did great acts of good with their wealth, such as build some of the greatest universities in Islamic civilization.

Right to work and equal pay

In Islamic law, women have the right to work in any field that they choose so long as the occupation lies within the moral guidelines of Islamic teachings — the same guidelines to which men must also adhere. In fact, the Koran even says that women must receive equal benefits as men for the work that they do (4:32).

However, according to the Koran, a woman's first responsibility is to ensure the moral upbringing of her family, which takes precedence over her right to work.

The Koran considers the family unit (see Chapter 15) an essential component to a spiritually and morally healthy society. As such, the honor of raising righteous homes has been given to the wife and mother. However, this doesn't mean that women must cook, clean, and do all the house chores. Following the example of Prophet Muhammad, who helped his wife in the home and sewed his own clothes, men are also obligated to help in the home. According to most scholars of Islamic law, a man must provide an assistant for house chores if his wife so demands.

Right to education

The Islamic tradition places great emphasis on obtaining knowledge, and the first commandment Prophet Muhammad received was, "Read!" (96:1). The Koran says that those who have true knowledge rank higher in the sight of God (58:11).

According to Prophet Muhammad, every Muslim, male and female, must receive an education. Islamic governments must work to make educational opportunities equally available for both sexes.

While women's education proves problematic in some poorer countries in the Muslim world, it is a myth that women aren't properly educated in that part of the world. Personally, I know many devout Muslim women who study in diverse fields from medicine to law, and everything in between.

Women in high places

During the time of Prophet Muhammad, many women, known as *Aslamiyyah,* practiced medicine in the Islamic community. Also, historically, women have served as Islamic scholars, judges, financial advisers, and even military and foreign policy advisers.

Right to social and political participation

Those few who argue that the role of women in Islamic societies is confined to the home seem to have not read the Koran properly. The Book quite clearly states that women have not only the right, but the responsibility to actively participate in society's affairs:

> "The believers, men and women, are friends of one another: they enjoin what is good, and forbid what is evil. They establish regular prayers, pay obligatory purifying alms, and obey God and His Messenger . . ." (9:71).

This also includes a woman's right to vote as a citizen in society.

Rights of marriage

A woman can't be forced to marry against her will (4:19). Marriage can't be legalized under Islamic law without the explicit consent of the woman (and the man) during the wedding ceremony.

Lineage is considered sacred in Islam, and a woman shouldn't change her last name after marriage. Rather, she should maintain her last name as a means of preserving lineage. However, if she so wishes, she can add her husband's last name to her last name.

Right to initiate divorce

The Koran forbids men to hold women in marriage against their will (4:19). As such, a woman has the right to go to a judge in an Islamic court and request a divorce.

Prophet Muhammad allowed women who came to him to divorce their husbands. In one famous case, Muhammad allowed a woman to divorce her husband on the grounds that she found him physically undesirable and could no longer stand to live with him. So, as you can see, women are well within their rights to initiate divorce. However, Islamic law generally discourages divorce.

Using birth control

According to the sayings of Prophet Muhammad, couples can use birth control so long as it doesn't harm the woman or any potential fetus. Both the husband and wife must make the decision to use birth control.

However, birth control doesn't include abortion, because the fetus is considered a life in the womb that has been made sacred. Abortion, according to most scholars, is allowed in the case where medical experts judge the woman's life to be in danger.

Right to bear witness to business transactions

In economic transactions, the Koran makes every effort to ensure just and fair dealing. The Koran says that witnesses must observe every business transaction in order to resolve any future disputes.

The passage that forms this law says that there should be two *male* witnesses to the transaction. But, if two men are not available, then one male witness and two female witnesses suffice, so that if one woman makes a mistake the other can remind her (2:282).

I know what you're thinking: two women witnesses and only one man! Critics of the Islamic tradition use this verse to claim that the Koran teaches that women are half of men. These critics also claim that this verse makes women appear intellectually inferior to men. Both of these claims are incorrect. You have to remember that at the time of revelation, women were largely unfamiliar with business practices as a sector that was mostly male dominated. (Unfortunately, the same holds true today for women in some parts of the world.) This stipulation about female witnessing performs a function of justice in fair business practices and doesn't represent female inferiority in any way.

If you look at other verses that require witnessing, this stipulation of needing two women to one man doesn't exist. For example, 24:6–9, about witnessing adultery, proves that, generally, witnessing is a gender-neutral act.

See Chapter 15 for more discussion about women's rights and roles within the context of family. This chapter also discusses hot topics, such as modest covering for women *(Hijab)* and polygamy. Also, I recommend the Web site for the Muslim Women's League (mwlusa.org/index.htm) if you want to read more about women in the Islamic tradition.

Chapter 20

The Koran and Modernity

In This Chapter

▶ Defining modernity

▶ Developing the modern mankind in the Koran

▶ Examining Islam's compatibility with issues of modernity

▶ Looking at Islam's compatibility with democracy

*E*very era brings the competition of new ideas and theories that shape the global community. Theology, sacred law, and ethical practice must also compete on the global stage.

In this chapter, I don't address whether the Muslim world is moving towards modernity or not — I leave that question to the sociologists and political scientists. Instead, I look at what aspects of Koranic teachings prove compatible or incompatible with modernity as a global movement.

I begin by exploring the meaning of modernity in relation to Islam. Then, I look at the role of Muslims in the age of modernization. Finally, I tell you about some key modern issues and the Koran's perspective on those challenges.

Differentiating between Modernity and Modern Culture

When investigating whether or not Islam is compatible with modernity, it's important to ask, "What is modernity?" Unfortunately, the answer to this question often reflects an ethnocentric worldview rather than the realities of modernity.

When some people ask, "Why can't Muslims modernize?" they really mean "Why aren't Muslims like us? Why do they dress differently? Why do they follow different social laws and customs?"

Such people often assume that "modernity" is good, and that everything that isn't "modern" is backward. Islam's compatibility with modernity clashes at this point; change does not always bring with it public and moral good, which is the fundamental concern of Koranic laws and teachings, according to the commentators of the Koran.

Modernity is rightfully credited with the progress of certain ideals (such as universal human rights) and inventions (such as efficient transportation) that have greatly improved the condition of the world. However, modernity has also brought with it phenomena (such as excessive waste) and inventions (such as nuclear weapons) that have the potential to destroy the world even faster than they build it.

Unfortunately, the Muslim world today often ignores the beneficial aspects of modernity. To act "modernized," Muslims sometimes pursue those aspects of Western culture (such as materialism) that result in more harm than good. Some corporations have tapped into this desire for "modernization" by exporting a growing culture of mass distraction rather than mass development.

Modernity, meaning social and political progress that benefits humanity, differs from modern culture, which reflects lifestyles not necessarily built around the notion of public benefit.

Promoting Social Progress

Since human beings drive modernity and social progress, I want to look at the role of man on earth from the Koranic perspective.

The Koran describes Adam, the first man, as having superior intellect among God's creations in his ability to name things that were shown to him (2:31). On earth, Adam received the honorary title of God's Representative or Vicegerent on earth. This title extends a responsibility onto every human being, male and female (2:30; 6:165).

Furthermore, God raised human beings above the rest of His creations by honoring His role and status. "We have honored the children of Adam. Provided them with transport on land and sea. Given them for sustenance things good and pure, and conferred on them special favors above a great part of Our creation" (17:70).

Mankind received the honors of intellect (2:31), eloquent speech (55:4), and free will (2:281; 2:286) to represent God on earth by building spiritual, moral, and ethical civilizations based on public benefit. The Koran describes the role of humanity on earth as socially progressive.

Advancing society through science

Muslims are responsible for developing new institutions and inventions that promote moral and scientific benefits. The early Muslim community understood this concept; Muslims developed some of the greatest inventions in world history, such as the paper industry that began with Chinese Muslims. The Muslim community also led in the science fields, especially with new discoveries in medicine (such as Al-Razi's treatment of measles and chickenpox), astronomy (the invention of the astrolabe, for example), and mathematics (such as Al-Khowarizmi, who is considered the father of Algebra).

However, the Book also acknowledges that mankind was "created weak" in resolution (4:28). Historically, humanity has shown a tendency to follow lower temptations rather than higher aspirations. The moral laws of God ensure that civilizations build on morally constructive foundations, rather than shortsighted whims and desires.

Muslims today stand in the middle of the road on issues of modernity. On the one hand, the Scripture mentions nothing that prevents Muslims from venturing into the sciences and arts that bring benefit to civilization. On the contrary — the Koran encourages such pursuits (see the sidebar "Advancing society through science"). However, modern Muslims also recognize that not everything "modern" translates into good.

Muslims in every era bear the responsibility of supporting progressive social change. At the same time, they must also warn humanity against ignoring the divine ethical and moral laws that balance scientific and artistic pursuits.

Focusing on Issues of Modernity

In the following sections, I take a closer look at issues of modernity that face the Muslim world in particular, and the Koran's perspective on these issues.

Public benefit, defined by Koranic principles of preserving life, religion, honor, family, wealth, and intellect, drives Islamic law. Change should not occur for its own sake, but only for public benefit. Also, Islamic law establishes that everything is permissible *(mubah)* as long as it is not explicitly forbidden *(haraam)* or does not contradict the spirit of Islamic law.

Science

The Koran holds in great esteem those who deeply reflect and study divine creation "in the heavens and the earth" (3:191). This constant call for man to come to know God through contemplation provides the moral basis for pursuing science in the Islamic tradition. For example, this call led to a deep interest in astronomy when Islamic civilization was at its peak. If the Muslim world again rises to such great heights, this call may lead to a new interest in pursuing space exploration.

Similarly, the Koran also asks people to "reflect within themselves" (30:8) and often pushes its reader to think about his or her own humble origins from a single sperm drop to a mature human being (22:5). These and other such reflections urge Muslims to explore the biological and medical sciences.

However, these scientific pursuits must find balance with the divine ethical laws that give priority to preservation of life over scientific pursuit. Ideally, the two interests marry. For example, in medicine, the marriage of these two priorities results in the sacred preservation of life.

The arts

The concept of *Ihsan* defines a beautiful relationship with God. (This word comes from the root "HUSN," which means beauty and goodness.) Those who practice *Ihsan* are called *Muhsin,* which in the spiritual tradition means "to make or produce beauty." The Scripture says that "God loves those who produce beauty (and goodness)" (2:195).

A *Muhsin* beautifies the world with good actions and struggles against any moral ugliness in society; a *Muhsin* produces physical beauty on earth that is consistent with divine ethics. The Koran even encourages human beings to wear "beautiful apparel at every time and place . . ." (7:31).

Prophet Muhammad taught his companions that "God is beautiful, and He loves to see beauty."

Development of the arts formed a great part of Islamic civilization in calligraphy (see Chapter 2) and architecture, a tradition that Muslims still celebrate today. Wherever you go in the Muslim world, you see great symbols of art, especially in places like Turkey, Spain, Egypt, Syria, and Morocco.

However, in the arts, the preservation and sanctity of religion precludes drawing humans and animals and creating idols (14:35). This prohibition helps Muslims down the road avoid falling into any sort of idol worshiping or polytheism.

While the Koran encourages beauty, it also warns against excessive waste by saying that "God loves not the wasters" (7:31). Finally, overindulgence in making great buildings while ignoring social justice is also condemned in the Koran as the practice of civilizations that were destroyed in the past (89:7).

Human rights

With the creation of the United Nations, the world moved closer to implementing a universal declaration of human rights. Indeed, the Koran (4:1) and the Islamic tradition are in agreement with most of these laws (see Chapter 17). In fact, Muslims would argue that Islam brought universal human rights to the world over 1,400 years ago, highlighted in Prophet Muhammad's farewell speech that calls for social justice, economic rights, women's rights, an end to racism, and equality of all humanity.

However, the Koran focuses on two institutions that human rights movements today sometimes ignore:

- Sanctity of family
- Sanctity of honor

The Koran strongly discourages and punishes sexual relations outside of marriage (25:68; 24:2) in order to preserve lineage and family ties. From the Koranic perspective, family preservation qualifies as a human right (4:1) that all children deserve and that all healthy societies need to function properly. Currently, the universal human rights movement does not include an emphasis on family rights.

Similarly, the Koran believes in preserving the sanctity of honor (17:70), because honor forms the basis of human rights in Islam. With the destruction or neglect of people's honor, society can create an array of social evils. Islamic law emphasizes a great need for laws that protect people from slander (49:12; 104:1), unproven accusations (24:4), name calling (49:11), invasion of privacy (24:27–28), and spying (49:12).

Also, Islamic law dictates much tougher and stricter punishments than modern laws on those who offend sacred law (see Chapter 17). These punishments act as a deterrent against actions that violate human rights in society.

Muslims today face a challenge when it comes to honest reform of human rights laws that were developed by Islamic jurists to reflect the condition of their own time period. Islamic jurists today must apply laws in the context of an ever-changing social and political climate to ensure the existence of the Islamic tradition.

For example, some Muslims question whether the inheritance laws, which give women half the inheritance of men, still apply in today's world. (See Chapter 15 for more information on the reasoning behind these laws.) Today, Muslim women sometimes find themselves the breadwinners for their families, taking on the role that men used to play in the past. This situation poses the following question for today's jurists: If the laws of inheritance seek to create justice in the family system, shouldn't the woman who has the family responsibility receive an equal, if not greater, share of the inheritance? Modernist interpreters would usually say yes, because the reasoning and spirit of the law seeks to maintain family justice. However, classical interpreters would say no, because the Koran provides a perfect model for life and society. As such, according to these scholars, society should reform to Koranic laws, rather than Koranic laws reforming to modern society.

These types of questions must be openly debated and resolved among Islamic jurists today. Sadly, the discourse is little, but the need is great.

Economics and free trade

The Koran encourages free trade as long as it complements *fair* trade: "O you who believe, eat not up property among yourselves in vanities. But let there be amongst you traffic and trade by mutual goodwill . . ." (4:29). As such, criminals who spread fear and instability in society to such an extent that they hinder economic trade face severe punishment in Islamic law (see Chapter 17).

Property is considered sacred in Koranic law. As such, the Scripture says, "And do not eat up your property among yourselves for vanities . . ." (2:188). The Book also condemns and strongly punishes stealing (5:38) in order to preserve the sanctity of people's property.

The Islamic economic model does not believe in socialism or communism. The government cannot control the finances of any citizen other than to require the payment of purifying alms (see Chapter 12) that are spent in helping the poor and needy in society, or contribute to other public benefit programs, such as education and health care.

The Book honors individual wealth and calls for equal pay for equal work for both men and women (4:32). Free trade and work are encouraged by the Koran when it says, "And when the prayer is finished, then you may disperse through the land, and seek of the bounty of God . . ." (62:10).

The key to the economic model found in the Koran lies in its principal of balance and moderation (17:29; 18:46). Consumption is permissible (2:168), while lavishness (17:27), miserliness (35:29), and wastefulness (6:141) are strongly discouraged and condemned. The pursuit of livelihood (*Surah* 106), satisfaction (42:36), and beautification (7:31) are all encouraged so long as wealth does not distract from important moral obligations (*Surah* 102) and from the remembrance of God who "is the best of providers" (62:11).

Some citizens will always be wealthier than others; each economic level offers a test from God. The rich face the test of charity and kindness (2:270–271), while the poor have the test of patience (2:153–157). However, an Islamic society must not discriminate against the poorer members of society by restricting their ability to open businesses and pursue free trade. To make trade fair, the Koran lays down laws that ensure ethical business practices. For example, all business transactions must occur in the presence of two or three witnesses (depending on the situation), and be written down on paper to avoid future conflicts (2:282–283). Similarly, the fulfillment of oaths and obligations is commanded (2:177, 5:1). There is also a prohibition on fraud (2: 267; 26:181) and the Koran's insistence on establishing clear and just standards in trade (55:9).

Perhaps the greatest barrier between Islamic teachings on business and the modern economy is on the issue of usury, a form of interest. Usury is strongly condemned and forbidden by the Koran (2:275). The Koran says that "God will deprive usury of all blessing, but will give increase for deeds of charity" (2:276). From the Koranic perspective, usury results in added burdens on the poor and those who are in debt. (If you are still paying off your college loans, like I am, then you know what I am talking about.) The Koranic prohibition of usury has its basis in economic justice.

This prohibition poses problems for modern Muslims who live in a world dominated by banking systems based on usury. This prohibition confounds Muslims who want to purchase homes, for example. Many scholars say that because usury is unavoidable, it becomes permissible for Muslims to engage in it, due to the "law of necessity" derived from Koranic law. (Scholars of Islamic law define necessity as food, drink, and shelter.) Also, usury is only permitted in cases where an alternative does not exist. However, scholars maintain that it is prohibited to engage in usury for the sake of simply increasing your wealth.

Morality and secularism

The Koran rejects the culture of *moral relativism,* in which social trends dictate morality. Rather, morality in the Koran is eternal and absolute. God does not consider something moral one day and then immoral the next. The Koran serves as the criterion for judging between what is good and evil, right and wrong, just and unjust (25:1).

Secularism has various meanings and definitions. In the United States, secularism is defined more or less as the separation of church and state. In other words, the church stays out of the public affairs, and the state stays out of the private affairs of religious communities. This form of secularism, advocates argue, protects corruption of religion by the state, and protects corruption of state policies by religion. Some scholars of Islamic political theory actually favor this model, because they too are weary of the government's potentially corrupting influence on religion.

Another form of secularism, which is sweeping across Europe, severely restricts freedom of worship. This form of secularism teaches not only separation of church and state, but rather prohibition of religious expressions and symbols in public — thereby making freedom of worship rather difficult. Advocates of this system may argue that religion best functions in the private sphere, and no one in the public sphere should feel intimidated by another person's expression of faith. Muslims have a hard time with that concept, because Islam's concept of worship *(Ibadah)* extends beyond formal rituals that take place inside a mosque or home (2:177). The Koran says that "Islam" is a state of being that cannot be switched on and off. Rather, teachings of the Koran form the purpose of life itself (2:208).

Secularism in both forms (especially the second) violates the sacred teaching that says, "There is no authority or law, except God's." Also, for Islamic law to work, government has to have some role in implementing laws and forming policies out of the principles of Islamic law (4:59). To form human laws that clearly contradict divine law is considered a sin in the Islamic tradition (3:185). It proves difficult to marry secularism to the ideals of the Koran.

If you want to read more about Islam and issues of modernity, I highly recommend that you visit Minaret (www.minaret.org), a Muslim think tank on the importance of liberty and free markets in society.

Imagining an Islamic Democracy

With the topple of regimes in Afghanistan and Iraq, and the development of democracy in Muslim countries like Malaysia, Sudan, and Iran, the question of whether Islam and democracy can coexist has never been more hotly debated.

Some advocate a secularization of the Muslim world as the only means to achieve democracy. However, this idea emboldens ideological fundamentalists and radicals who say that the West is out to destroy Islam and its role in the world.

At this stage in world history, Islamic democracy is as much a theory as it is a practice, since democracy is still in its early years of development. Recent political developments in the Muslim world, coupled with an intense desire for freedom from oppressive regimes, make this a perfect time to imagine how an Islamic democracy will work.

For democracy to succeed, Muslims must find a way to connect the tradition of Islamic principles to democracy. Only then can the idea of democracy gain popular legitimacy among Muslims, who still overwhelmingly define their faith as a complete way of life. If the sources of Islam, including the Koran, and democracy can't connect in the minds of Muslims, then the work of academics will remain just that, without any practical application.

Debating the rule of law between citizenry and God

Some people argue that the difference between the ideals of democracy and Islamic law is that democracy is the "rule of man" while Islam is the "rule of God." However, this simplistic model mistakenly assumes that Islam advocates a *theocracy* (a government ruled by a religious authority that speaks on God's behalf) — the opposite of a democracy.

Theocracy is the rule of religious authority. In a theocracy, a central figure (such as a pope) or a group of people (such as priests) have a special line of communication with the Divine by which they come to know God's Will, and which they subsequently implement on society.

However, the overwhelming majority Sunni tradition doesn't recognize a sole communicator with God, or a class of religious people who have special access to God's Will. No real religious authority exists whose rulings are absolute, necessarily binding, and unquestionable.

Rather, the rulings of those who interpret divine law only gain authority or credibility if they can show that their rulings derive from the words or wisdom of the Koran and prophetic tradition. In Islam, determining God's Will is a thoroughly human intellectual process that by its nature remains open to debate, unless a clear mandate exists in the Koran and prophetic tradition.

In fact, the Koran strongly criticizes the Jews and Christians for taking "their rabbis and their monks to be their lords beside God . . ." (9:31). In other words, the Koran feels that past religious communities began blindly following their religious leaders instead of the laws of God.

Also, the Koran cautions against a hierarchical religious establishment that over time can become corrupt, stealing the wealth of pious worshippers, and distracting people from the true path of God (9:34).

The Koran does not believe in establishing a theocracy on earth. Rather, its system of governance focuses on the following three concepts:

- ✔ **Unity of God:** God's Oneness brings together His attributes of Creator, Sustainer, and Master, which make God sovereign over all His creation (23:116; 57:2; 7:54; 10:31). As such, God has the primary authority to create personal and social laws that govern human life.

- ✔ **Prophecy:** Prophecy communicates and presents the modeled life and path built on divine laws and guidance (4:79–80; 7:157–158).

- ✔ **The role of mankind as God's vicegerent on earth (2:30, 6:165):** A religious elite or a single religious figure does not claim ownership to this role — it belongs to the entire community that lives under divine laws of rights and responsibilities. As such, all citizens in a community have equal rights and equal accountability under the law, whether they are leaders or farmers. No one is above the law, and no one person is designated as interpreter of God's Will.

Men and women, as a collective body, must nurture God-conscious civilizations that enjoin moral good and social benefit and struggle against moral evil and social harm (9:71; 22:41). As new legal issues arise for the ever-progressing community, the community must actively take part in an intellectual struggle (*Ijtihad*) to determine God's Will.

While an Islamic state follows divine laws, humans must determine and implement those laws, which takes place under a system of mutual consultation, known as *Shura* (42:38). Here, an elected body of legislators (such as members of parliament or congress) debates and decides affairs of the state in light of the Koran, prophetic teachings, and other sources of sacred law (see Chapter 17).

Key differences exist between a Western-style democracy and an Islamic democracy. Western democracy places the sovereignty or authority of rule in the people, who form the constitution to determine rights and responsibilities for citizens. An Islamic democracy places sovereignty or rule of law in God, Who places rights and responsibilities on the people (4:1). In Western democracy, people make their own laws that reflect the trends of time and place. Islamic democracy runs according to divine laws that are based on eternal principles. Western democracies serve the will of the people. Islamic democracy serves the Will of God. But, in the end, both systems share the essence of democracy: Government by the people, expressed through popularly-elected representatives.

Just as man's ability to make laws in a democracy is limited by the words and principals of a constitution, man's ability to govern is limited in an Islamic democracy by its constitution that is based on the divine principles of the Koran and prophetic tradition.

Expressing the will of the people through elections

Democracy must represent the will of the people. Citizens express their will through elections. Does the Koran provide a basis for such elections? The answer is yes:

- ✔ Since all human beings are vicegerents of God on earth (2:30), which makes them responsible for the state of affairs in the world, it is only logical that leaders and representatives of the people will be elected by the people.

- ✔ The Koran mandates mutual consultation or consent (42:38), which is the essence of democratic elections.

- ✔ The Koran teaches Muslims to "pay heed to God, and pay heed to the Messenger, and unto those from among you who have been entrusted with authority . . ." (4:59). This third category clearly says the trust comes "among you" and is not imposed "upon you," which makes it clear that leaders must be chosen by the people and must come from the people themselves — not dictated upon the citizenry.

Interestingly, early Islamic history provides some answers and models that give the theory of elections strong credence.

When Prophet Muhammad was on his deathbed, his companions anticipated that he would name a successor who would become leader of the *Ummah,* or Muslim community. But, to the surprise of many, the Prophet remained silent on the matter. Since Muhammad didn't give a clear mandate, the *Ummah* was left to decide (or if you will, *elect*) a leader for the community.

Three companions were nominated: Abu Bakr, Umar, and Saad bin Abadah. Abu Bakr emerged as the clear choice and was elected as the first *Caliph* of Islam. The next three *Caliphs* (Umar, Uthman, and Ali) were also elected by the *Ummah* in a similar fashion that represented the will of the majority in the Muslim community.

As such, elections are not only compatible with an Islamic system of government, but an essential part of Islamic governance.

Holding public officials responsible

In order for a democracy to function properly, the people must be able to hold their elected leaders and representatives accountable. *Shura,* or mutual consultation (42:38), plays a key role in this process. The concept of mutual consultation ensures that a representative of the people works with the consent of the people, rather than in a dictatorial fashion.

Skeptics of Islamic democracy, however, argue that *Shura* cannot be likened to democratic institutions, because they are non-binding. Advocates of Islamic democracy argue that *Shura* is in fact binding on representatives, an opinion overwhelmingly held by the majority of scholars, practice of Prophet Muhammad, and the first four authentic *Caliphs*.

Secondly, the Koran lays out the responsibility of an elected representative and leader in the following passage: "God does command you to render back your trusts to those on whom they are due. And when you judge between people, that you judge with justice . . ." (4:58). The elected representative is entrusted by the people and must live up to that trust. He or she must also govern with justice. If the representative fails to live up to these two standards, then he or she loses the confidence of the people and is no longer fit to govern.

Thirdly, legislation that is passed by representatives cannot be based simply on their whims and desires. Rather, legislation must stay in line with the Koran and prophetic tradition (4:59) — the two main sources of an Islamic constitution. For this, an independent council of jurists would be formed to ensure a system of checks and balances that would reject laws that violate the constitution. These jurists themselves would be checked by other jurists in order not to give a single jurist too much authority. And, all the representatives and jurists would be held responsible by the people to whom the trust of leadership and representation is due (4:58).

The Koranic concept of governance does reflect this essential principle of democracy that holds public officials responsible.

Liberty and Koranic ideals

Democracy necessitates that people have certain liberties, including the freedom to propose laws, the freedom of speech, and the freedom to organize and assemble. Liberty must also go beyond the political realm to include such things as the freedom of religion. Other laws, such as the right to privacy, are still being vigorously debated in democratic societies even today.

As discussed in earlier sections in this chapter, freedom to legislate is not only a right, but also a responsibility within an Islamic society, because the Koran believes in humanity's role as vicegerent and representative of God on earth (2:30). As such, a man or woman's right to propose laws can never be taken away. But, of course, as in any democracy, these laws would have to be voted on and must pass the test of the constitution.

The Koran espouses social movements and institutions that act as a moral and ethical voice within the community: "Let there arise out of you a band of people inviting to all that is good, enjoining what is right, and forbidding what is wrong . . ." (3:104). The liberty to politically and socially organize is an important freedom that must be honored by an Islamic democracy.

Religious liberties are a major concern for those thinking about Islamic democracy. Religious intolerance does exist among some Muslim communities today, and the rights of religious minorities are extremely poor in others. However, some Muslim countries have very tolerant beliefs about religious freedoms. (You can also find a great number of historical examples where freedom of religion was honored in Islamic civilization — such as Islamic Spain, in which non-Muslims even rose to high government posts.)

The Koran does indeed honor religious freedom when it says, "Let there be no compulsion in religion . . ." (2:256). The Koran also establishes the freedom of worship and even calls on Muslims to defend houses of worship that may be under attack (22:40). So, this right is certainly consistent with Koranic ideals.

While the legitimacy of privacy laws is a hot debate in many Western democracies, the Koran is clear in its belief that privacy is an important element of a citizen's liberties. The Koran forbids spying (49:12), forbids entry of homes without permission (24:27), teaches Muslims to leave if they are not permitted entry (24:28), and requires permission even from within the household to enter private rooms (24:58). Islamic law sanctifies the private realm, an important concept in any Islamic democracy.

The government can justly fight public immorality, but the private sphere should be left private, since actions committed within the walls of a home are between inhabitants of the home and God.

You can argue that Islam has more conservative values that limit liberty, but that doesn't mean that democracy can't coexist with conservative morality.

For example, many skeptics of Islamic democracy argue that Islam is incompatible with democracy because women lack the freedom to dress as they like. But, in the West, too, standards for dressing exist, which are based on the culture's concept of modest dressing. Depending on the Muslim country, laws for dressing would also reflect the cultural interpretation of modest dressing that does vary from society to society. Muslim women don't all have the same interpretation on exactly what the modest dressing requires. But, in an Islamic democracy, the culture of the people would also reflect the law.

Social equality and Islamic law

Social equality is an essential part of a successful democracy. Sovereignty of citizens requires that no citizen be deprived of their rights to participatory democracy.

Also, every citizen should be equal under the law of the land and must have the same access to rights that all other citizens enjoy. This guarantees minority rights, which is especially important in societies that don't have enough minorities to form an influential political block.

The Koran contains several passages that speak of social equality; the concept of equality is also an essential part of Islamic law. For example, passage 49:13 address all of humanity in teaching gender and racial equality. Similarly, passage 60:8 calls for the kind and loving treatment of non-Muslims who do not fight the Muslim community.

Probably the only really challenging laws concerning social equality are the laws regarding a woman's testimony in business law, her inheritance, and divorce laws. In all three cases women are treated differently — though not necessarily less equal. In all three cases, Muslim have thoroughly defended the wisdom behind the laws that are not meant to discriminate, but rather act in accordance with the functions of social and family responsibilities in an Islamic society (see Chapter 15).

However, modernist Islamic interpretations call for reform of some laws in order to match the spirit of justice in Islamic laws to the realities of modernity. However, this alone should not prevent the development of democracy, because an objective look at the world shows that inequalities of some sort exist in every single country today. So, these social issues will take time to develop, but that should not prevent the growth of an Islamic democracy.

Finally, I should point out that while this section deals with the Koran's compatibility with democracy in the context of modernity, Islamic governments can also take other forms that can be as free and just. From the Koranic perspective, diversity is the Will of God (49:13), which means that not every nation or community has to follow the same political or social structure in order for human progress to occur.

If you want to read more on the issue of Islam and democracy, I recommend the following resources:

- *After Jihad: America and the Struggle for Islamic Democracy,* by Noah Feldman (published by Farrar, Straus, and Giroux). A brilliant analysis of Islamic democracy. A must-read for all students of Islam.

- *Islam and Democracy,* by John L. Esposito and John O. Voll (published by Oxford University Press). Excellent case studies of the Muslim world's experiments with Islamic democracy.

- *American Muslims: Bridging Faith and Freedom,* by Muqtedar Khan (published by Amana Publications). An interesting analysis on the notions of freedom and tolerance in Islam.

- **Center for the Study of Islam and Democracy** (www.islam-democracy.com). A very resourceful site with many interesting articles.

Part VI
The Part of Tens

The 5th Wave — By Rich Tennant

© RICHTENNANT

My parents are Muslim. We live by the Five Pillars.

Cool. I have an uncle who lives by the Six Flags.

In this part . . .

This part contains two chapters full of fast, but vital, information that you can take with you as you continue to explore the Koran. The first chapter explodes ten myths about the Book. The second chapter tells you about resources to turn to as you look deeper inside this deep well of knowledge called the Koran.

Chapter 21

Ten Misconceptions about the Koran

In This Chapter

▶ Clearing up misconceptions about the Koran's authorship and style of communication

▶ Looking at some theological misconceptions about the Koran

▶ Dispelling common misconceptions about Koranic practices

*O*ftentimes, misconceptions separate people with differing worldviews, presenting minds and souls with seemingly valid excuses to not engage people of other faiths.

In this chapter, I deconstruct ten common misconceptions that people have about Koranic scripture, theology, and practice.

Misconception #1: Muhammad Wrote the Koran

As with all previous divine revelations, the Koran too was scrutinized by the community of Arabs who were the first recipients of the Book.

Those who rejected Muhammad's call to Islam argued that Muhammad was simply preaching "tales of the ancients" (16:24, for example). The Scripture responds to this demand for proof of divine authenticity by producing an eloquent form of Arabic that to this day remains unsurpassed by even the most articulate poets and writers of the Arabic language.

The Koran is so confident of its divinely-inspired language that it challenges those who question the Koran's authenticity to bring all the masters of literature together to produce even one chapter that achieves the same level of linguistic eloquence as the Koran (10:37–38; 17:88).

Also, the Koran argues that if the Scripture was man-made, contradictions and omissions would crop up in the Book, rather than coherence, consistency, and completeness (4:82; 39:23).

Muslims accept the Koran's majestic literary form as a sure sign of divine revelation, especially because Muhammad never participated in the influential poetry culture of the Arabs before the revelation of the Koran.

Muhammad is even known as the "unlettered Prophet" in the Koran to indicate that he had no knowledge of reading or writing (7:157–158).

The Koran quotes rejecters of the Koran as calling Muhammad a "poet" (21:5; 37:36), but firmly denies this title by saying, "It is not the word of a poet" (36:37).

The Scripture also forcefully argues that Muhammad has no authority to change the words of God, and speaks only that which was directly revealed to him through Angel Gabriel (53:1–10).

Defenders of the Islamic tradition also argue that had the Koran been the eloquent articulation of Muhammad, he would surely have displayed the same level of eloquence in his collected sayings, known as the *Hadith*. While the *Hadith* are often beautifully worded and full of wisdom, they come nowhere close to the high literary standard of the Koran, which revolutionized the Arabic language with its eloquence.

Misconception #2: The Koran Is Incoherent and Unorganized

Many non-Muslim readers, such as the British historian Thomas Carlyle, view the Koran as rather unorganized and difficult to comprehend.

Most Western literature is linear and non-oral in nature. Non-Muslims, especially those familiar with the Biblical narrative, expect books to contain a narrative form with a beginning, middle, and end.

The Koran, on the other hand, has a nonlinear style. For example, the Book begins with a declaration of God's attributes; moves into a supplication; begins the next chapter (or *Surah*) with an introduction to the Koran's belief system; then moves into describing the hearts of believers, rejecters of faith, and hypocrites; then defends its own Scriptural authenticity against the attacks of skeptics; briefly argues the case for God's existence; and, finally, describes the beginning of time and creation with verse 30 of *Surah* 2. Later, the Koran returns to the subject of creation at different times throughout the Book.

The Koran's literary structure can prove challenging to anyone who is used to a linear, structured body of text, whether sacred or secular in nature. However, the Koran's structure is not randomly pieced together, nor is it as unstructured as you may initially find it to be. Rather, the Koran's structure is built on a worldview that sees history as a part of human moral experience, rather than human moral experience as part of history.

In other words, the Koran's style centers around mankind's relationship with God. The Book views the history of creation and prophets as part of that intellectual and moral discourse, rather than the primary subject at hand.

The Koran is, in fact, quite structured in terms of moral and ethical lessons and guidelines. The history of creation, prophets, and civilizations appear as examples and points of reference for the overall Koranic argument. For example, the story of Prophet Moses appears in 44 different places throughout the Book whenever Moses' story fits the moral context of Koranic discourse.

Reading the Koran is no simple task if you're used to Western literature. When reading the Koran, you need to strip yourself of any preconceived notions of how narrative structure works. Approach the Koranic narrative like a baby and attempt to experience the world with a newfound freedom.

Misconception #3: The Koran Is Void of Reason

Muslims are often portrayed as only interested in a set of rituals, declining intellectual debate and reason. Those who espouse this view link it to the Koran as the basis for Muslim intellectual life. However, the Koran places great emphasis on intellect and reason as a way of coming to know God.

In fact, the Koran asserts in several passages that guidance is for those who "ponder" (16:12) and "reflect" (30:21). The Book also says that its message is for "men (and women) of understanding" (12:111). Entire *Surahs* in the Koran are almost exclusively dedicated to inspire man's intellect (*Surah* 55, for example).

Prophet Abraham, who is honored as a role model of true faith (16:120–123), comes to the worship of God alone through reason (6:76–79) and preaches faith also through the use of reason (2:258; 21:51–67). Other heroes in the Koranic narrative, such as Luqman the sage (*Surah* 31), are praised for their deep wisdom and intellect.

Also, the Koran seeks to respond with reason to the questions and arguments of those who rejected Prophet Muhammad's call to accept Islam. For example, the pre-Islamic Pagan Arabs had no belief in a Hereafter and would mockingly question Muhammad, "Who can give life to bones and decomposed ones?" (36:78). The Koran responds by saying, "He will give them life who created them for the first time, for He fully knows all creation . . ." (3:79). In other words, the Koran logically concludes that if God made man out of nothing, then surely He can remake man in the same form.

To argue that the Koran expects its readers to believe and act without thinking is wrong. In reality, the entire Koranic argument proceeds from the notion of reason as the way of coming to faith.

Misconception #4: The Koran Espouses Polytheism

One of the greatest untruths spread about the Koran is that it teaches anything other than worship and servitude to One God alone, without associating any partners with Him. In fact, the entire religion of Islam is built on Oneness of God, known as *Tawhid*.

Academic scholars of Islam, whether they admire or criticize the Islamic tradition, have noted that the teaching of God's absolute Oneness in the Koran is so strong that Islam's belief system can be referred to as the strictest form of monotheism in religious traditions today.

Those who argue that Islam does not teach monotheism make two erroneous claims:

✔ **They argue that Muslims worship the "moon god."**

The myth of Islam worshiping a moon god comes from the belief that "Allah" was the name of a moon god among the pagan Arabs. While the pagan Arabs did believe in a set of smaller gods, the Koranic dialogue recognizes that the pagan Arabs had a concept of a universal supreme God, who they called Allah in Arabic.

Another proof that Allah is simply the name of God in Arabic is the fact that Arabs of all other faiths, including Jews and Christians, call God "Allah." In fact, in Aramaic — the language of Jesus — the name for God is Allaha, which is close to Allah since both Arabic and Aramaic come from the same family language. Similarly, Eloh, or Elohim — the name for God in Hebrew — also comes from the same roots as Allah.

The crescent moon that you see on mosques is not even originally part of any Islamic symbol associated with the Islamic faith. In fact, Islam was originally void of any symbols at all because of the fear that later generations would fall back into pagan practices of worshiping idols and symbols, rather than God alone.

The crescent symbol, from most historical accounts, became Islam's "symbol" when the Turkish Ottoman Empire became the capital of the Islamic civilization and decided to leave the age-old crescent moon on their flag and other government institutions.

✔ **They argue that Muslims worship Muhammad and not God.**

This belief comes from pure ignorance, and not any sort of misunderstanding of history, as the case may be for the "moon god" argument.

Perhaps this myth stems from the reasoning that, just as Buddhists worship Buddha and Christians worship Jesus, Muslims probably also worship Muhammad.

Also, Orientalists who studied Islam in earlier generations referred to Islam as "Mohammadanism." The Book completely rejects such a concept.

The Koran tells Muhammad to teach his companions that "I am but a mortal man like all of you. It has been revealed unto me that your God is the One and Only God . . ." (18:110). The Scripture also warns Muslims not to leave the worship and service of One God after the death of Muhammad (3:144).

Abu Bakr, the first *Caliph* of Islam after Prophet Muhammad, exemplified this teaching when he stood in front of the large congregation that had gathered upon hearing of Muhammad's death, and said: "Those of you who worshipped Muhammad know that Muhammad is dead. But, those of you who worship God know that He is Living and will never die."

Misconception #5: The Koran Says That God Belongs to One People

The second verse of the Koran gives God a universal attribute: "Praise be to God, the Sustainer of all the worlds" (1:2). Furthermore, the Book says several times that God is the Lord of the East and the West (73:9, for example).

The Scripture teaches that all prophets throughout history form a single community of brotherhood under the Lordship of God alone (23:51). The Koran teaches His universality as the Sustainer of not only every human being, but of all the universe, including animal life, plant life, all the constellations in the solar system, and so on.

See Chapter 8 for a more complete understanding of God in the Koran.

Misconception #6: God Is Wrathful and Unloving in the Koran

Some critics of the Koran say that the Book describes God as full of wrath and rage, and not of love and mercy. I often wonder if these people have ever even picked up a Koran, as that claim is completely false and baseless.

Some Christian missionary books say that the Koran mentions the concept of love only twice. In fact, the Book mentions the concept of love about a hundred times, if such statistics really even mean anything.

After declaring God's universality, the Koran describes God as "most Merciful, most Compassionate" (1:3). In fact, every single *Surah* except one begins with this declaration about the divine nature.

God is also known in the Scripture as "Full of Loving-Kindness" (11:90; 85:14). It is with the attribute of divine Love that the Koran most often seeks to directly create a relationship with humanity by encouraging those actions that bring God's love and discouraging those actions that extinguish God's love.

Without doubt, the Koran also mentions God's wrath for those who reject faith after clear signs have come to them, and upon those who are bent on spreading evil and corruption on earth. But, as Prophet Muhammad said while quoting God himself, "My Mercy prevails over My wrath."

Misconception #7: The Koran Preaches Fatalism

The Scripture itself creates a complex debate over predestination versus free will. The Koran presents verses that seem to advocate fatalism, and other times free will. This has led critics to argue either that the Koran contradicts itself, or that the Koranic worldview on this issue heavily sides with fatalism.

To see this debate from a Koranic perspective, you have to understand the Koranic worldview that says, "Every human being is bound to taste death, and We test you (all) through the bad and the good by way of trial: and unto Us you all must return" (21:35).

In other words, the life of this world serves as a test for every soul in both good and bad things that happen in life. Both the good and the bad cannot occur without the permission and Will of God, which come to men and women in the form of a trial. Faith, by its very nature, must be tested in order to be proven true.

The Koran says that all of humanity will be tested on the Day of Judgment for all the good they did and all the evil they did. However, none will be tested or asked to account for how long they lived, how much wealth they had, or where they were born, because these factors are, for the most part, not within human control.

The Koran offers a balance between divine measurement, known as *Qadr* in the Koran, and free will.

Misconception #8: Jihad Means "Holy War"

Jihad is almost always wrongly translated as "Holy War." The Arabic word *Jihad* actually means "to struggle" or "to exert one's utmost."

In the context of the Koran, *Jihad* means the struggle for good against all evil. This struggle also includes the suppression of the lower self in order to reach a state of higher God-consciousness that leads to a pure soul.

Jihad can take place in many forms, including speaking out against injustice or spending your wealth in the cause of public good, such as alleviating poverty. *Jihad* does also include armed struggle, which at times becomes necessary in order to protect the weak and to establish freedom of religion. (*Jihad* in the context of armed struggle is known as *Qital.*)

Critics of the Koran love to quote passages such as 9:5 of the Koran, which calls for taking up arms against those who ascribe partners with God. Most often, these critics fail to recognize the context of such passages. It's misleading to simply cut and paste verses out of their context in order to erroneously prove a point.

All verses in the Koran that deal with armed struggle advocate the use of force only for self-defense in the widest sense possible, such as freeing the oppressed and establishing the freedom of worship.

The Scripture clearly says that fighting in the path of God does not include converting people by the sword. The Koran emphatically declares, "Let there be no compulsion in religion" (2:256).

All legitimate scholars recognize this essential ethic as one that Muslims must abide by, even during times of war.

Misconception #9: The Koran Discourages Interfaith Dialogue and Cooperation

Critics often say that the Koran shows a hostile attitude towards non-Muslims and discourages friendship with anyone outside the Islamic tradition.

Some people get this misunderstanding from passages, such as 5:51, that discourage Muslims from taking Jews and Christians as their *Awliya'*, a word often mistranslated as "friends," but in which in fact means "allies" or "protectors" or "defenders."

Verses, such as 60:8–9, make it crystal clear that the Koran only discourages mutual cooperation and friendship with those unbelievers who fight Muslims because of their faith, or unjustly expel them from their homes, or aid others in causing oppression to the Muslim community (60:9). Otherwise, the Koran actually says that Muslims should engage peaceful unbelievers with justice and kindness (60:8).

Furthermore, the Koran calls for dialogue between religions, cultures, and civilizations regardless of faith, in order to know one another, and by implication become close friends in mutual kindness (16:125; 5:5; 49:13).

Other passages that sometimes lead people to believe that the Koran is hostile towards other faiths include those that condemn *Kafirs* to hellfire.

The Arabic word *Kafir* doesn't mean "unbeliever" or an even worse translation "infidel." Rather, the term *Kafir* at its root means one who is ungrateful. The term describes an individual who is so ungrateful of God that he rejects Him and turns away from worshiping and serving Him. The word also describes an individual who is ungrateful towards God and therefore begins worshiping other idols besides Him, including idol worship, worship of the lower self, worship of intellectual concepts that defy divine ethics and morality, or associating with God anything such as a mother, son, or wife (98:1).

Some critics have accused the Koran of referring to Jews and Christians as apes and pigs, therefore providing "proof" of the Scripture's hostility towards these two religions.

However, the Koran does not call Jews or Christians "apes" or "pigs," but rather refers to a physical (and moral state) that a small group of "evil worshippers (5:60)" from among the Jews and Christians fell into.

This is by no means a sweeping accusation of all Jews and Christians, but only of that small group who fell into evil practices and beliefs of ascribing partners with God. While many commentators, such as Qurtubi, believed it to be a physical state, some famous commentators, such as Mujahid, believed that "apes and swine" refers to a moral (not physical) state of worshipping lust rather than God.

Furthermore, the Koran provides stories about errant peoples in history not merely for the sake of criticizing or making fun, but for the serious purpose of warning followers of the Koran not to take similar paths of hypocrisy.

The Koran warns against making unfair generalizations about Jews and Christians among whom there are such that stand for justice, pray to God all night, and do good works (3:113–115). The Scripture even espouses a close affinity of love with the Christians who are praised for their dedication to learning, simplicity, and humbleness (5:82).

You should also recognize that theological rejections of another faith do not in turn espouse worldly hostility. Just because the Koran strongly rejects Paganism in no way means that Muslims should treat peaceful Pagans (and other faith groups) with injustice and unkindness, as is pointed out in 60:8.

Misconception #10: The Scripture Values Men More Than Women

Some people view verses about women in the Koran outside of their context, giving rise to misunderstandings about the status of women. Another problem is that the Arabic words used in the case of sensitive marital issues are very sophisticated terms that are more often than not mistranslated in the English language.

The Koran, in fact, argues that women are completely equal to men in the sight of God, and that both men and women will be rewarded solely according to their deeds, and not due to any sort of preference for one gender over the other.

The Koran says, "Verily, for all men and women who have surrendered themselves unto God, and all believing men and believing women, and all truly devout men and truly devout women, and all men and women who are patient in adversity, and all men and women who humble themselves, and all men and women who give in charity, and all men and women who keep fast, and all men and women who remember God constantly: For all of them has God prepared forgiveness of sins and a mighty reward" (33:35).

See Chapters 15 and 19 in order to gain a full understanding of family roles and women in the Koran.

Chapter 22

Ten Ways to Dig Deeper into the Koran

. . . .

The Islamic tradition describes the Koran as a vast ocean of knowledge that never ceases in its wisdom, no matter how much you study it. You may want to continue investigating the Koran, looking for new perspectives, challenges, and insights, long after you finish reading this book.

In this chapter, I tell you some avenues to pursue as you continue your voyage on the vast ocean that is the Koran.

Comparing "Translations"

You can find several "translations" of the Koran at any major bookstore.

Don't rely on a single translation of the Koran, but rather get two or three that you can compare and contrast.

Of course, the Arabic never changes, but the translation of it into English is based as much on interpretation as it is on "translation" — because no one word can fully reflect the depth of many concepts found in the Arabic language.

Translators often vary in how they choose to translate or interpret these Koranic concepts. Comparing and contrasting two or three "translations" helps you gain a broader depth of the Koran's meaning.

The following "translations" best reflect the Koran's Arabic and original meaning, in my opinion:

> ✔ *The Holy Qur'an: English Translation of the Meanings and Commentary,* **by Abdullah Yusuf Ali; published by King Fahd Holy Qur'an Printing Press.** This famous translation was endorsed for a long time by the Saudi royal family.
>
> Ali, a British convert to Islam, does a good job of reflecting the Koran's eloquence, and his footnotes are for the most part brilliant.

The translator uses old-style English, which makes it a bit difficult to read for the modern reader. But, if you can read old-English literature, such as Shakespeare, then you may feel comfortable reading Ali's translation as well.

Finally, Ali's work has a fairly good index that can aid you in your research on the Koran.

✔ *The Message of the Qur'an,* **translated and explained by Muhammad Asad; published by Maktaba Jawahar ul uloom Publishers and Distributers.** The introduction to this translation provides a great analysis of the Koran in relation to the Western experience.

Asad's unique translation uses several words to express important Koranic concepts that draw out the words' full meanings, or at least more so than other translations.

Asad, a Polish Jew who converted to Islam, also does a masterful job of understanding his audience and of using words that are best understood in the context of a Western experience with Scripture.

This translation uses eloquent, mostly easy modern English, which makes it easier to read than Yusuf Ali's translation for most modern English readers.

Asad also draws on several famous classical commentaries that offer a broad perspective on the various interpretations of the Koran.

However, some criticize a few of Asad's unorthodox views about certain passages in the Book, and also his heavy use of allegorical interpretations.

Finally, Asad's four appendixes discuss some critical issues about the Koran in a very thoughtful manner.

Asad's work doesn't have an index, which makes it difficult for researchers who want to study specific topics in the Koran.

✔ *The Meaning of the Glorious Koran,* **an explanatory translation by Mohammed Marmoduke Pickthall; published by Maktaba Jawahar al Uloom.** This translation is usually sold in pocket-size editions, which makes it a good travel companion.

Pickthall, a British convert to Islam, mixes simplicity of language with eloquence. His work has almost no footnotes, and the index is not very comprehensive.

However, his lack of commentary and excellent translation prove a great combination if you want to read and understand the Koran for yourself before venturing into the interpretation of the interpreters.

✔ *The Majestic Quran,* **by Abdal Hakim Murad, Mostafa al-Badawi, and Uthman Hutchinson; published by the Nawawi Foundation.** This book offers a unique combination of simple, easy-to-understand English with great elegance to reflect the rhythm of the Koran. It contains over 800 footnotes that draw from the classical tradition of Koranic interpretation.

> ✔ ***The Essential Koran,* by Thomas Cleary; published by Castle Books.**
> This marvelous translation of selected passages in the Koran features
> excellent footnotes designed to introduce the Koran to non-Muslims
> living in the West. Cleary is also working on a highly anticipated com-
> plete translation of the Koran, called *The Qur'an: A New Translation.*

Before you begin reading a translation (or interpretation) of the Koran, you
should check into the qualifications of the translator. Most good translations
are done by those who have an expert command of the Arabic and English
language. Also, translators who are thoroughly familiar with Western culture
are usually more reliable.

Most early translations of the Koran into English (and other European languages) were done by Christian missionaries who introduced several alien
and often derogatory concepts into the Koran. As such, you may want to
avoid these translations if you want to discover the authentic message and
teachings of the Koran.

Listening to the Koran

The message of the Koran can be understood by its reading, but the best way
to experience the powerful soul of the Koran is by listening to its beautiful
recitation.

Non-Arab speaking Muslims are as awed by the Koran voice as are Arab
speaking Muslims who can understand the meaning as it is being recited.
Many non-Muslims, such as authors Michael Sells and Karen Armstrong, also
speak fondly of the almost therapeutic affect of Koranic recitation on its listeners. As such, your experience of the Koran cannot be complete without
listening to its magnificent voice.

Muslims often debate which reader has the best recitation. My personal
favorite is Shaykh Mishari al-Ifasi. Probably the most famous recitations in
the Muslim world are by Shaykh al-Minshawi, Shaykh al-Hussary, Shaykh
Abdul Basit, and Shaykh Saad Al-Ghamdi.

You can listen to these and other recitations on the Web:

> ✔ www.islamweb.net/php/php_arabic/eqerraa_qaree.php: Part of
> the Koran section at Islamweb.net. You find over 130 reciters to choose
> from on this site. The names are listed in English, so it's easier to choose
> a reciter.

> ✔ http://english.islamway.com/sindex.php?section=erecitorslist:
> Part of the Koran section at Islamway.com. Contains the most famous
> reciters known in the Muslim world.

Looking at Different Interpretations

The interpretation of the Koran is a science that has been mastered and used throughout Islamic history. By reading different interpretations of the Koran, you can gain important depth in your understanding of the Book.

Sadly, classical interpretations of the Koran have rarely been translated into the English language. Hopefully, as the interest and influence of Islam grows in the English speaking world, these classical works will soon be translated. For the time being, however, you can read the following interpretations available in English:

- *The Qur'an and its Interpreters,* **by Mahmoud M. Ayoub; published by State University of New York Press:** This excellent collection of 13 different classical commentaries includes two post-colonial interpreters on almost every single verse of the Koran.

  Volume One of this collection gives short biographies and introductions to these famous commentators of the Koran. So far, only the first three *Surahs* of the Koran have been completed, but more are on the way. This collection proves indispensable for any serious student of the Koran.

- *Tafsir Ibn Kathir,* **by Ibn Kathir; published by Darrusalam Publications:** Translation of one of the most famous classical commentaries on the Koran, and most referred to in the Muslim world today. This abridged version takes out Ibn Kathir's references to Jewish stories and weak prophetic traditions.

- *Towards Understanding the Qur'an,* **by Sayyid Abul A'la Mawdudi and translated by Zafar Ishaq Ansari; published by The Islamic Foundation:** Insight into one of the most brilliant minds on the Koran of the twentieth century. His commentary of the Koran and other writings prove very influential on Muslims of today, especially in the Indian subcontinent and Muslims living in the West.

  Mawdudi's work is part of the post-colonial experience, and many of his ideas on the Koran's role in a social movement reflect this experience. He draws on several classical interpretations, but his writings reflect his own deep conceptions about the Koran as a guide for life and society.

- *In The Shade of the Qur'an,* **by Sayyid Qutb and translated by M.A. Salahi and A.A. Shamis; published by The Islamic Foundation:** An interesting look at one of the most influential and controversial Muslim figures of the twentieth century.

  His commentary and other writings have enormous impact on Muslims, especially in the Arab world today. Qutb counts among the famous post-colonial interpreters of the Koran, and much of his lifelong struggles reflect his deep understanding of the Scripture's passages.

✔ *A Thematic Commentary of the Qur'an,* **by Shaykh Muhammad al-Ghazali; published by the International Institute of Islamic Thought:** Another great work on the Koran in the post-colonial era. Al-Ghazali is highly respected as one of the most brilliant scholars of the twentieth century. His work offers a unified reading of each *Surah* while explaining how each *Surah* is linked together in its message and teachings.

Many of the translations that I recommend earlier in this chapter contain heavy footnotes that reflect classical interpretations of the Koran.

Reading Books

Reading a book or two, such as this one, gives you an introduction to the Koran's literary style, structure, and message.

Many books are being published about the Koran these days. I recommend the following ones:

✔ *Approaching the Qur'an,* **by Michael Sells; published by White Cloud Press:** A beautifully written book that translates early *Surahs* and provides a compelling account of a Western experience with this often mystifying Book. Also, this book features a well-produced CD with recitations by some of the most famous reciters of the Koran.

✔ *The Way to the Quran: A Guidebook for studying the Quran,* **by Khurram Murad; published by The Islamic Foundation:** This excellent guide offers step-by-step techniques in developing a personal relationship with the Koran. Although it was originally written for Muslims, many non-Muslims also find it interesting to see how the Koran relates to the life of a devout believer and how many Muslims today study the Koran.

✔ *The Koran: A Very Short Introduction,* **by Michael Cook; published by Oxford Printing Press:** A good introduction for Western audiences on the structure, origin, and meaning of the Koran. Also, this book explains controversial issues in the context of a Western framework and compares the Koran to other sacred Scriptures.

✔ *Struggling to Surrender* and *Even Angles Ask,* **by Jeffery Lang; published by Amana Publications:** An interesting experience of a Western man who converted from Atheism to Islam. The author explains the Koran's emphasis on reason and attempts to answer several questions regarding the Book in the same logical manner. Also, this book includes a very compelling account of the American Muslim experience.

✔ *Qur'an and Woman,* **by Amina Wadud; published by Oxford University Press:** An important contribution to the study of the Koran. This book re-examines selected passages of the sacred Scripture from a woman's perspective.

Also read the introductions to *The Message of the Qur'an* and *Towards Understanding the Qur'an* (see the previous sections). The two introductions give an excellent summary of the Koran's message and literary style.

Studying Arabic

Arabic is the language of the Koran. With the enormous depth that this beautiful language carries, you can't fully grasp the teachings of the Koran without understanding the Arabic language.

In the following list, I offer some advice if you want to study the Koran's language:

✔ If you live near a university, most schools offer introductory Arabic courses. These classes provide a good way to familiarize yourself with the alphabets and basic grammar.

✔ Pick up a copy of *The Dictionary of the Holy Qur'an,* by Abdul Mannan Omar, published by Noor Foundation International, Inc. Omar accurately translates and fully explains the meaning of Arabic words found in the Koran. Also, the appendix gives a nice introduction to the Arabic language and its grammatical structure.

Studying the Koran

The following tips can help you become more familiar with the Scripture:

✔ Begin reading the Koran from its last part *(Juz'),* where some of the shorter, more concise *Surahs* belong. This way you can learn about the basic teachings in the Koran before tackling the longer *Surahs* that posses several themes and shift from story to story.

✔ Keep a journal of your thoughts and reflections as you read the Koran. This helps in expanding your thought process about the passages that you've read. Also, keeping a Koran journal can help you express your feelings, initial reactions, and questions that may come to mind.

✔ Study the Koran as a group. Often, by studying the Scripture in a sort of Koranic study circle with friends who are also interested in the Book, you can gain added perspectives while creating an avenue through which some of your questions can be answered.

Surfing Web Sites

The following Web sites can provide some great opportunities for additional information about the Koran:

- www.quran.org.uk: An excellent resource that contains hundreds of articles and links to other Web sites about the Koran. On this site you find several English translations of the Koran. The site also offers a nice sampling of beautiful Koranic recitations, in audio files, by some of the best reciters in the world.

- www.jannah.com/quran: Provides information on Koranic memorization, the Book's translation and transliteration, recitation of the Koran, and some great audio files.

- www.islamicity.com/mosque/quran: Part of an award-winning site called IslamicCity.com. This site offers excellent tools for searching topics and phrases in the Koran — it's the only site on the Web that offers a phonetic search of the Book.

  Here you can see translations of the Koran in over 20 different languages and also listen to Koranic recitation from the Holy Mosques of Mecca and Medina.

- www.islamonline.net/surah/english/quran.shtml: Part of a larger site, known as IslamOnline.net. This site features great research tools, including a word search of the Koran, a browser, an index, and a nice introduction to every *Surah* in the Book.

Buying resources on the Web

You can find a lot of good material about Islam and the Koran at Islamic Web sites that sell books and audio. These sites have really great sales around the time of Ramadan:

- **Sound Vision** (www.soundvision.org): Tons of material about Islam, and several documentaries concerning various topics.

- **Astrolabe** (www.islamicmedia.org): A diversity of resources about the Islamic tradition from various schools of thought.

- **Islamic Bookstore** (www.islamicbook store.com): A comprehensive collection of books, audio, and video about the Koran and other Islamic sciences.

- **Alhambra Productions** (www.alhambra productions.org): Material on traditional Islamic teachings, including lectures by Hamza Yusuf, a leading scholar of Islam in America.

Taking Classes

Islamic Studies courses, which many universities and colleges now offer, can help you discover more about the Koran and Islam in general.

Understand, though, that academic study of religion is different than studying Muslim life. If you are more interested in knowing how Islam is lived and in discovering traditional understandings of Islam, your time may be better spent talking to Muslims or reading books about the Koran and Islam.

Also, if you live in or near a major city, you can usually find a center of knowledge where Muslims and non-Muslims gather to study the Koran and Islam. For example, if you live in the Bay Area in California, you can look into attending classes at the Zaytuna Institute (www.zaytuna.org), which offers courses on Koranic sciences and Islam in general. If you live in the Chicago area, you may want to try taking courses with the Nawawi Foundation (www.nawawi.org), which offers one course per semester, and is open for both Muslims and non-Muslims.

Talking to Muslims

Conversing with Muslims about the Koran provides a great way to find out more about how traditional Muslims understand and interpret the Book.

Most, but not all, Muslims are quite comfortable in discussing their faith with non-Muslims. However, you should remember that not every Muslim has a good level of knowledge about the Koran. You may have to talk to a few before you can gain insight into the Scripture from a Muslim's perspective.

If you don't know Muslims personally, you can find your local mosque through www.islamicfinder.com. Contact the people at your local mosque, who are often quite open to putting you in touch with a Muslim or a few Muslims.

If you live on or near a college campus, you can contact Muslims through their respective campus organization, usually known as the Muslim Students Association.

Visiting Your Local Mosque

Sometimes the best way to find out about any tradition is to meet people of the faith and to visit their places of worship. Visiting your local mosque can give you an intriguing insight into how Muslims live the Koran in worship and social interactions. Here you can often locate an *Imam* or religious leader who can discuss the Koran with you.

However, the *Imam* is not always trained in Islamic sciences even though he may have a lot of Koran memorized. Don't expect all your questions to get answered, and see if you can talk to other people in the community who have good knowledge about the Scripture.

Contact your local mosque beforehand to set up a visit. Feel free to address any questions that you may have about your visit over the phone, since different mosques expect different things from their visitors. Cover yourself modestly before you visit the mosque, regardless of whether you are male or female.

Appendix A

Glossary of Koranic Terms

- -

*I*n this appendix you find Arabic terms that appear often in the Koran. These terms form an important part of the Koranic worldview.

I also include some terms that don't surface in the Koran, but are an integral part of the Islamic tradition.

Adhan: The call for prayer.

Ahl Dhimmah: Means "those who are protected." Represents the non-Muslim population in Muslim lands.

Ahmad: Short for Muhammad, by which the Prophet is also called in the Koran.

Akhira: The next life, afterlife, Hereafter.

Alim: A scholar of Islamic Sciences.

Allah: Name for God in Arabic. Arab Jews and Christians also call God by Allah.

Ansar: Muslim residents of Medina who welcomed the Muslims to the city after their migration from Mecca.

Aqida: Muslim creed that represents basic beliefs and practices.

Arabic: The language of the Koran.

As-Salaamu'Alaykum: "Peace be upon you." Greeting that all Muslims use when they meet each other. Also, the greeting of all past Prophets and of the angels. Represents the core of Islamic teachings on human relationships.

Ayah: Literally means "sign." Represents the verses of the Koran, which Muslims consider to be signs from God.

Batin: The hidden, esoteric meaning of *Ayat* in the Koran.

Becca: Another way of saying Mecca, which is also referred to in the Bible (Psalms 84:3–6).

Bid'a: Innovations in religion that corrupt Islam from its original teachings and practices. Considered a sin in Islam.

Bismillah: "In the Name of God, the most Gracious, the most Merciful," which appears at the beginning of every _Surah_ except _Surah_ 9.

Caliph: Title of the Muslim ruler in the Islamic tradition.

Da'wa: Calling people to the path of Islam.

Deen: Translated loosely as "religion," but more accurately means a "complete way of life."

Dunya: Worldly life. The Koran warns against running after the worldly life to the neglect of the Hereafter; instead, the Koran advocates maintaining a balance between the two.

Faqih: A jurist of Islamic law.

Fardh: Those aspects of faith and practice that are obligatory on all Muslims.

Fatwa: A non-binding legal opinion that can be issued by a trained scholar of Islamic law.

Fiqh: The scholarly science of Islamic law.

Fitna: Corruption that Muslims are taught to fight against in the world.

Fitrah: Natural inclination that God places in the heart of every human to worship and obey Him.

Hadith: Collection of Prophet Muhammad's sayings and actions.

Hadith Qudsi: Words or acts of God related to Prophet Muhammad that do not appear in the Koran.

Hafidh or Qari: One who has memorized the entire Koran. A unique oral form of preserving the Koran throughout history.

Hajj: Pilgrimage to Mecca that represents the spiritual and physical path of Prophet Abraham. All able Muslims are required to do this once in their lifetime.

Halaal: Those actions that are permissible in Islamic law.

Haraam: Those actions that are forbidden in Islamic law.

Hifdh: To memorize the entire Koran. An oral tradition that is still very much alive today.

Hijab: Modest head covering that Muslim women wear.

Hijra: "Migration." Represents the historical migration of Muhammad and his companions from the oppression of Mecca to the welcoming city of Medina. Also, signifies a spiritual and moral journey from evil to good. The year of *Hijra* marks the beginning of the Islamic Calendar.

Hudood: The Islamic penal code that punishes grave immoral actions.

Ibada: Any act of worship that is for God.

Iblis: Proper name of Satan in the Koran.

Ibrahim: Arabic equivalent for Prophet Abraham.

Ihram: Two pieces of white cloth that represent simplicity and humility before God, and unity with man. Worn by men during the Hajj.

Ihsan: Defined in the Islamic tradition as "To worship God as though you see Him, and while you don't see Him, to know that He surely sees you." Represents the most beautiful spiritual state that a human can achieve.

Ihtisab: Accountability of self and public figures.

Ijtihad: Intellectual struggle to determine the Will of God.

Ikhtilaf: Juristic differences of opinion on areas that are left gray by the Koran and Sunnah.

Imam: In the Sunni tradition, one who leads prayers in a congregation of worshippers. Generally considered a role model in the community. In the Shi'ite tradition, an Imam has more authority as a religious leader.

Iman: Literally means "faith." Theologically, to have complete trust and sense of security in God and His teachings. Includes belief in the angels, Books of revelation, Messengers of God, Day of Judgment, and fate.

Injil: Name of the original Gospel revealed to Prophet Jesus.

Insha'Allah: Means "God Willing." Used by Muslims when talking about the future.

Isa: Arabic equivalent of Jesus.

Islam: Submission or surrender to the Will of God. Theologically, to testify that that there is no god but God, and Muhammad is the Messenger of God. To pray five times a day, fast during the month of Ramadan, give purifying alms annually, and make pilgrimage once in your lifetime.

Isnad: Chain of narrators designated to every *Hadith.*

Jahannam: Hellfire.

Jahil: One who lives in ignorance of Islam.

Jahiliyya: Time of ignorance of Islam and period of Pagan worship in Arabia.

Jannah: Paradise.

Jihad: Means "to struggle" or "strive." Represents an inner struggle against evil impulses and behavior. Also represents an external struggle for good against evil. This includes armed struggle to defend Muslims against hostilities, for the freedom of faith, and for freedom from oppression and tyranny.

Jinn: God's creation made out of smokeless fire. Able to travel large distances in a short time. In the Koran, Satan belongs to this group of creation and is not considered a fallen angel. However, *Jinn,* like humans, can be both good and evil.

Jizya: A protection tax exemption that non-Muslim men pay in an Islamic state.

Juz': Part or section of the Book. The Book is divided into 30 parts; each Juz' constitutes one part.

Ka'ba: House of God first built by Prophet Adam, then rebuilt by Abraham and his son Ishmael. Prophet Muhammad purified the House from idol worship to rededicate it to the worship of One God after years of Pagan practice in Arabia.

Kafir: One who rejects God and His teachings.

Kalaam: Islamic theology.

Khalifa: Refers to the nature of man on earth as God's representative or vicegerent.

Kitab: Literally means "book." A name that the Koran uses to describe itself.

Koran: Literally means "The Recited" or "Recital." Represents the divine revelation for all Muslims.

Kufr: Rejection of God and His teachings.

Makruh: Those actions that are disliked, but not forbidden or prohibited in Islamic law.

Malaikah: Means "angels." One of the six articles of belief for all Muslims.

Mansoukh: Means Abrogated, or verse that is abrogated by the abrogating verse.

Mathl: A literary device used often in the Koran to give a similitude in order to make concepts and teachings easier to understand.

Matn: Contents or body of *Hadith*.

Mecca: The Holy city where the first House of God was built. Also, the birth-place of Prophet Muhammad.

Medina: The Holy city where Muhammad and his companions took refuge from the oppression of Mecca.

Millat: Path or way that the Koran refers to especially in reference to Prophet Abraham.

Mubah: Those actions that are allowed, but not obligatory in Islamic law.

Mufti: One trained in Islamic law who has the ability to issue non-binding legal opinions.

Muhajir: Migrants from Mecca to Medina who forged a relationship of brother-hood with the residents of Medina (Ansar).

Muhammad: The last prophet of God in a series of prophets who were sent to humankind throughout history. Muhammad also represents the perfect role-model human for Muslims.

Muhkamat: Those verses of the Koran that are clear and firmly established in their meaning.

Muhsin: One whose deeds represent the beauty of a true relationship with God.

Mumin: One who has complete trust in God and his teachings.

Munafiq: A hypocrite who declares belief in God, but proves otherwise through his or her actions.

Musa: Arabic equivalent of Prophet Moses.

Muslim: One who submits or surrenders to the Will of God by believing and practicing God's teachings in the divine revelation. Represents the faith of all prophets and their true followers throughout history.

Mutashabihat: Those verses of the Koran that are ambiguous, and can hold several different interpretations.

Muttaqi: One who possesses *Taqwa*.

Naasara: Refers to Christians in the Koran. Literally means "helpers," referring to the true followers of Jesus who helped him to follow the path of God.

Naasikh: Abrogator, or verse that abrogates another verse.

Nabi: Prophet of God.

Nafs: The Islamic term for soul.

Naskh: Abrogation of verses in the Koran. A method of Koranic interpretation that replaces earlier injunctions with later injunctions in order to understand the Koran as a gradual revelation over 23 years.

Qadi: An Islamic judge in an Islamic court.

Qadr: Fate.

Qalb: Islamic term for the heart, which acts as the kingdom of faith.

Qital: A form of *Jihad* (struggle in the path of God), known as armed struggle.

Qiyam: Standing humbly before God in prayer.

Qiyas: Juristic analogy used in Islamic law for progressive reasoning.

Ramadan: Holy month in which God began revealing the Koran to Prophet Muhammad through Angel Gabriel. Muslims commemorate this month with fasting and extra devotional prayers.

Rasul: Messengers of God who received a divine Book of guidance.

Riba: Usury or interest that is prohibited in Islam.

Ruh: Islamic term for spirit.

Ruqu: The bowing position in the Muslim prayer. Believed to be shared by all prophetic communities as a way of showing respect to God.

Sadaqa: Charity.

Salat: Arabic term for the prayers that Muslims perform.

Sawm: Arabic term for fasting from dawn to sunset. Obligatory during the month of Ramadan for all able-bodied Muslims, but optional throughout the year.

Shahadah: To testify in the Oneness of God and belief in Muhammad as the Messenger of God.

Shaitan: Name of the devil, Satan.

Shariah: Literally means "path to the well of water that never runs dry." Represents the sacred path or law of Islam.

Shia: The second largest branch of Islam, comprising of about 10 to 15 percent of all Muslims.

Shirk: Associating partners with God. Considered the worst sin one can commit.

Sirat Al-Mustaqeem: Known as the "straight path" that defines the nature of the Islamic way of life in the Koran.

Sufi: A follower of the mystical interpretations of the Koran and Islamic tradition.

Sufism: Mystic thought and practice in Islam.

Sujjud: Act of prostrating before God. Mentioned in the Koran as the internal state of being in all of God's creation, except for humans who have strayed from the original path.

Sunnah: The practice or way of Prophet Muhammad. Constitutes both his actions and sayings, which play an active role in Islamic law.

Sunni: The largest branch of Islam that represents the teachings of Prophet Muhammad and his companions.

Surah: A chapter of the Koran.

Tafsir: Commentary or interpretation of the Koran.

Taqwa: A spiritual state of God-consciousness that acts as a shield against inner and outer evils.

Tawba: Means "repentance." Returning to God.

Tawhid: Belief in the Oneness of God.

Ulama: The community of Islamic scholars.

Ummah: Refers to the Muslim community as a whole.

Wahy: Divine revelation.

Wudu: An act of purification using water that all Muslims are required to make before each prayer.

Yahud: Refers to Jews in the Koran. Literally means "those who repented," meaning those who repented and took to the guidance of the Torah under the Prophecy of Moses.

Yum Al'Deen: Day of Judgment.

Zabur: Psalms of David.

Zahir: The open, clear meaning of *Ayats* in the Koran.

Zakat: Arabic term for purifying alms that are given to the poor and needy annually by all financially-able Muslims.

Appendix B

Finding Prophets in the Koran

*T*he lives and teachings of prophets make up a major portion of the Koranic message (see Chapter 8).

This appendix helps you find where the Scripture mentions all the prophets, except for Prophets Abraham, Moses, Jesus, and Muhammad, whose stories appear elsewhere in this book:

- **Prophet Aaron (Harun in Arabic):** 2:248, 4:163, 6:84, 7:122, 7:142, 7:150, 10:75, 10:89, 19:28, 19:53, 20:30, 20:45, 20:70, 20:90–94, 21:48, 28:34, 37:114–120

- **Prophet Adam:** 2:31–37, 3:33, 3:59, 5:27, 7:11, 17:61, 17:70, 18:50, 19:58, 20:115–121, 36:60

- **Prophet David (Dawud in Arabic):** 2:251, 4:163, 5:78, 6:84, 17:55, 21:78–79, 27:15, 34:10–13, 38:17–30

- **Prophet Elias (Ilyas in Arabic):** 6:85, 37:123–130

- **Prophet Elisha (Al Yasa' in Arabic):** 6:86, 38:48

- **Prophet Enoch (Idris in Arabic):** 19:56, 21:85

- **Prophet Ezekiel (Dhul Kifl in Arabic):** 21:85, 38:48

- **Prophet Hud (not mentioned in Bible):** 7:65, 11:50, 11:53–58, 11:60, 11:89, 26:124, 46:21

- **Prophet Isaac (Ishaq in Arabic):** 2:133–140, 3:84, 4:163, 6:84, 11:71, 12:6, 12:38, 14:39, 19:49, 21:72, 29:72, 37:112–113, 38:45

- **Prophet Ishmael (Ismail in Arabic):** 2:125–127, 2:133–140, 3:84, 4:163, 6:86, 14:39, 19:54, 21:85, 38:48

- **Prophet Jacob (Yaqub in Arabic):** 2:132–140, 3:84, 4:163, 6:84, 11:71, 12:6–113, 12:38, 12:66, 12:83, 19:6, 19:49, 21:72, 29:27, 38:45

- **Prophet Job (Ayyoub in Arabic):** 4:163, 6:84, 21:83, 38:41

- **Prophet John the Baptist (Yahya in Arabic):** 6:85

- **Prophet Jonah (Yunus in Arabic):** 4:163, 6:86, 10:98, 37:139

- **Prophet Joseph (Yusuf in Arabic):** All of *Surah* 12 (known as the Most Beautiful Story), 40:34

- **Prophet Lot (Lut in Arabic):** 7:80, 11:70–77, 11:81–89, 15:59, 15:61–68, 21:71–74, 22:43, 26:160–167, 27:54–56, 29:26–33, 37:133, 38:13, 50:13, 54:33–36, 66:10

- **Prophet Noah (Nuh in Arabic):** 3:33, 4:163, 6:84, 7:59, 7:69, 9:70, 10:71, 11:25, 11:32, 11:36, 11:42–48, 11:89, 14:9, 17:3, 17:17, 19:58, 21:76, 22:42, 23:23, 23:26, 25:37, 26:105–6, 26:116, 29:14, 33:75–79, 38:12, 40:5, 40:31, 42:13, 50:12, 51:46, 53:52, 54:9, 57:26, 66:10, 69:11, 71:1, 71:21–26

- **Prophet Salih (not mentioned in Bible):** 7:73, 7:75–79, 11:61–66, 11:89, 26:142, 27:45, 54:27

- **Prophet Solomon (Suliman in Arabic):** 2:102, 4:163, 6:84, 21:78–81, 27:15–44, 34:12, 38:30–34

- **Prophet Zechariahs (Zakariyya in Arabic):** 3:37–38, 6:85, 19:2–11, 21:89

Index

•••

• A •

Aaron (Prophet), 339
Aawj, 217
Al-Abadillah (companion of
  Muhammad), 94
Ibn Abbas (companion of Muhammad),
  94, 95
Abduh, Muhammad (scholar), 103, 128
Abdullah ibn Al-As (companion of
  Muhammad), 94
Abdullah ibn Umar (companion of
  Muhammad), 94, 95
ablution, 174–175, 176
abortion, 205, 294
Abraham (Prophet)
  advice to father, 225–226
  details added to life of, 75
  Ka'ba and, 19
  as Muslim, 121
  pilgrimage and, 186
  reason and, 125, 313
  story of, 50–51, 120–122
  testing of, 121–122
  view of, 69
Abrahamic faiths
  covenant of God and, 73
  divine laws and, 67–69
  historical narrative and, 70–71
  Jesus, view of, 77
  Mary, view of, 76
  Muhammad, view of, 75–76
  overview of, 65
  prophetic stories and, 69–70, 73–75

reforming laws and, 72
reforming rituals and, 72
unity of God and, 67
view of, 65–66
abrogating passages, 90–92, 281
Abu Bakr (Caliph)
  Ali and, 104
  Book and, 28
  death of Muhammad and, 27, 315
  election of, 305
  inaugural speech of, 244
  Tafsir and, 94
  teachings of, 277
Abu Hanifa, An-Nu'man Thabit
  (jurist), 270
Abu Lahab, wife of, 290
accountability of deeds, 13, 18
Adam (Prophet)
  Eve and, 284–286
  finding in Koran, 339
  human nature through, 129–130
  Jesus compared to, 126
  message of Koran and, 12
  sin of, 198
Adhan, 172, 173–174, 331
adoption, 205–206
adultery, 197–198, 269–270
*After Jihad: America and the Struggle
  for Islamic Democracy* (Noah
  Feldman), 308
Afterlife, 25
Ahl' al-Kitab. *See* People of the Book
Ahl Dhimmah, 251, 331
Ahmad, 331. *See also* Muhammad
  (Prophet)

Aisha (wife of Muhammad), 89

Akhira, 331

alcohol, ban on. *See also* intoxicants
  Muslims in secular lands and, 164
  in pre-Islamic Arabia, 23, 24
  reasons for, 209
  use as medicine and, 204

Alhambra Productions Web site, 327

Ali, Abdullah Yusuf, *The Holy Qur'an:
    English Translation of the Meanings
    and Commentary*, 57, 321–322

Ali (Caliph), 104–105, 251, 280

Alim, 331

Allah, 109–110, 314, 331

almsgiving
  balance and, 235
  giving alms, 183, 252
  as pillar of faith, 19, 23, 338
  receiving alms, 184–185

*American Muslims: Bridging Faith and
    Freedom* (Muqtedar Khan), 308

Amilina 'alayha, 184

Amin, 54

angels. *See also* Gabriel (Angel)
  belief in, 18
  functions of, 141
  heaven and, 145
  Salam and, 179

animals, 138, 140, 189–190

An-Naasara, 148

Ansar, 331

Approaching the Qur'an
    (Michael Sells), 325

Aqida, 331

ibn Arabi, Muhyi al-Din (interpreter), 98

Arabia, pre-Islamic, 23

Arabic language
  Koran as standard for, 15, 311–312
  preservation of, 32, 56
  reverence for, 53

studying, 326
  translations of, 56–57
  transliterations, 2–3
  triliteral roots of, 54–55

Arafah, 189

arrangement of Surahs, 38

arrogance, 202, 208, 248

arts, 298–299

Asad, Muhammad, *Message of the Koran*,
    57, 97, 322

Aslamiyyah, 293

As-Salaamu'Alaykum, 331

associating partners with God, 149,
    209, 226

Astrolabe Web site, 327

astrology, 134

audience of Koran, 16–17

authenticity of Koran, 311–312

Awilya', 156

Ayah, 331

Ayat (verses)
  definition of, 2
  general and specific, 88–89
  interpreting from viewpoint of laws,
    86–88
  about Muhammad, 159–163
  structure of, 37–38

Ayoub, Mahmoud M., *The Qur'an and
    its Interpreters*, 324

Aziz, wife of, 289–290

• *B* •

baatin, 86, 88

baby, soul of, 199

backbiting, 195, 196, 206

al-Badawi, Mostafa, *The Majestic
    Quran*, 322

balancing worldly and spiritual in
    society, 234–235

Al-Baqara, 38

Basit, Abdul (reader), 323

Batin, 331

Battle of Yamama, 27

bearing witness to truth, 237–238

Becca, 186, 331

bees, 138

belief, six pillars of, 17–18

believers as audience of Koran, 16

Bible, view of, 66

Bid'a, 332

Big Bang Theory, 134–135

Al-Birr, 153, 226, 250

birth control, 294

Bismillah, 332

Book. *See* Koran

bridal gift, 219, 229

brotherhood of man, 241–243

Al-Bukhari, Ismail (collector of Hadith), 261

business
  ethics of, 206, 301
  women and, 291–292, 294

• C •

calendar, Islamic, 135

Caliph, 244, 332. *See also specific Caliphs, such as Abu Bakr*

calligraphy, 35–36

Carlyle, Thomas (historian), 312

Center for the Study of Islam and Democracy Web site, 308

change through God's mercy, 193

chapters, 2. *See also* Surahs

charity, 185, 211–212, 336

chastity, 196, 223–224

children
  inheritance and, 228
  parental responsibilities to, 227
  raising righteous, 224–225, 226–227
  responsibilities toward parents, 225–226

Children of Israel
  Jesus and, 127
  Moses and, 124–125

Christianity. *See also* Abrahamic faiths; Bible, view of; People of the Book
  status of Jesus in, 149–150
  view of, 318–319

citizens
  obligations of, 246
  responsibilities of Islamic government toward, 245
  rights of, 247–249

Clark, Malcolm, *Islam For Dummies*, 2

Cleary, Thomas, *The Essential Koran*, 323

cloud formations, 137

collecting Surahs as book, 27–28

community, building. *See also* Islamic law
  almsgiving and, 183
  bearing witness to truth and, 237–238
  enjoining good and forbidding evil, 238–240, 246
  middle path and, 233–237
  prayer and, 172
  Ramadan and, 182
  rope of God and, 240–243

contentment, 211

controversial passages on interfaith relations, 153–156, 318–319

Cook, Michael, *The Koran: A Very Short Introduction*, 325

creation
  patterns of, 134
  story of, 198

crescent moon symbol, 315

The Criterion, 14

criticism of Hadith, 262

crucifixion, 77, 128
cutting hair, 190

● D ●

David (Prophet)
  fasting of, 182
  finding in Koran, 339
  Goliath and, 274
  Sheba and, 74
Da'wa, 332
Day of Judgment
  accountability on, 13
  angels and, 141
  belief in, 18
  description of, 143–144
  intercession and, 112–113
  Meccan phase of revelation and, 25
  mountains and, 137
  Muhammad on, 165
  Pharaoh and, 51
  pilgrimage and, 189
  rain as parable for, 137
  Satan and, 142
  souls and, 200
  Wudu and, 175
death, 200
debate in society, 257, 303–304
deception, 207
declaration of faith, 19, 170
Deen, 332
Deen Al-Fitrah, 199
defaming another, 195
democracy
  holding officials responsible in, 305–306
  liberty and, 306–307
  overview of, 302–303
  resources on, 308
  rule of law between citizenry and God,
      debating, 303–304
  social equality and, 307–308
  Western versus Islamic, 304
  will of people, elections, and, 305
dhahir, 86, 88
Dhikr, 212–213
Dhimmies (Ahl al-dhimmah), 251, 331
diacritical marks, 29–30, 34–35
dialects of Koran, 25, 28–29
The Dictionary of the Holy Qur'an
      (Abdul Mannan Omar), 326
dietary laws, 204, 260
dignity, 247
disabled, honoring, 248
disbelief, Koranic concept of, 17
discrimination, 249, 251, 301
diversity, respect for, 152–153, 241
Divine. *See* God
divine law. *See* Islamic law
divine signs, moral narrative through, 47
divorce, 229, 293. *See also* marriage
"Domestic Terrorism in the Islamic Legal
      Tradition" (Sherman Jackson), 268
dress
  modesty and, 223–224, 307
  for pilgrimage, 187
Dua', 179
Dunya, 332

● E ●

ears, 194–195
ease, law of, 259
economic model, 300–301
education
  for children, 227, 245
  for women, 292
elections, 305
Elias (Prophet), 339
Elisha (Prophet), 339
Enoch (Prophet), 339

equality
  human rights and, 247
  of mankind before God, 240–241
  social, 307–308
  social rights based on, 249
  of women, 284–290, 319
Esposito, John
  Islam and Democracy, 308
  *Unholy War: Terror in the Name
    of Islam*, 282
The Essential Koran
    (Thomas Cleary), 323
eternal nature of God, 111
ethical principles
  armed struggle and, 277
  honor, preserving, 206–207
  life, preserving, 204–205
  lineage, preserving, 205–206
  overview of, 14, 203
  property, preserving, 206
  religion, preserving, 203–204
  Shariah, 264–265
  warfare, 102, 155, 248, 275
Eve (wife of Adam), 130, 284–286
Even Angels Ask (Jeffery Lang), 325
evil. *See also* penal code; Satan
  fighting against, 12–13, 142–143, 274
  forbidding, 238–240, 246
  Jihad and, 252–253
extremes, avoiding, 236–237
eyes, 195–196, 224
Ezekiel (Prophet), 339

● *F* ●

faith. *See also* Abrahamic faiths; religion
  declaration of, 19, 170
  freedom of, 254
  hardship as condition of, 236
  pillars of, 17–19
  rejecters of, 17, 151, 202

false testimony, 270
falsehood, 207
family. *See also* children; marriage
  God-consciousness and, 215–216
  laws dealing with, 260
  overview of, 215
  preservation of, 270, 299
  spouse, searching for, 216–217
  women, work, and, 292
Faqih, 332
Fardh, 332
al-Faruqi, Ismail Raji, *Islam and
    Other Faiths*, 156
fasting
  applications of, 89
  outside Ramadan, 182
  as pillar of Islam, 19
  purpose of, 180–182
  reform of, 72
fatalism, 316–317
Al-Fatihah, 176
Fatwa/Fatawah, 257, 332
fear of wrath of God, 234
Feldman, Noah, *After Jihad: America
    and the Struggle for Islamic
    Democracy*, 308
Fiqh, 257, 332
Fi'r Riqab, 184–185
Fi-sabili 'llah, 185
Fitna, 332
Fitrah, 199, 332
Five Pillars of Islam, 18–19
forbidden actions, 265
Forbidden Tree, 284
forgiveness, 118, 189, 210–211
fornication, 197–198, 269–270
free trade, 300–301
freedom
  of choice, 152
  of faith, 254
  of religion, 275–276, 307

freedom *(continued)*
  as right of citizenship, 245, 247–248
  of worship, 251, 302
funeral prayer, attending, 242
Fuqaha', 257
Fuqara, 184

• G •

Gabriel (Angel)
  Hagar and, 188
  Mary and, 126
  Muhammad and, 22, 24, 162
gambling, 209, 258
generosity, 118, 166
al-Ghamdi, Saad (reader), 323
Al-gharimin, 185
Al-Ghazali (jurist and theologian), 61
al-Ghazali, Muhammad (*A Thematic
    Commentary on the Qur'an*), 103, 325
ibn Ghazali, Zain (interpreter), 99
God. *See also* unity of God
  as Allah, 109–110, 314, 331
  associating partners with, 149, 209, 226
  attributes of, 113–117, 150, 212
  balanced approach to, 234
  extending covenant of, 73
  as having son, 127
  judgment and, 149
  knowing, 117–119
  Koran as revelation from, 9
  love of, 316
  mercy of, 145–146, 165, 193, 234, 316
  Muhammad on, 165–166
  narrative told from perspective of,
    62–63
  nature and, 134
  nature of, 110–113
  oaths of, 60
  punishment of, 165

reckoning of, 165
relationship with, 166
teaching children about, 226
women in service to, 286–287
worship and service to, 11
wrath of, 146, 234
God-consciousness
  creating with prayer, 171
  family and, 215–216
  fasting and, 180
  overview of, 18
  Taqwa, 55
good, enjoining, 238–240, 246
government. *See also* democracy;
    Islamic state
  Islamic law and, 266
  in religion, 239
gradual law, 102
gratitude
  for favor, showing, 242
  to God, showing, 171, 181
group prayer, 172, 173
guidance
  divine, interpretation and
    application of, 257
  to spiritual path, 12, 13–14
Guidance, Book of, 13–14
guilt, admission of, 270

• H •

Hadith
  divine Will and, 160
  Isnad, 262
  levels of authenticity of, 262–263
  literary standard of, 312
  Matn, 262
  overview of, 15, 27, 261–262
  Sunnah and, 261–263
Hadith Qudsi, 198, 332

Hadr, 34
Hafidh/Huffadh, 31–32, 332
Hafsa (wife of Muhammad), 28
Hagar (wife of Abraham), 186, 188
hair, shaving or cutting, 190
Hajj, 19, 332. *See also* pilgrimage
Halaal, 332
Hanafi School of Law, 270–271
Hanbal, Ahmad Ibn (jurist), 272
Hanbali School, 272
handling Koran, 30–31
hands, 196–197
Haq, 247
Haraam, 332
hardship as condition of faith, 236
head-covering, 69
The Healing, 16
hearing, 194–195
heart, spiritual
    ears, tongue, and, 194–195
    eyes and, 195–196
    gates to, 194
    hands, legs, and, 196–197
    as part of self, 191–193
    purifying, 212–213
    sexual organs and, 197–198
    sin and, 199
    stomach and, 197
heaven, 144–145
hellfire, 145, 201
Hifdh, 332
high treason, punishment for, 267
Hijab, 69, 333
Hijra, 164, 333
Hirabah, 267
historical narrative, 70–71
*The Holy Qur'an: English Translation
    of the Meanings and Commentary*
    (Yusuf Ali), 57, 321–322
honey, 138

honor
    interaction and, 207, 213
    preserving, 152, 206–207, 259, 299
    rights and, 247–248
hope in God's mercy, 234
horse, wild, and rider analogy, 192–193
house chores, 292
Hud (11), 49
Hud (Prophet), 50, 339
Hudood, 333
human beings. *See also* vicegerent role
    angels and, 141
    as audience of Koran, 16
    caretaker role of, 139–141
    Divine and, 118
    guides for, 11–12
    nature and, 139–140
    role of, 11, 100, 131, 296
    as servants of God, 111
    status and nature of, 128–130
human rights, 299–300
humility, 226
hunting, 140
Huqquq, 247
al-Hussary (reader), 323
Hutchinson, Uthman,
        The Majestic Quran, 322
hypocrisy, 208, 318–319
hypocrites
    as audience of Koran, 17
    Medinan Surahs and, 26

Ibada, 333
Iblis. *See* Satan
Ibnu 'Sabil, 185
Ibrahim. *See* Abraham (Prophet)
idle talk, 195
al-Ifasi, Mishari (reader), 323

Ihram, 187
Ihsan, 18, 226, 298, 333
Ihtisab, 333
Ijaza, 257
Ijma', 263
Ijtihad, 257, 333
Ikhtilaf, 257, 333
Ikhwan al-Muslimeen, 99
ill
  honoring, 248
  visiting, 242
Imam
  advice to, 235
  Sunni versus Shi'ite tradition,
    104–105, 333
  talking with at local mosque, 329
Iman, 17–18, 333
immigrants and hosts, relationship
    between, 26
imminence of God, 118
immortality, deceptive quality of, 130
In the Shade of the Qur'an (Qutub),
    103, 324
infanticide, 205
"infidel", 154. *See also* Kafir
influence of good company, 214
inheritance, laws of
  Islamic laws and, 228–229
  kinship ties and, 48
  modernists and, 300
  women and, 291
Injil, 66, 126, 333
injustice, 208. *See also* justice
innocent until proven guilty concept, 248
Insha'Allah, 213, 333
insulting another, 195
intellect, preserving, 259
interaction and honor, 207, 213
intercession, 112–113
interfaith relations, controversial
    passages on, 153–156, 318–319

interpretations of text. *See also* Tafsir;
    translations
  abrogating passages, 90–92, 281
  circumstances of revelation and, 90
  classic works of, 96–98
  companions of Muhammad and, 94–95
  comparing, 324–325
  controversial passages on interfaith
    relations, 153–156, 318–319
  differences of opinion, basis of, 82
  diversity of, 3
  general and specific applications, 88–89
  inner meanings, 88
  key terms of, 82–84
  Mawdudi and, 99–101
  muhkamat or clear verses, 85, 86–88
  mutashabihat or figurative verses,
    85–86, 88
  outer meanings, 86–88
  out-of-context, 153–154
  overview of, 81
  post-colonialist, 98–103
  qualifications of interpreter,
    checking, 323
  Qutub and, 101–103
  Shi'ite, 105–106
  in successive generations, 95
  teaching of, 84
  translations as, 56–57
intimacy in marriage, 222–223
intoxicants. *See also* alcohol, ban on
  reasons for prohibition on, 209
  struggle against as Jihad, 253
  successive stages of prohibition on,
    154, 258
invitation, accepting, 242
Iqra, 10
Iraq, interpreters from, 95
Isa. *See* Jesus (Prophet)
Isaac (Prophet), 339
Ishmael (Prophet), 75, 120, 186, 339

Islam. *See also* Islamic law; Islamic state
  almsgiving in, 19, 23, 183–185, 338
  as complete way of life, 164
  concept of, 12
  declaration of faith in, 19, 170
  definition of, 10, 333
  fasting, 19, 72, 89, 180–182
  Five Pillars of, 18–19
  Ottoman Empire and, 98
  pilgrimage, 19, 186–190
  prayer, 170–180
  preservation of, 203–204
  six pillars of belief, 17–18
  triliteral roots of, 55
  as universal faith, 147, 315
Islam and Democracy (John Esposito and
    John Voll), 308
Islam and Other Faiths (Ismail Raji
    al-Faruqi), 156
Islam For Dummies (Malcolm Clark), 2
Islamic Art Network, 36
Islamic Bookstore Web site, 327
Islamic Brotherhood, 239
Islamic law. *See also* penal code; Shariah
  Abrahamic faiths and, 67–69
  ease, law of, 259
  everyday, 68
  family and, 260
  Fridays and, 72
  government and, 266
  gradual, 102
  Hanafi School of Law, 270–271
  Hanbali School, 272
  inheritance and, 48, 228–229, 291, 300
  Islamic state and, 244
  Malike School of Law, 271
  Muhammad and, 10
  necessity, law of, 301
  overview of, 255
  principles of, 259–260
  purity and, 72, 213–214
  Qital and, 279
  religious practice in, 260
  remission, law of, 266
  sexual relations, unlawful, 269–270
  Shafi'i School of Law, 271
  social equality and, 307–308
  Sunnah and, 261–263
  Women's rights in, 290–291
Islamic movement and Qutub, 101–103
Islamic state. *See also* democracy
  concept of, 113
  failures of, 282
  non-Muslims in, 249–252, 278
  obligations of citizens in, 246
  political identity, forming, 244–245
  responsibilities of, 245
  rights of citizens in, 247–249
  warfare and, 253–254
Isnad, 262, 334
Israliyat, 84, 96
Itifaq, 257

● **J** ●

Jackson, Sherman, "Domestic
    Terrorism in the Islamic Legal
    Tradition", 268
Jacob (Prophet), 339
Jahannam. *See* hellfire
Jahil, 334
Jahiliyya, 99, 101–102, 334
Jamaat Islami, 99
Jamarat, 189
Jammat, 172
Jannah, 334
Jesus (Prophet). *See also* Mary
    (mother of Jesus)
  birth of, 287
  foretelling of Muhammad and, 75–76

Jesus (Prophet) *(continued)*
   Gospel and, 66
   status of, 149–150
   story of, 125–128
   on Torah, 66
   unity of God and, 127
   views of, 77
Jihad. *See also* Qital
   as armed struggle, 102, 253–254,
      273–278
   definition of, 12, 252, 317, 334
   forms of, 273
   Islamic law and, 279
   practicing, 214
   Qutub and, 102
   as struggle against evil, 252–253
   in today's world, 280–282
   triliteral roots of, 55
Jinns, 142, 202, 334
Jizya tax, 252, 278, 334
Job (Prophet), 339
John the Baptist (Prophet), 339
Jonah (Prophet), 339
Joseph (Prophet), 74, 289–290, 339
journal, 57, 326
Jtihad, 264
Judaism, 148, 318–319. *See also*
      Abrahamic faiths; People of the
      Book; Torah, view of
judgment, 149
jurisprudence, 257
just retribution, 204, 235, 266–267
justice
   economic, 184
   establishing, 12–13, 244–245
   God's wrath and, 146
   non-Muslim citizens and, 251
   revenge and, 280
   in society, 235
Juz', 39–40, 334

• K •

Ka'b Al-Quradi (interpreter), 95
Ka'ba
   Abraham, Ishmael, and, 19, 120
   Muhammad and, 334
   pilgrimage and, 186, 188
Kafir
   as rejecter of faith, 17, 151, 334
   Satan as, 202
   as ungrateful, 318
Kalaam, 334
ibn Kathir, Ismail
   as interpreter, 96
   Tafsir Ibn Kathir, 324
Khadija (wife of Muhammad), 22, 292
Khalifa, 334
Khan, Muqtedar, *American Muslims:*
      Bridging Faith and Freedom, 308
ibn Al-Khattab, Umar. *See* Umar (Caliph)
Al-Khidr (sage), 123
Khilafat, 100
kindness, 166, 179, 225, 250
kinship ties, 48
Kitab, 334
Kital, 253
knowing God, 117–119
knowledge, divine, 113
Koran
   audience of, 16–17
   dialects of, 25, 28–29
   divine creation of, 22
   handling, 30–31
   meaning of, 10
   names of, 13–16
   printing of, 29–30, 31
   as revelation from God, 9
   self-preservation of, 58
   as standard for Arabic language,
      15, 311–312
   themes of, 11–13

The Koran: A Very Short Introduction (Michael Cook), 325
Kufr, 57, 334
Kursi, 88

• L •

Lailatul' qadr, 21
Lang, Jeffery
  Even Angels Ask, 325
  Struggling to Surrender, 325
language, 84. *See also* Arabic language
laws. *See also* Islamic law
  abrogation and, 91–92, 281
  divine, 113, 164
  ethical principles and, 203
  interpreting verses from viewpoint of, 86–88
  in Koran, 258–260
  man-made moral, 102
  moral narrative through, 47–48
  secular, 164
  specification of, 92
  transgression and, 209
leader, selecting, 244, 246
leadership of family, 220–222
legislation, 306
legs, 197
letters, disjointed or mysterious, 61–62
liberation, war of, 254
liberty, 306–307
life
  preserving, 204–205, 259
  purpose of, 131
life, leading good
  discouraged behaviors, 207–209
  encouraged behaviors, 210–212
Light upon Light, 12
lightning, 137
lineage, preserving, 205–206, 259, 270
listening to recitation, 323

literary style
  disjointed or mysterious letters, 61–62
  muhkamat or clear verses, 60–61, 85, 86–88, 335
  mutashabihat or figurative verses, 60, 85–86, 88, 335
  non-historical narrative form, 63, 71
  nonlinear, 312–313
  oaths, 60
  overview of, 57–59
  perspective, 62–63
  sayings, 59
  simile, 59
Lot (Prophet), 50–51, 340
Lot, wife of, 290
love of God, 316
lowering of eyes, 224
Luqman (sage), 226, 313

• M •

maasum, 120
Madyan, People of, 51
Mahr, 219, 229
The Majestic Quran (A. H. Murad, M. al-Badawi, and U. Hutchinson), 322
Makruh, 334
Malaikah, 334. *See also* angels
Malik ibn Anas (jurist), 271
Maliki School of Law, 271
man/mankind. *See* human beings
Mansoukh, 335. *See also* abrogating passages
marriage
  as basis of family, 219–220
  bridal gift, 219
  divorce, 229, 293
  forced, 216, 218
  harm to, 270
  intimacy in, 222–223
  leading family, 220–221

marriage *(continued)*
  obeying and rebelling within, 221–222
  with People of the Book, 250
  polygamy, 218
  protecting family, 221
  providing for family, 220
  restrictions on, 217–218
  rights and responsibilities in, 220
  sexual relations and, 197–198
  spouse, searching for, 216–217
  women and, 293
martyrdom, 279–280
Mary (mother of Jesus), 76, 126, 286–288
Masakin, 184
Mash'Allah, 213
Masum, 74
materialism, 211
Al-mathani, 38
Mathl, 335
Matn, 262, 335
Al-Mawdudi, Abdul
  as sayyid, interpreter, 99–101
  Towards Understanding the Qur'an,
    99, 101, 324
meals, 197, 250
The Meaning of the Glorious Koran
  (Mohammed Pickthall), 57, 322
meat, forbidden, 197
Mecca
  Abraham and, 75
  description of, 335
  interpreters from, 95
  pilgrimage to, 19
Meccan Surahs, 24–25
Medina, 95, 335
Medinan Surahs, 24–25, 26
memorization, 26–27, 29, 31–32
mercy
  of God, 145–146, 165, 193, 234, 316
  of Muhammad, 161–162
  showing to others, 166
  in society, 235

message of prophets, 119
Message of the Koran (Muhammad Asad),
  57, 97, 322
messengers, 119, 127
middle path between spiritual and
  worldly, 233–237
Millat, 335
Mina, 189
Minaret (think tank), 302
al-Minshawi (reader), 323
miracles of Jesus, 126–127
misconceptions of Koran
  as authored by Muhammad, 311–312
  as claiming God for one people, 315
  as devaluing women, 319
  as discouraging interfaith dialogue and
    cooperation, 318–319
  as espousing polytheism, 314–315
  as incoherent and unorganized,
    312–313
  on meaning of Jihad, 317
  as portraying God as wrathful and
    unloving, 316
  as preaching fatalism, 316–317
  as void of reason, 313–314
Al-mi'un, 38
moderation, 192, 233–237
modernity
  arts and, 298–299
  economics, free trade, and, 300–301
  human rights and, 299–300
  modern culture compared to, 295–296
  morality, secularism, and, 301–302
  reform of laws and, 308
  Rida (interpreter) and, 103
  science and, 298
  social progress and, 296–297
modesty
  elements of, 211
  honor and, 206
  lowering eyes and, 196, 224

public, and dress, 223–224
teaching to child, 227
moon, function of, 135–136
moon god, 314
moral narrative
conclusion of, 51–52
history and, 71
as non-historical form, 63
presentation of, 46
of shorter Surahs, 52
through divine signs, 47
through laws, 47–48
through stories of past, 48–51
moral relativism, 14, 301–302
Moses, mother of, 288
Moses (Prophet)
appearance in Koran, 313
Children of Israel and, 124–125
magic and, 125
Muhammad compared to, 70, 122
Pharaoh and, 51, 124, 240
story of, 122–125
Torah and, 66
mosque, visiting, 329
mother, position of, 225, 285
Mothers of the Believers, 94
Mount Arafah, 19
mountains, 137
Muadhin, 173
Mu'allafati Qulubuhum, 184
Mubah, 335
Mufasir, 83
Al-mufassal, 38
Mufti, 335
Muhajir, 335
Muhammad (Prophet). *See also* Hadith;
Sunnah
on achieving nearness to God, 198
on animals, 140
on backbiting and slandering, 196

Cave of Hira and, 22
on charity, 185
companions of, 94–95
compared to Abraham, 75
compared to Moses, 70, 122
death of, 93–94
divorce and, 293
on evildoers, 239
as example, 161, 163–165
on excess in matters of religion, 236
on family, 216
"Farewell Sermon", 241
on fasting, 181
fasting of, 182
first word revealed to, 10
Gabriel and, 22, 24
on God, 165–166
on heart, 193
on Jihad, 273
as last prophet, 15, 162
on leadership, 246
mercy of, 161–162
mission of, 160–161
on moderation, 192
proof of prophethood of, 14–15
prophecy of, 75–76
rebuke of, 248
revelation and, 21, 311–312
role of, 10–11
as Seal of prophets, 162–163
as servant of God, 160
on speech, 195
Sunnah Salat and, 179
transmitting revelation to community,
26–27
on treatment of neighbors, 243
verses about, 159–163
on virtue, 166–167
wives of, 94
on women, 285

muhkamat or clear verses, 60–61, 85, 86–88, 335

Muhsin, 298, 335

Mujahid (interpreter), 95, 319

Mumin, 54, 335

Munafiq, 335

Murad, Abdal Hakim, *The Majestic Quran*, 322

Murad, Khurram, *The Way to the Quran: A Guidebook for Studying the Quran*, 325

murder, 235, 266–267

Musa. *See* Moses (Prophet)

Mushrikun, 154

Muslim
  Arabic language and, 53
  definition of, 12, 19, 54, 148, 335
  population of, 20
  Shi'ite, 104–106, 337
  as state of being, 201–202
  Sunni, 104–105, 257, 337
  talking to, 328

Muslim Brotherhood, 99

Muslim ibn al-Hajjaj (collector of Hadith), 261

Muslim Women's League, 294

The Muslim World, 268

Mustalah al-hadith, 262

mutashabihat or figurative verses, 60, 85–86, 88, 335

Mu'tazali theology, 106

Muttaqi, 336

mutual consultation. *See* Shura

mystics. *See* Sufis

N •

Naasara, 336

Naasikh, 336

Nabi, 336

Nafs, 191–193, 336. *See also* souls

Nafs al-Ammarah Bis-sou, 193

Nafs al-Lawwamah, 193

Nafs al-Mutma'innah, 193

names
  of children, 227
  of God, 113–117
  of Surahs, 40–46
  of things, Adam and, 129
  of women after marriage, 293

Naskh, 336

nature, divine ways of
  animals, 138, 140
  deep seas, 136–137
  humans, 139–140
  mountains, 137
  overview of, 133–134
  patterns of creation, 134
  plants, 137–138
  sky, 137
  stars and planets, 135
  sun and moon, 135
  universe, creation of, 134–135

Nawawi Foundation, 328

al-Nawawi (scholar), 241

necessity, law of, 301

neighbor, treatment of, 243

Al-Nisaa' (4), 48

al-Nisaburi, Nizam al-Din (interpreter), 98

Noah (Prophet), 49–50, 340

Noah, wife of, 290

non-Muslims in Muslim lands, 249–252, 278. *See also* Ahl Dhimmah; Jizya tax

numbers of Surahs, 40–46

• O •

oaths, 60, 242

obedience
  to God, 166, 286–287
  to parents, 225

obligations, personal and communal, 264
ocean, 136–137
olive tree, 138
Omar, Abdul Mannan, *The Dictionary of the Holy Qur'an*, 326
opinion, differences of, 257
opposites, Universe as made of, 146
oppression, 242, 274–275
oral tradition. *See also* memorization; recitation
  Muhammad and, 26–27
  Tafsir and, 95
  teacher-student relationship and, 32
  as way of preservation, 29
Orientalists, 249
original sin, 198
orphans, 23
Ottoman Empire, 98
ownership of God, 112

• P •

Paganism, 319
paradise, 201
Party of Islam, 239
patience
  as encouraged behavior, 210
  Muhammad on, 166
patterns of creation, 134
pay for work, women and, 292
penal code
  murder and, 266–267
  overview of, 265–266
  spreading of violence and, 267–268
  theft and, 268
  unlawful sexual relations and, 269–270
People of the Book. *See also* Christianity; Judaism
  as audience of Koran, 16–17, 147
  friendship with, 156, 318

marriage of women from among, 152–153
  Medinan Surahs and, 26
  relations with, 250–251
permissibility, concept of, 264–265, 272, 297
Pharaoh, wife of, 288
Pickthall, Mohammed Marmoduke, *The Meaning of the Glorious Koran*, 57, 322
pilgrimage
  Abraham and, 186
  answering call, 187–188
  asking for forgiveness, 189
  camping at Mina, 189
  death during, 186–187
  dressing in humility and equality, 187
  hurrying between two hills, 188–189
  making sacrifice, 189–190
  overview of, 186
  as pillar of Islam, 19
  stoning Satan, 189
  walking around House of God, 188
planets, creation of, 135
plant life, 137–138
poetry, regarding Koran as, 58
political identity for Islamic state, forming, 244–245
polygamy, 218
polytheism, 149, 314–315
pork, 204
pornography, 253
poverty, 301
prayer. *See also* Salat; supplication
  approaching, 172, 174–175
  At-tahiyyat position for, 178
  balance and, 235
  call to, 172, 173–174
  outer and inner meaning of, 175–180
  overview of, 170

prayer *(continued)*
  as pillar of Islam, 19
  position of sun and, 136
  purpose of, 171–172
  Qiyam, 176–177
  reform of, 72
  Ruku, 177–178
  Salam, 179–180
  Sujjud, 178
  supplementary, 179
  Takbir, 176
preservation
  of Arabic language, 32, 56
  of family, 270, 299
  of honor, 152, 206–207, 259, 299
  of intellect, 259
  of Islam, 203–204
  of Koran, 31–32, 58
  of life, 204–205, 259
  of lineage, 205–206, 259, 270
  of property, 206, 247, 259
  of religion, 203–204, 259
pretension, 208
priesthood, 257
printing of Koran, 29–30, 31
privacy, 248, 269, 307
The Proof, 14–15
property. *See also* inheritance, laws of
  preserving, 206, 247, 259
  protection of, 268
  right to own, 249
  women and, 291–292
prophecy, 304
prophets. *See also specific prophets,*
    such as Abraham
  agreements among faiths on stories of,
    69–70
  belief in, 148
  as brotherhood of faith, 148
  description of, 119–120

differences among faiths on stories of,
    73–75
  Islamic law and, 261–263
  role of, 11–12
  as sinless, 74
prose, rhythmic, 58
protecting family, 221
providing for family, 220
Psalms, 74
public benefit, concept of, 259, 297
punishment, collective, 248
purity
  controlling passion and, 214
  of heart, 193
  Islamic law and, 213–214
  keeping company with pious people
    and, 214
  laws of, 72
  of Mary, 287
  pilgrimage and, 187
  prayer and, 171–172, 174–175
  remembering divine and, 212–213
Purity of Faith, 110–111

Qadi, 336
Qadr, 336
Qalb, 191–193, 336
Qari, 31, 332
Qisas, 266
Qital
  to defend human rights and freedom of
    worship, 275–276
  to defend life and religion, 274–275
  definition of, 273, 336
  Islamic law and, 279
  passage 9:5 and, 276, 278
  passage 9:29 and, 278
Qiyam, 176–177, 336

Qiyas, 264, 336
The Qur'an and its Interpreters
(Mahmoud M. Ayoub), 324
Qur'an and Woman (Amina Wadud), 325
Quraysh dialect, 28
al-Qurtubi, Muhammad ibn Ahmad Abu
'Abdullah (interpreter), 97, 318–319
Qutub (sayyid, interpreter), 101–103, 324

● *R* ●

racism, 249
Al-Rahman (55), 47
rain, 137
Ramadan
description of, 336
fasting and, 19, 180–182
Juz' and, 39–40
rape, 269
Rasul, 336
al-Razi, Fakhr al-Din (interpreter), 97
reader as audience of Koran, 17
reason, 313–314
recitation, 33–35
reform of laws, 308
rejecters of faith, 17, 151, 202
relationship with God, 166
religion. *See also* faith; freedom, of
religion; *specific religions*
academic study of, 328
avoiding extremes in, 236–237
disagreement about, 251
forced, 247, 251
preserving, 203–204, 259
role of government in, 239
religious diversity, respect for, 152–153
The Reminder, 15
remission, law of, 266
repentance, philosophy on, 54
researching topics, 154, 325–329

respect
for diversity, 152–153, 241
showing to parents, 225
for women, 285
responding in kind, 242–243
responsibilities of brotherhood, 242–243
revelation
beginning of, 22
circumstance of and interpretation, 90
Koran as completion of past, 12
Meccan phase of, 25
Medinan phase of, 24–25, 26
Muhammad and, 21
names and qualities in, 13–16
previous, view of, 65–66
protection of, 21
stages of, 24–25
transmitting to community, 26–27
revenge, 280
reverence for Koran, 9
Riba, 336
Rida, Muhammad Rashid
(interpreter), 103
righteous children, raising, 226–227
rituals, 131, 169
rope of God
brotherhood of man, 241–243
equality and, 240–241
overview of, 240
Ruh, 191–193, 336
Ruku, 177–178
Ruqu, 336

● *S* ●

Sabians, 148
Sadaqa, 185, 336. *See also* charity
Sa'ee, 188–189
Sahaba, 83
Saja', 58

Salaam, 55
Salam, 179–180
Salat, 19, 183, 336. *See also* prayer
Salih (Prophet), 50, 340
Salim, 55
Sanders, Peter (photographer), 36
Satan
  Adam, Eve, and, 129, 284
  purpose of, 142–143
  stoning, 189
  story of, 202
Saudi Arabia, 84
Sawm, 19, 336
sayings, 59
science
  advances in, 297
  Koran and, 298
  worship of, 134
scribes, 27, 28
Scripture. *See* Koran
search engine, 154
seas, 136–137
secularism, 301–302
seeking God's love, 166
self, parts of, 191–193
self reflection, 210
self-defense, war for, 253–254, 274–275
self-restraint, practicing, 214
Sells, Michael, *Approaching the Qur'an*, 325
sexual relations. *See also* adultery; fornication
  marriage and, 197–198
  unlawful, 269–270
Shafi' (jurist), 264
al-Shafi'i, Muhammad bin Idris (jurist), 271
Shafi'i School of Law, 271
Shahadah, 19, 170, 337
Shaheed, 279–280

Shaitan. *See* Satan
Shariah. *See also* Islamic law
  consensus of scholars and, 263
  definition of, 11, 255–256, 337
  ethical standards and, 264–265
  jurists and, 257, 264
  Koran and, 258–260
  Medinan phase of revelation and, 26
  Muhammad and, 160
  overview of, 213–214
  prophetic tradition and, 261–263
  sources of, 258
shaving head, 190
Sheba (queen), 74, 289
Shia, 337
Shi'ite Muslims, 104–106
Shirk, 102, 209, 337
Shu'aib (Prophet), 51
Shukr, 16
Shura, 221, 304, 305–306
sibling inheritance, 228
simile, 59
simple living, 211
sin
  Adam and, 129–130
  Christian view of, 71
  forbidden action as, 265
  harm to marriage and, 270
  Muhammad on, 166
  original, 198
  philosophy on, 54, 77, 130, 198–199
  prophets and, 74, 120
  rejecting Truth as, 150–151
  Satan and, 142
sincerity, 210
Sirat Al-Mustaqeem, 337
Six Pillars of Belief. *See* Iman
slandering, 195, 196, 206
smoking, 265
social behavior, 260

social change
  Koran and, 12–13, 23, 238
  Meccan Surahs and, 25
social equality, 307–308
social progress, 296–297
Solomon (Prophet), 289, 340
souls. *See also* Nafs
  accounting of, 143–144, 200
  Day of Judgment and, 200
  earthly life and, 199–200
  five stages of, 201
  grave and, 200
  hereafter and, 201
  of newborn babies, 199
  pre-worldly existence of, 199
  sacredness of, 151
Sound Vision Web site, 327
speech, 194–195, 207
spiritual experience
  Day of Judgment and, 143–144
  heaven and, 144–145
  hellfire and, 145
spouse. *See also* marriage
  inheritance and, 228
  searching for, 216–217
stars, creation of, 135
stomach, 197
stories of past, moral narrative through
  Abraham and Lot, 51–52
  Hud, 50
  Moses, 51
  Noah, 49–50
  overview of, 48–49
  Salih and people of Thamud, 50
  Shu'aib and people of Madyan, 51
structure of Koran
  Ayat, 37–38
  Juz', 39–40
  nonlinear, 312–313
  Surahs, 38

struggle
  armed, 102, 253–254, 273–278
  against evil, 252–253
Struggling to Surrender (Jeffery Lang), 325
study group, 57, 326
studying Arabic, 326
studying Koran
  by comparing interpretations, 324–325
  by comparing "translations", 321–323
  by listening to recitation, 323
  by reading books, 325–326
  by taking class, 328
  by talking to Muslims, 328
  tips for, 326
  by visiting mosque, 329
  Web site resources, 327
submission to God
  Abraham and, 121
  declaration of faith and, 170
  as message of Koran, 12
  pilgrimage and, 188
Sufis, 98, 123, 337
Sufism, 337
Sujjud, 178, 337
sun, function of, 135–136
Sunnah
  description of, 83, 160, 161, 337
  as source of Islamic law, 261–263
Sunnah Salat, 179
Sunni Muslims, 104–105, 257, 337
supplication. *See also* prayer
  of Abraham, 120–121
  of Adam and Eve, 284–285
  for divine knowledge, 113
supporting parents in old age, 225
Surahs (chapters)
  collecting as book, 27–28
  definition of, 2, 337
  early, 23

Surahs (chapters) *(continued)*
  Meccan, 24–25
  Medinan, 24–25, 26
  moral narrative of, 46–52
  names and themes of, 40–46
  overview of, 38
  as self-explanatory, 85
al-Suyuti, Jalal al-Din (interpreter), 97–98

• T •

al-Tabari, Ibn Jarir (interpreter), 96
al-Tabarsi, Abu Ali al-Fadl ibn Hasan
    (interpreter), 105–106
al-Tabataba'i, Muhammad Husayn
    (sayyid, interpreter), 106
Tabi'un, 83
Tafsir. *See also* interpretations of text
  abrogation and, 90–92, 281
  Abu Bakr and, 94
  classic works of, 96–98
  definition of, 82
  oral tradition and, 95
  Shi'ite Muslim, 105–106
  Sunni compared to Shi'ite traditions,
    104–105
Tafsir al-baatin, 86
Tafsir al-dhahir, 86
Tafsir al-manar, 103
Tafsir bil-'Ishara, 83
Tafsir bi'l-ra'y, 83
Tafsir bil-riwaya, 94
Tafsir Ibn Kathir (Ibn Kathir), 324
Tafsir madhmum, 83
Tafsir mahmud, 84
Taif, 162
Tajweed, 33, 34
Tajweed Tahqiq, 34
Takbir, 176

Talbiya, 187–188
Taliban in Afghanistan, 236–237
Taqwa, 55, 226, 337
Tarawih, 182
Tartil, 34
Tawaf, 188
Tawba, 54, 337
Tawbah, 213
Tawhid, 25, 337. *See also* unity of God
Ta'wil, 82
tax on non-Muslims, 252, 278, 334
Ibn Taymiyah, 96
teacher-student tradition and
    memorization, 32
teachings, universality of, 162
television, 196
Ten Commandments, 67–68
terrorism, 101, 102, 103
Thamud, People of, 50
theft, punishment for, 268
A Thematic Commentary on the Qur'an
    (al-Ghazali), 103, 325
themes. *See also* moral narrative
  of Koran, 11–13
  of Surahs, 40–46
theocracy, 303
theology, inclusive, 149–151
Throne of God, 113
thunder, 137
Al-tiwal, 38
tolerance, religious, 307
tongue, 194–195
Torah, view of, 65–66
touching Koran, 30–31
Towards Understanding the Qur'an
    (Mawdudi), 99, 101, 324
traffic laws, 259
transcendence of God, 118
transgression, 209

translations. *See also* interpretations of text
  comparing, 321–323
  notation on, 32
  reading, 56–57
transliteration of Arabic terms, 2–3
transmitting revelation to community, 26–27
travel and waves of ocean, 137
treason, punishment for, 267
Treaty of Hudabiyya, 278
trust in God, building, 171
truth, bearing witness to, 237–238
Truths, 148, 150–151
tyranny, 208

• *U* •

Udhiya, 189–190
Ulama, 337
Umar (Caliph)
  Ali and, 104
  as leading by law, 244
  on perception of God, 111
  preservation of Scripture and, 27, 28
Ummah, 73, 83, 337
Unholy War: Terror in the Name of Islam (John Esposito), 282
unity of God. *See also* Tawhid
  Abrahamic faiths and, 67
  governance and, 304
  inclusive theology and, 149
  Jesus and, 127
  Muhammad on, 165
  overview of, 11, 15, 110–111
  as pillar of faith, 17–18
  teaching to children, 226
universality of teachings, 162

universe, creation of, 134–135
University of Virginia, search engine, 154
usury, 23, 301
Uthman (Caliph), 28, 104
Uthmani version, 28–29

• *V* •

Verse of the Throne, 111–113
verses, 2, 37–38. *See also* Ayat
vicegerent role, 131, 139, 296, 304
violence, spreading of, 267–268
virtue, 166–167
voice of narrative, 62–63
Voll, John, *Islam and Democracy*, 308
vowel marks, 29–30

• *W* •

Wadud, Amina, *Qur'an and Woman*, 325
al-Wahidi, Abu al-Hasan 'Ali ibn Ahmad (interpreter), 96
Wahy, 22, 337
Waraqa ibn Nawfal (cousin of Khadija), 22
warfare. *See also* struggle, armed
  circumstances of, 253–254
  ethics of, 102, 155, 248, 275, 277
  laws of, 260
wastefulness, 209, 299
water, 256
waves, 137
The Way to the Quran: A Guidebook for Studying the Quran (Khurram Murad), 325
wealth
  test of, 301
  women and, 291–292

Web sites
  for buying resources, 327
  calligraphy, 36
  Center for the Study of Islam and
    Democracy, 308
  Minaret (think tank), 302
  Muslim Women's League, 294
  The Muslim World, 268
  Nawawi Foundation, 328
  recitations, 323
  for studying Koran, 327
  Tafsir of Tabataba'i, 106
  University of Virginia search
    engine, 154
  Zaytuna Institute, 138, 328
winds, 137
wine in pre-Islamic Arabia, 23
women
  business transactions and, 294
  divorce and, 293
  dress and modesty, 223–224, 307
  education of, 292
  equality of, 249, 284–290, 319
  Eve and, 130
  head-covering of, 69
  health and wellbeing of, 222–223
  inheritance and, 228–229, 291, 300
  Koranic worldview of, 285, 287–288, 289
  laws of purity and, 72
  marriage and, 293
  as mothers, 225, 285
  names of after marriage, 205
  in pre-Islamic Arabia, 23
  property, business, wealth, and,
    291–292
  respect for, 285
  rights granted to, 290
  social and political participation of, 293
  work, pay, and, 292, 293

work and women, 292
worldview
  of radical groups, 281
  structure of Koran and, 313
  of women, 285, 287–288, 289
worship
  of Muhammad, 160, 315
  service to God and, 11, 131, 302
wrath of God, 146, 234
written tradition, 27, 35–36
Wudu, 174–175, 176, 338
Wuquf, 189

• Y •

Yahud, 148, 338
Yum Al'Deen. *See* Day of Judgment
Yusuf, Hamza (scholar), 327

• Z •

Zabur, 74, 338
Zahir, 338
Zaid bin Aslam (interpreter), 95
Zaid bin Thabit (scribe), 27–28
Zakariya, Muhammad (calligrapher), 36
Zakat
  balance and, 235
  giving alms, 183, 252
  as pillar of faith, 19, 23, 338
  receiving alms, 184–185
al-Zamakhshari, Abu al-Qasim Jar Allah
    Mahmud ibn Umar (interpreter), 97
Zamzam water, 188
Zaytuna Institute, 138, 328
Zechariahs (Prophet), 340
Zoroastrians, 274